AF378227

VOLCANIC 7 SUMMITS

DREAMS OF THE UNKNOWN

Seven Journeys to the
Continents' Highest Volcanoes

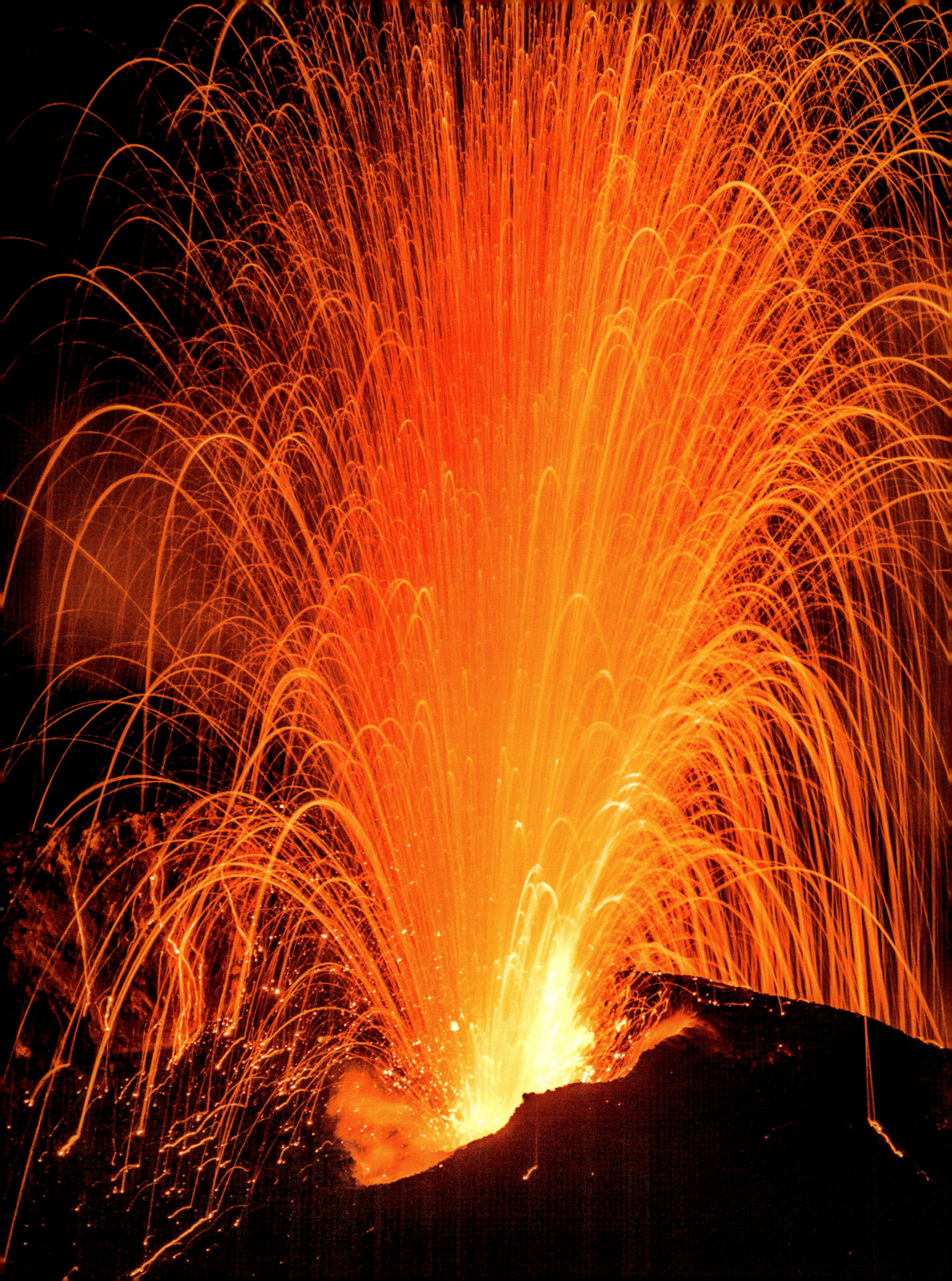

VOLCANIC 7 SUMMITS

DREAMS OF THE UNKNOWN

Seven Journeys to the
Continents' Highest Volcanoes

teNeues

CONTENTS

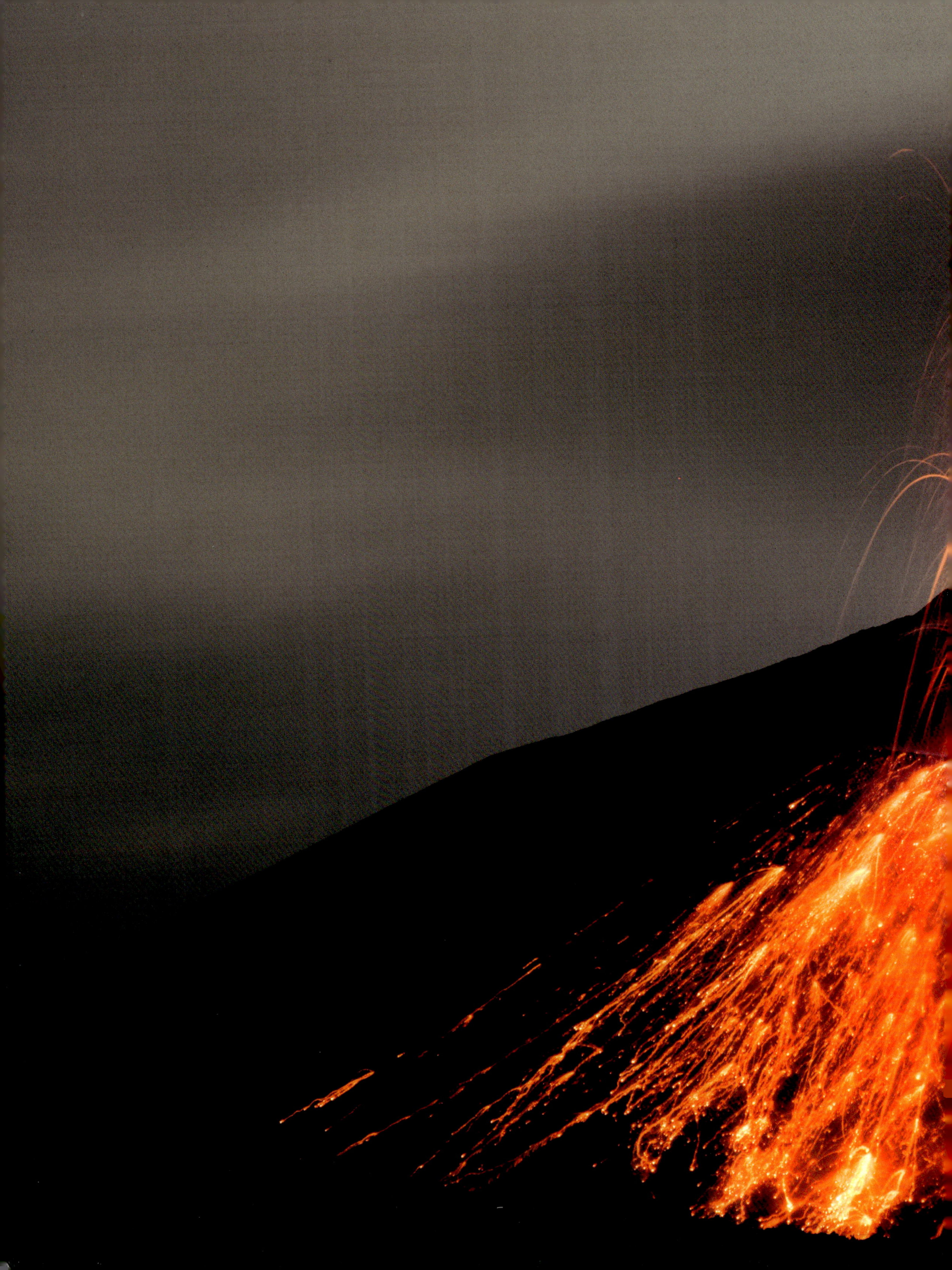

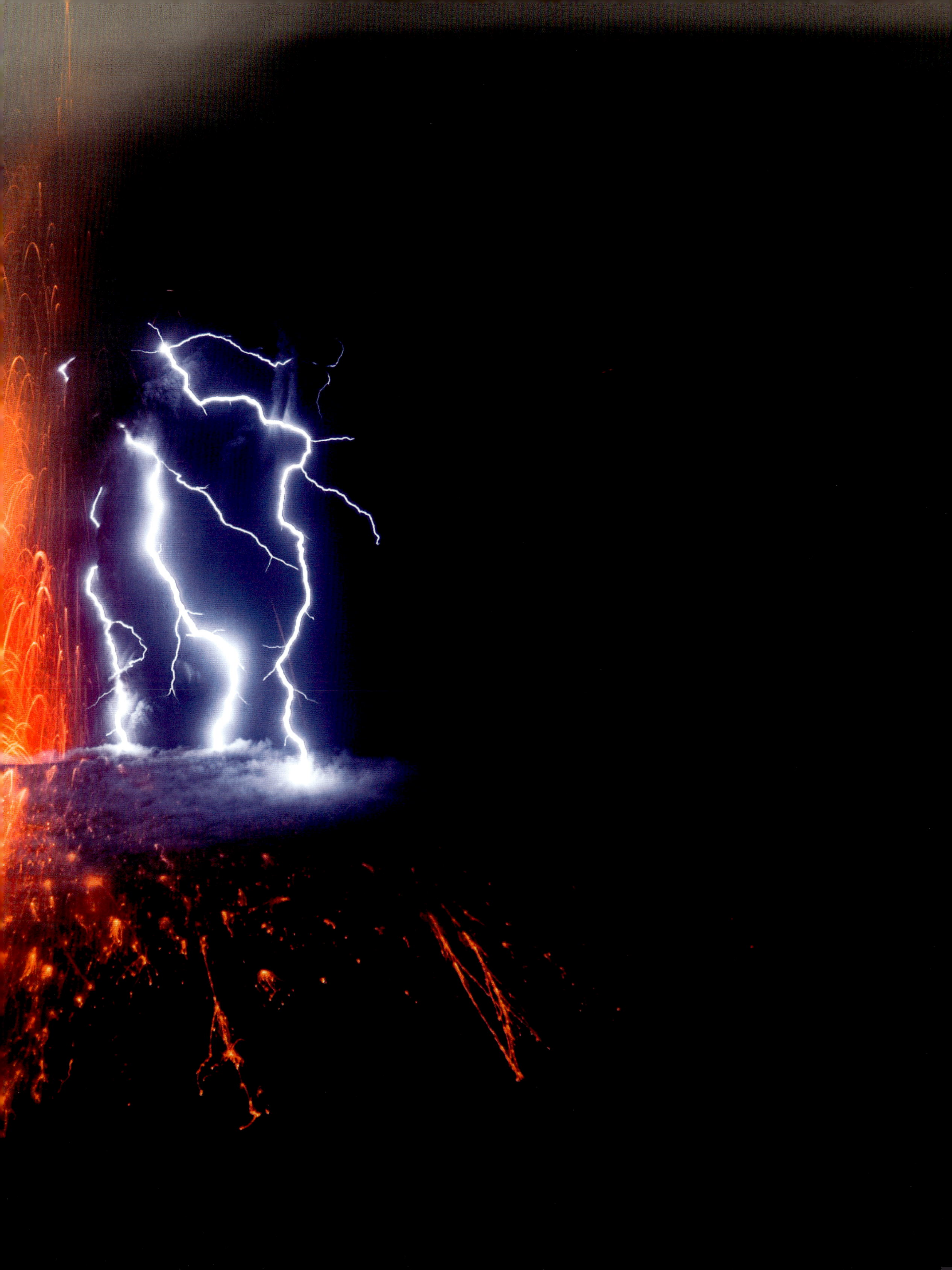

LIVING MY DREAM

Once upon a time …
Midnight, perfect silence. Nothing but the faintest hint of moonlight stands between me and pitch-black darkness. The damp, aggressive cold has penetrated my thick jumper, two jackets, and woolen hat and has chilled me to the bone. I fear I may fall asleep right here as I stand. It is a mere ten minute walk to the comparative comfort of my warm, dry rental car—paradise on earth, or so it appears to me right now. Yet the fear of missing the next eruption keeps me here, keeps me awake.

About two miles ahead, Mount Sakurajima towers silently in the mist—it is one of Japan's most active volcanoes. One of its unusual features is that volcanic lightning may appear in its plume. Even today, scientists are not quite sure how or why these so-called "dirty thunderstorms" arise. The assumption is that friction between dust and miniature ice particles within the plume play a role. Yet for me, the underlying science is secondary; what counts is the visual spectacle. Thus I have been waiting for hours—for four nights in fact—for the mountain to live up to its reputation. "Come on!" I urge the dark, mute giant, "Do something!"

At first, Sakurajima appears to be ignoring my plea. The only signs of life are intermittent flashes of headlights, restless midnight drivers in the distance. Then, as if it had heard me after all and had just been teasing me for a couple of seconds—punishment for my impatience, no doubt—a thick cloud of ash suddenly comes rolling towards me. I remain wary though: these events are now unfolding for the umpteenth time, just as I find myself covered in layers and layers of unhealthy, dusty grey flakes for the umpteenth time. My eyes are burning and I am shaken by a relentless coughing fit—yet again. For a second I can hardly see a thing in the thick fog of black ash, and I become acutely aware of the smell of burning soil. Then, just as suddenly as it began, the eruption halts, and silence returns.

For two more hours, all I can do is wait. Then, without warning, Sarukajima begins to steam; gently at first, but the longer I wait, the steam issues with more speed and force. White and grey clouds of vapor rise fast and dissipate in the wind. Several volcanic rocks (solidified, cold lava) rattle down the slopes. I can still hear their echoes bouncing off the surrounding rocks as I take a bite of my last Japanese rice cake.

And then suddenly it happens: the rim of the crater glows red and mere fractions of a second later, countless fiery lumps come flying up into the air, 600, 700 feet above the rim, and seemingly in silence. Seconds later, the sound waves of the eruption have reached my vantage point. My ears are ringing and I recoil, quite pointlessly, from the enormity of the sound. Hearing the explosion, all I can think of is a giant giving one fierce clap of his mighty hands. Almost simultaneously, a powerful shockwave blasts into me and a cloud of volcanic ash shoots up high into the sky; the lava's fiery light that illuminates it rather than lessens its darkness. As if nature were intent to prove the vast extent of her full power, the hiss and crackle of electricity now permeate the eruption. Lightning bolts in various, eerie shades of blue cut through the cloud in jagged lines. There it is at last: my own personal Twilight of the Gods; my private fireworks display. The volcano has granted my wish.

I recall the period of my childhood during which I devoured books on nature, natural phenomena, volcanoes, and dinosaurs. I even found some children's drawings of erupting volcanoes, which were somewhat distorted and misleading, but good enough to serve as proof for my early passion for the subject. As I grew older, I

Sakurajima is a volcano in Japan. It sits on the Pacific "Ring of Fire", a string of volcanoes that form an arc around the Pacific Ocean on both sides. About two thirds of the world's active volcanoes are located on this ring.

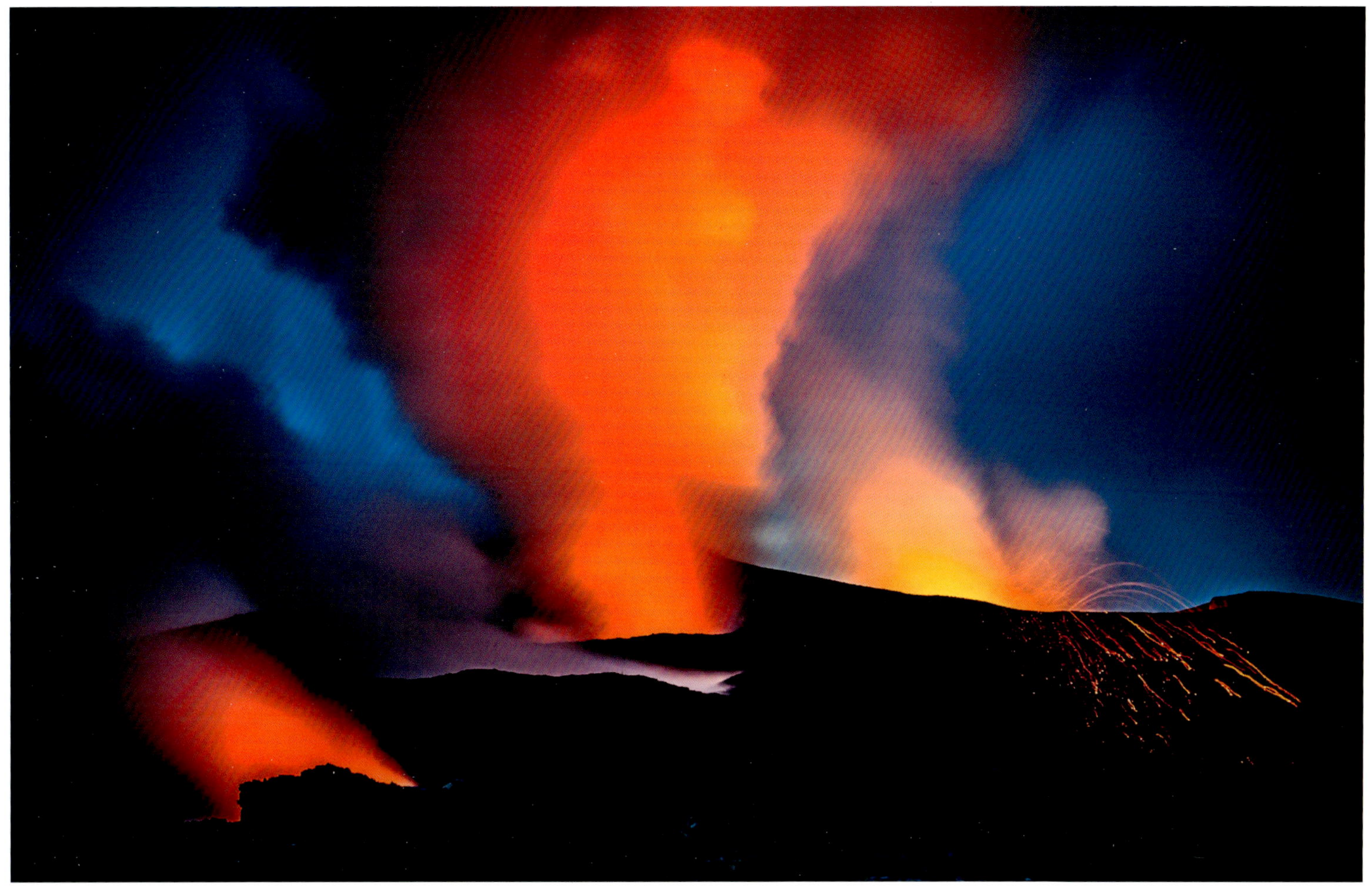

would go to the local library and take out any book on the topic of explorers and pioneers that I could find. Columbus, Magellan or Cook: books on globetrotters and people who had to fight and suffer in order to realize and live their own personal dream; people who did not care about or submit to the opinions and demands of others. And so I, too, started dreaming dreams of my own. Dreams of my own discoveries, of travels to far away, exotic countries, of tropical adventures and, ever since having watched my very first Star Wars movie at age twelve in 1981, dreams of space travel, leaving earth and exploring foreign planets.

Yet 20 years would pass before I had the opportunity to actually climb my very first volcano, and even then the circumstances were fortuitous. El Misti, an active volcano in Peru, stands at over 19,000 feet. On the day of the climb, El Misti's charms were not forthcoming and it just sat there, for all the world as if it were extinct, but I could still feel it simmering deep inside. The change wrought within me was permanent: I became completely entranced by volcanoes and their surrounding untouched landscapes. There is no real substitute for the feeling of the power of nature in this setting. There is a primordial quality to nature's vitality. Of course, as a photographer, it is the visual spectacle and the exploding fireworks that captivate me. In the past ten years I have shifted my focus in my photography work towards the sense of adventure that surrounds the glowing giants and so I became a "lava hunter"—in Kamchatka (eastern Russia), Indonesia, Sicily, Guatemala, Hawaii, Japan, Iceland, and Ethiopia.

As is often the case in life, one thing leads to another: towards the end of 2015, just as I was in the middle of my preparations for the next trip to Dallol and Erta Ale, two volcanoes in Ethiopia, I received an e-mail from a fellow photographer who mentioned in passing: "I found a tour announcement for the volcano Mount Sidley, surely that would be just the thing for you". I have to admit, I had, at the time, never heard of that volcano before and so I was curious. Following the link my colleague had

To date, fewer than 20 people have climbed all seven of the Volcanic Seven Summits. Fewer than five people have climbed both the Seven Summits and the Volcanic Seven Summits. The feat was first achieved in 2011.

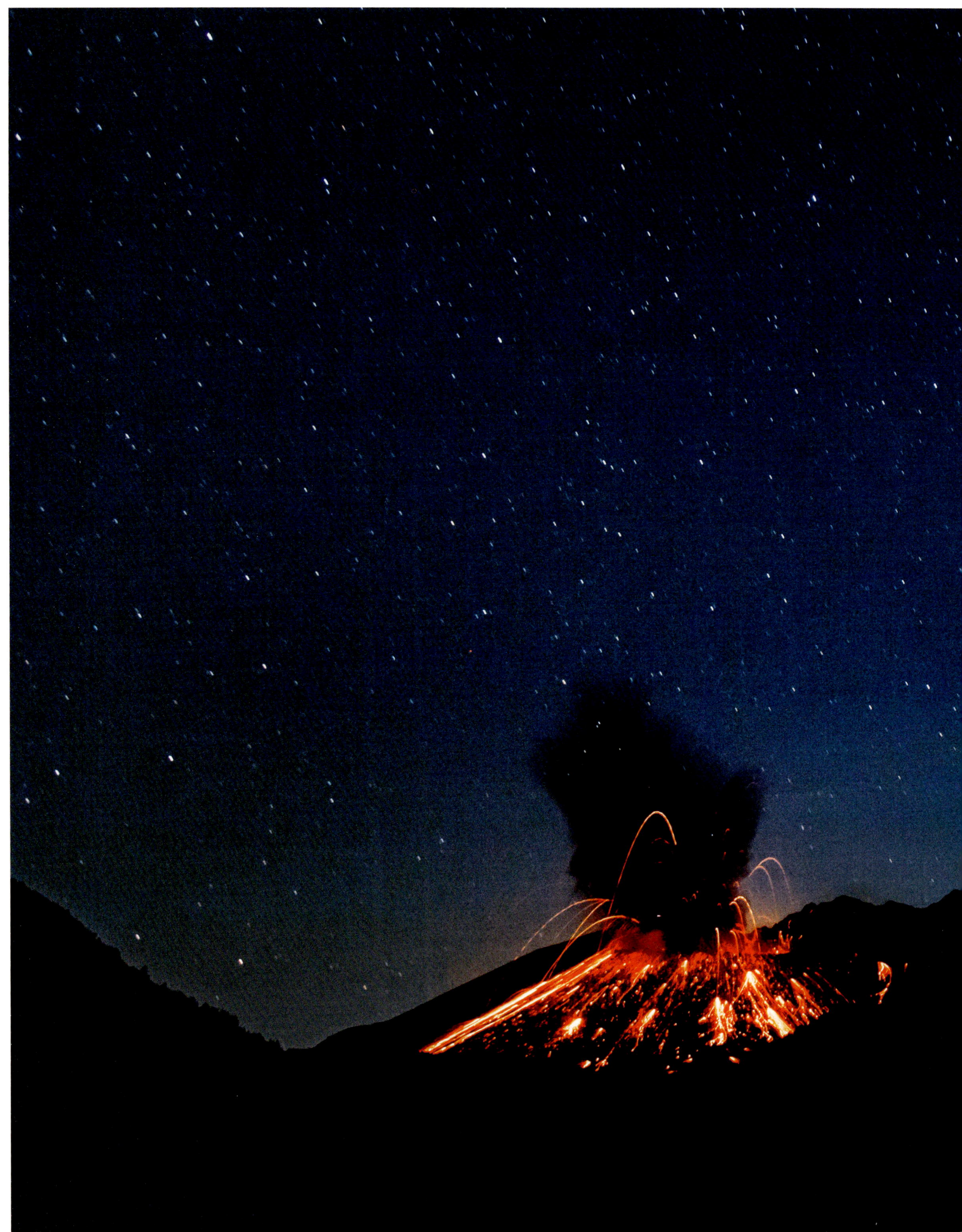

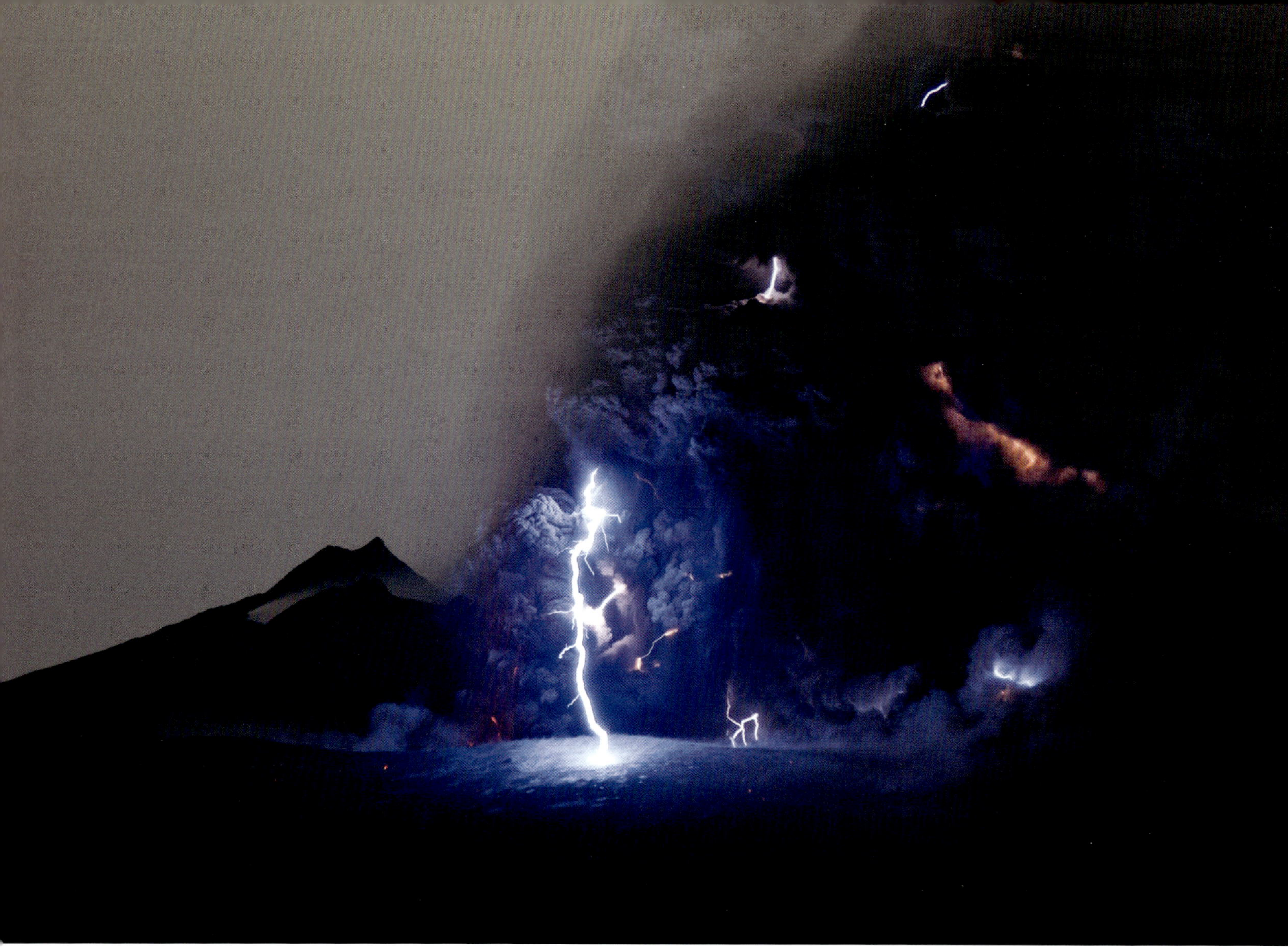

The tallest volcanoes in Europe and Africa, Mount Elbrus and Mount Kilimanjaro, are also the tallest mountains on their respective continents.

included in his e-mail, I read about Antarctica being "more inaccessible than the moon," the "most remote and least frequently climbed western summit" and how it is "Earth's vastest natural playground". Each sentence sounded as though it were addressed to me personally; the sense of adventure sent shivers of pleasure down my spine. After further research, I discovered that Mount Sidley was the highest volcano in Antarctica, and thus was one of the renowned "Volcanic Seven Summits". I had never heard of them before and I instantly knew: this will be my project, my dream of discovery and exploration, which ever since childhood I had never quite been able to abandon—the Volcanic Seven Summits, the highest volcanoes on each of the seven continents.

Of course I knew about the famous "Seven Summits", the highest mountains of each continent. They include Mount Everest in the Himalayas (Asia), the Aconcagua in Argentina (South America), and the Denali in Alaska (North America), and are unquestionably among the most difficult tasks a mountaineer can set out to do. In 1985, the American mountaineer Dick Bass was the first to succeed in setting foot on every single one of the seven peaks. In Germany, Reinhold Messner also managed the feat, as have just over 400 other climbers so far. How do the Volcanic Seven Summits compare? So far, they are not at all well-known; fewer than 20 people have climbed them to date. An Italian man was the first to succeed: in 2011 he had managed all seven. In 2018 a record was set when a man of 71 years of age, the oldest yet, managed the seven peaks. At the beginning of 2019, the youngest climber finished aged only 35. Yet my research showed that so far, not a single photographer had attempted this project. What an opportunity! What a task!

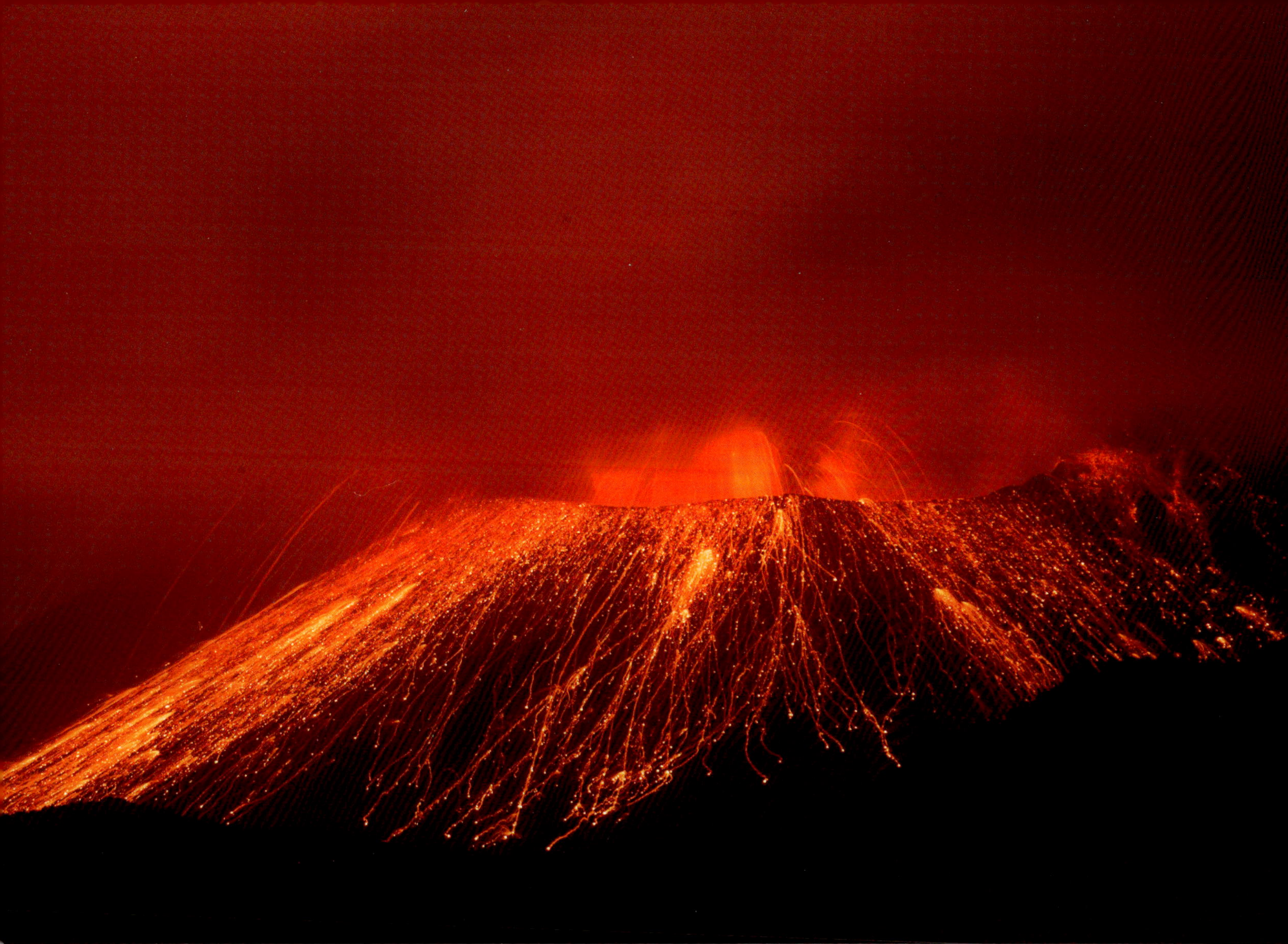

Although the Volcanic Seven Summits are not the most active volcanoes on earth, the tremendous primal fascination they engender captivated me immediately. I had seen enough fire on my previous tours. The seven different mountain ranges and the surrounding landscapes encompassing seven countries and cultures attracted me uniquely for the compelling opportunities to both document and photograph such wonders.

I knew from the beginning that setting foot on the summit of each of the seven volcanoes would not be my primary goal—I am too much of a photographer and not enough of a mountaineer. What would count, so I thought, would be the photographs I took and the stories I could tell. Furthermore, I had made a promise to my family never to take any unnecessary risks. Of course, the thrill of danger is part of climbing difficult summits, particularly volcanoes. So even if I cannot always stay true to my promise, I can honestly say I tried …

So here I sit, alive and well, and in this book I tell the story of how an innocent e-mail made me travel all seven continents in only two years. Driven by a pioneering spirit and the desire to explore the unknown, I visited the most remote corners of the earth. While I was at the edge of civilization, I would often reach my personal limit, too. At the same time, my travels have enabled me to take amazing photographs, experience adventure, meet new people and make new friends. At last I had the opportunity to live my childhood dream, the dream of the unexplored. Fire away!

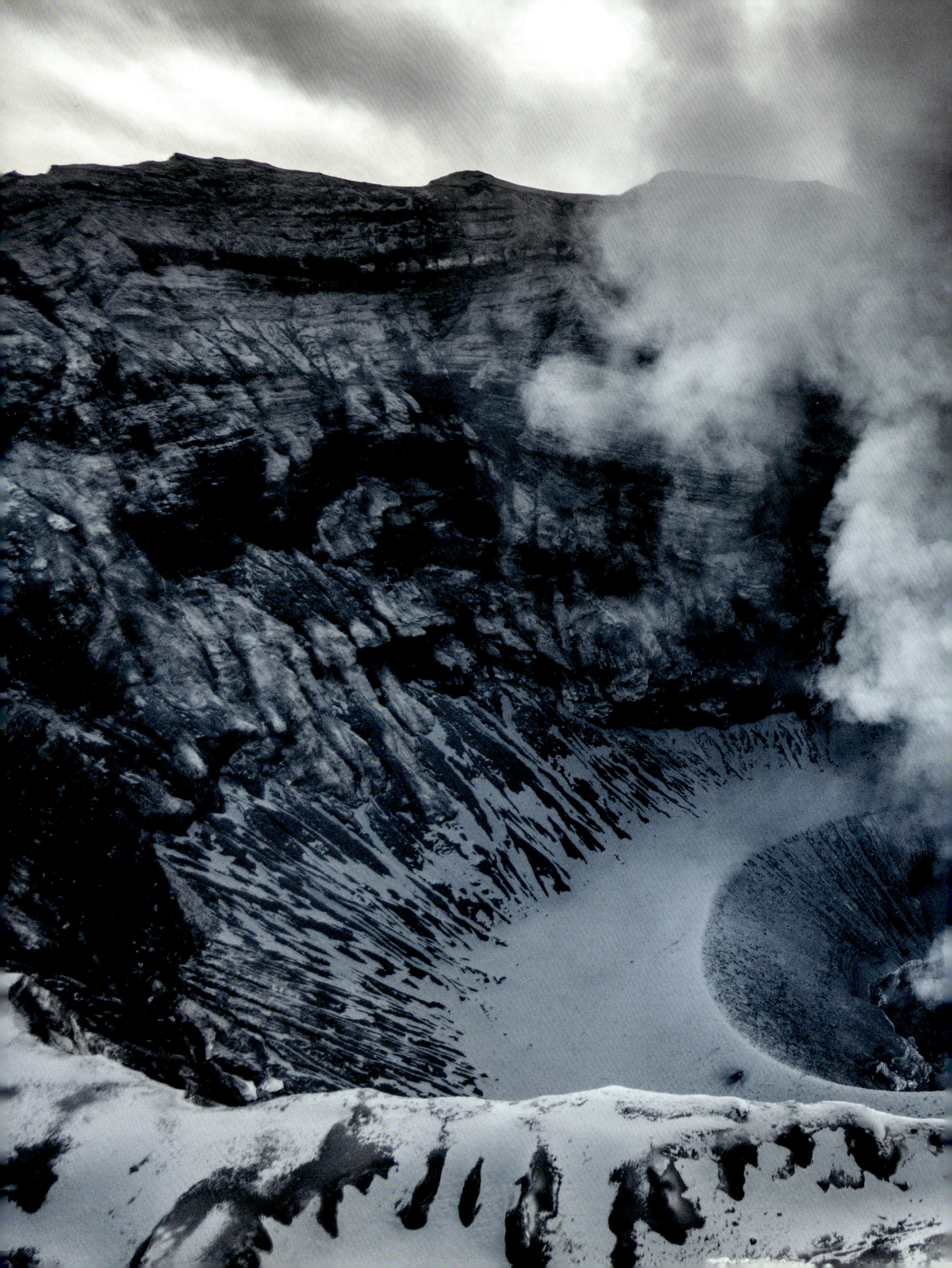

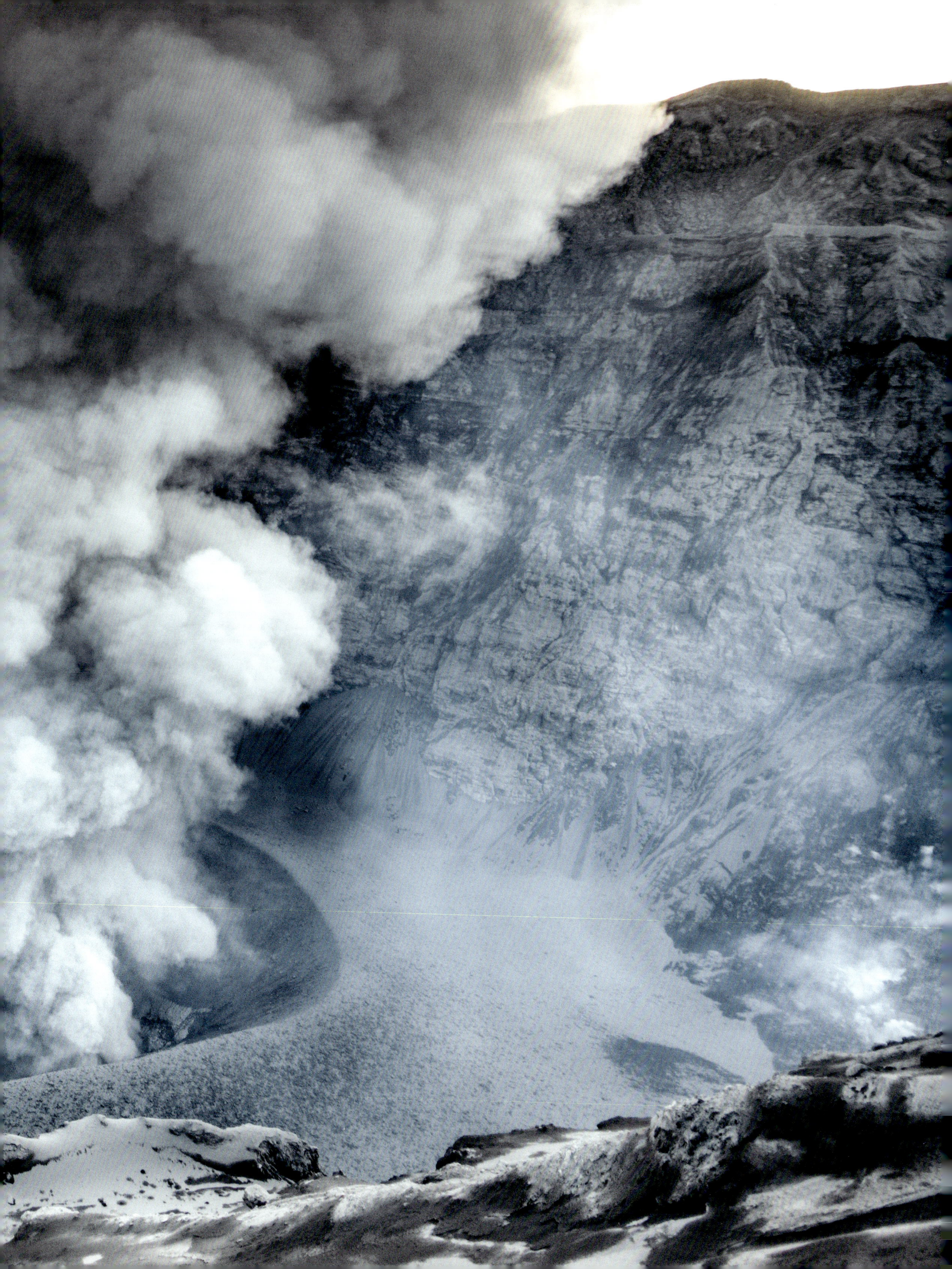

Volcanic 7 Summits

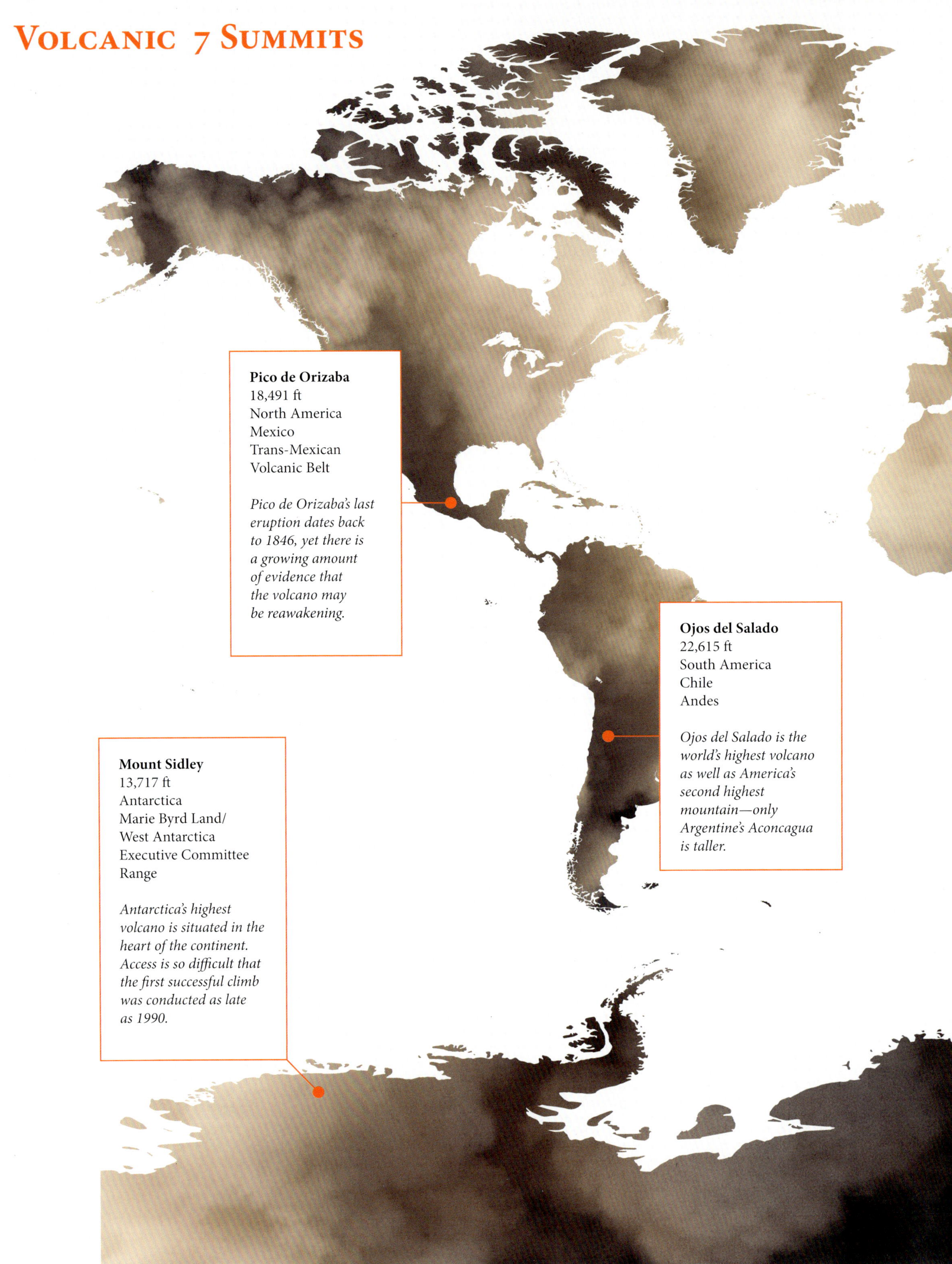

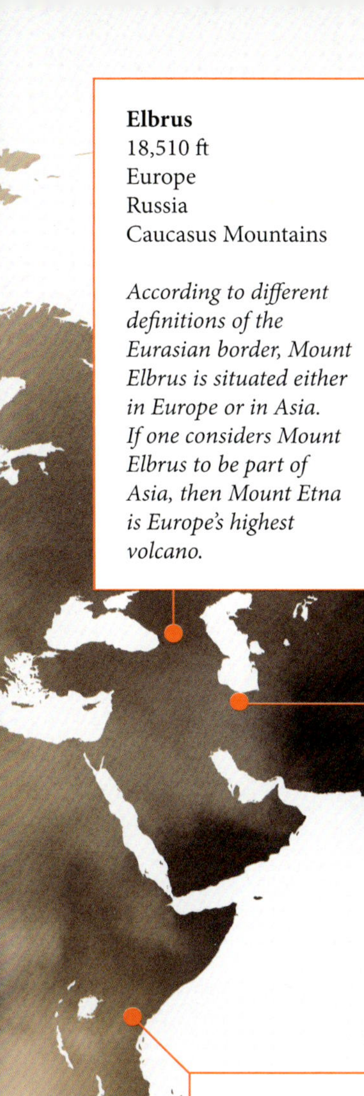

Elbrus
18,510 ft
Europe
Russia
Caucasus Mountains

According to different definitions of the Eurasian border, Mount Elbrus is situated either in Europe or in Asia. If one considers Mount Elbrus to be part of Asia, then Mount Etna is Europe's highest volcano.

Mount Damavand
18,386 ft
Asia
Iran
Central Alborz Mountains

Mount Damavand towers over all its surrounding mountains. Due to its impressive height, it has always played an important role in Persian folklore and literature.

Mount Giluwe
14,330 ft
Oceania
Papua New Guinea
Bismarck Range

Mount Giluwe is the world's highest volcano that is situated on an island.

Mount Kilimanjaro
19,341 ft
Africa
Tanzania
Kilimanjaro Massif

Mount Kilimanjaro is both the highest mountain and the highest volcano in Africa. It is considered to be one of the world's tallest free-standing mountains.

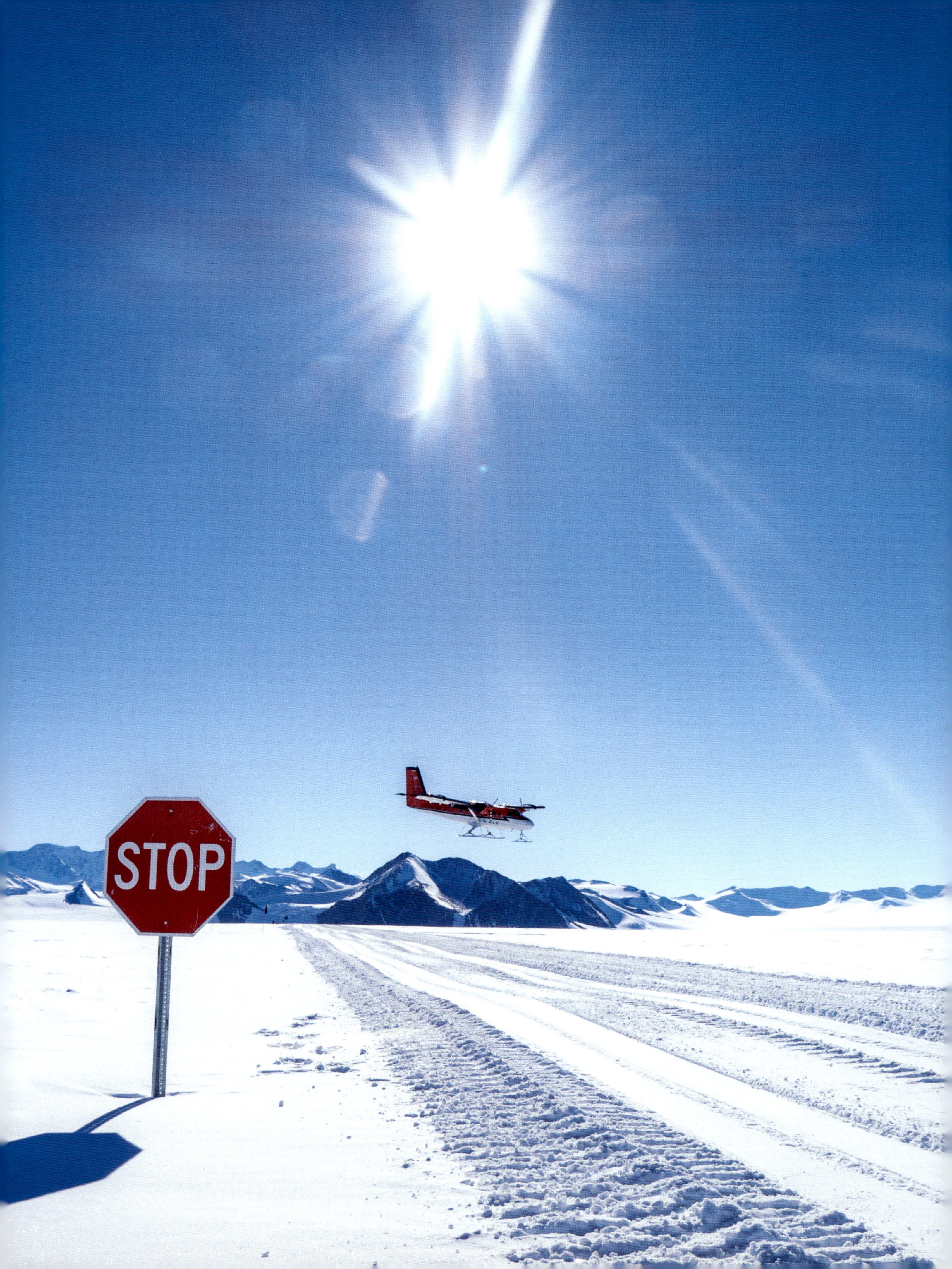
STOP

1

MOUNT SIDLEY

Like on a different Planet

Antarctica

"I am an astronaut!" I scream into the vast void. For that is exactly how I feel: like an astronaut walking the surface of a strange, faraway planet, a planet of ice and snow. Right now I must be the most isolated person on earth—and it feels good, more than just good. Right at that moment I am living up to my own personal life motto: "Die with memories, not dreams." I am adamant that when I go, I want to be looking back at my memories, not at missed opportunities. Right in front of me towers the mighty volcano's steep glaciated crater. Below my clunky polar boots, a floor of ice that feels as hard as diamond is glowing in the pale blue light. Behind me is a plain of seemingly endless snow that stretches to the horizon. In my thick red-and-blue polar suit, black sunglasses and furry hood that covers my head almost entirely, I like to think I even look a bit like an astronaut.

The only trace of earthly life is located about 150 feet away from me: bright red tents, pitched right on the ice, and the airplane, which despite the crystal clear air, I can only just about make out in the distance. Two days ago it brought us here, and now it sits on the plain below me, waiting patiently for my return. Here we are—Marie-Byrd-Land, the largest single unclaimed territory on earth, right in the western part of Antarctica. No other place on earth is further removed from civilization.

I take a deep breath, taste the unadulterated air and drink in the view of my surroundings. Through the dark lenses of my sunglasses, the sky seems as blue as the deepest ocean. The sun hangs in the air like a burning white and perfectly foreign flying object. The wind whips up small, intricate ice crystals, and the silence here is so profound that I can hear a hushed sound as they hit my polar suit. Suddenly I find myself moved to tears by the quiet, peace, and beauty that surrounds me, and I wish I could stop the clocks, and make this moment last a little longer. I am hopelessly lost in thought… And in my head I travel back in time, back to what happened five days ago.

Fly Me to the Moon

Even the journey here felt more like a mission to the moon than a journey on the surface of our own planet. I sat squeezed in a supremely uncomfortable row of seats like a Russian astronaut in a Soyuz capsule. Above me hung a precarious-looking crane-like fixture, around me all was dented, scuffed metal, and behind me there was an old, rather ragged curtain. There was not a single window. And yet I was on an aircraft, or to be more precise, I was on board a Russian transport plane, an Ilyushin IL76. It was built for flights in extreme conditions of up to -94 degrees. That is to say, for the coldest territories on earth. This beast of an airplane was to carry us from the bleak airport in Punto Arenas, southern Chile, to Antarctica. Destination "Union Glacier, Antarctica," as my boarding card proclaimed. The only element that stood out in these generally rather utilitarian surroundings was the large flat screen that was mounted just above the cockpit door. At first I was hopeful for an in-flight entertainment program, but I quickly realized my mistake as the four engines came to life. They screamed and screeched just as loud as I had imagined a rocket to be, and the sound filled the plane, where sound-proofing appeared to have been an afterthought—so movies were out of the question. The large screen was the cabin crew's only means of communicating with us. The captain's greetings, security instructions, information on our destination; everything was done via written messages that appeared on the screen. "Please fasten your seatbelts," it read

> Even the journey here felt more like a mission to the moon than a journey on the surface of our own planet.

In 2017, researchers discovered the area containing the densest concentration of volcanoes in the world beneath the West Ice Shelf in Antarctica. More than 100 volcanoes are located in a comparatively small area —with the peaks of tallest amongst them breaking through the glacial covering.

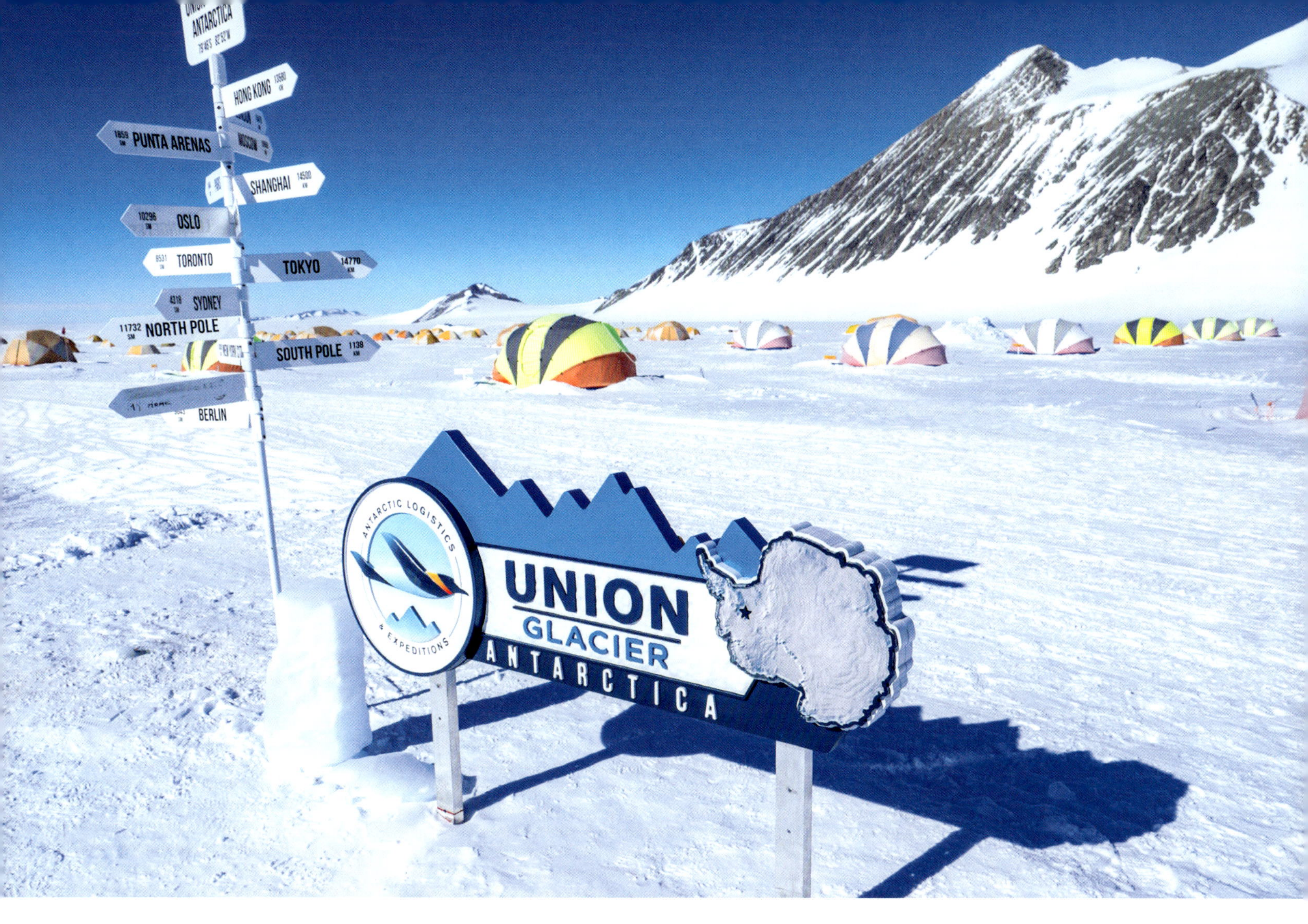

UNION
ANTARCTICA
HONG KONG
PUNTA ARENAS
SHANGHAI
OSLO
TORONTO
TOKYO
SYDNEY
NORTH POLE
SOUTH POLE
BERLIN
ANTARCTIC LOGISTICS
& EXPEDITIONS
UNION
GLACIER
ANTARCTICA

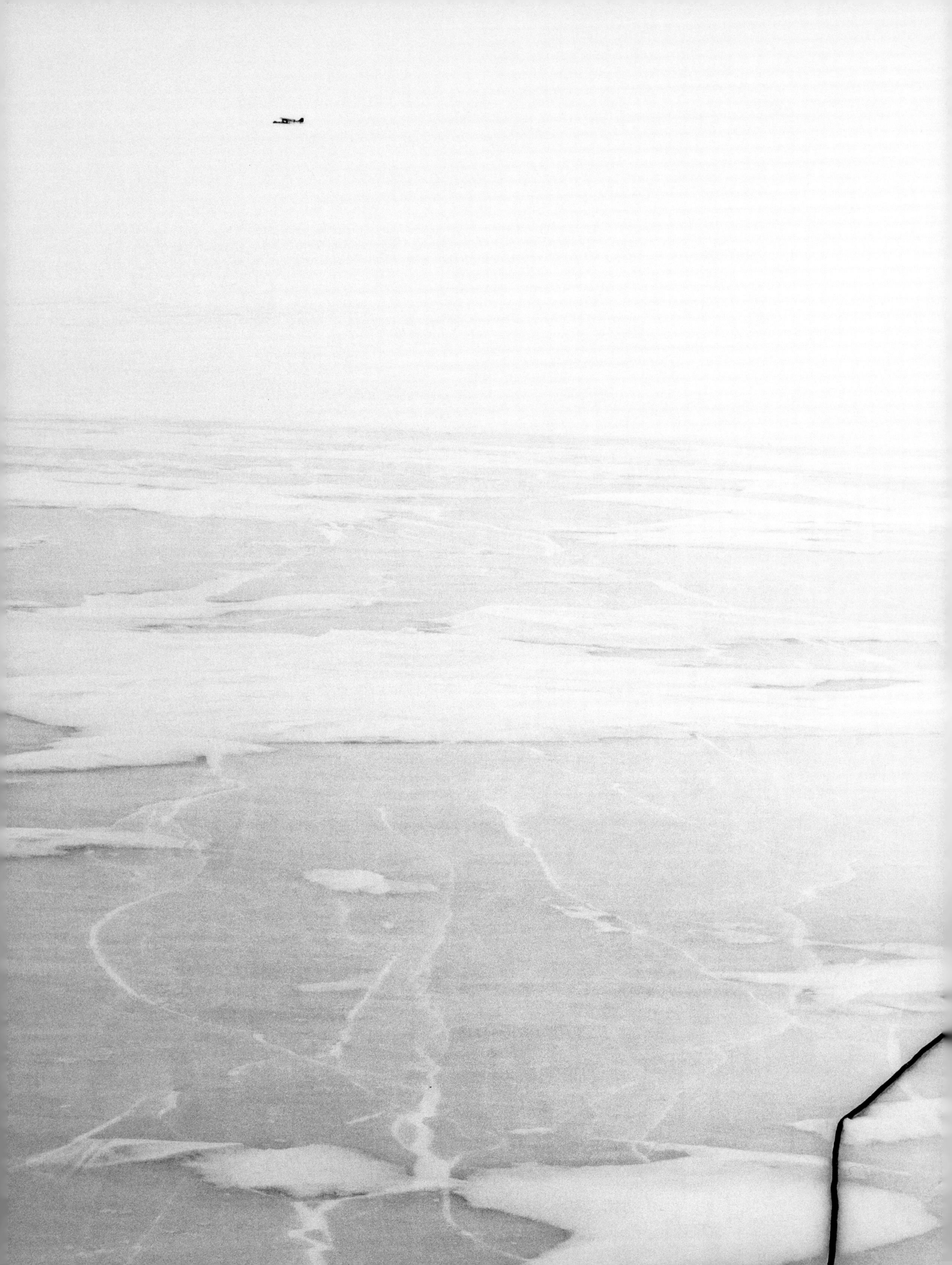

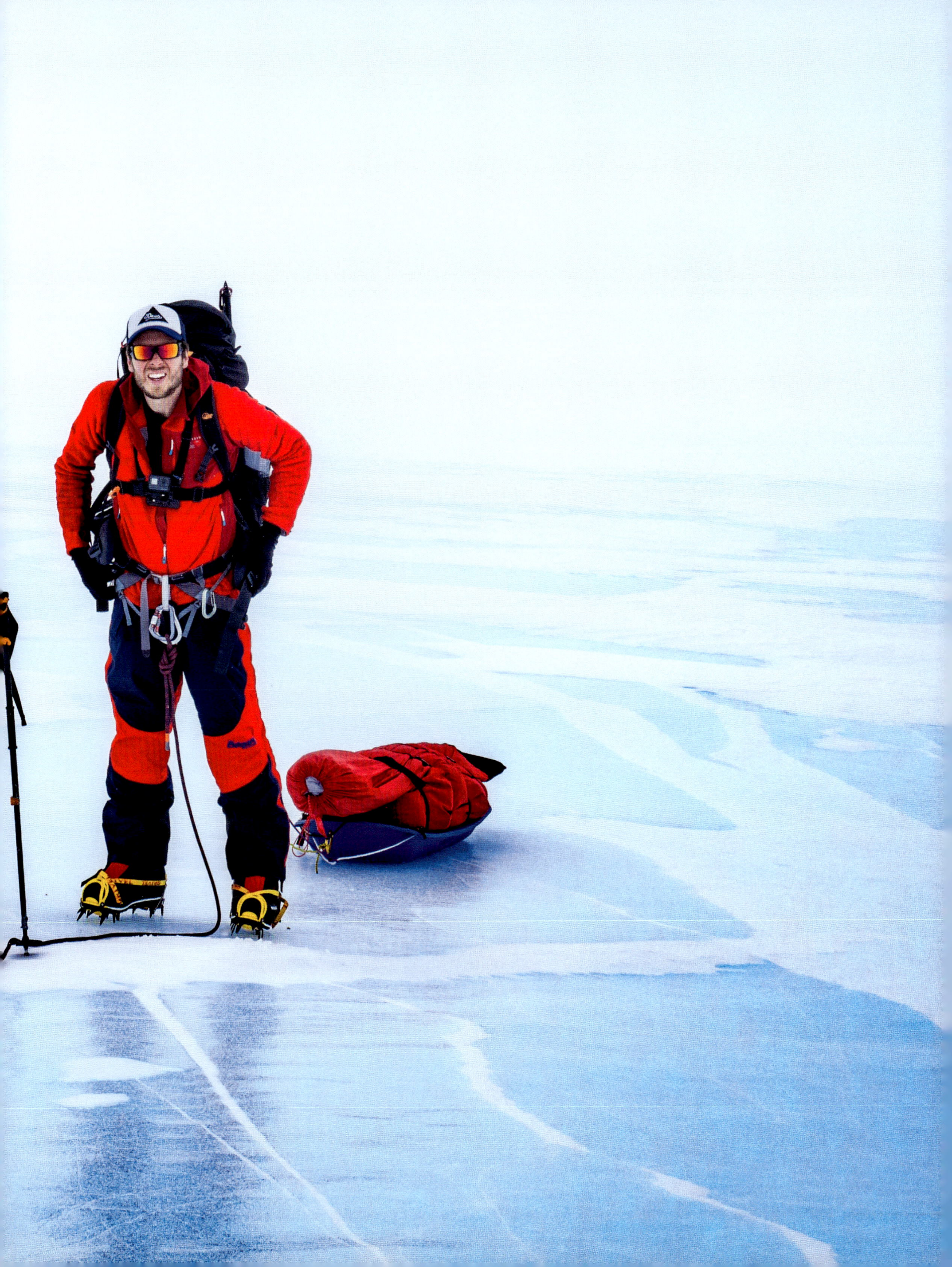

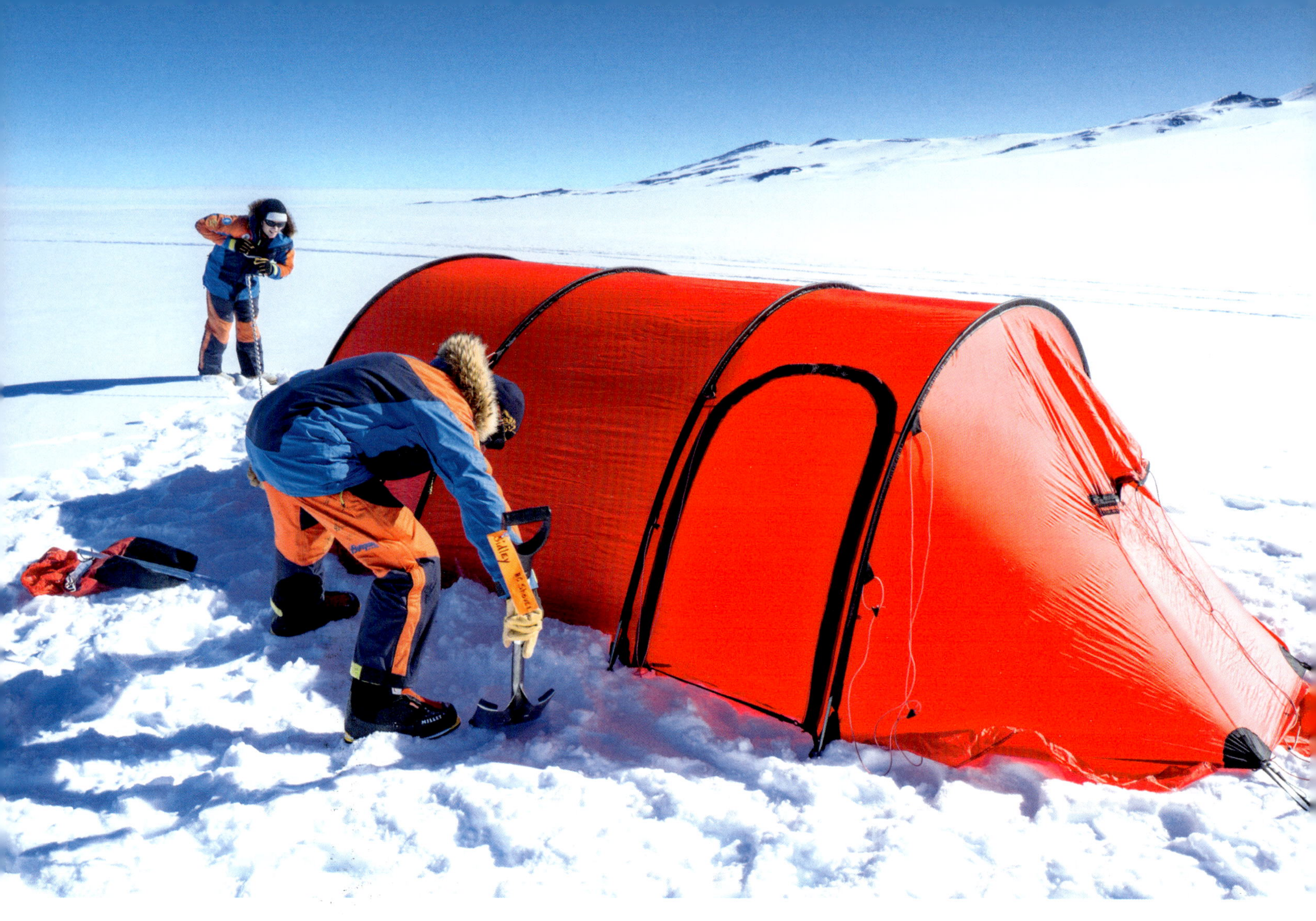

now. A good sign, and very sound advice, for as it turned out, the engines were just as powerful as they were loud. The take-off was abrupt; the plane leapt forward and pressed me even deeper into my hard seat Within seconds we were effortlessly airborne. Looking back at take-offs in normal passenger airplanes, they felt like a leisurely train ride by comparison. I tried to get as comfortable as my narrow seat, thick polar suit and boots would allow me, and began to concentrate on the somewhat bewildering in-flight entertainment (which they did have after all). They were showing, and this is the honest truth, Pretty Woman. Who would have thought that Julia Roberts would accompany me on my five hour flight to Antarctica? A smart move by the cabin crew, actually, for every single person on board had seen the film already and so nobody cared much that there was no sound, just pictures—the engines' roar was simply too loud.

As the credits were rolling and the man next to me sighed a barely concealed "Finally!"

the atmosphere on board gained an element of tension. For one, the temperature inside the Ilyushin was dropping slowly in order to prepare us for the arctic cold that awaited us. What is more, we were already approaching the Ellsworth Mountains. They make up Antarctica's highest mountain range, 224 miles long and 30 miles wide, with several summits at over 13,000 feet of altitude. At the foot of the 220 miles long and 30 miles wide Union Glacier lay our first destination, the Union Glacier Camp.

The flat screen switched to the cockpit camera and I could watch the heavy Ilyushin touch down on the Union Glacier Blue-Ice Runway. It is a runway made of a stretch of shining, perfectly smooth ice surrounded by blindingly bright, clean white snow. As a stark contrast, steep mountains created from pitch black stone rose in the distance, though the clear air made it seem as if they were so close you could touch them. Antarctica seemed a manifestation of beauty. Yet I knew that Union Glacier Basecamp

Monday, January 9th,

Taking a plane to Antarctica is unlike taking
a plane to any other place in this world. It feels
like flying to another planet. I will now have the
opportunity to leave earth and our society for ten
days. Ahead of me there is ice, adventure, a never
ending void, and freedom without borders as far as
the eye can see. It's a dream come true!

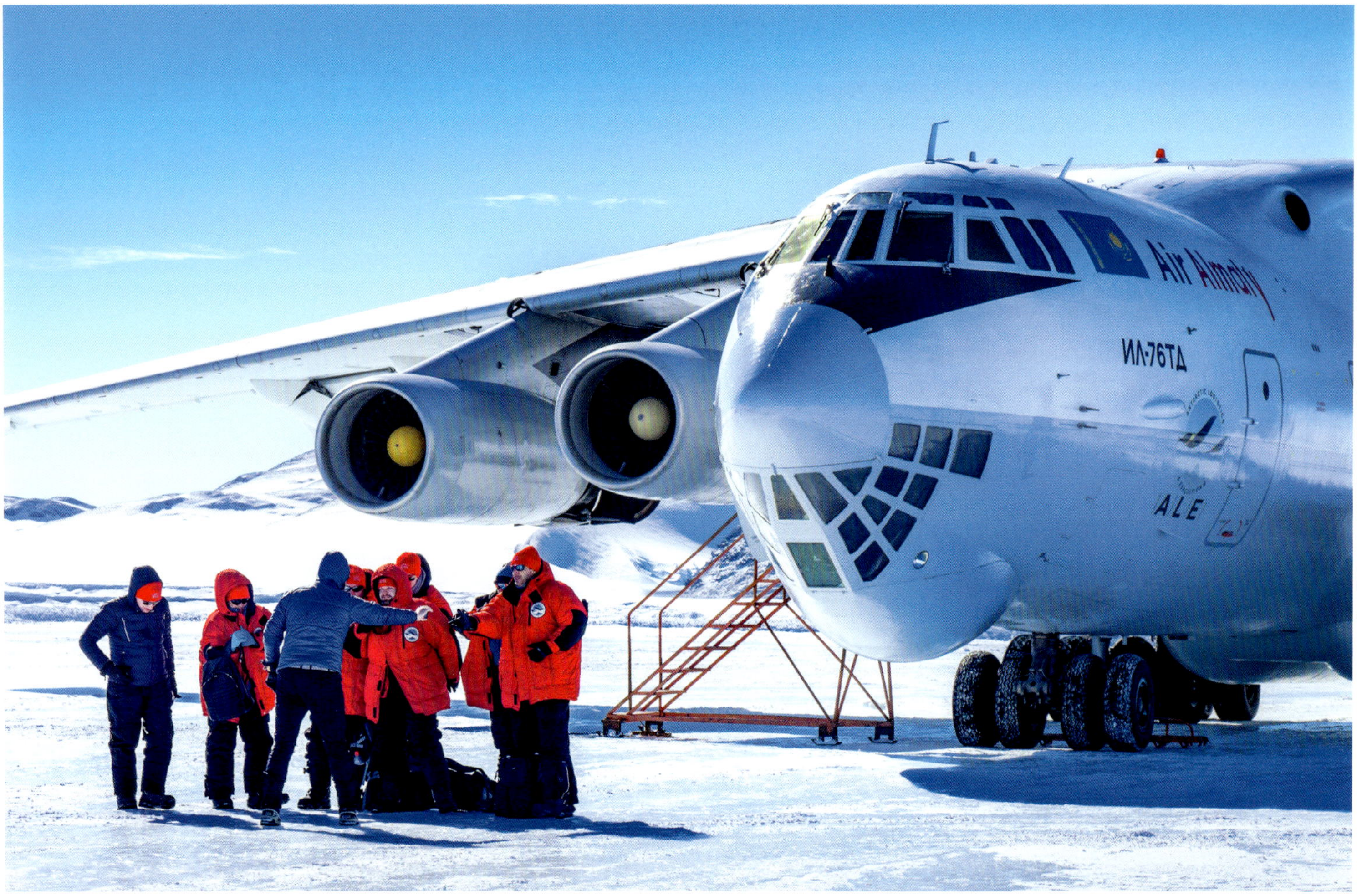

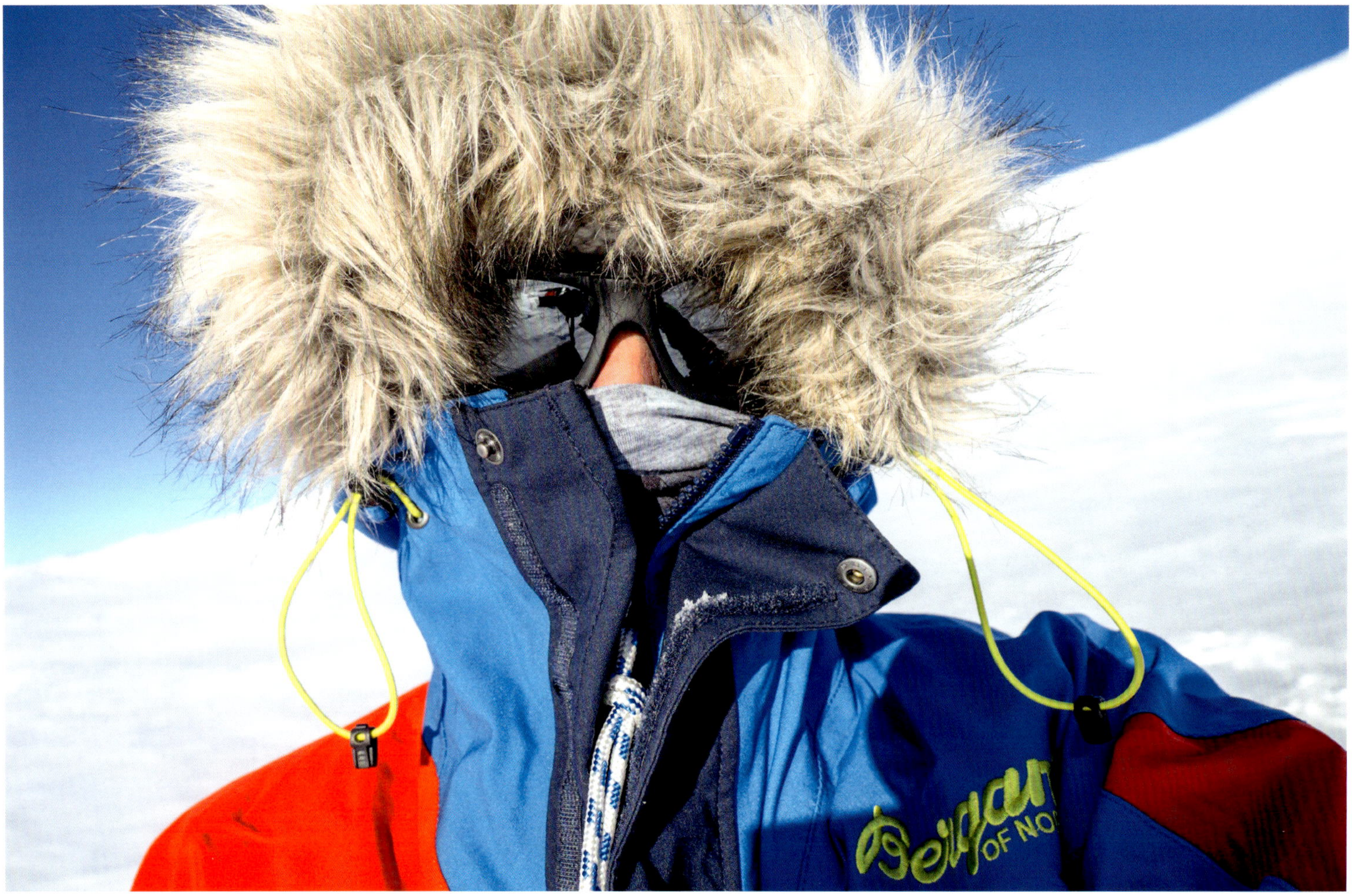

would not be the final destination of my journey. In a few days I would continue, deeper and deeper into the heart of the ice.

Luxury at the End of the World

I return from my flashback, tear my gaze away from the small airplane in the distance below me and duck back into my spacious bright red tent which is part of the camp here at the foot of the volcano. I squeeze past the clothes line and the socks dangling off it and reach for my large thermos. Despite the sunshine, which feels surprisingly warm, temperatures are nevertheless sub-zero and if I were to keep my water in any other container, it would freeze in no time. In this cold climate I rarely feel thirsty, but I still force myself to take a few large gulps in regular intervals for fear of dehydration. Our camp is located at 10,000 feet of altitude, and at these heights it is essential to keep hydrated at all times. Into the lukewarm water I stir a foul-smelling powder—a small portion of one of the artificial-looking instant expedition meals which luckily taste a lot better than they look. Yet I still miss the quality and variety of provisions we had at Union Glacier Basecamp.

Union Glacier Camp is the transport hub for tourism in Antarctica. The high season during summer lasts for about three months, from November until February. During this period, a few hundred tourists visit the camp. They can choose between trips to the South Pole via airplane, on skis, or even—and this sounds both incredible and crazy to me— in a pickup truck, as well as climbing Mount Vision, the highest mountain in Antarctica. Another option is a flight to the coast, to see the large penguin colonies. Mount Sidley, the place I want to go to, seems to be one of only a few sights that have not made it on the list. Not many attempt what we are setting out to do; this expedition is special.

And I have been planning accordingly: during the run-up to Christmas, just before my departure, I actively tried to gain six to eight pounds of weight by eating excessive amounts of cookies and gingerbread, thinking I'd lose the additional weight more or less immediately in the arctic cold. The strategy seemed sound at the time, though it had a vital flaw: I hadn't considered the excellent chefs at Union Glacier Camp. Three times a day, anything you might wish for was on offer in copious quantities at the long buffet. "Look at that, they even have beer and wine!" I could not help but blurt out the first time we had dinner. There were large bowls of nuts, cookies, chocolate, and other snacks at every table. It was a gourmet's paradise at a place where I had been least expecting to find it. By the time the tour was over, I would not have lost an ounce.

Food aside, Union Glacier Basecamp was full of surprises. I had been expecting to spend my time here living the relentlessly tough life full of hardship that seems inevitable when you are on an expedition. Yet the American camp offered a few unanticipated luxuries: spacious double tents with cheerful stripes in yellow and red, furnished with neoprene rubber floors and actual bedframes. Later I would tell my family: "I've been to expensive hotels that were not as comfortable as this." The toilet stalls could be locked, were deep blue on the outside, very clean on the inside, and I would not have been surprised if you had told me they had heated seats. Besides, there were hot showers, a small shop, a telephone booth, a large tent that served as common room, a volleyball net, and a selection of mountain bikes with thick snow tires. After my first day there, I titled my diary entry "Union Glacier Holiday Camp" and smiled. Another element that was reminiscent of a holiday camp was the constant activity and the sound of motors. Orange track vehicles that were suitable for driving in polar regions and what looked like monster trucks with big ballooning tires cut through the camp. Sometimes there were small, quick skidoos. On top of that, amusing little red Twin Otter prop planes regularly touched down and took off on the small landing strip near the camp.

The largest tent served as the common room where we would all hang out. Just like the other

It is a runway made of a stretch of shining, perfectly smooth ice surrounded by blindingly bright, clean white snow.

The coldest ever temperature recorded on Earth found in Antarctica on July 23rd, 2004, in a small valley in the east of the continent: -145,5 degrees. At this temperature, almost breathing is life-threatening.

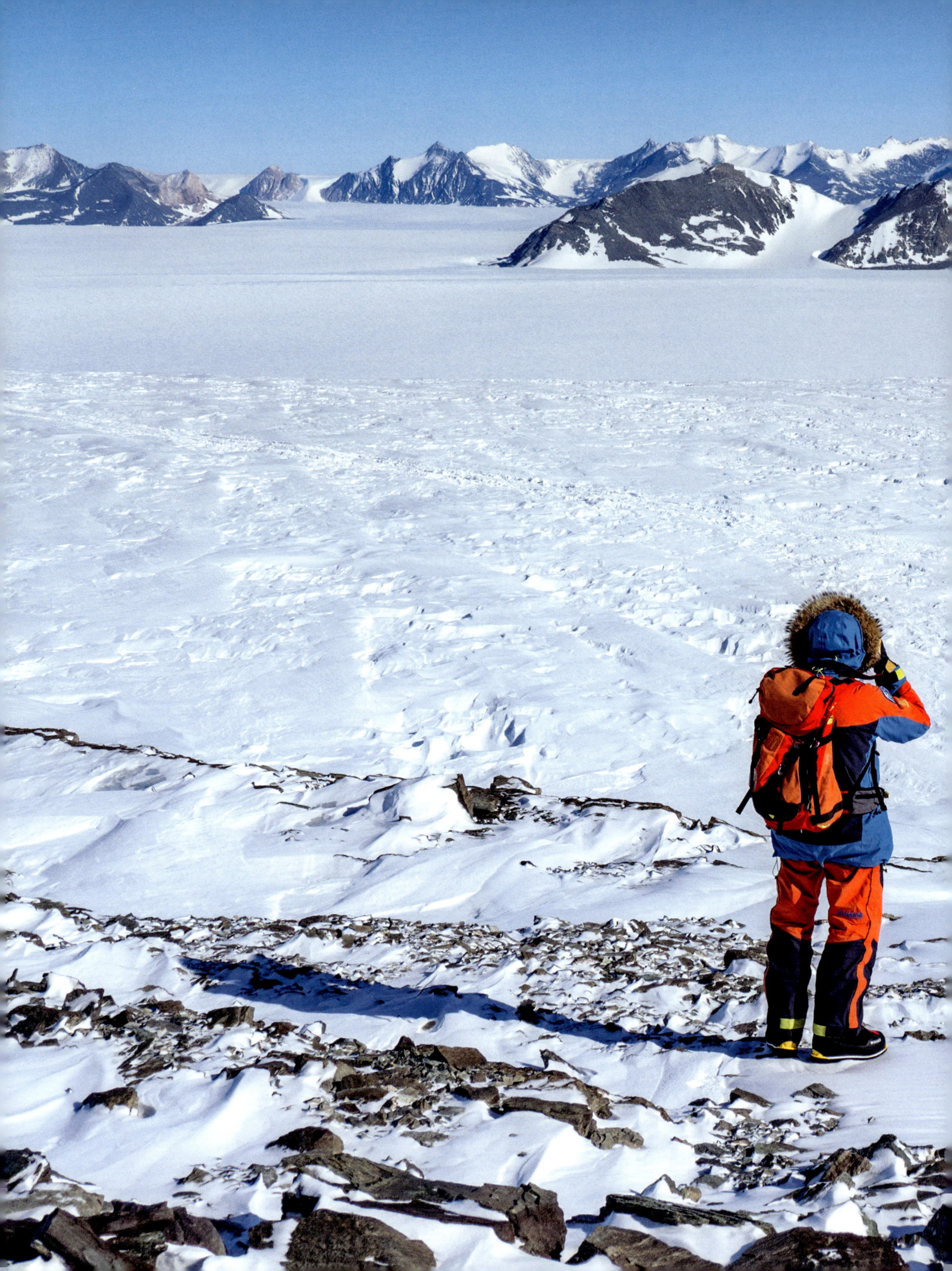

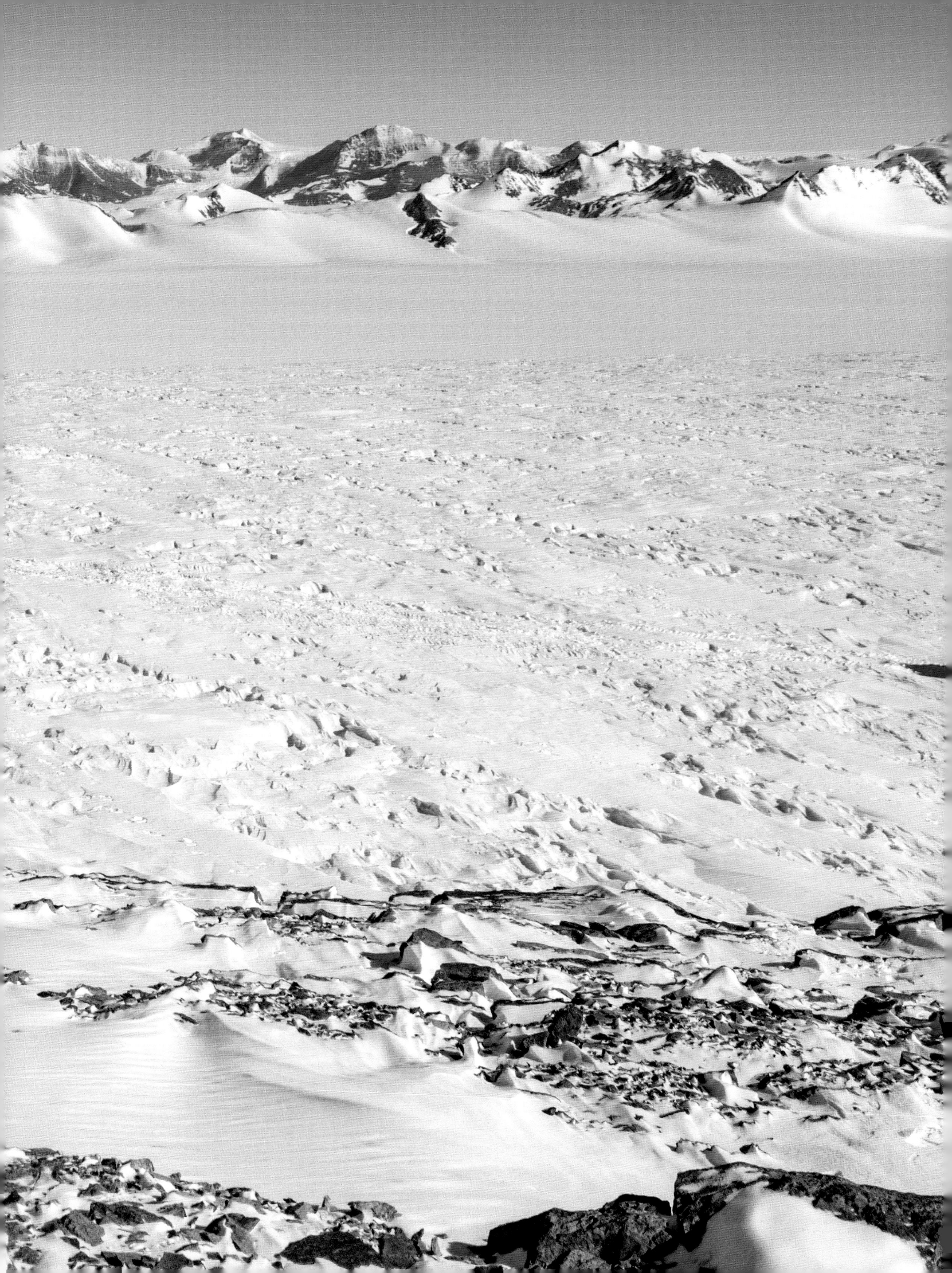

tourists, I spent many hours there. For on this continent, weather rules over all comings and goings. Due to frequent and rapid temperature changes and powerful storms of nearly 200 mph, plans in Antarctica often had to be revised at the last minute, or thrown out altogether. That was the case for us, too. The sun was shining here at Union Glacier, but the second leg of our journey had to be postponed several times. "Bad weather at Mount Sidley right now, unfortunately," said Eric, our bearded, perpetually cheerful Belgian meteorologist with his bright eyes and cheeky smile. "It looks like there might be a more favorable weather window opening up in a couple of hours, though," he added. To keep us up to date, Eric brought us weather updates in six hour intervals. From my layman's perspective, he and his team did an incredible job. Mount Sidley is more than 600 miles away from the closest weather station, and so, based on nothing but satellite photos and weather models, Eric and his team had to calculate precise hourly predictions for a comparatively tiny area. An incorrect or even just an imprecise calculation risked us wasting kerosene twice—and that was the best case scenario. In the worst case, a wrong weather forecast can have fatal consequences here in Antarctica.

In a few days I would continue, deeper and deeper into the heart of the ice.

"Your Weather Window Has Arrived!"

Just as I was getting settled in and expecting to spend a few more comfortable days at the "Union Glacier Holiday Camp", my "holiday" came to an abrupt end. Eric rushed into the common room and proclaimed: "Come on now, get ready, your weather window has arrived!" That was our signal: we jumped up, started running to our tents and packed as fast as we could. Shortly afterwards I boarded the next plane, a DC3 prop plane which had undergone some alterations for deployment in Antarctica, with room enough for no more than 14 passengers. From my seat I could look directly into the open cockpit in which our Canadian pilots, who seemed daring but confident, were getting ready. Their safety instructions were rather unusual: "Please wrap up warm and tell us immediately if you are experiencing any signs of altitude sickness." Before I could ask what they meant by this, they gave us the explanation: "We will be flying at roughly 13,000 feet of altitude—without pressure equalization and without heating." "Great," I sighed, "down at Union Glacier they're probably fitting heated seats right now and here we're flying with open windows, pretty much." Again we received the obligatory earplugs as the propeller began to scream and turn and the plane moved slowly across the endless ice and then slowly up into the sky.

While the engines were as loud as ever, the team on board was unusually quiet. Throughout the flight I too was lost in thought, torn between fear of the unknown and an explorer's gleeful anticipation. Whenever I glanced out of the window I was presented with the same view: a bare plain of ice that stretched right up to the horizon, occasionally interrupted by hills and mountainous glaciers. It was bleak but fascinating.

After a roughly four hour flight, the tension on board erupted into something like euphoria. One of the passengers two rows ahead of me suddenly screamed: "There it is, there it is!" Through the small scuffed window I could make out majestic Mount Sidley in the distance. The five million year old volcano's imposing crater, over three miles wide and 4000 feet deep, slowly came into view. Its flanks were a mixture of white and bright blue ice, and even from our poor vantage point, it made an overwhelming, almost otherworldly impression. In all of human history up until this point, there had only been five previous expeditions to this remote region, this seemingly endless stretch of ice.

In my head, the phrase "I can't believe this is happening!" was playing on repeat. This was a dream come true! And not just any dream— my dream, my own personal moon landing. Just as the airplane began its descent, I suddenly thought of Neil Armstrong's words as he took his first step on the moon. Although I have to admit that in my case, the more appropriate phrase was: "That's one giant leap for me, one small step for mankind." Luckily, Eric's weather

Researchers suspect that there may be several freshwater lakes located below Antarctica's ice sheets, which are several miles thick. Those subglacial lakes have remained untouched for millions of years and may contain unique, completely unknown forms of life.

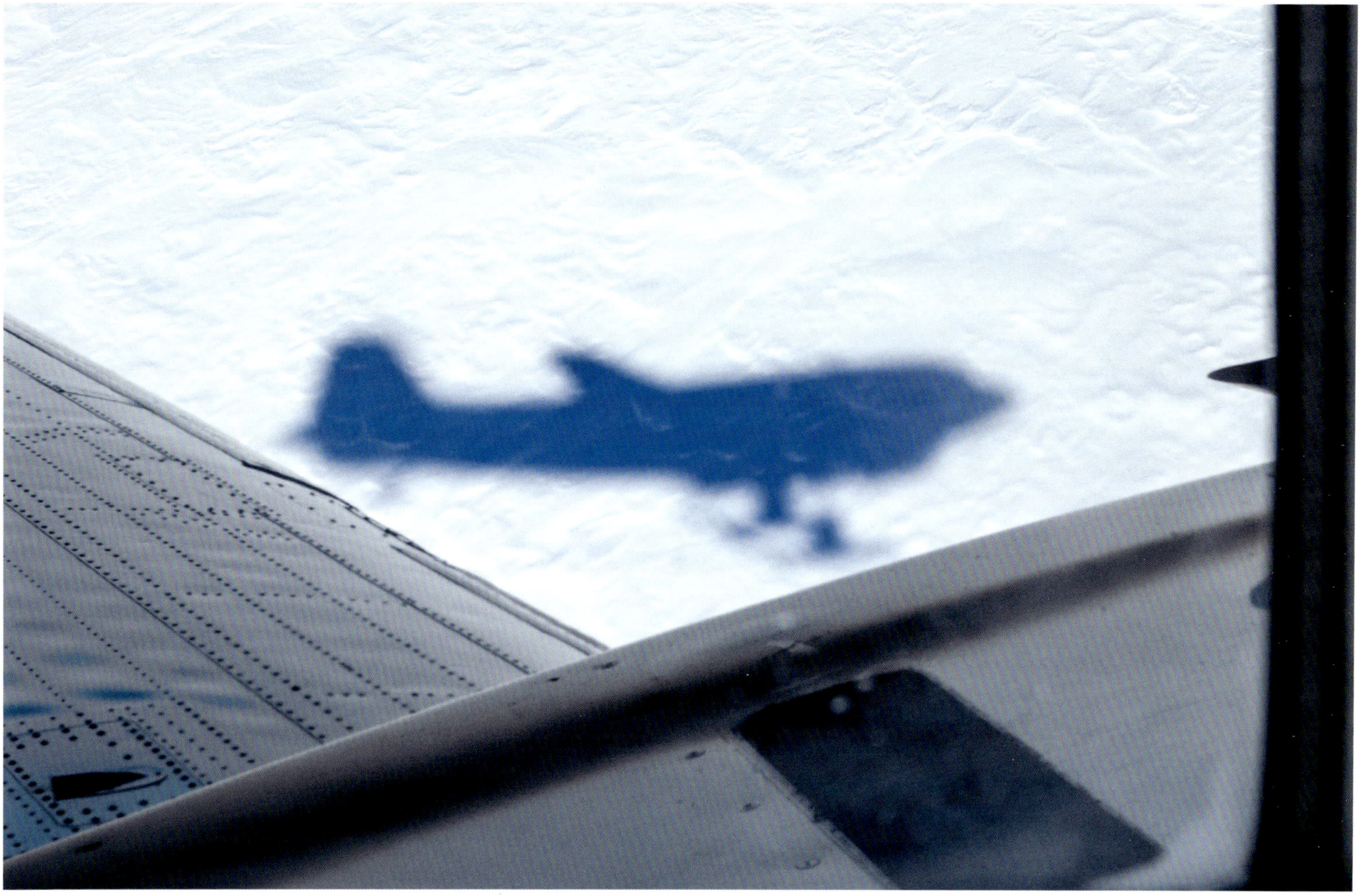

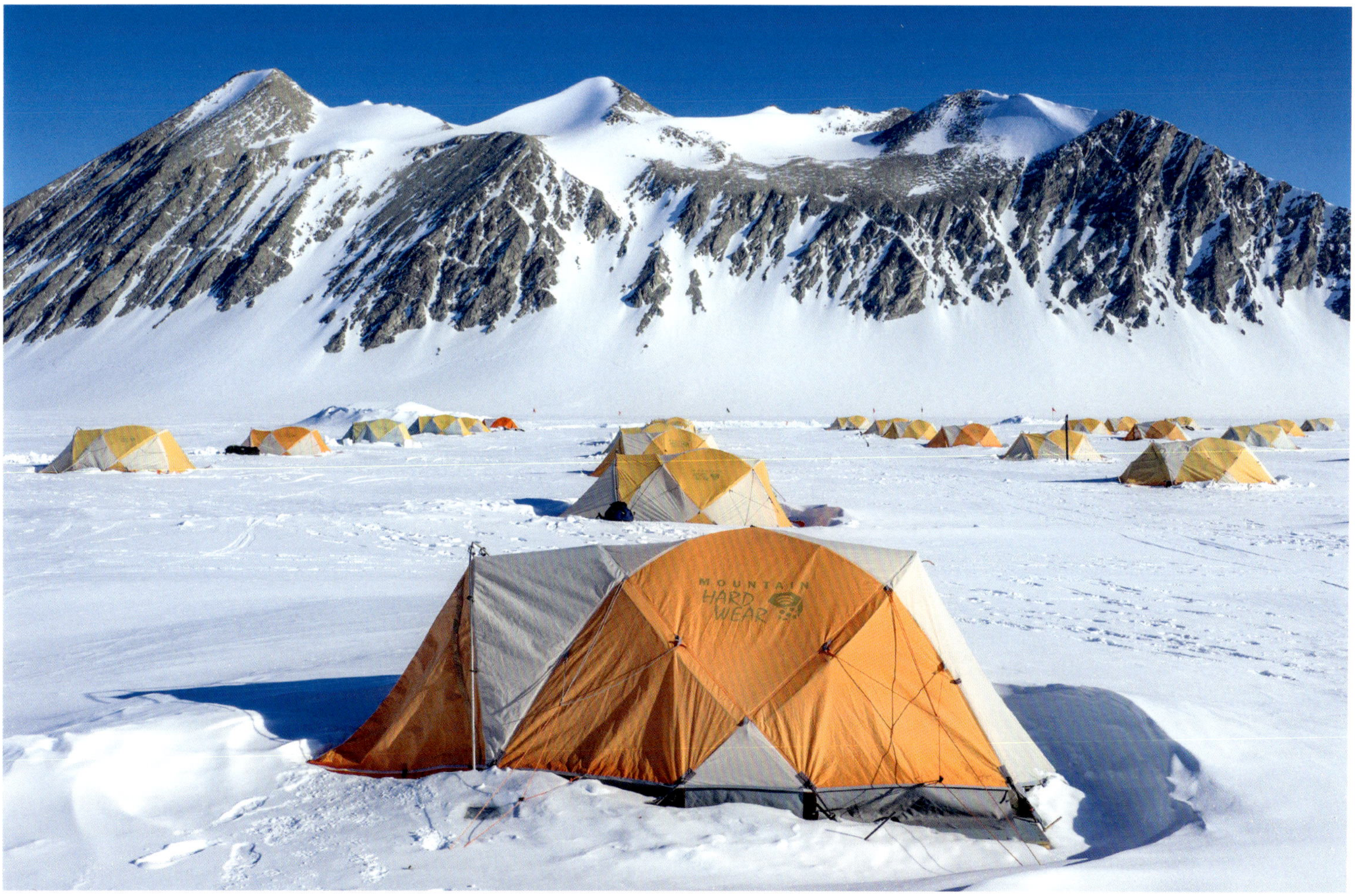

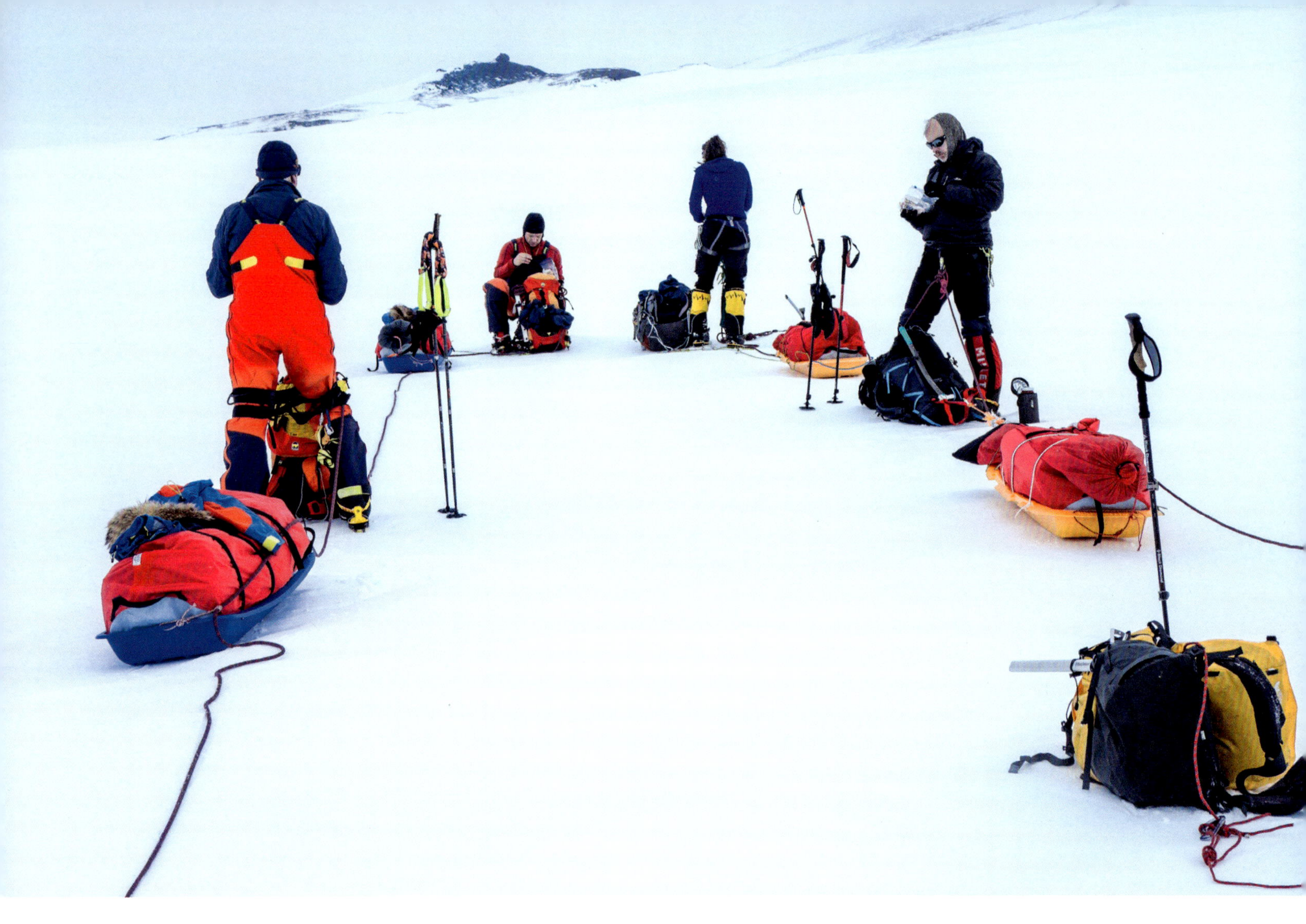

forecast was correct and the bright sunshine created enough contrast for the pilots to search this desert of ice and snow for a suitable place to land. It still took three attempts, three descents which were aborted halfway through, before the plane was taxiing at the foot of Mount Sidley and slowly came to a halt.

My Own Personal Nightmare

I resurface from my thoughts and realize that my hands are as cold as ice. It had suddenly become a lot darker inside my tent, too. "It can't be the setting sun," I think, because the sun never sets during an Antarctic summer. "Strange," I continue to think, reach for my thick hat and stick my head outside.

Immediately, what is exposed of my face is covered in melting, feathery snowflakes. It is snowing, and all that is left of any horizon or the infinite stretches of white is a few feet of visibility. "This is not good," I can hear my own thoughts, and immediately I am reminded of the notorious and lethal phenomenon of "whiteouts": a snow-covered ground and diffuse light conditions combine to make the entire field of vision appear perfectly smooth and featureless. The horizon disappears; the ground and the sky blend into each other, and ultimately, a person may feel as if they are in empty, infinite space. Right now I can still distinguish what is above and what is below me without any issues, but the snow seems to fall faster and faster, and in my head, scenes like from a horror movie begin to roll.

The rest of our small team is currently somewhere in these unknown surroundings on their way to the summit of Mount Sidley. Even when conditions are excellent, this expedition is dangerous. With falling snow and poor visibility, the risk of an accident is greatly increased. Mentally I see scenes of both roped teams suddenly slipping and falling into a glacier crevasse just below the summit. I imagine the climbers trying desperately to scramble back up, fighting for their lives, but they lose their footing time and again. When after hours of waiting there is still no sign of them, it is beginning to dawn on me that I am all alone, the only person here at the high camp, trapped in this Antarctic storm. Should I try to descend on my own, down to the base camp, to the airplane? With the amount of glacier crevasses, that would be suicide. Should I hope for the pilots to come and save me? The brave little DC3 and its crew are waiting for us while we are attempting the expedition, but the Canadians have not brought any equipment for an ascent. It could be days before a rescue team from Union Glacier might reach me. I do have sufficient supplies to wait for them if necessary, but the prospect is less than tempting.

So how come I am sitting here all on my own, in a camp halfway up a mountain that is considered to be one of earth's most remote in the first place?

Calling off a Dream

Just about ten hours ago, this camp was anything but lonely. The sun was shining brightly and the mood amongst the team was good as we were busy making preparations. Backpacks were filled with equipment and provisions, sharp crampons were strapped to polar boots, gloves were fastened with loops to wrists to make sure they would not be lost, and finally we all linked together with ropes. Slowly we began to move and step by step we climbed the sheer, ice-covered slope ahead. There was about ten feet of rope between me and the person in front of me, and behind me the next person followed at roughly the same distance. Thus, even though we were linked by the rope, it felt like we all were on our own. Nobody tried to make conversation, since talking would use up too much precious energy which we needed for our ascent. I trudged through the white landscape and enjoyed the sound of the crampons crunching deep into the tough ice: a sound not unlike crumbling cereal. It was a blessing for me, since I cannot stand the grating sound of snow under boots—it never fails to make me shiver with every step. I smiled as I remembered the tour leader's face as I had told

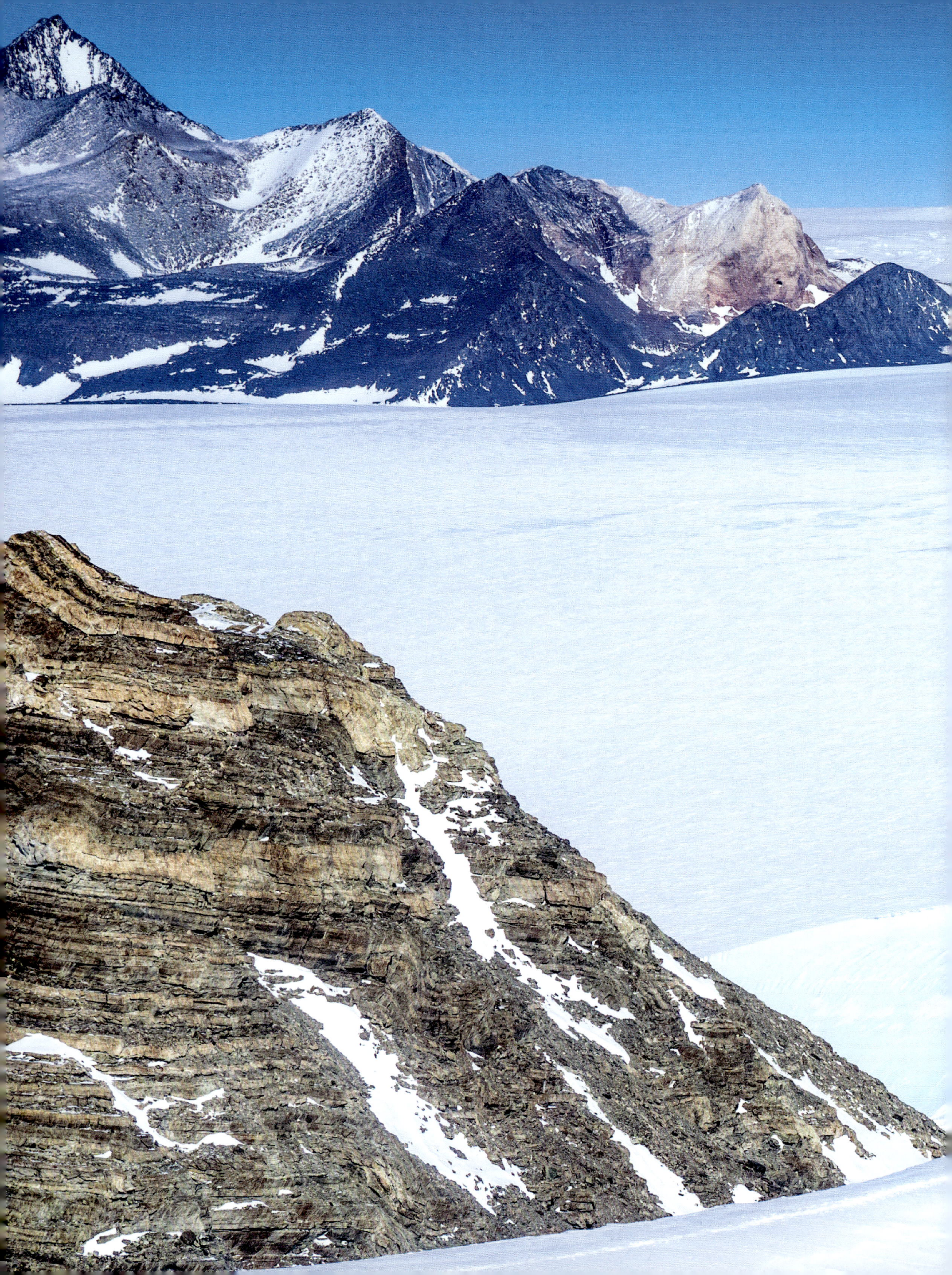

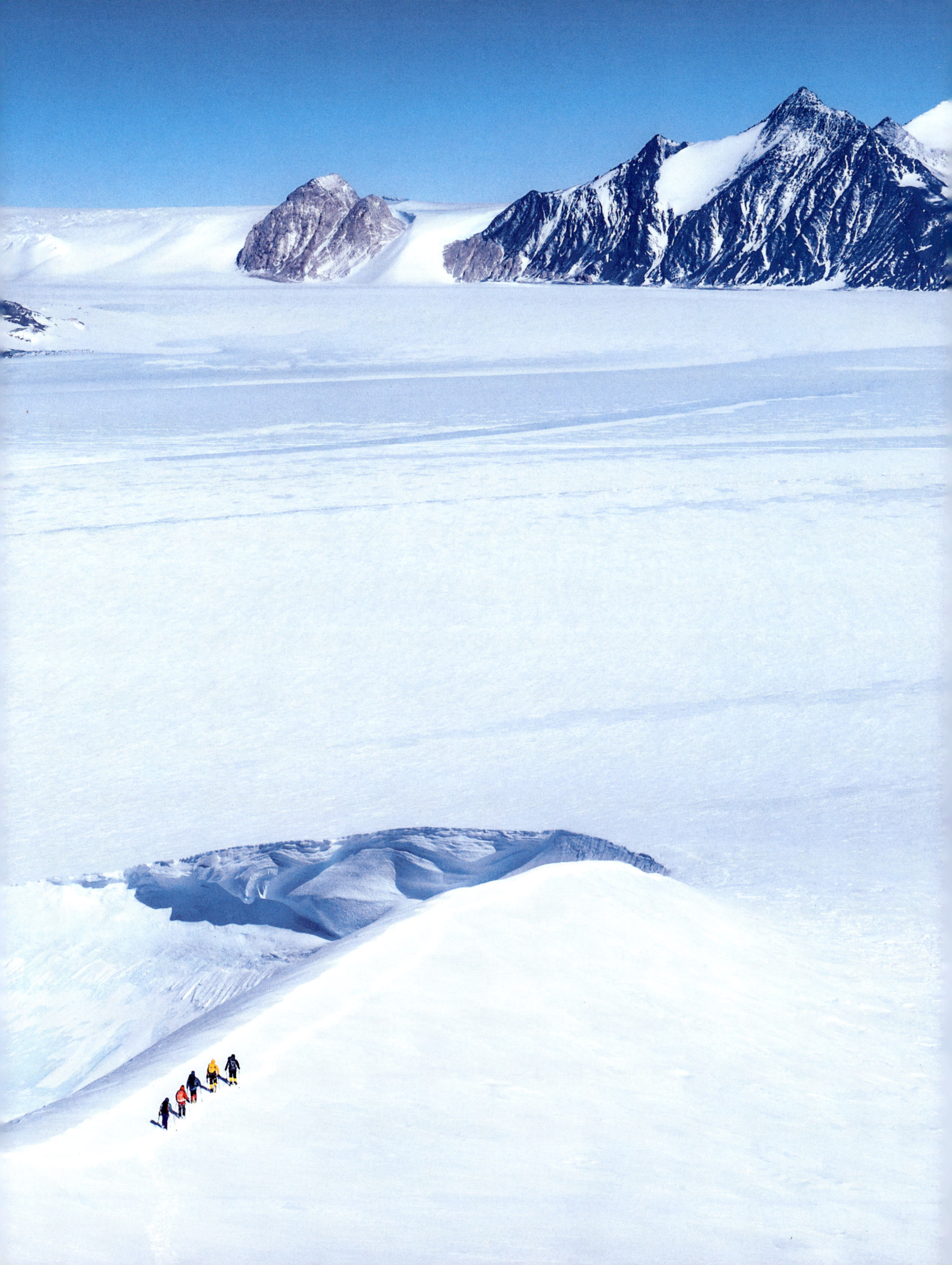

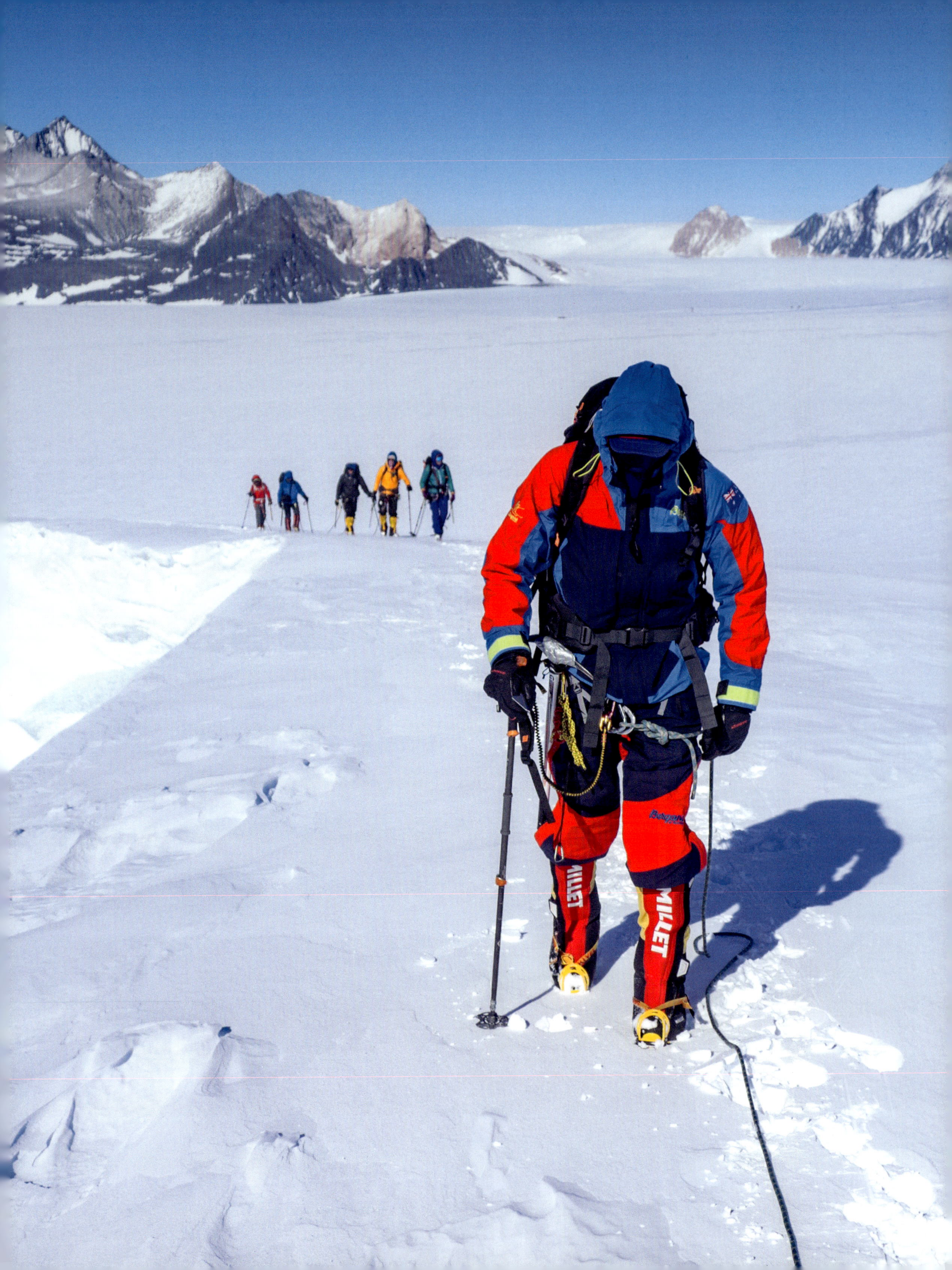

him about this personal aversion of mine during the preparation period for our journey.

An hour later we took our first break. We rested for five minutes and I took the opportunity to drink from my thermos and take a couple of bites of my surprisingly tasty energy bar. I was not aware of it at the time, but later I learned that snacking is one of the more dangerous activities one can engage in while in Antarctica. Apparently, at least six climbers each season will lose a tooth when they bite into a solid frozen energy bar. One of the most important rules for climbers in these climates is therefore: whichever snack or meal is to be consumed at the next stop must be carried in the warm inner pocket rather than the backpack during the hike.

Our five minutes of rest were over in a heartbeat—I had barely finished my energy bar when our tour leader urged us to continue. The human body can stay warm even in these climates—as long as it keeps moving. During periods of rest, it can become dangerously cold within minutes. So we continued our single file trudge, climbing increasingly steep terrain. Quickly, one of my biggest issues as a mountaineer became very apparent: I am not very tall, and so I usually take smaller steps. If I wanted to keep up with the speed of the other three, who were considerably taller, I had to more or less break into a run. Due to the rope, falling behind was not an option—I was, in a sense, "trapped". For a rope party, finding a rhythm for the ascent is essential. Nobody can slow down the person in front of them, or force them to stop. An exhausting task.

While I was already struggling with the hike, the worst case scenario began to unfold: out of nowhere, the weather turned. An icy wind started to blow and made the strenuous hike even less enjoyable. Tiny, sharp ice crystals cut into exposed bit of skin on my face. I pulled up my scarf to cover my chin and nose but it froze almost immediately with the condensation of my breath, so I had to pull it back down again soon afterwards. This again exposed my skin to ice and wind, and it was hard to say which of the two elements was the least unpleasant.

An endless back and forth began: pulling my scarf up, pulling it down again, pulling it up, and pulling it down again. I muttered curses into the damp, cold cloth that covered my face. Soon the first doubts began to nag in my mind. "What happens if the weather gets even worse? What if there's a real storm?" I began to realize that the training that I had undergone in the run up to this expedition—hikes across the snow-covered alps, first attempts at ice—could not make up for my complete lack of experience climbing mountains under these conditions.

My mountaineering experience thus far consisted of hikes and climbs in warmer climates. I was worried I might make mistakes and slip, which meant I would put not only myself but the whole rope team at risk. A rope team which, with the exception of myself, boasted weathered mountaineers with years of experience, several polar expeditions, and even a successful climb of Mount Everest. As the weather conditions continued to worsen, I kept pondering these thoughts.

In my mind, adventure and reason were having an argument which went something like this:

A: "If you call off the expedition right now, you're probably never going to climb the Volcanic Seven Summits. Calling off this mission means calling off the whole project."

R: "You're not one of those self-aggrandizing mountaineers who ticks off summits like a shopping list. You don't need to prove anything here."

A: "You could be the first German and the first photographer to climb the highest volcanic summits in each of the continents. Wouldn't that be amazing?"

R: "Do you still remember the promise you gave to your family? You swore you'd be careful and that you'd come home to them safe and sound."

At that moment, a picture of my family appeared quite clearly in my head. I didn't have to think twice before I knew what would be the right thing to do. "I'm going back," I said to the others, and I stopped.

My team members looked embarrassed, but

An icy wind started to blow and made the strenuous hike even less enjoyable.

Emilio Palma, born in 1979, is the first person to have been born on mainland Antarctica. He holds a Guinness World Record for being the only person in this world who is recorded as having been the first person to have been born on any continent.

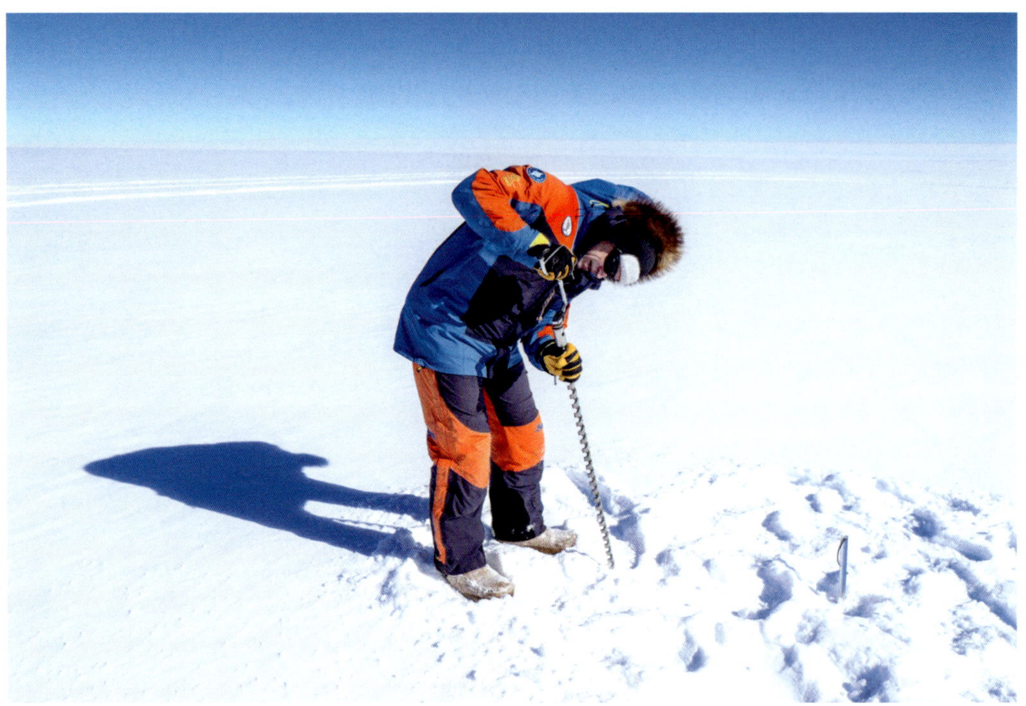

the fact that they didn't reply at all told me that they shared my assessment of the situation. I had made the right decision. And so I really did turn around, I unhooked my carabiner from the rope and started to walk downhill. With each step I took, I began to feel lighter. Luckily our tents were still clearly visible from up here, so there was no risk of me losing my way. We had not encountered any crevasses on the way up here either, and so my tour leader let me head back on my own.

My decision turned out to be the right one in more than just one way. It was not just a decision against reaching the summit, but also a decision for another, similarly intimidating task. Here I was in the world's vastest uninhabited region, as remote from any civilization as I could possibly be—all on my own. My dream of exploring foreign territory was at my fingertips. Up until that point, I had always had my team to depend on. Now, in a liberating moment, I was walking with a happy spring in my step towards absolute solitude.

A so-called katabatic wind with extreme speeds is moving towards Antarctica.

The Dream Lives On

All this happened a few hours ago now; hours during which I did nothing but sit and enjoy this extraordinary feeling that is still the closest I have had to being an astronaut; hours during which I jumped through the snow like a child and left traces in the untouched snow; hours during which I first tasted, then feasted on Antarctica's beauty and her incredible silence.

As much as I enjoyed the feeling of remoteness, I am beyond relieved when after nine hours of waiting I finally hear faint, faraway voices. It still takes another hour for my fellow mountaineers to reach the camp again, but I am waiting for them with a profound feeling of calm and a perpetual smile on my face. After our hellos have been said and I congratulated them on their incredible feat, they tell me about their experience at the summit. "Don't worry about it, you didn't really miss much," they comforted me. "It was all cloudy up at the summit, there was no visibility whatsoever." On top of that, they tell me about the relentless winds, their frozen hands, and brutal temperatures of up to -22 degrees. The ice in their beards and their visible exhaustion were sufficient proof of just how difficult a climb it had been.

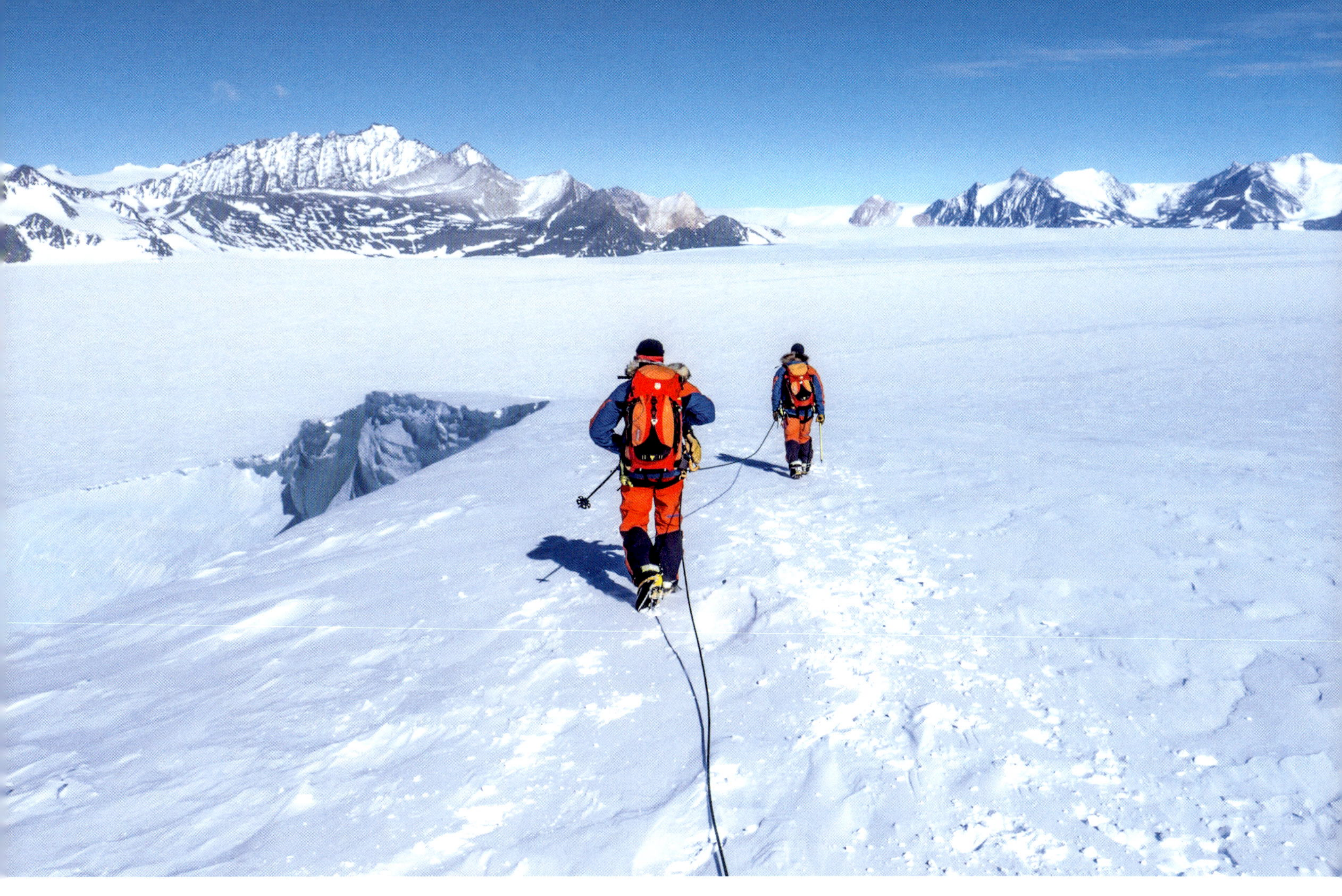

There is not much time to recover though. Eric contacts us from Union Glacier via satellite phone with bad news regarding the weather forecast. A so-called katabatic wind with extreme speeds is moving towards Antarctica. We have to leave Mount Sidley and even Union Glacier as quickly as possible. Thus my dream of adventure on this extraordinary, underexplored continent ends a few days sooner than I had planned. I am not sad though and I have no regrets. My time here left me with many incredible impressions and memories as well as a deep sense of longing and hope to maybe return one day and explore this special place on my own.

Maybe next time I will visit the top of my current wish list, Mount Erebus on Ross Island, an island near mainland Antarctica. It is an active volcano with the peculiar feature that one of only nine currently known permanent lava lakes bubbles inside it. This possibility of a glance inside the simmering heart of the earth right amidst a sea of ice embodies nature's fiercest extremes and speaks to my fascination for fire and ice. On my flight back—destination Tierra del Fugo, how appropriate for a trip of ice and fire—I am not only reminiscing about my extraordinary adventures in Antarctica's eternal ice, I am also recalling my three-day encounter with the lava lake Erta Ale in the Danakil Desert, Ethiopia.

> Maybe next time I will visit the top of my current wish list, Mount Erebus.

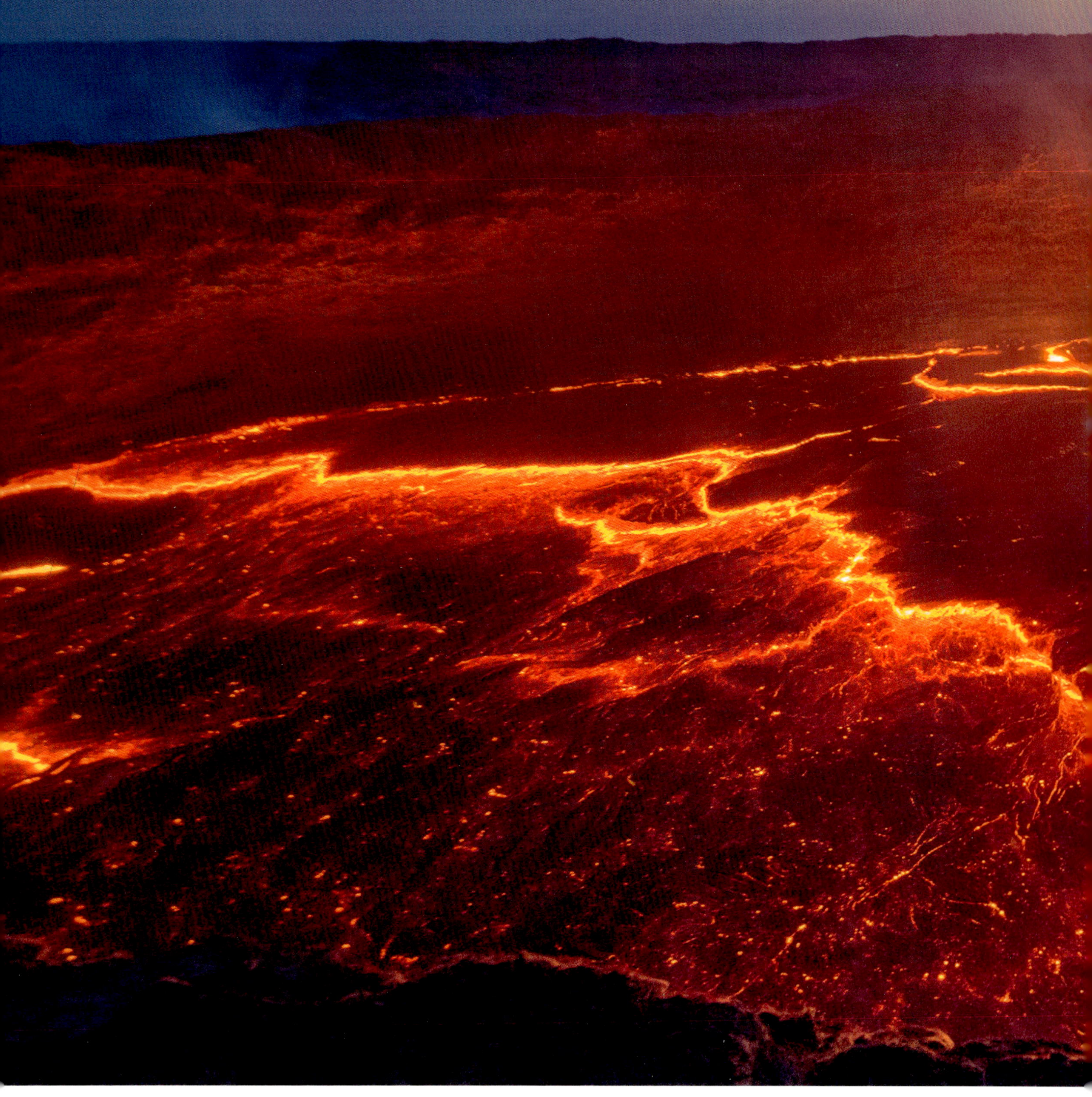

As I was standing there at the crater, the heat was so relentless I had to turn away at regular intervals. The gas that came pouring out of the crater had me in coughing fits and my forearm was still bleeding from a fall I had taken earlier on sharp, rocky ground. Still, I felt in my element. The thermometer which I had pointed at the lake showed temperatures of above 1000 degrees. Imagine an experience like that, but surrounded by snow and ice, far away from civilization, at Mount Erebus in Antarctica. Maybe one day…

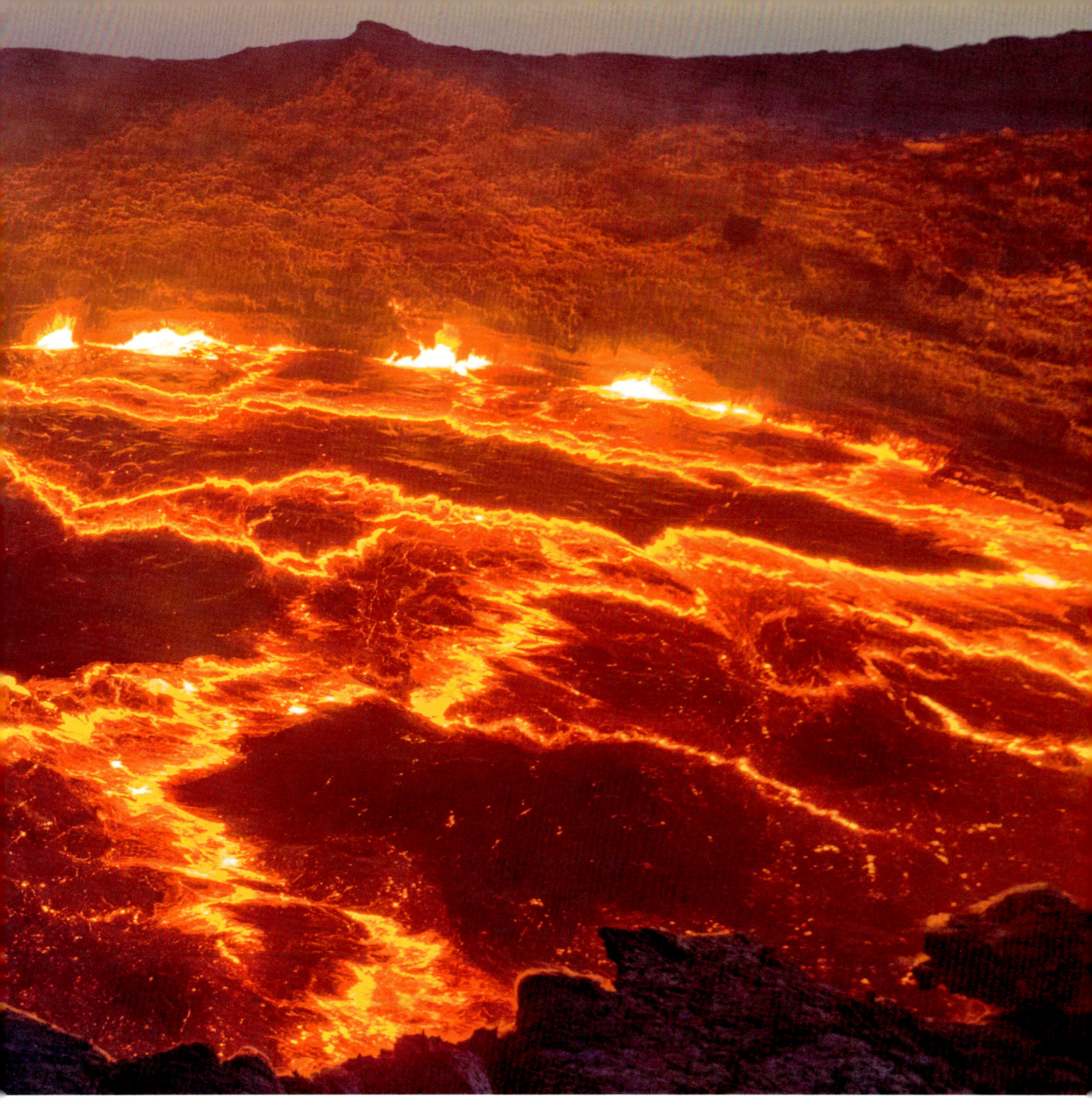

Lava lakes are a rare phenomenon; very few of them maintain their molten state for a long period of time or permanently. In 1979, the space probe Voyager 1 discovered lava lakes on Io, one of Jupiter's moons.

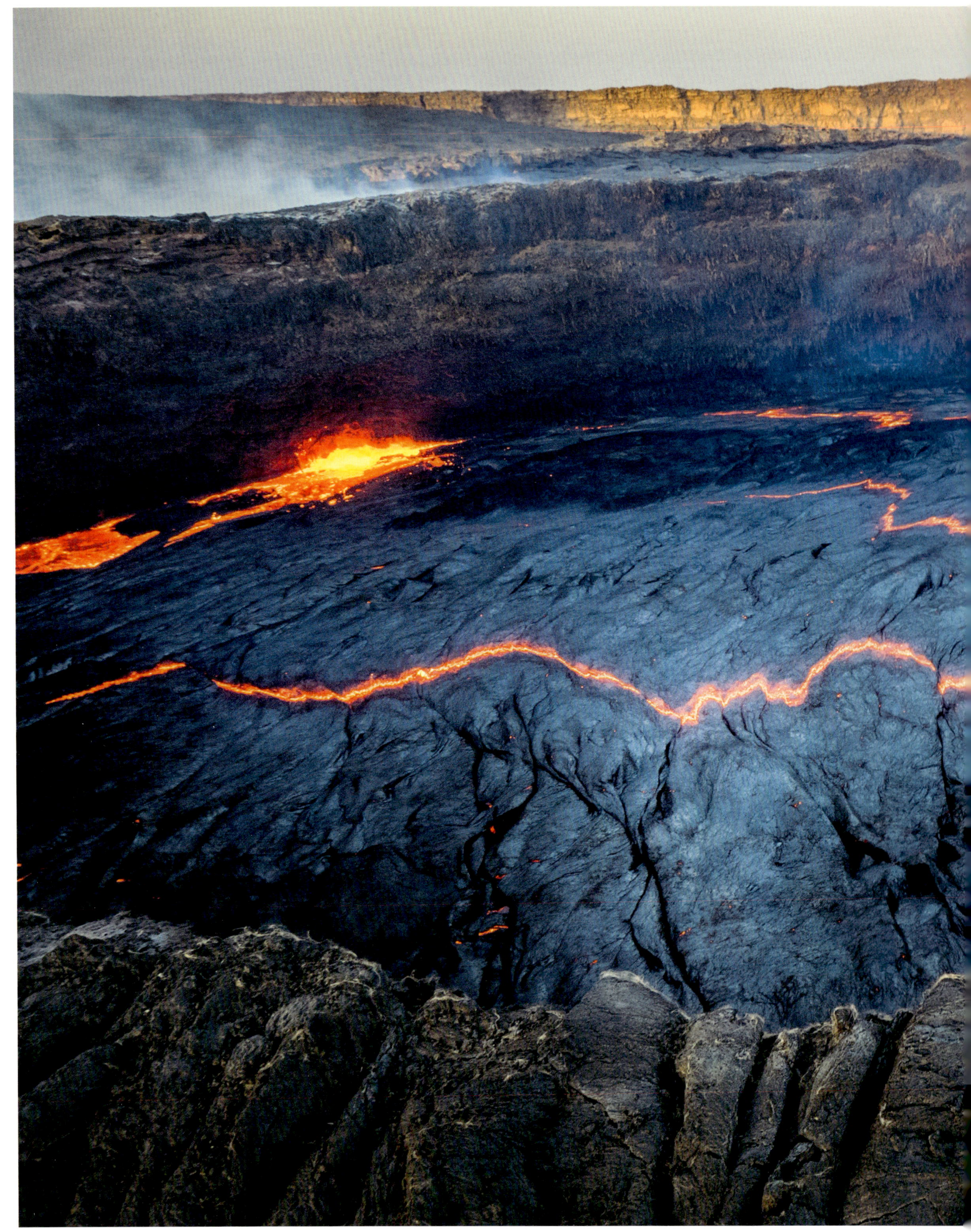

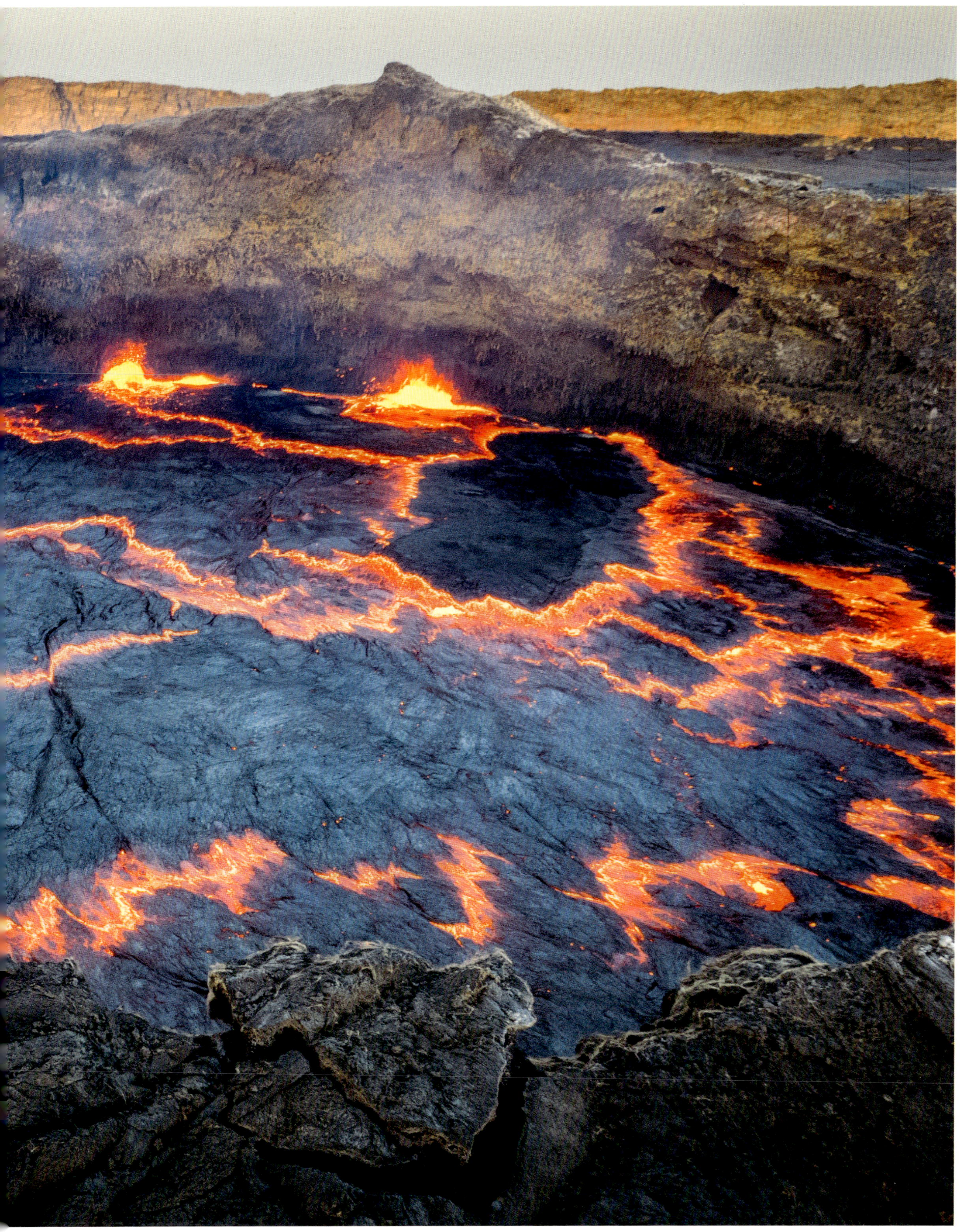

 Antarctica | Mount Sidley

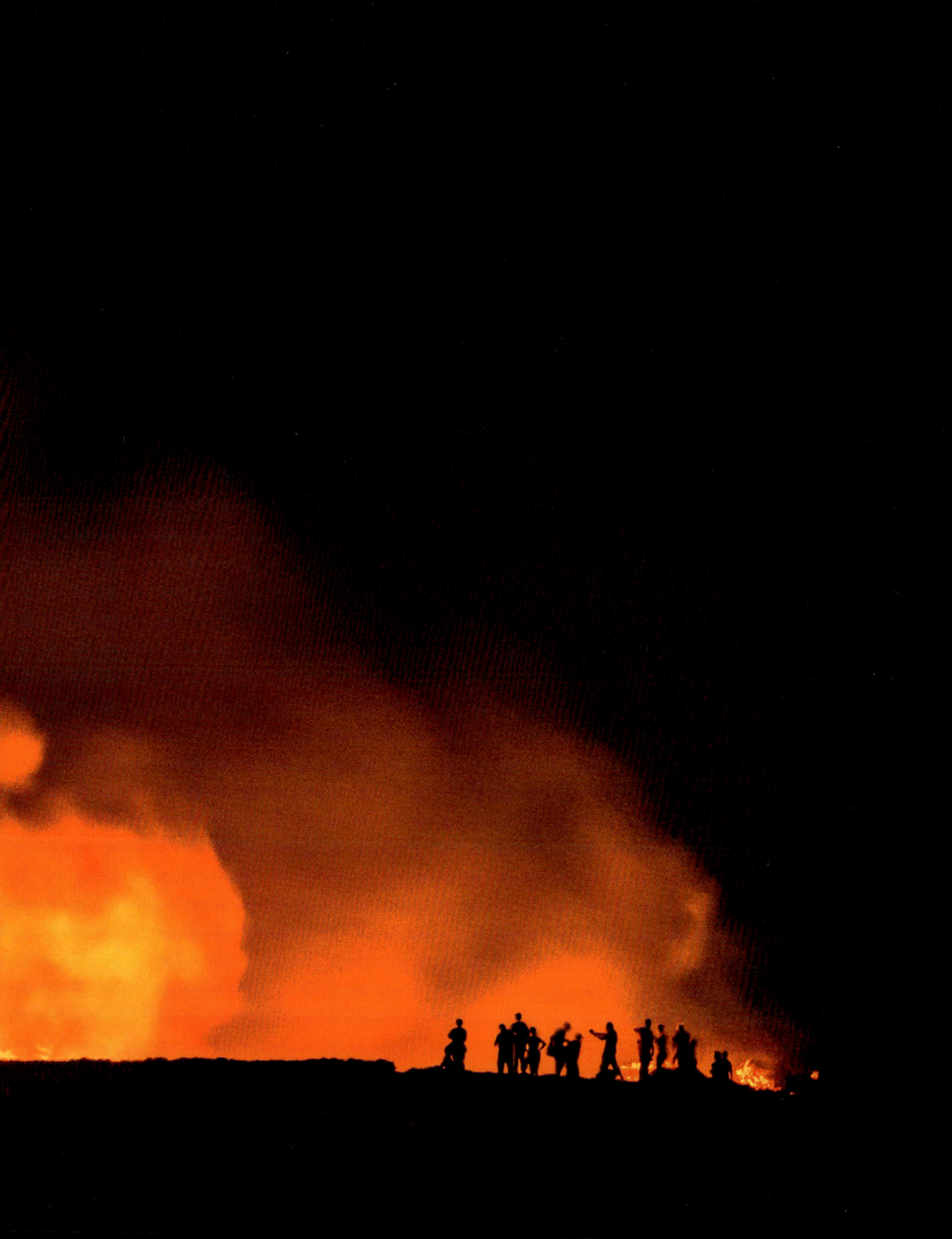

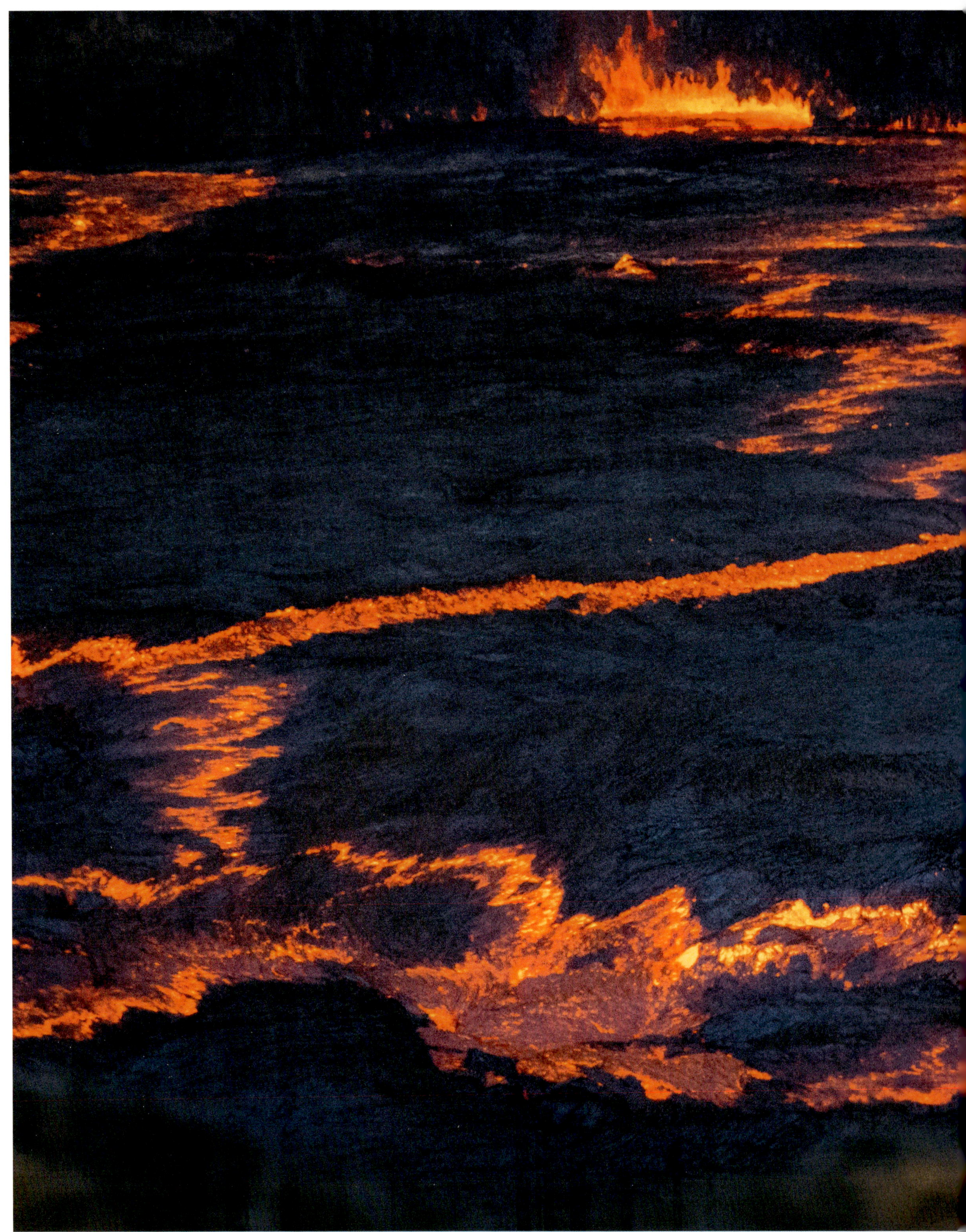

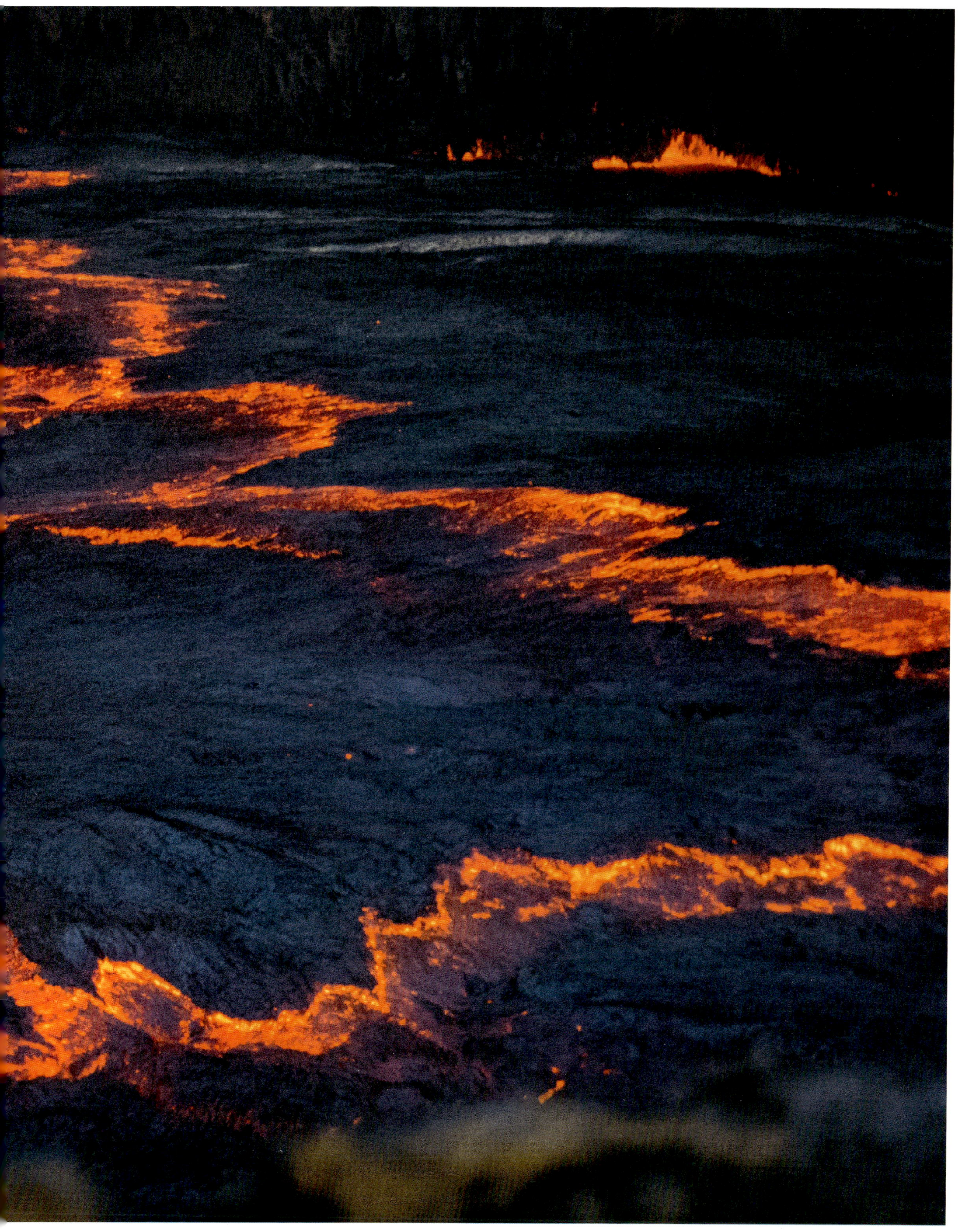

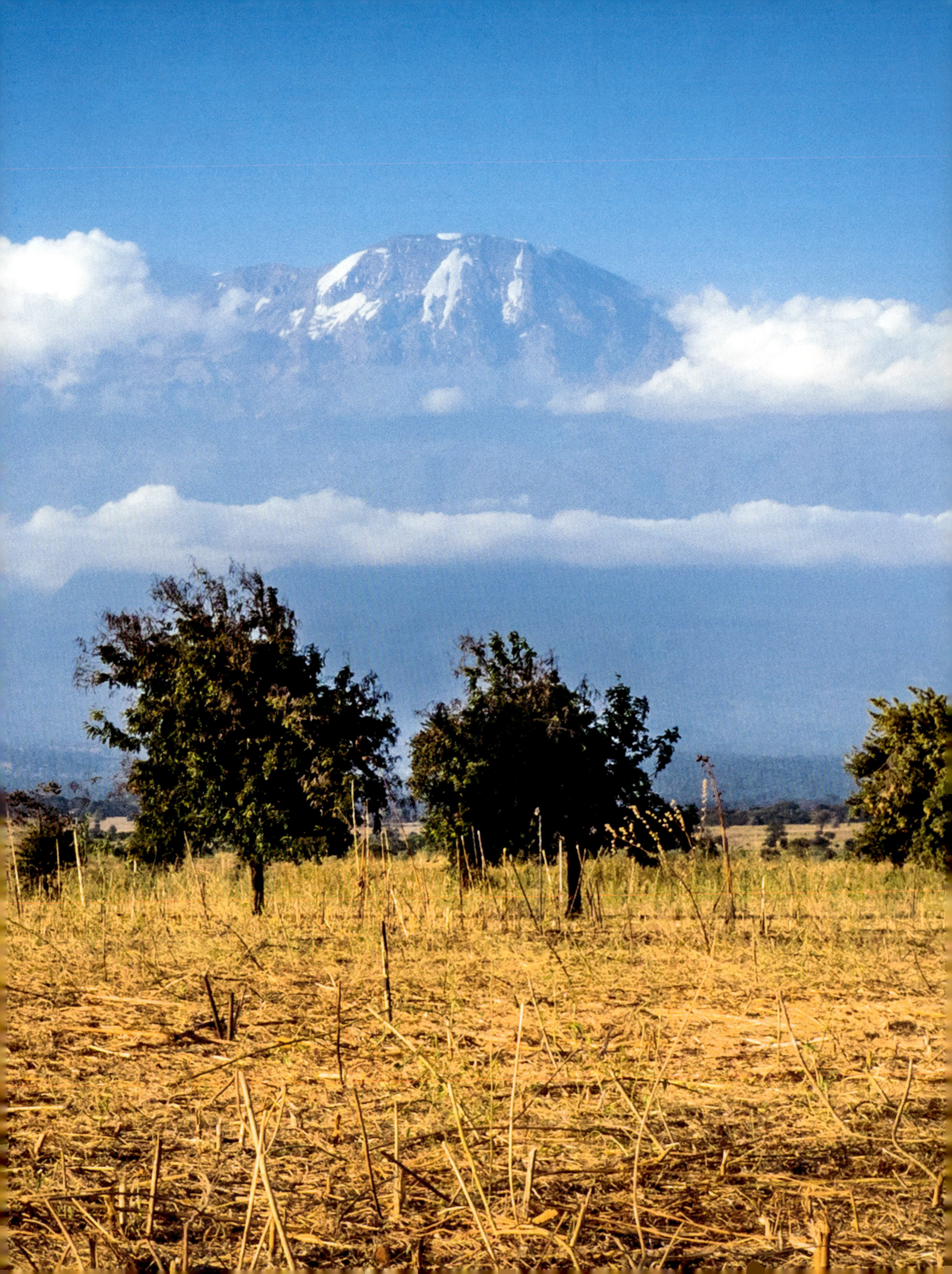

2

KILIMANJARO

Pioneers on the Roof of Africa

Tanzania

Mount Kilimanjaro in north-eastern Tanzania is located in a tropical zone some hundred miles south of the equator. In theory, I could not be much further from the icy poles. Yet here, within our planet's hottest latitudes, I encounter thick, age-old layers of ice as well as permafrost. I am currently at an elevation of 20,000 feet and just a few feet away from a rugged, towering glacier. I am cycling. Yes, I am actually cycling up here—or rather, I am riding an e-bike, at 20,000 feet. This feeling of freedom combined with the surrounding natural beauty makes me blurt out: "Are you sure this is not a dream?" Roman, my friend and companion on this journey, smiles and replies: "Absolutely, it's all real." It is so real, in fact, that after a few more rotations of the pedals we cannot help but jump off our bikes and hug each other in euphoria. We have reached one of the world's most well-recognised signposts, although it looks more like a wooden fence. It says: "Mount Kilimanjaro. Congratulations, you are now at Uhuru Peak, Tanzania. Africa's Highest Point". Roman and I have made it—and we have done something nobody has done before us. We are the first people to have reached the roof of the world by e-bike.

"The Future Doesn't Exist"

A few days ago we had all but given up hope of our pioneering project. It was just this little "e" before the "bike" that almost caused our plans to fail. Roman and I were sitting on uncomfortable wooden chairs in a restaurant whose tables were draped with ugly plastic tablecloths. We were watching the waiter, who was wearing the region's traditional clothes, as he balanced two bottles of beer on a tray. There was not much else for us to do. "How did we even come up with such a stupid idea?" I asked Roman, exasperated.

„Congratulations, you are now at Uhuru Peak, Tanzania. Africa's Highest Point"

Going on an e-bike expedition in Tanzania, in a country where the closest e-bike seller is more than 6000 miles away, in a country where, according to our waiter at least, "anything is possible, there's always a way", but where things just move so much more slowly than they do back home in Germany. The problem was that our e-bike batteries, which we had decided to ship over, still had not arrived, and there was no sign of them doing so in the near future. Every day for the past five or six days we had been told they would probably arrive "tomorrow". The local shipping company's manager, whom I called daily, sometimes twice a day, remained perfectly calm throughout this ordeal. He did not seem to care that we had been sitting around with nothing to do but wait for several days now.

"Here's to tomorrow!" I rolled my eyes and held out my beer bottle to Roman. "To a future that doesn't exist yet," Roman replied in a sarcastic tone and clinked his beer bottle against mine. Thomas, our hotel's extremely well-dressed manager, had just explained to us this afternoon that in Africa, things move at a different pace. "Things that will happen tomorrow, that is to say, in the future, don't concern us today. It's tomorrow, after all." He smiled a cryptic smile, and we felt as though we were talking to a philosopher. Optimistic people would call this way of life "deceleration". For us, the African approach to time was nothing short of infuriating. Yesterday we had already seen Mount Kilimanjaro, whose name translates as "White Mountain". It was nothing but a glimpse really, far away from the edges of Moshi, a city with a population of 150,000. Yet Mount Kilimanjaro was unmistakable with its three striking main craters: Shira, the oldest and shortest of the three, measures 13,140 feet; Mawenzi, sheer and jagged, sits at 16,893 feet; at 19,341 feet, gently sloping Kigo is the highest of the three summits.

Mount Kilimanjaro is one of the world's tallest freestanding mountains. It sits at 19,341 feet above sea level and 14,000 feet above the Maasai Steppe that surrounds it. The second-highest mountain in Africa is Mount Kenya, located just over 200 miles away from Mount Kilimanjaro.

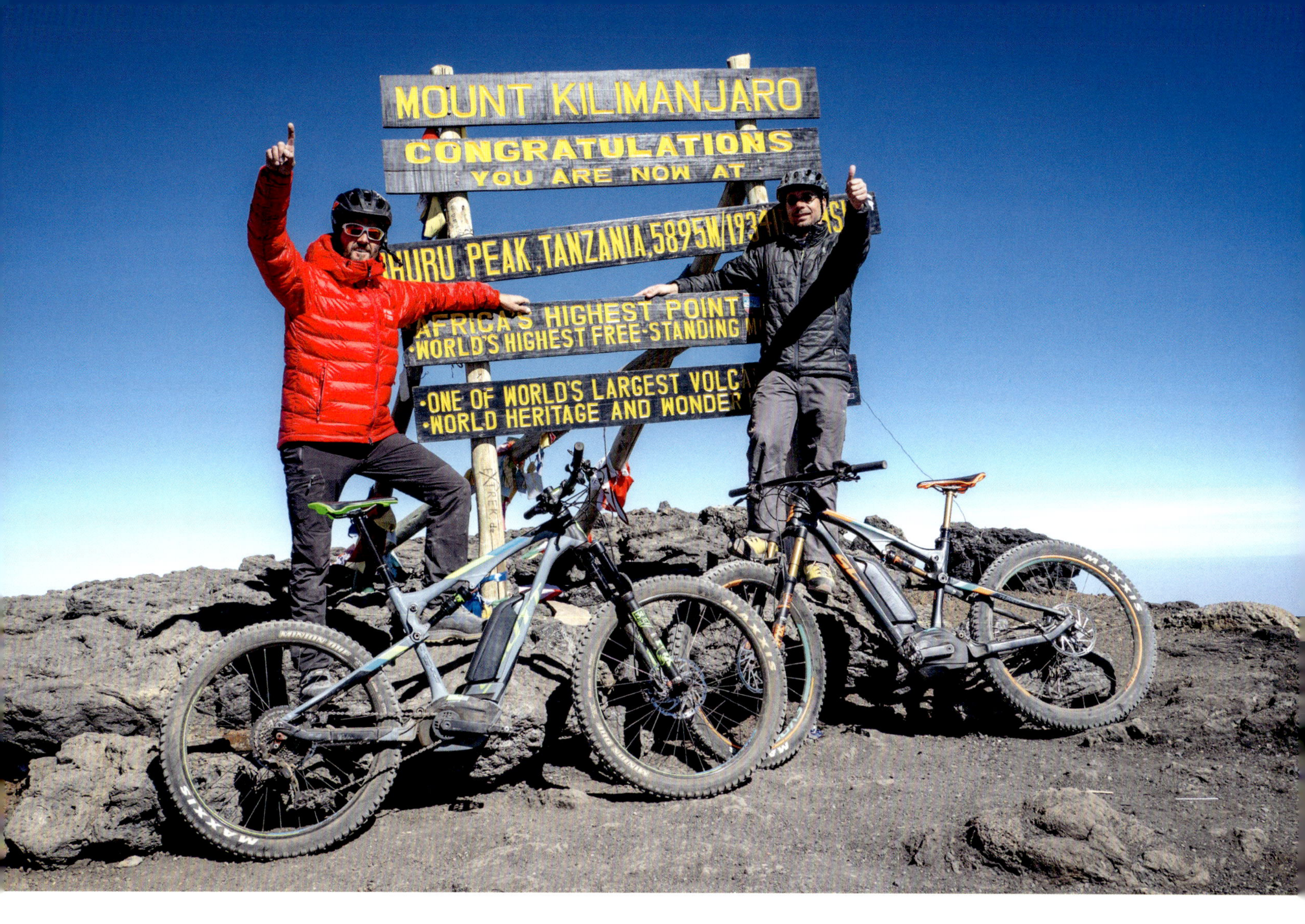

MOUNT KILIMANJARO
CONGRATULATIONS
YOU ARE NOW AT
UHURU PEAK, TANZANIA, 5895M/193
AFRICA'S HIGHEST POINT
WORLD'S HIGHEST FREE-STANDING M
ONE OF WORLD'S LARGEST VOLC
WORLD HERITAGE AND WONDER

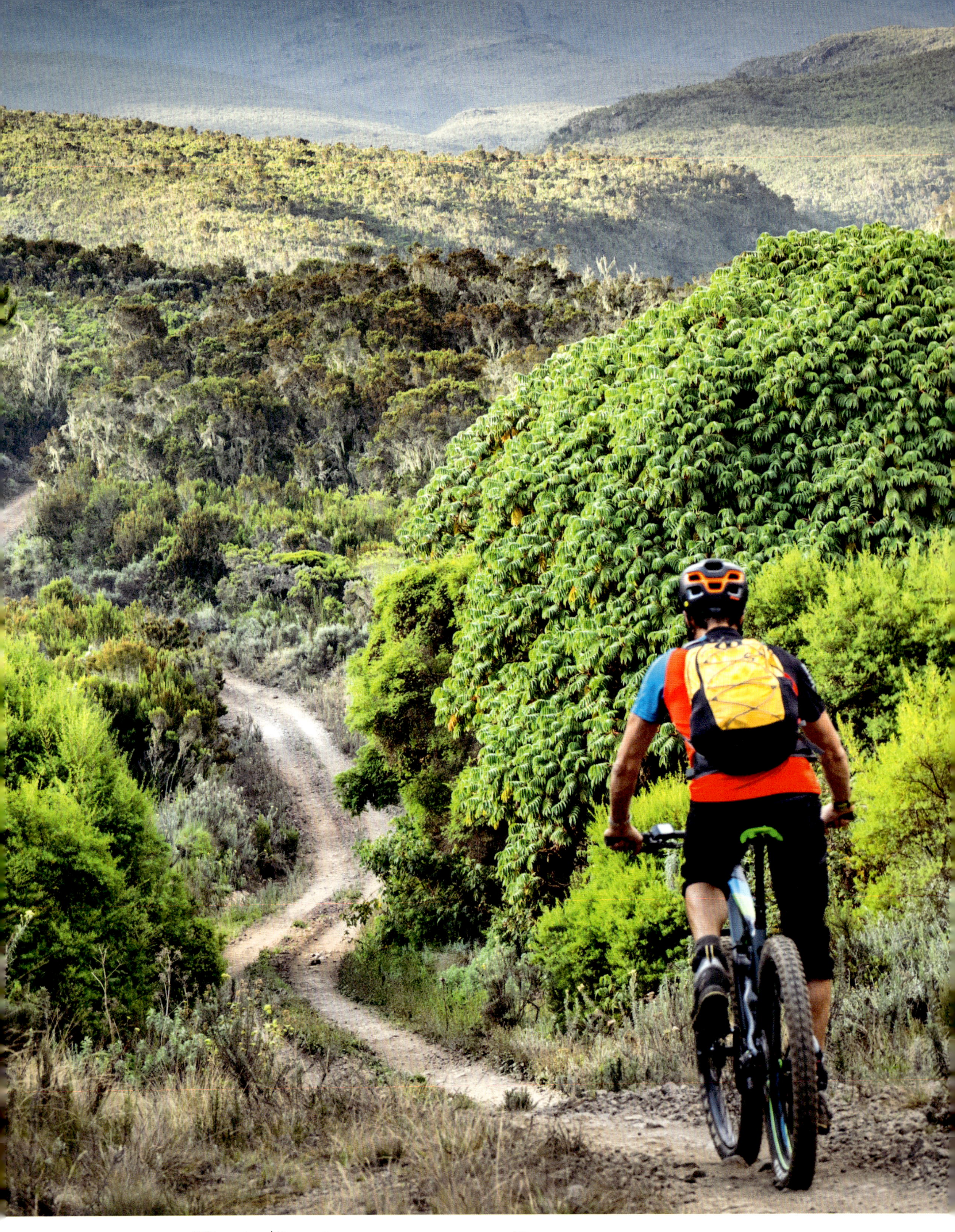

The remarkable thing about Mount Kilimanjaro is that it is not only Africa's tallest mountain and volcano; it is also the tallest free-standing mountain in the whole world. Anyone who wants to climb it has to pass through six distinct climate zones. Even from such a distance, they were clearly visible:

Straight ahead, the golden savanna and its famous baobab trees.

Right behind it, the fertile zone, which is ideal for plantations.

The humid, green rainforest zone with the striking line of clouds at roughly 10,000 feet, which is where the real climb up Kilimanjaro begins.

Above the clouds, another fertile zone that is covered in bright green heather and moorland.

The ash-grey desert region between the summits.

The craggy arctic zone with intermittent glaciers up toward Kibo. This is the summit, that right now seems all but out of reach to us.

After four more stressful days of countless phone calls and muttered curses, the African future finally reaches us in our European present. The day the shipping company director knocked on our hotel doors at 5am is the day on which, according to the original schedule, we should have been back home with our families. At last we received our eagerly anticipated batteries.

"Let's go!" Roman cheered. Our two Tanzanian tour guides with the unusual names Goodluck and Nikolaus were just as delighted as we were. They finally had the opportunity to earn the money we had promised them at our arrival. What is more, they too were quite excited to see the e-bikes in action.In Europe, e-bikes are becoming increasingly popular. In other parts of the world, they are still a rarity, and Tanzania is one such place. A few months ago, Goodluck and Nikolaus had led a group of mountain bikers up the Kibo summit, but they had never seen e-bikes in real life before—only in videos. "They were world-famous professional cyclists," they told us proudly the first time we met, one day after our arrival. In their small, chaotic office they showed us the route on a faded map. "This part here will be steep, even for you and your e-bikes," Goodluck explained and pointed at a passage just below the Horombo Huts. "I don't think you'll be able to cycle up there."

"We'll see," I thought.

First Zone: Rainforest

Originally we had thought that our journey through the first zone, the rainforest, would be ideal for testing the power of our e-bikes. Roman and I had been looking forward to this part of the journey the most. We had read accounts of humidity, deep mud, and thin roots which stretched across narrow paths.

Yet for a long time after our departure, we saw little of this wild, untouched nature. Every now and then there was a rich green plant, or occasional tree; yet the majority of the vegetation on the side of the road was covered in grey specks of dust. The sounds were not reminiscent of the jungle, either. Occasionally there was a faint, faraway bird call, but we did not hear the screams of monkeys that we had found described in so many guide books.

For cyclists, the Kilema-Route is the only official route up Mount Kilimanjaro. As it turned out, it was also the official route for a trusty jeep which served as an ambulance around here, and which later went speeding past us honking its horn. Given the amount of noise and traffic, it did not come as a surprise that there were no monkeys to be seen. It did not matter though, for soon we reached a steep path of small rocks and loose pebbles. The road there seemed ideal for a little demonstration of what our e-bikes could do. We gave Roman's bright green bike to Goodluck, who

Anyone who wants to climb it has to pass through six distinct climate zones.

Even though Mount Kilimanjaro is located only about two hundred miles south of the equator, it is one of only two mountain ranges in Africa that still have glaciers. Yet in recent years, the glacial ice has been melting rapidly and researchers predict that soon the glaciers will vanish altogether.

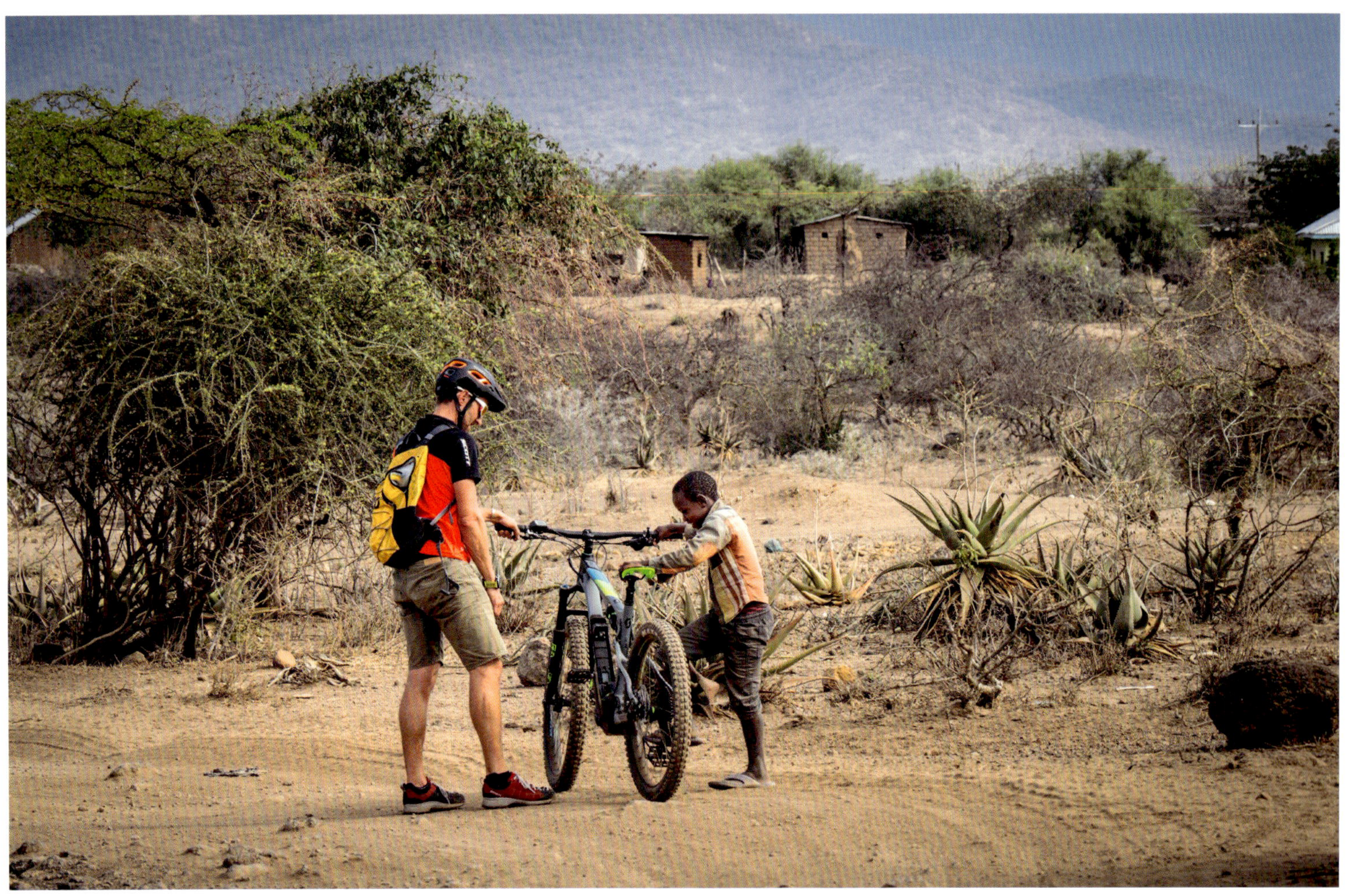

climbed the slope laughing with joy. "That's not an e-bike, that's an r-bike," he said laughing after he had finished his test run. "That's a real Rocket-Bike!" On that day, we had climbed up to just about 10,000 feet, so there was no need for our rocket-propulsion just yet.

We set up our first camp in the area where rainforest gave way to moorland. Even though we were not far away from the road, in a small clearing, it felt as though we were deep in the heart of nature. Pale grass that reached our knees covered the clearing. Small, thin trees with tangled branches and covered in vivid green lichens stood at the entrance to the near-impenetrable tropical forest. It grew rapidly darker as night fell.

Our bikes weighed more than 45 pounds, so we struggled to heave them across some tree branches and up into the trees. According to Goodluck, there were mice in this forest which would come out at night to gnaw away at the tires if we kept our bikes right here on the ground. I wondered what else we might encounter in these woods. As the daylight faded, we set up our camouflage-green tents. We hooked our bikes' batteries up to a brand-new car battery to charge overnight. Then we sat down at a camping table covered with food, with the Milky Way glowing above us. The fresh evening air cooled us down as we devoured large portions of vegetables seasoned with African spices and cooked to perfection—not too soft, not too hard. At last it felt as though we had found the famously unspoiled wilderness of Mount Kilimanjaro.

Second Zone: Heather and Moorland

Mount Kilimanjaro's natural delights kept us captivated throughout the following days of our journey. Thanks to our rocket-bikes we made our way up without much effort and so we still had time to take regular breaks, allowing us to admire the endless wonders and variety we were in the midst of. Although botany is most decidedly not a forte of mine, I enjoyed the

Mount Kilimanjaro is located near the famous "East African Rift". In this area of high volcanic activity, the African Plate is slowly splitting into two tectonic plates over the course of millions of years. In some places, the resulting valley is deeper than 3000 feet.

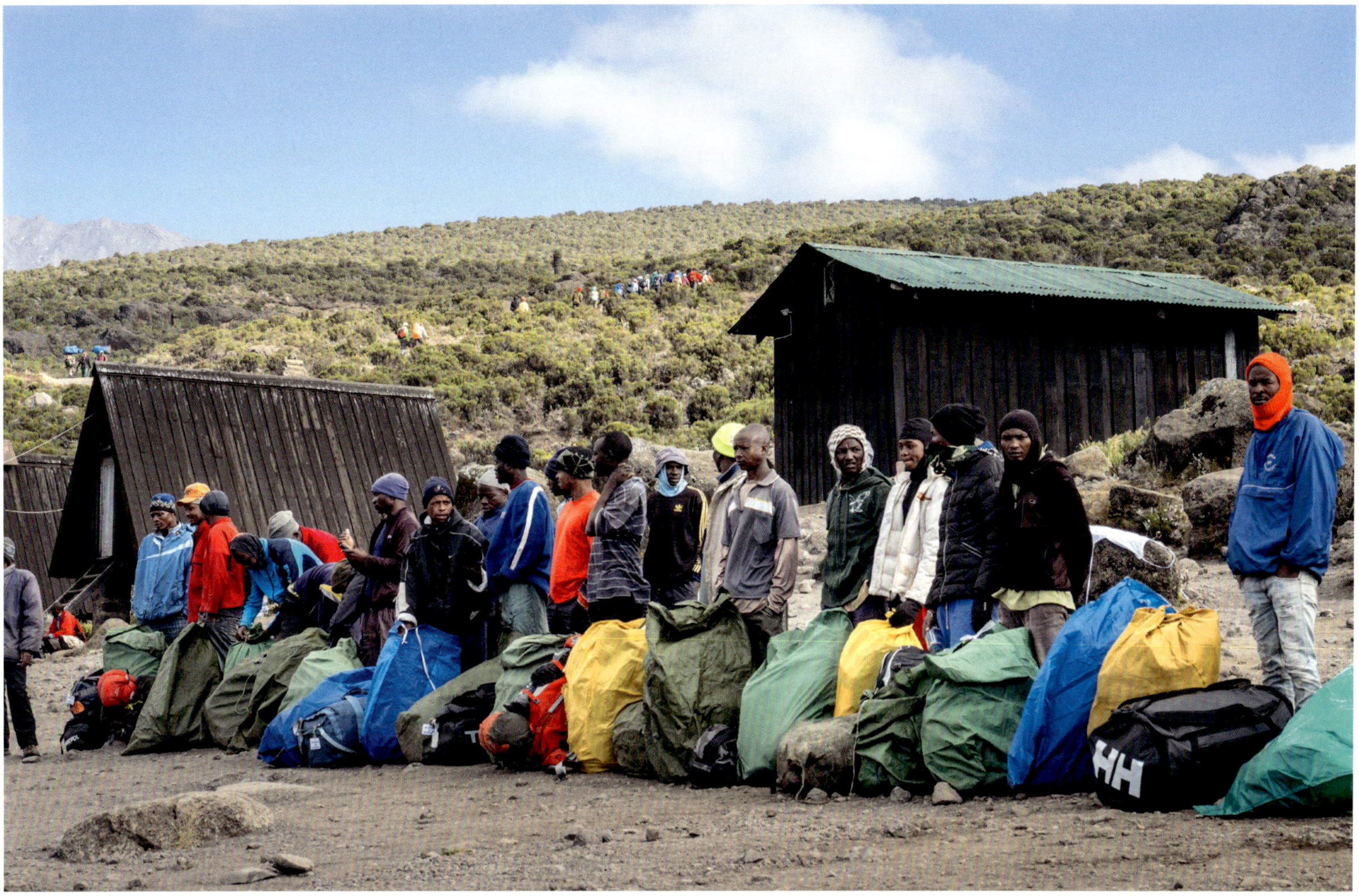

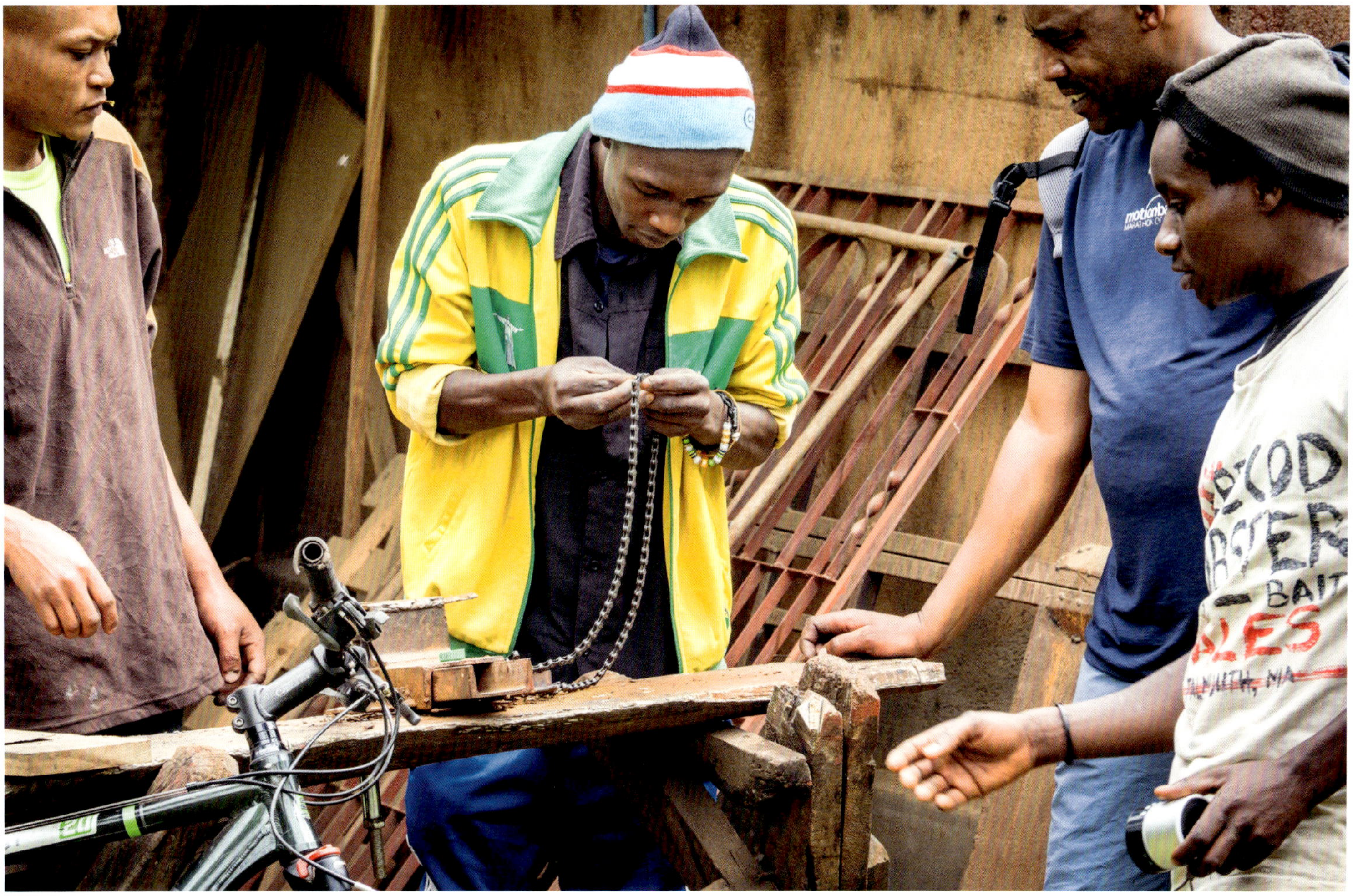

　　　　　　　　　　Tanzania | Kilimanjaro

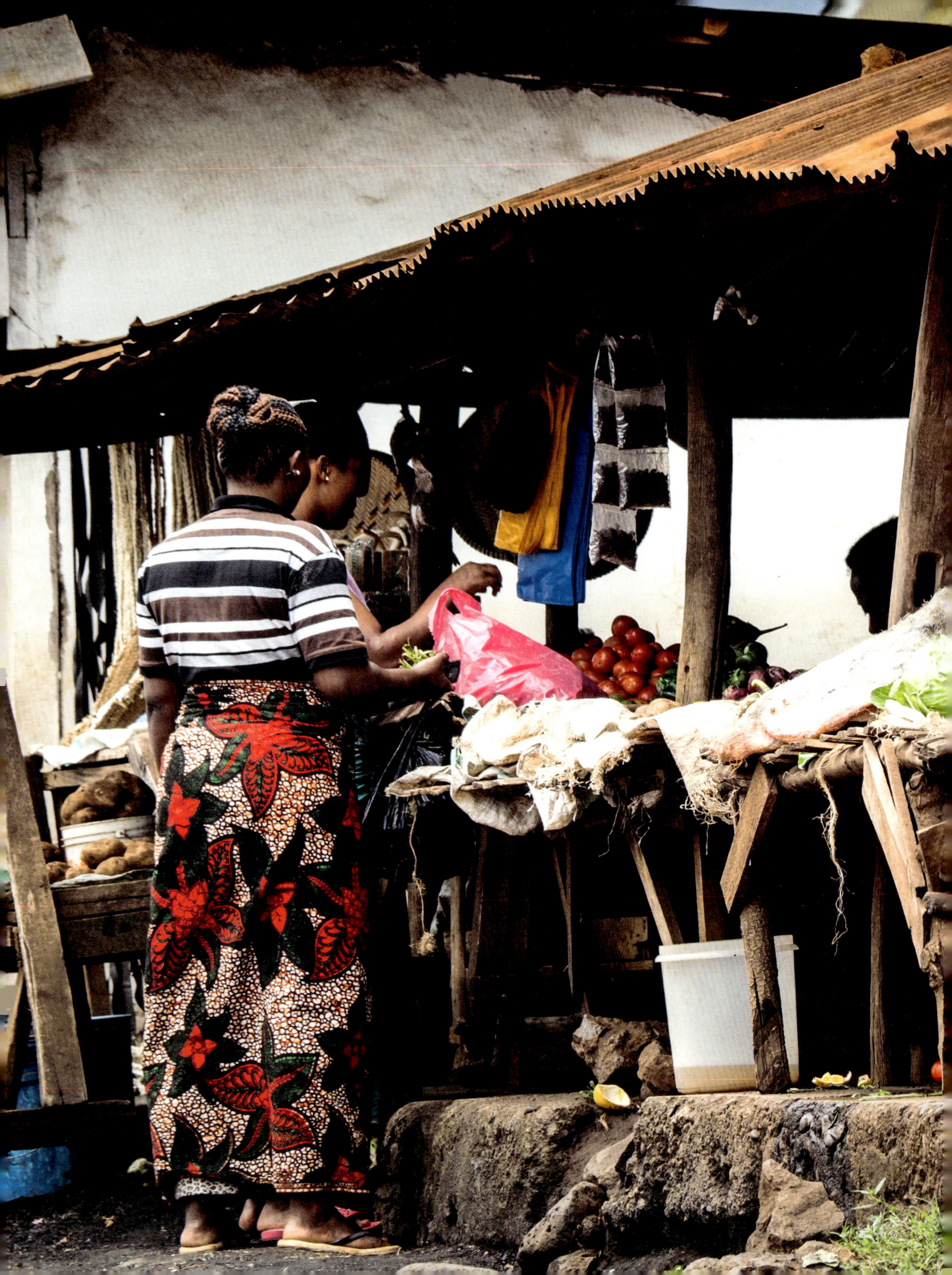

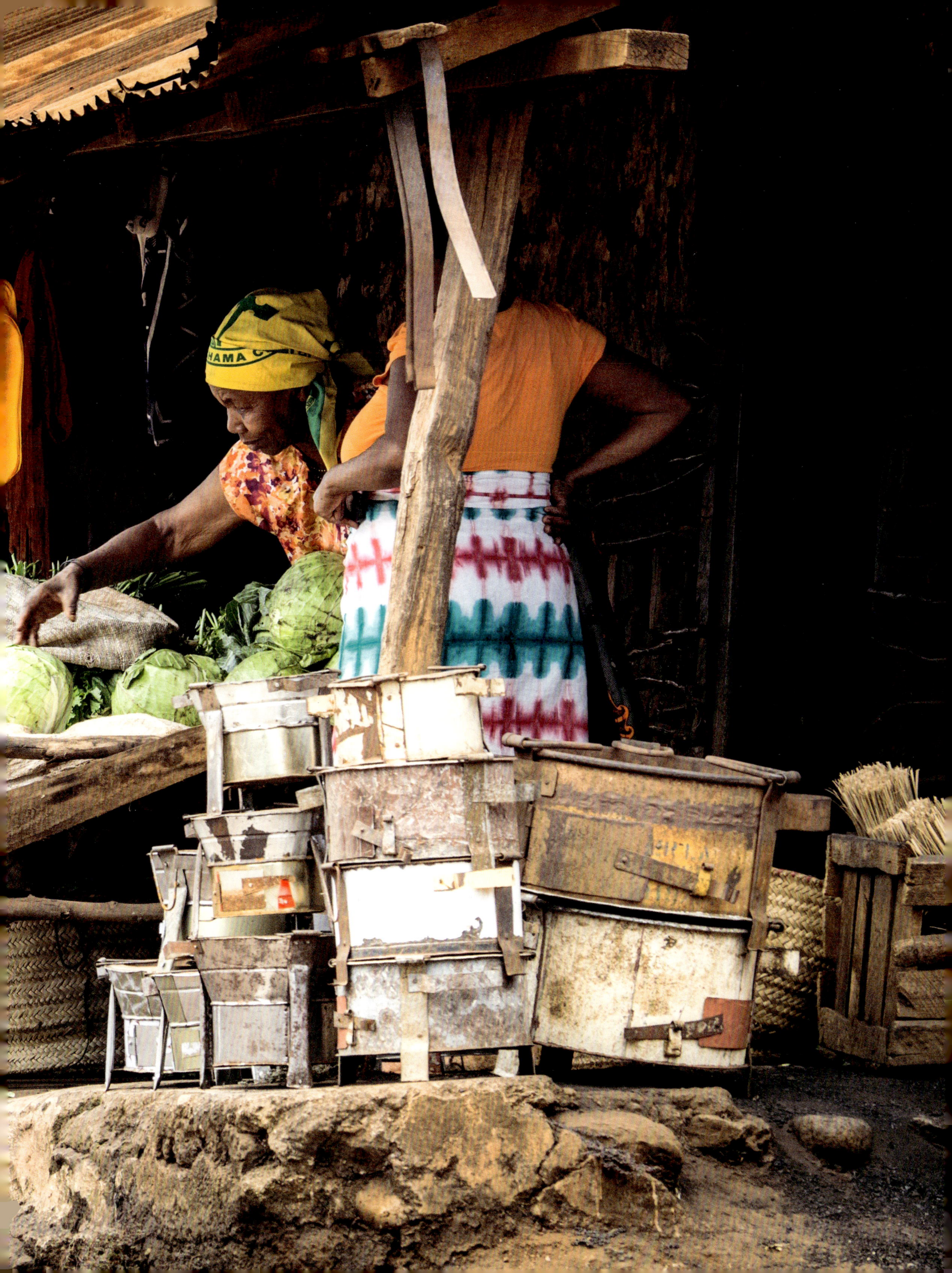

HAMA

Friday, September 23rd,

The ascent really took it out of us—we would never have been able to do this without our Tanzanian friends and guides. What an amazing team! I will never be able to get my head around the selfishness I often encounter in mountaineers. Why are humans so determined to be the first, the best, the only one to have done something? Without help and support from local guides, many a milestone in mountaineering history would never have been set…

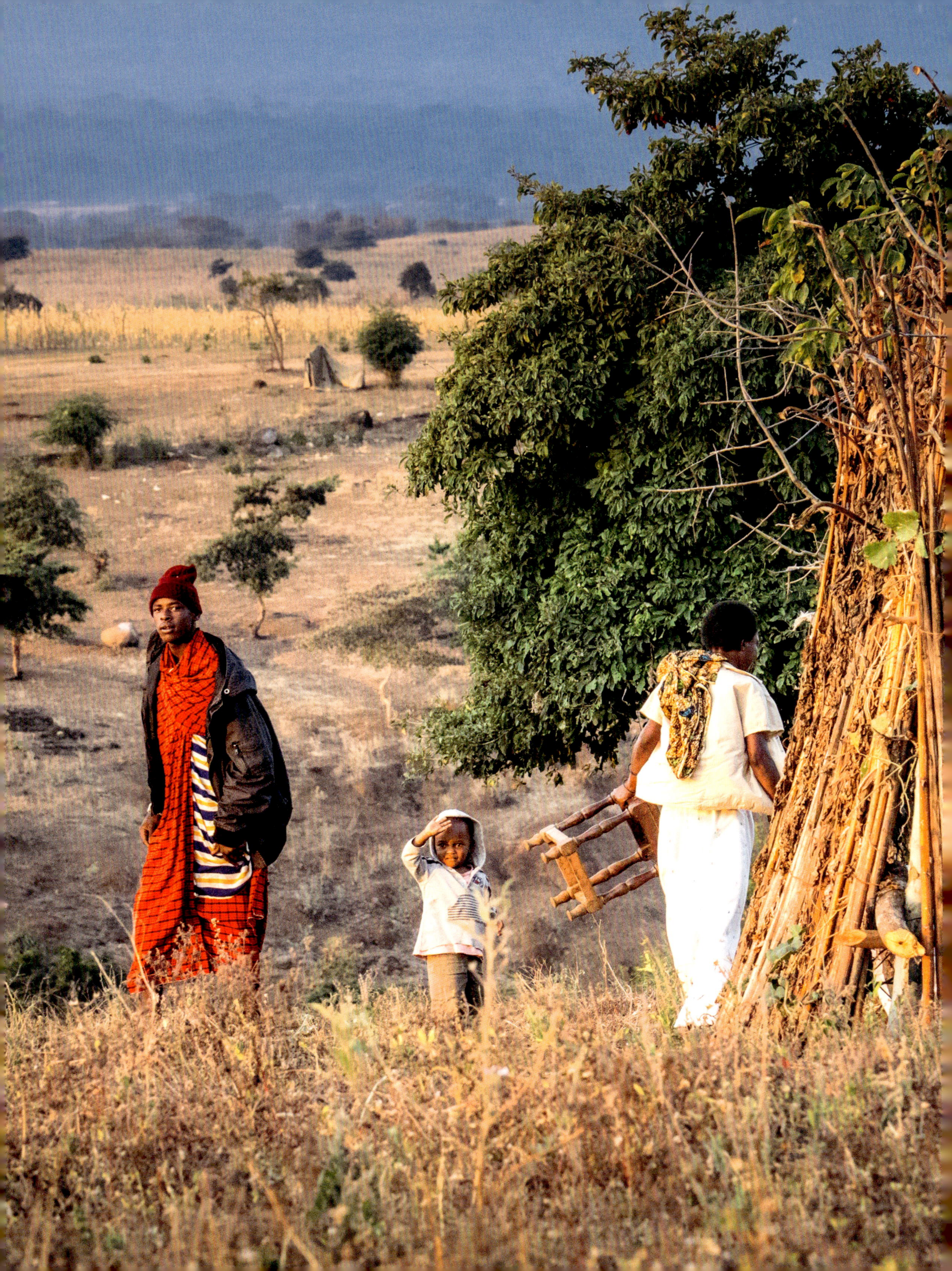

sheer variety of colours in this lively, invigorating landscape nevertheless. The sandy ground was a greyish brown, the orange lichens glowed in the trees; there were black volcanic rocks, green shrubbery, and bright purple seas of flowers surrounding tufts of yellow grass. Yet the strangest—and most exotic—plant I saw was a cactus-like tree with multiple bulbous trunks and tough, pointy leaves at the top.

"Giant Groundsels," Goodluck helped me with my lack of botanical knowledge. We stopped and admired a particularly large specimen. "The bulging trunks can store water and protect the tree from the cold and against evaporation." I checked my small GPS watch and found that we had reached an altitude of 11,500 feet. "In this region here, there is very little rainfall," Goodluck continued. "During the day, the sunshine is intense, and at night, temperatures often drop below freezing. These are difficult conditions for any form of life."

Third Zone: Alpine Desert

At just over 13,000 feet, whenever there is any rainfall or snow, it just sinks into the porous stone without leaving a trace. Here in the high desert on the saddle between the Mawenzi and Kibo summits I felt right at home. Everything was familiar. Even though every summit has its own individual charm, there are certain patterns and formations that are very similar in any crater region. Personally I thought that the yellow, grey and brown plain of sand, ashes, and countless black pebbles of volcanic rock was the most beautiful landscape I had seen throughout this tour. The area is infamous for it heat, storms, and dust by day, while the nights are bitterly cold. This place made you feel as if you were walking on the surface of the moon. Tufts of grass emerged from the ashes; not a great deal, but those that survived here were particularly hardy. Sharp, palm sized rocks were lying scattered in a strange, random formation. To me they looked like meteorites that had fallen from space. The volcanic pebbles made a crunching noise like breaking glass under my rugged tires. Behind us, we left deep furrows in the soft desert ground. I imagined what it would be like to be the first person to ride a bicycle on the moon. In a way, this daydream was not too far from the truth. I suppose that these lands, which are over half a million years old, are unlikely to have seen many bicycles.

Summit Zone

We traversed the saddle and the cinder cone that leads up towards the Kibo summit. Here we reached the last and the highest of the zones. In this polar region at over 16,000 feet, there is never any liquid water, and consequently there are no plants, either. Just ashes, sand, and rocks as far as the eye can see. The slope here was so steep and the ground so soft, we ended up taking one step forward only to find ourselves sliding two steps down again. So we followed a serpentine path up the snow, snaking back and forth as we slowly ascend the last few feet, towards the Uhuru Peak. Cycling has long ceased to be an option, despite our rocket engines. Yet even just pushing the heavy bikes up the hill proved to be a challenge. "This would be impossible if we didn't have any help," Roman moaned as we took a short rest and watched small pebbles tumble down the hillside. We all had to help each other out as we pushed the 45 pound bikes slowly upwards. My hands were holding onto the handlebars while Goodluck pushed from behind, holding the saddle. Together we struggled on, drenched in sweat despite the cold, slowly conquering the summit.

Just below the edge of the crater, the volcanic landscape appeared even rougher, and we trudged past increasingly large rocks and boulders. At that point, the ground had become so uneven and the slope so steep, we had to carry the bikes. All of a sudden, we reached a labyrinth of rocks. It was time to take another break, have an energy bar, and look back at what we had achieved already. The view was overwhelming. The Kibo Hut's green roof was

In this polar region at over 16,000 feet, there is never any liquid water, and consequently there are no plants, either.

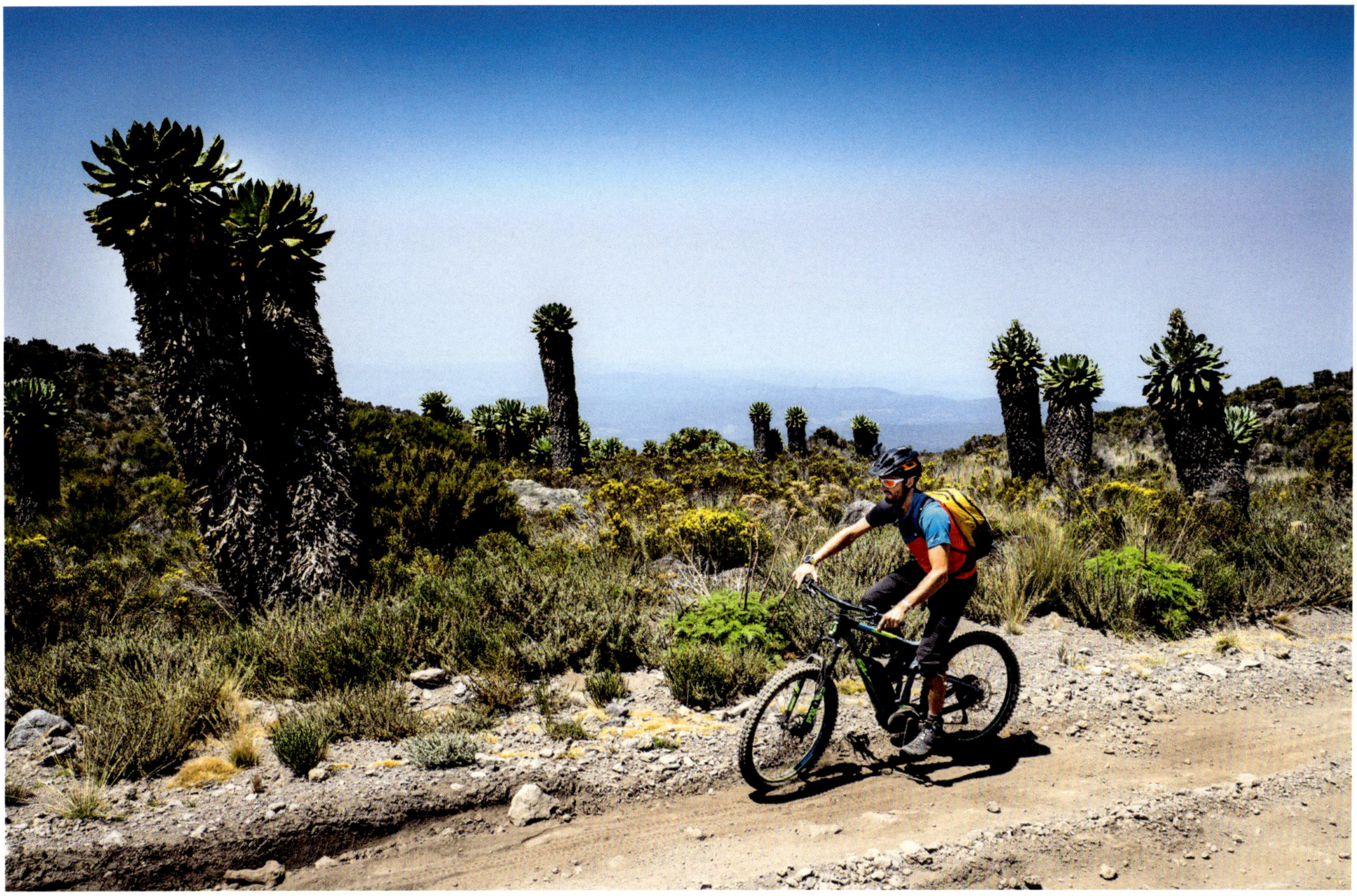

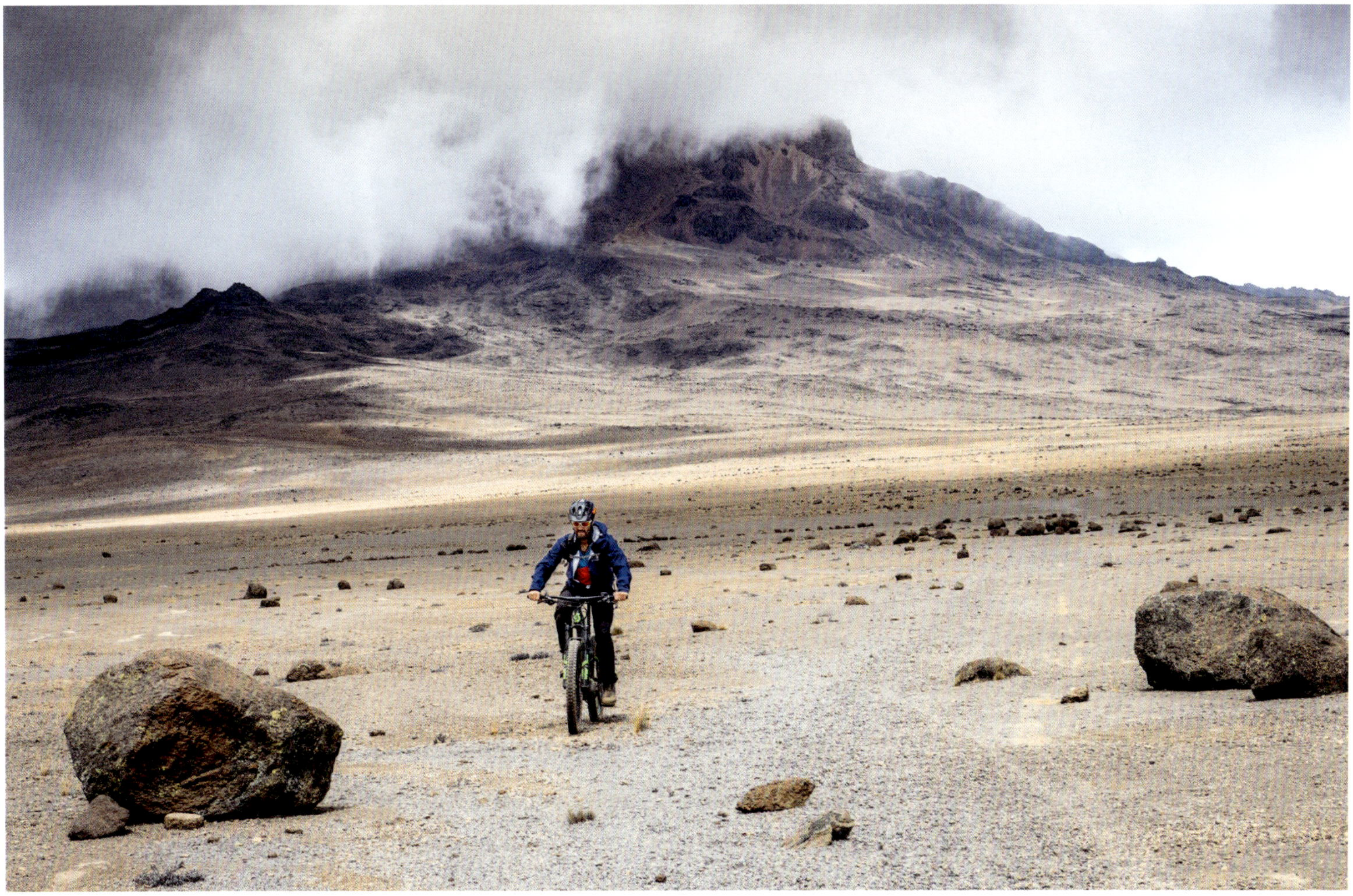

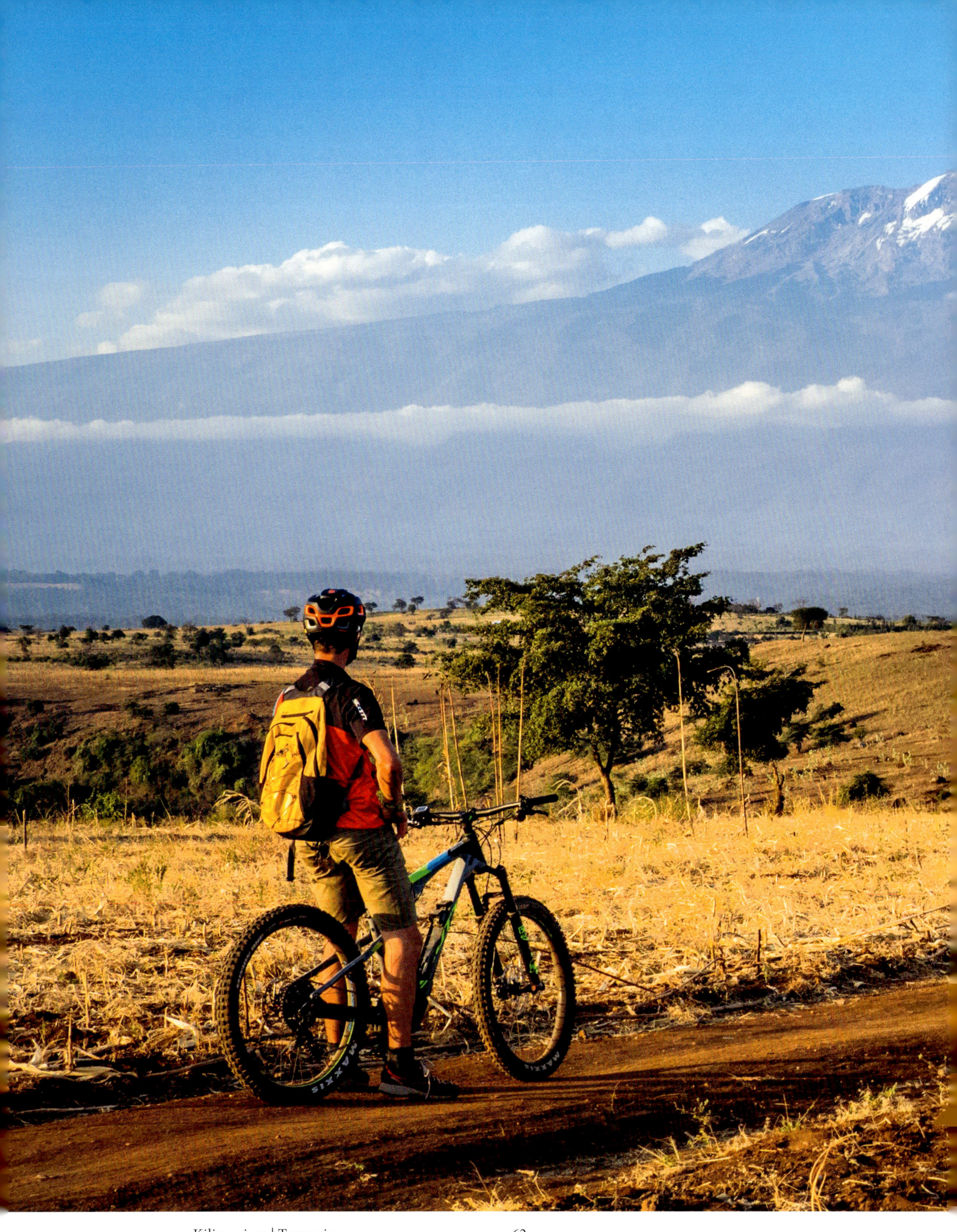

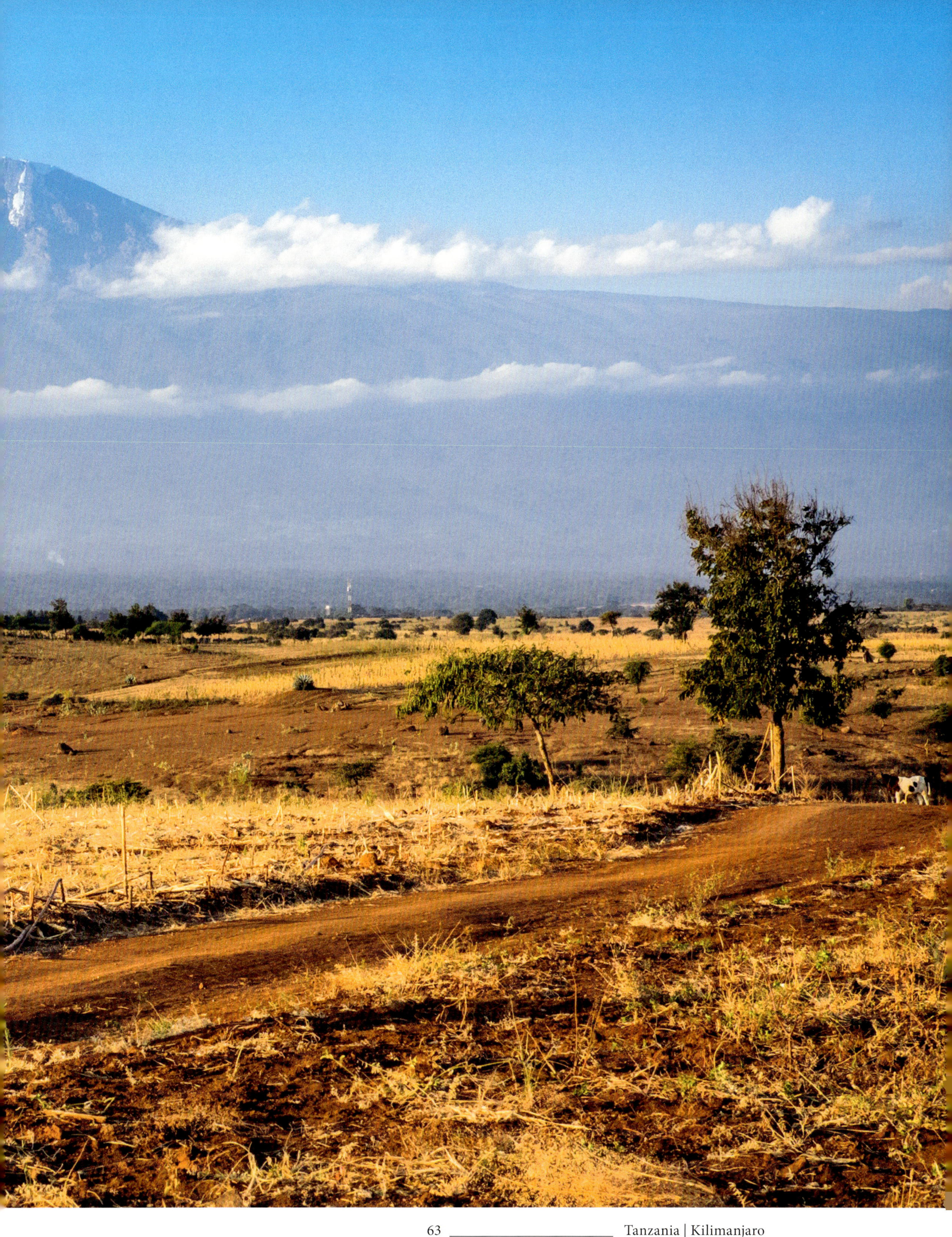

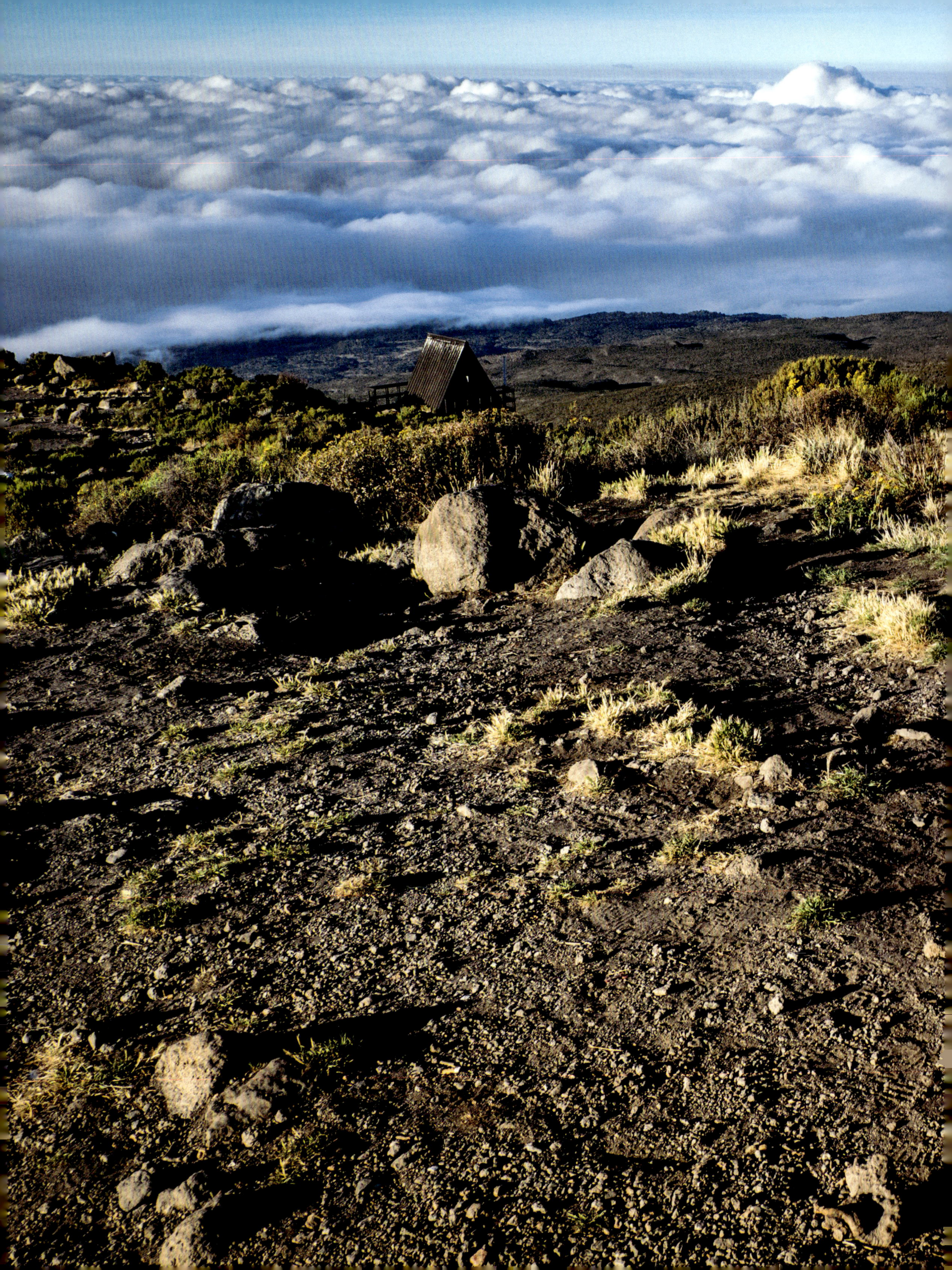

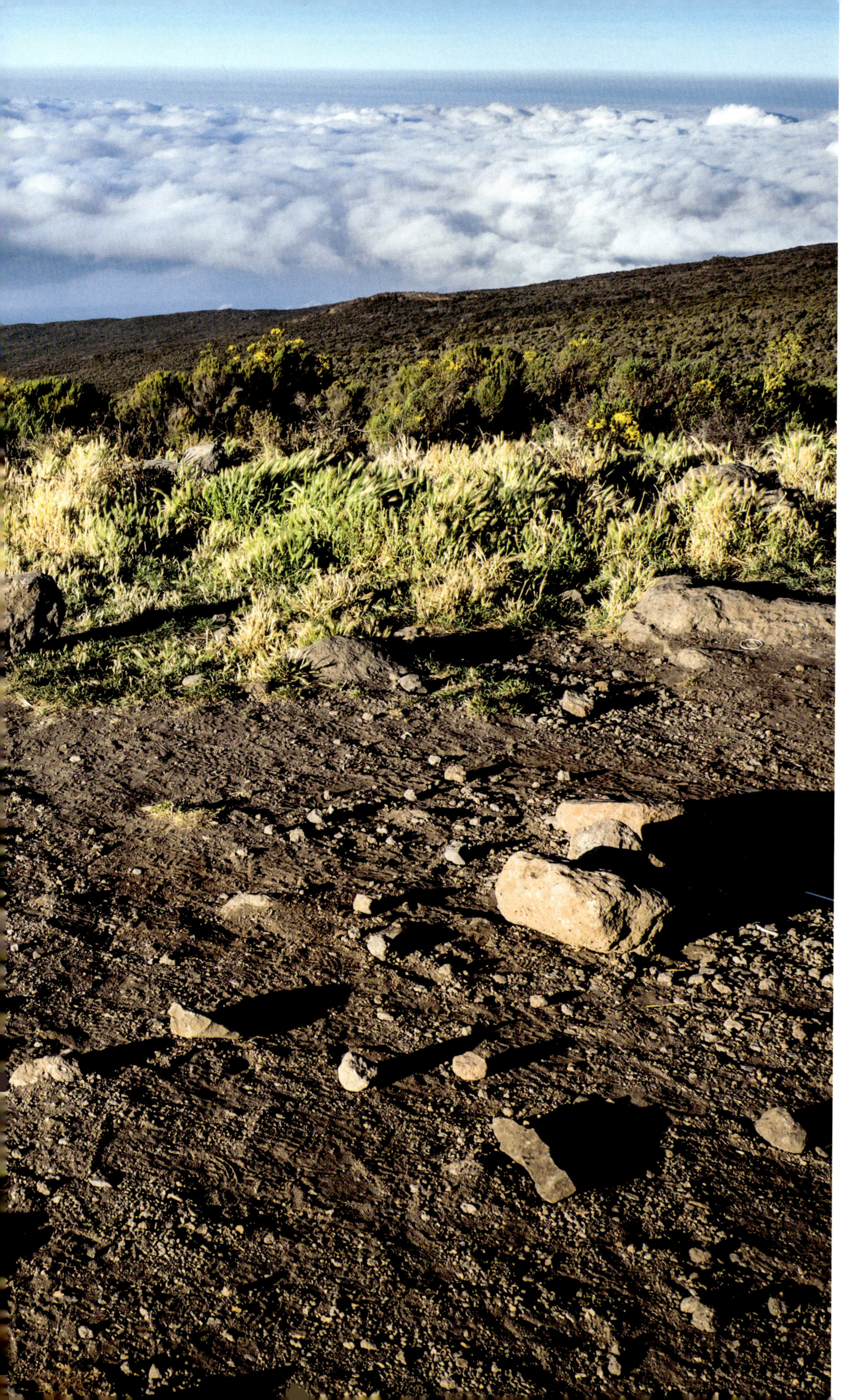

still just about visible at the bottom of the long, sheer, stone-grey slope of ash. The Marangu Route, Kilimanjaro's most popular, was clearly visible in the sandy brown lunar landscape below. Behind it, the Mawenzi peak towered majestically. To its right the view was unimpeded by clouds and I could see Tanzania's beauty stretch out. To its left lay the Amboseli national park behind the Kenyan border. Somewhere down there, lions, zebras, and giraffes were seeking shelter from the burning sun under broad-shouldered baobab trees. There was a shimmering, like a reflection of sun on the water, at the far end of the plain. It may have been a waterhole, perhaps surrounded by elephants that were cooling down in muddy waters.

There was no need for us to cool down up here. Not that we were complaining: we knew that the conditions we had encountered throughout our climb at Uhuru were ideal. At this altitude, icy winds and snowstorms are frequent phenomena, but the weather gods were kind to us and instead sent us sunshine and agreeable temperatures. It did not take long for us to reach the outer edge of the summit's caldera, which measured roughly 1.5 miles in diameter. It stretched out before us like a giant, dried-up lake. An imposing ice-blue, ash-grey, and snow-white glacier sat on the opposite shore. We followed a narrow path along the crater's edge, towards the Uhuru Peak. At last we could mount our e-bikes again and cycle, though we had to be careful. To the right, the crater was a sheer drop of at least 300 feet, whereas to the left, there was a risk of getting caught on one of the sharp rocks and losing balance. Just below the summit, which in Germany in the 1960s had been referred to as the "Kaiser Wilhelm Summit", the path became broader. We passed the rugged glacier and, once we had finished our triumphant ride at the Uhuru Peak, we took a group picture.

Up until 1964, Mount Kilimanjaro was named after Wilhelm II, the last German Kaiser: Kaiser-Wilhelm-Spitze ("Kaiser Wilhelm Peak"). Up until 1918, the mountain was situated in a German colony—it was the highest summit in the German Empire.

> Somewhere down there, lions, zebras, and giraffes were seeking shelter from the burning sun under broad-shouldered baobab trees.

"Get Out of My Way!"

The most exciting experience of all was the final ride downhill. Lugging a 45 pound bike all the way up the highest volcano in Africa must have its perks, after all. Within hours we would pass through all the various climate zones, from the poles back to the equator—what an experience. "Get out of my way!" Roman shouts as he overtakes me on the steep grey slope of ash and dust.

Our hands squeezing the brakes, the bikes' wheels not even turning, we slide downhill as clouds of dust trail behind us. Soon we can see the Kibo Hut's green roof again and after less than an hour, we are greeted there with a big round of applause. Our small team is suddenly surrounded by people, everyone wants to congratulate us, and for a while, we feel like celebrities. "I hope you brought some official autographs," I say jokingly to Nikolaus.

There is no time to rest and celebrate, however, so we keep cycling, following the tracks we made yesterday. Later we reach another difficult point where we have to somehow get down about a dozen steps, each of them roughly 1.5 feet high. Now we have to stop admiring the landscape and start concentrating on the road. In the run-up to this trip I completed intensive preparatory training for mountain biking in the Alps and so I manage this stretch without difficulty—and the same goes for our trusty e-bikes. Although they seem to be in dire need of a shower—another thing we have in common with the bikes—they still run as if they had come straight off the production line. We would love nothing more than to watch our bored waiter balance two cool beers on a tray and bring them over that same night; yet despite our rapid downhill progress, our descent is still a two-day journey. At times we may have had the impression that Nikolaus and Goodluck were running on e-shoes, yet they obviously could not complete the entire descent on foot in one day. So we take another rest at 12,000 feet and spend one last night on Mount Kilimanjaro.

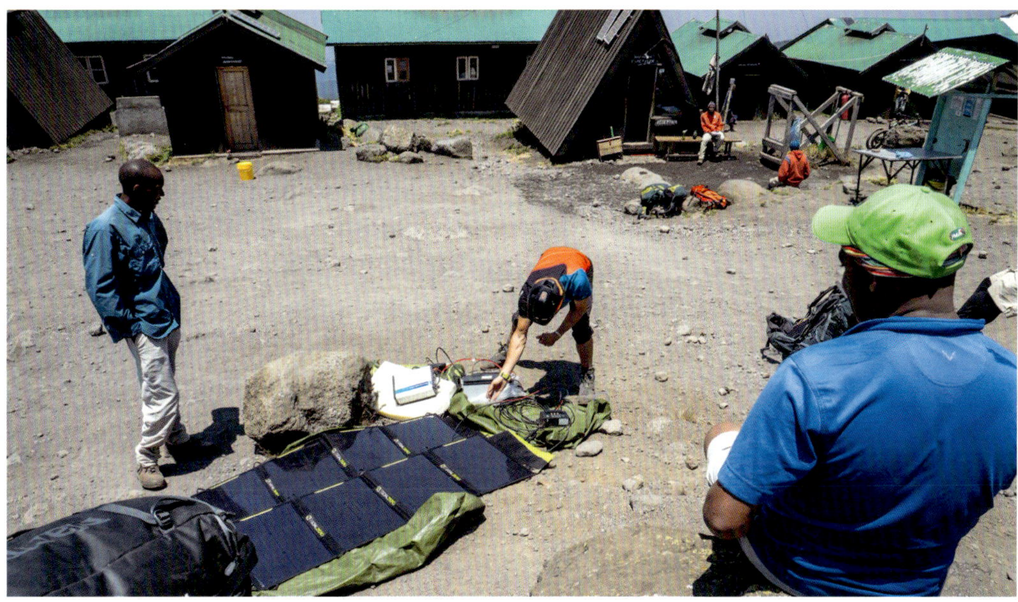

Here at the Horombo Huts we get another taste of the overwhelming amount of tourism here at the mountain. On summit day, we had already passed quite a few "mountaineers" who were not so much hiking as they were being dragged onwards by their tour leaders, looking on the brink of consciousness. Every year, far too many tourists—up to 60,000 annually—try to climb this mountain without the necessary preparation, training, or planning.

They often do not seem to realize the importance of acclimatization, the right gear, personal fitness, and experience. One of the issues is that local guides offer very cheap tours and present Mount Kilimanjaro as if it were nothing but a pleasant hike and suitable for hobby climbers. Der Spiegel, a German weekly news magazine, recently referred to Mount Kilimanjaro as the "world's toughest walk". Compared to other mountains of a similar height, Mount Kilimanjaro may be relatively easy to conquer, but climbing it is still an extreme challenge—and it is not without its risks.

We sit down on the steps leading up to tonight's accommodation which looks a bit like a wooden tent. Then we put on our sunglasses and stretch our freshly showered legs out to feel the warming rays of the slowly setting afternoon sun. As if the mountain wanted to reward us for our feat, the sunset paints the landscape a deep golden hue, partly concealed by the clouds below us. We are still looking at all the exhausted faces and shaking our heads at jeans and t-shirts rather than proper climbing gear when we suddenly overhear part of a conversation. "In ten years I bet they will ride up this mountain on e-bikes," an older man says. Roman and I grin at each other. Yet again we have brought the future to the present here in Africa.

> Compared to other mountains of a similar height, Mount Kilimanjaro may be relatively easy to conquer

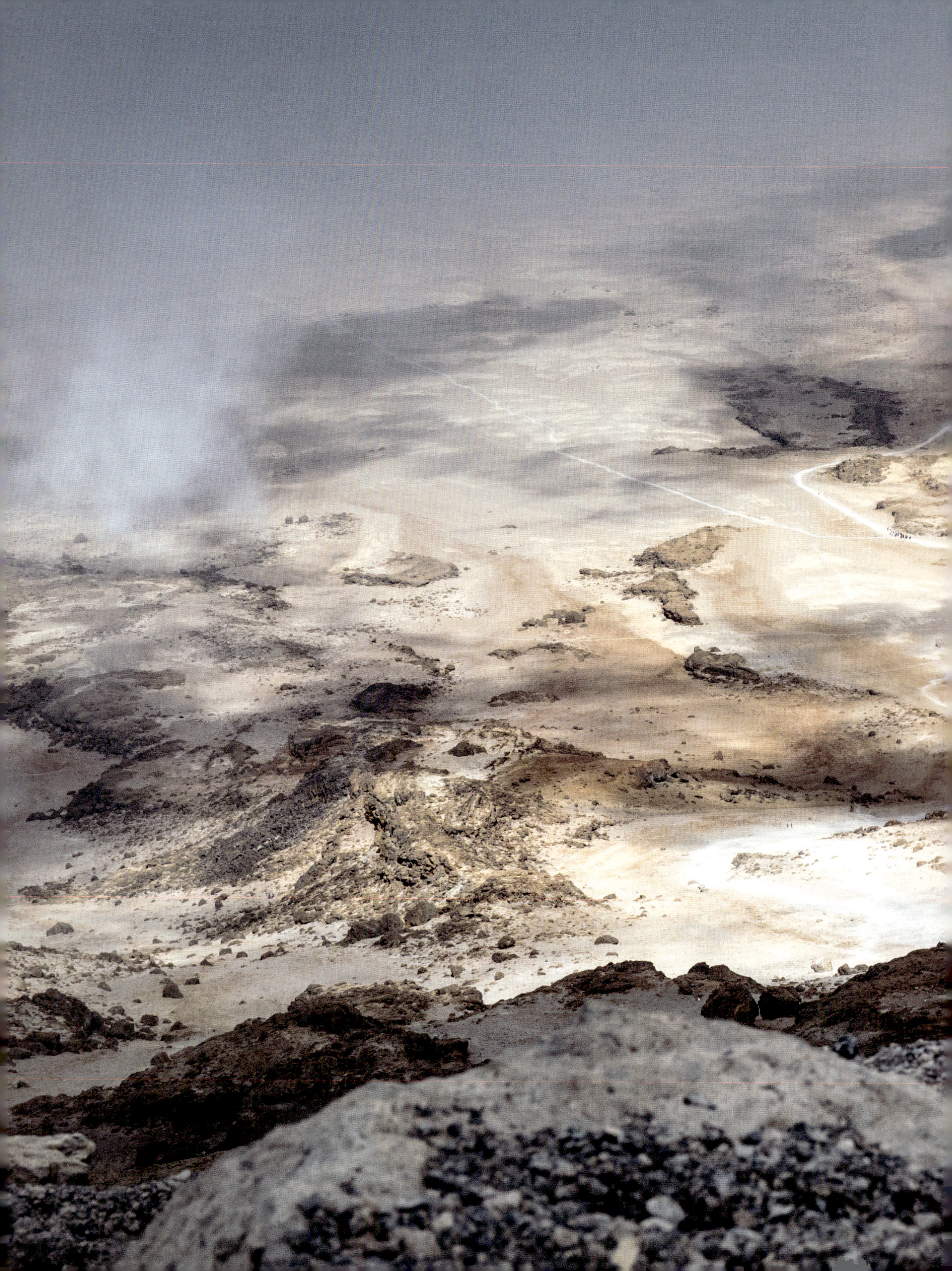

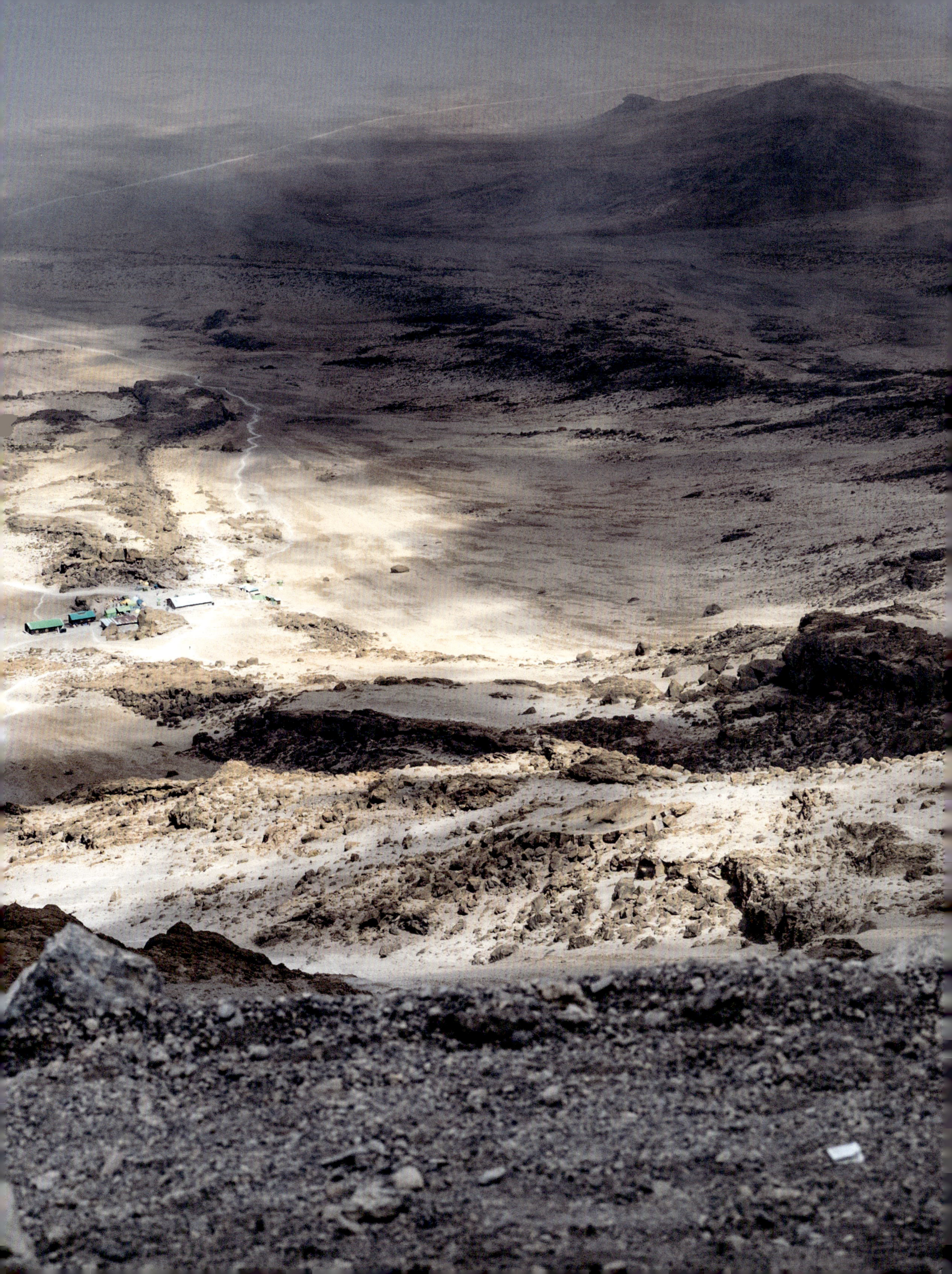

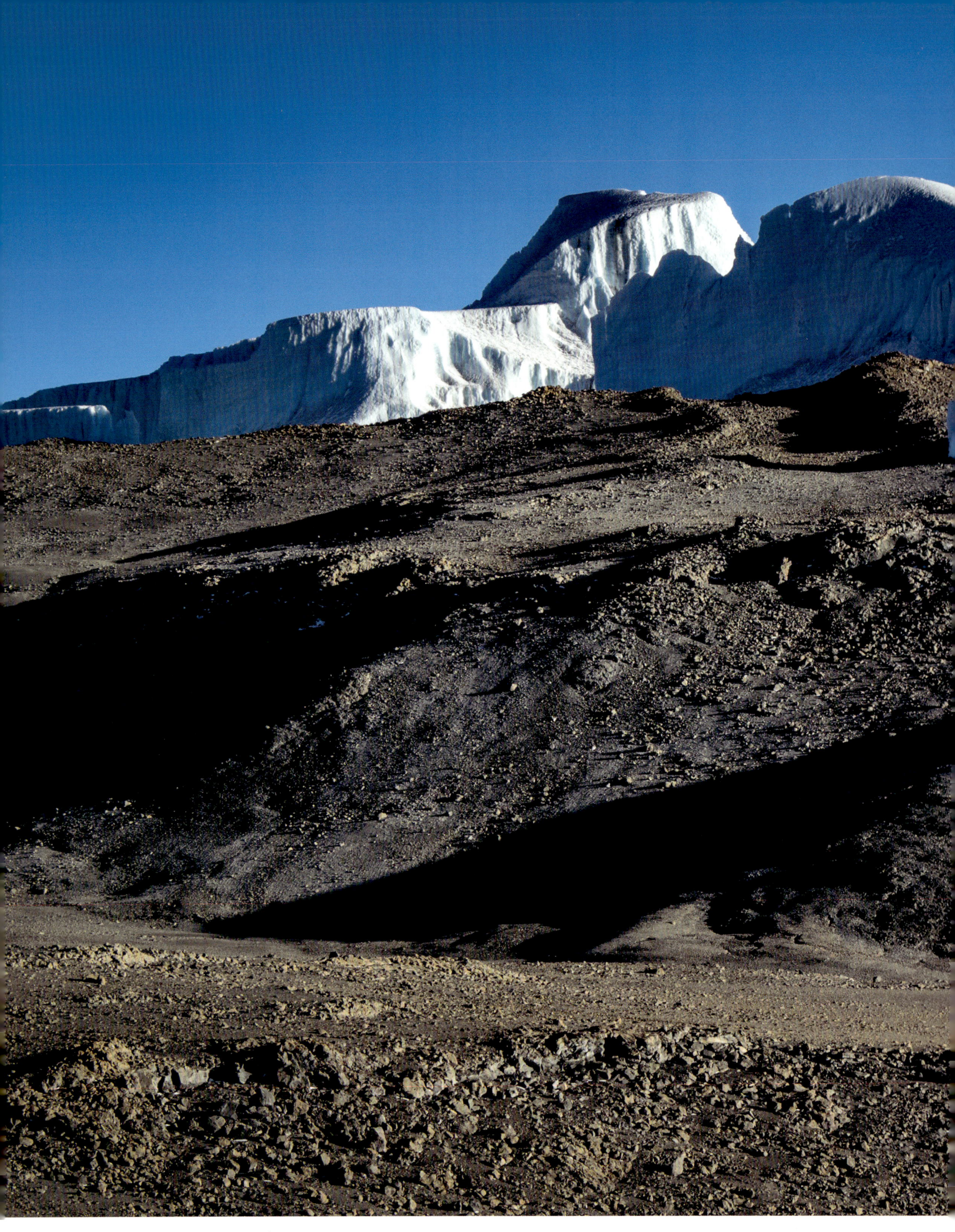

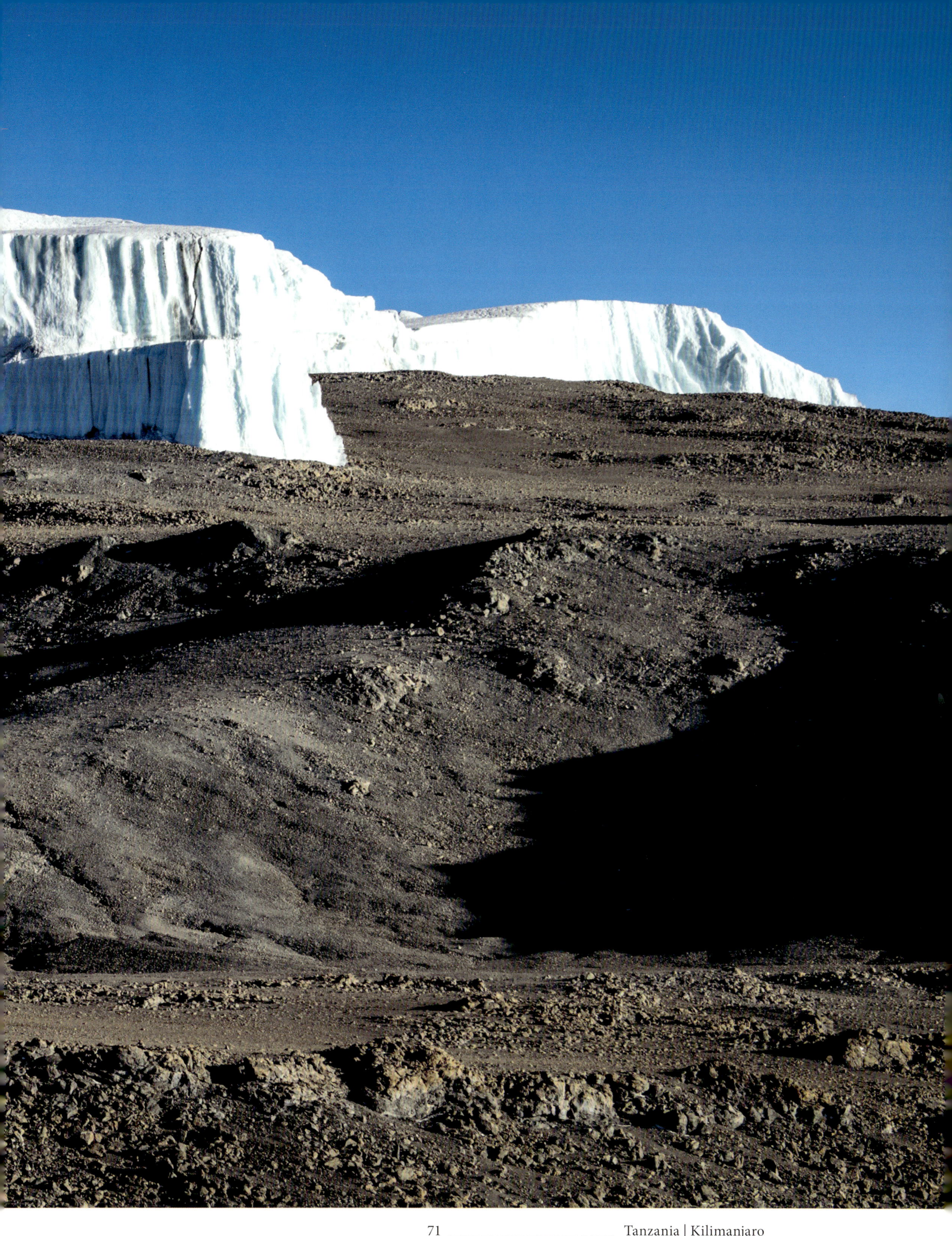

 Tanzania | Kilimanjaro

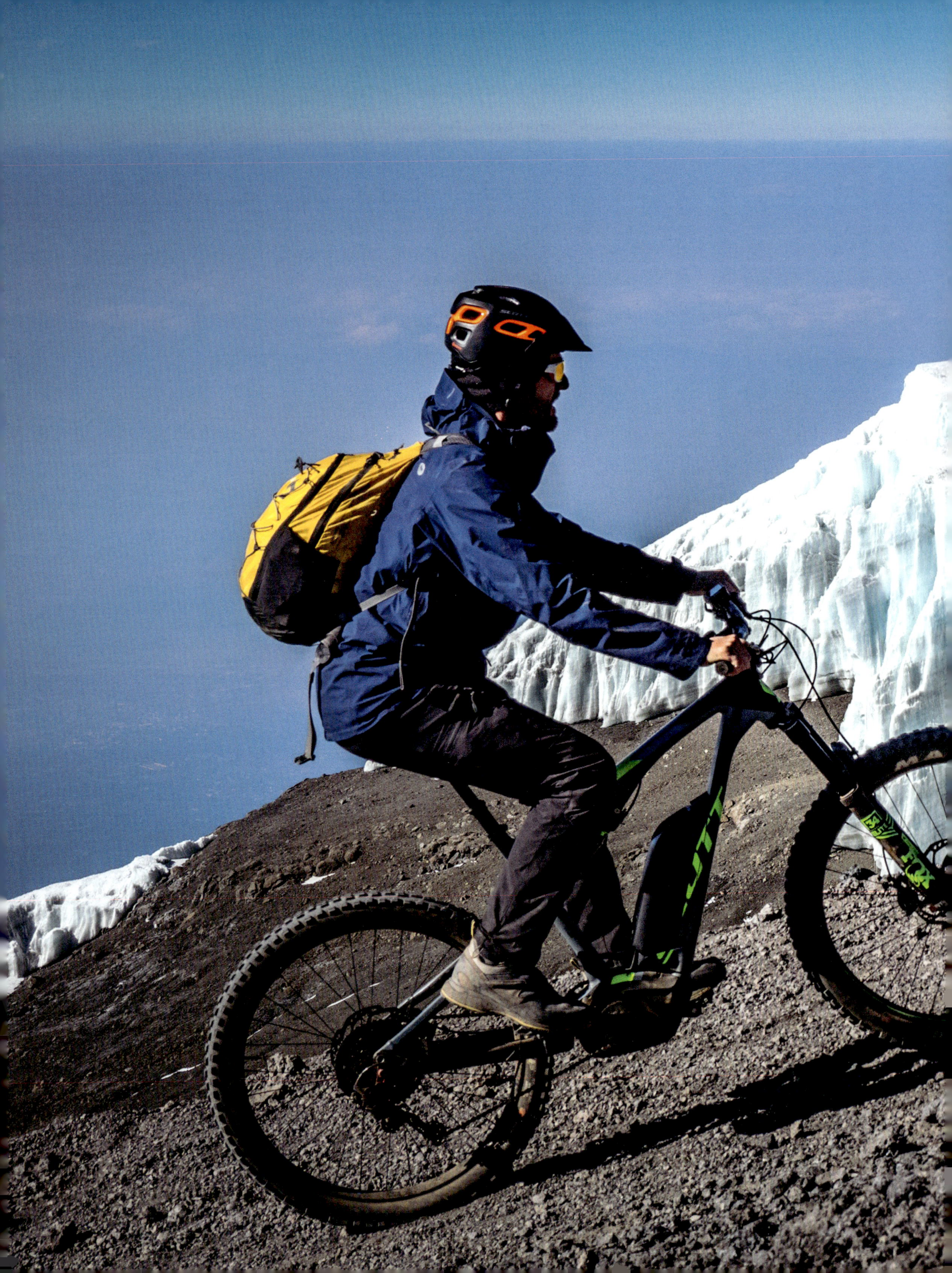

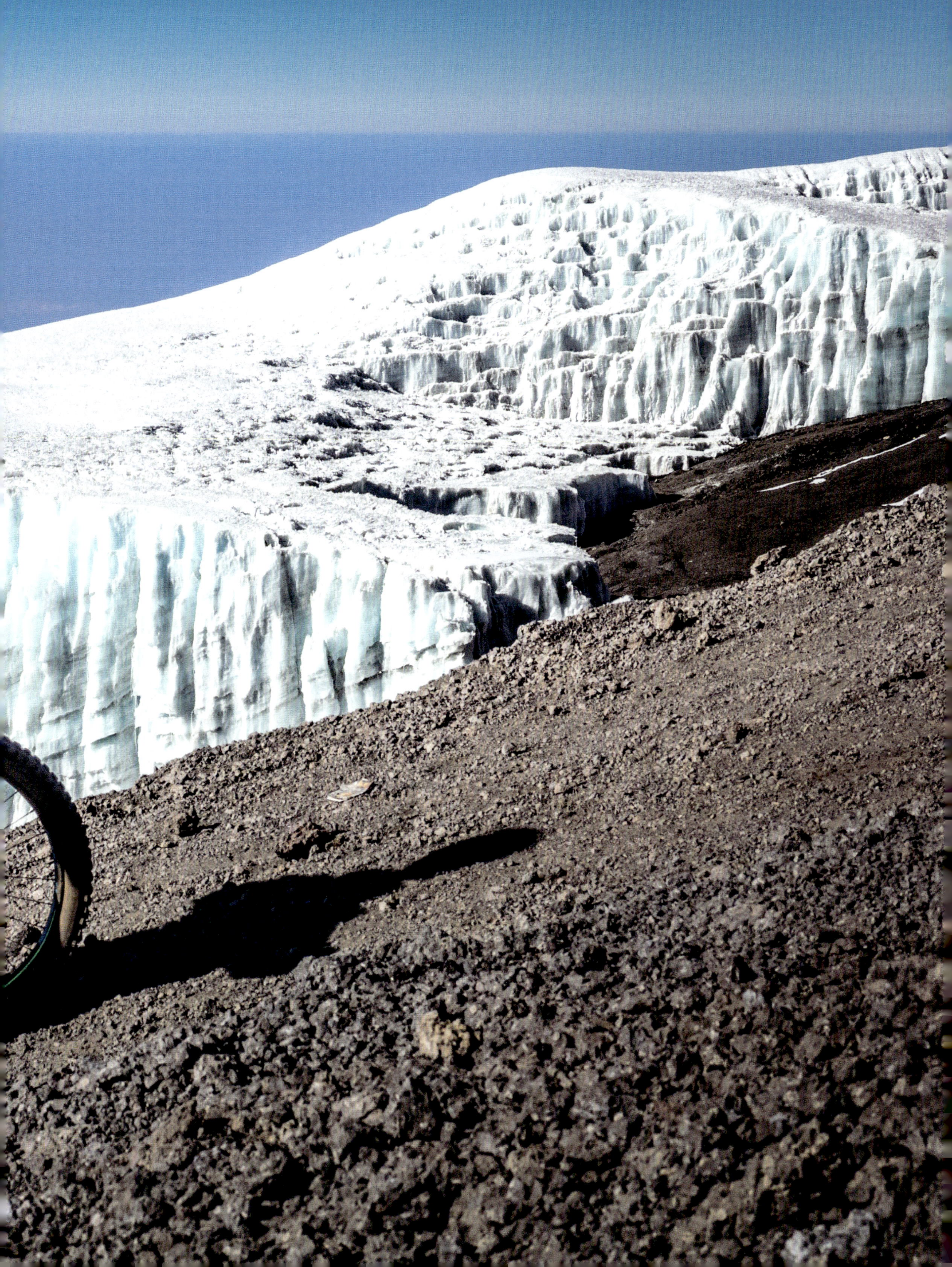

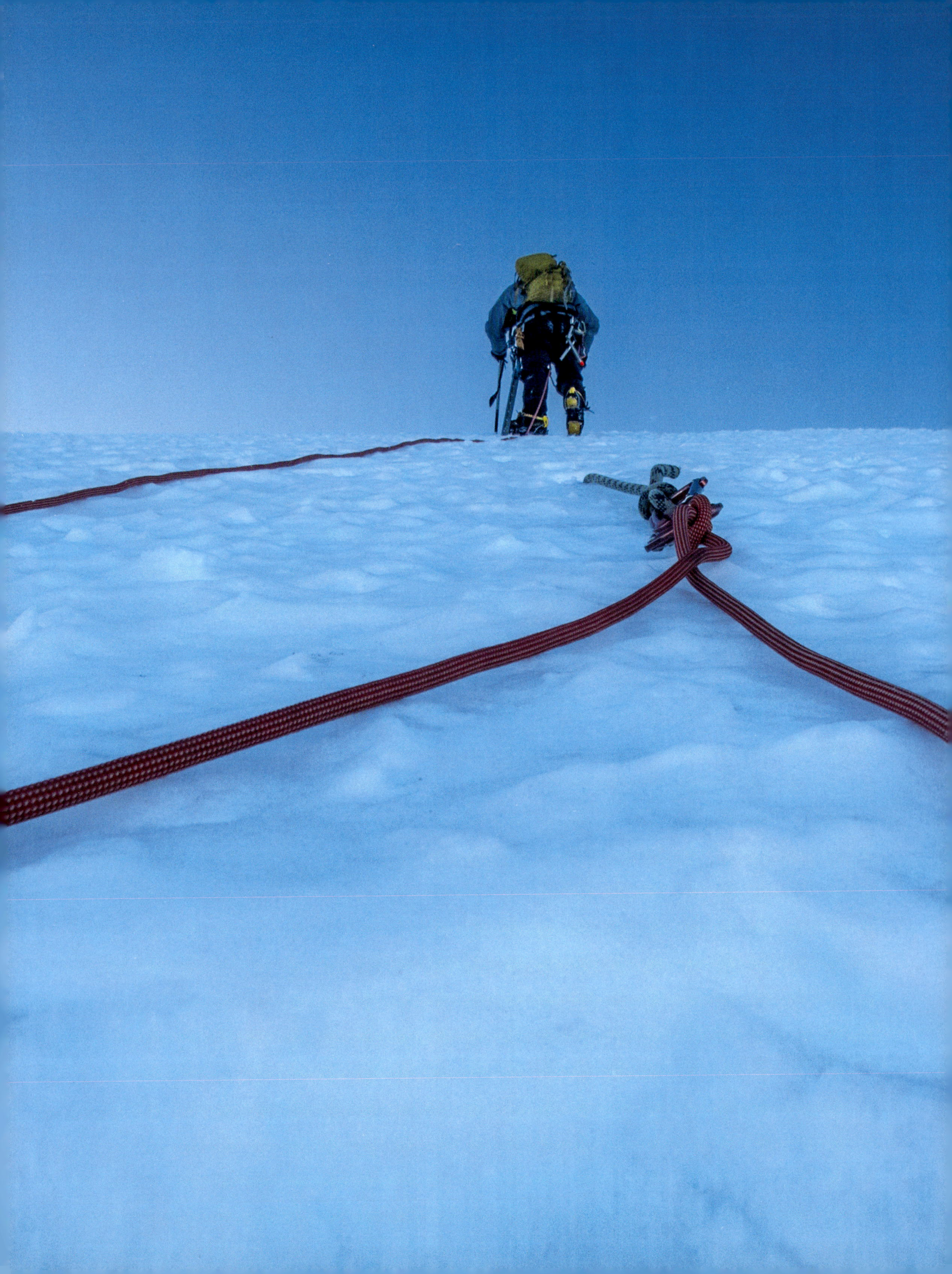

3

PICO DE ORIZABA

SHADOWS AND LIGHT
Mexico

"Boom!" The sound of the explosion makes me wince. For a few seconds, the whole building seems to shake as if during an earthquake. Luckily I know where the sound came from, for I have been hearing it all afternoon: it is a Mexican carnival musket. People in colorful costumes parade through the streets displaying their hand carved weapons and firing them into the air—using only gunpowder, no ammunition, of course. Yet these celebrations are all but harmless. A couple of times today I have found myself standing right next to a musket being fired, and the sound is deafening.

Earlier today, my travel companions Chris and Karl-Heinz accompanied me on a stroll through the carnival festivities in Mexico City. We were fascinated and delighted with the imaginative costumes and countless delicacies —you could get anything from tortillas to a pig's head—and began to join in with the celebrations. Our hotel's quirky owner had warned us not to stay out after nightfall though. Despite the security personnel and police, the streets would be dangerous, he said. Under the cloak of darkness, people felt more anonymous, and were often already very intoxicated, he explained. At that point, robbery and violent attacks were increasingly common, unfortunately.

I find this hard to believe, for over the past two weeks of my stay, I have found Mexico to be a cheerful, welcoming, and friendly country. Prior to our journey, we had read many fearmongering reports about drug-related gang wars, but our experience here showed that these reports could not have been further from the truth. "The only shots we have heard or seen fired came out of carnival muskets," I say with a smile as we watch the first purple shadows of sunset tint the Mexican sky. "What do you think, should we go back to the hotel now?" I ask my fellow travelers.

> For a few seconds, the whole building seems to shake as if during an earthquake.

Chris, Karl-Heinz and I have the same idea: we will make a small detour to one of the many corner shops in our district and stock up on beer. Tonight, the three of us will have a relaxed boys' night in in our hotel. Outside, the shouts, gun shots, and drunken, off-key chants continue while we are getting comfortable on our hotel's beautiful green roof terrace. The cool beer bottles are covered in condensation, and every time we take a sip, they leave a ring of moisture on the table. I am getting comfortable in my wicker chair and begin to sort through and organize the photographs I have taken over the past two weeks. Chris and Karl-Heinz watch me, and the images bring back memories…

There is a picture of the volcano Popocatépetl: it is illuminated by the setting sun, the landscape around it is vibrant, and small clouds are gathering around the summit. The volcano is located 43 miles southeast of Mexico City; Mexicans know it as El Popo. Although it is not one of the Volcanic Seven Summits, it is nevertheless the second tallest volcano in North America. Its melodic name alone would be reason enough for me to climb it. Its meaning in English sounds very promising to me: the smoking mountain. It is one of the continent's most active volcanoes and it is famous for its frequent eruptions, some smaller, some larger. The roughly 30 million people living in its vicinity fear and respect the mountain.

Our main destination in Mexico was the tallest volcano in North America: Pico de Orizaba. Yet we all agreed that El Popo would be ideal for some acclimatization expeditions. Of course, I was secretly hoping to catch it on one of its active days—and maybe capture some fireworks.

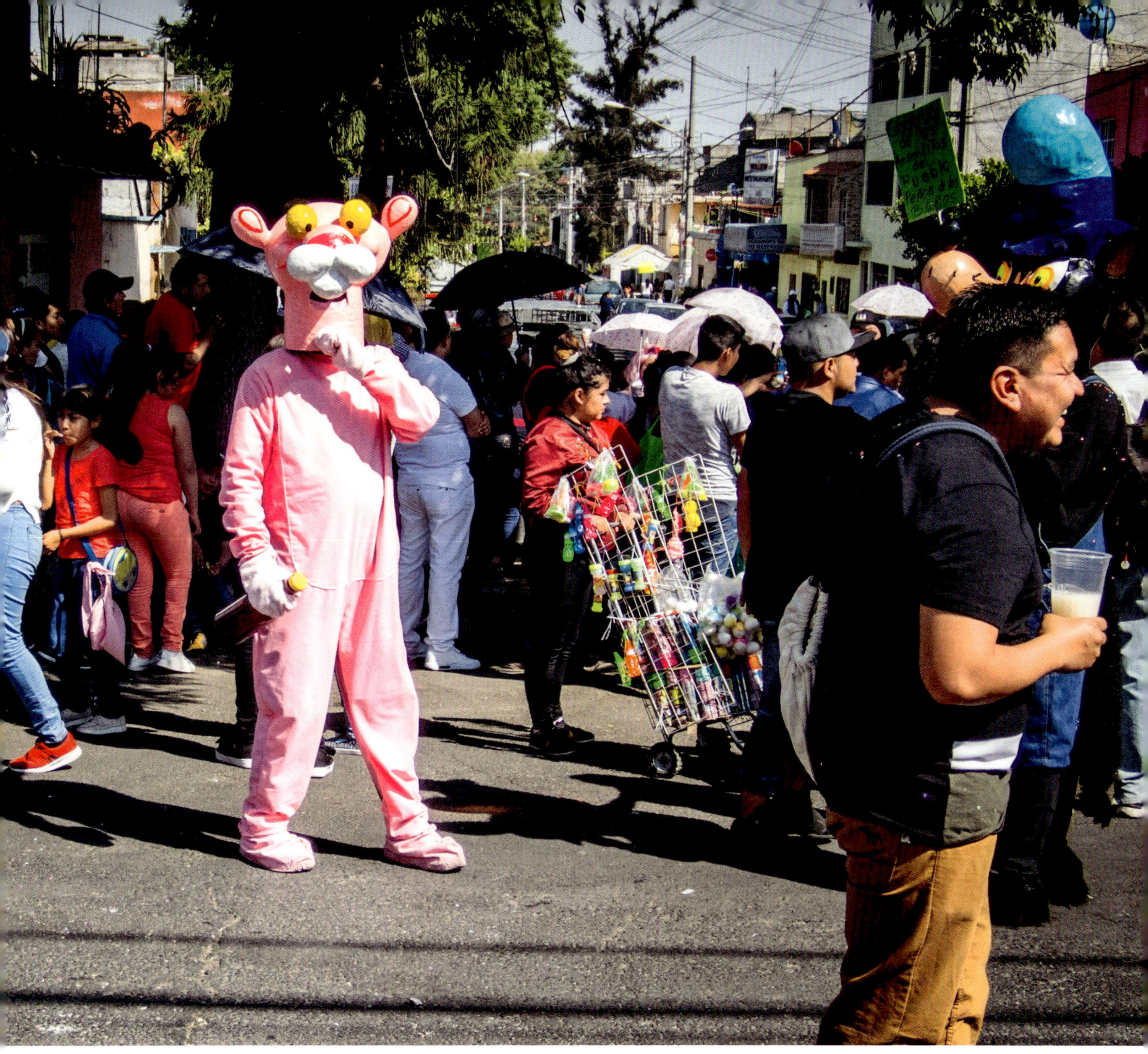

The capital of Mexico, Mexico City, has a population of over 20 million—it is one of the world's most populous cities. It was built on the ruins of Tenochtitlan, an old Aztec city, whose remains are still a major city center attraction. Until the 16th century, Tenochtitlan was the largest city in America and one of the biggest cities in the world.

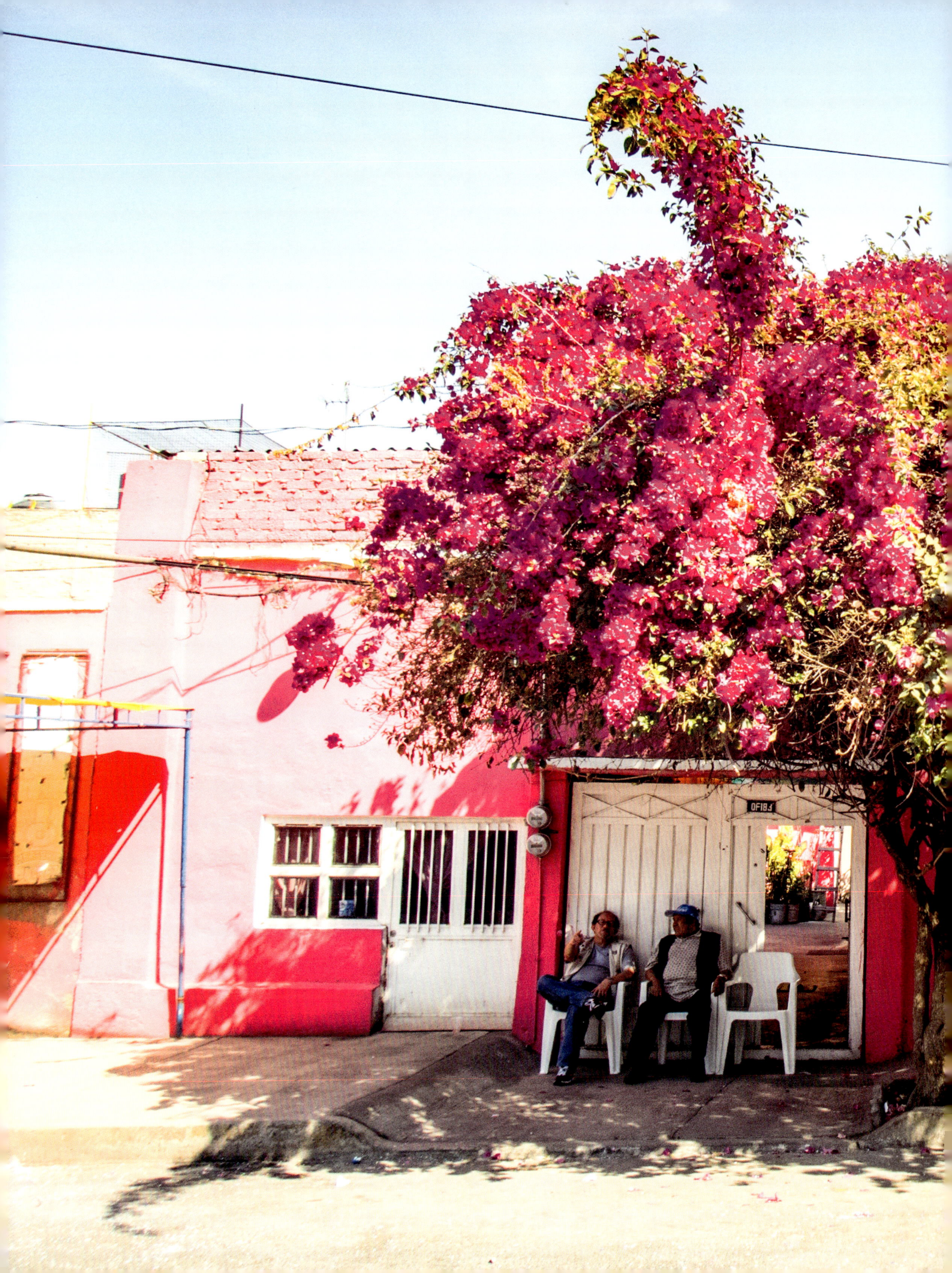

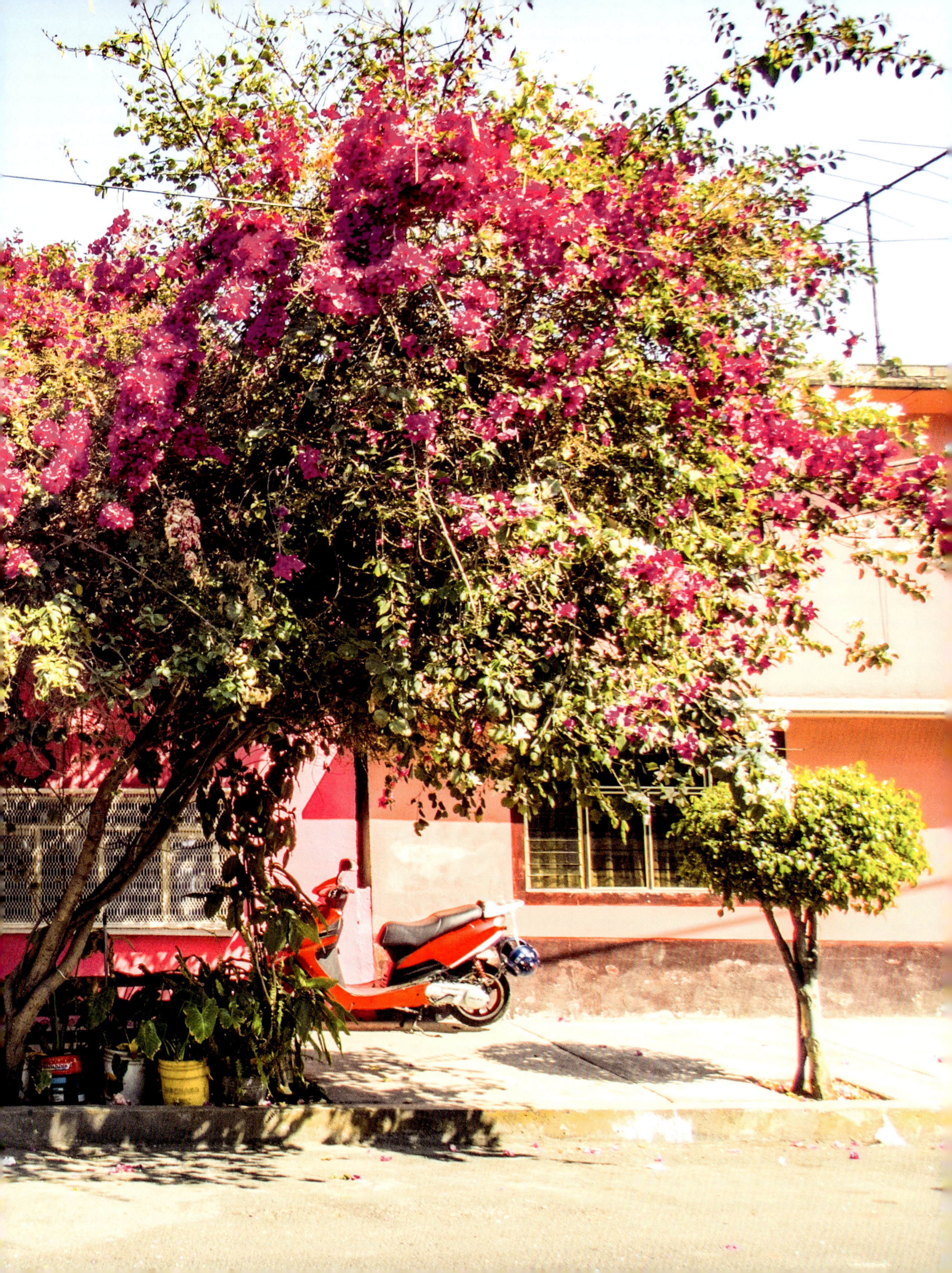

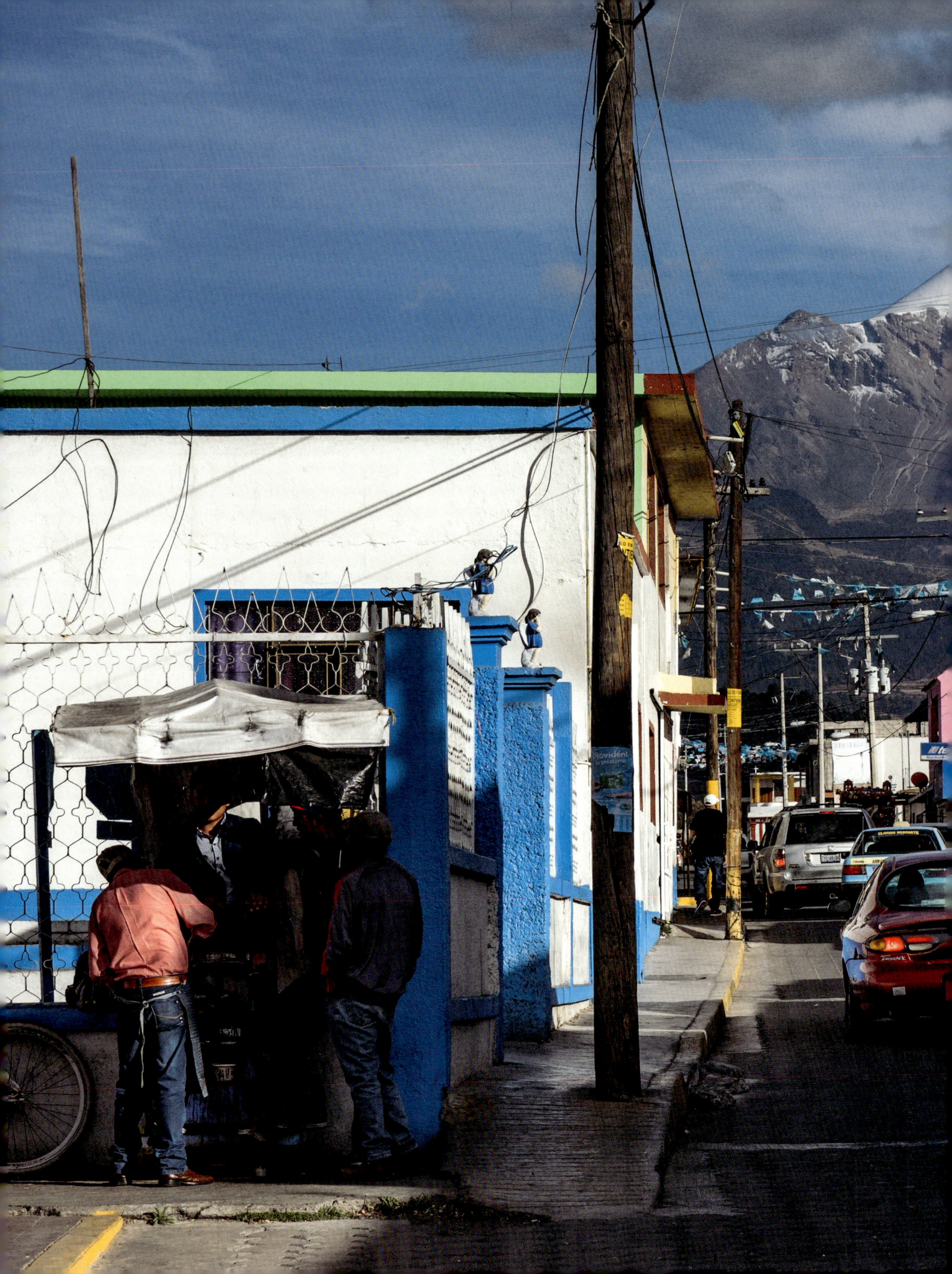

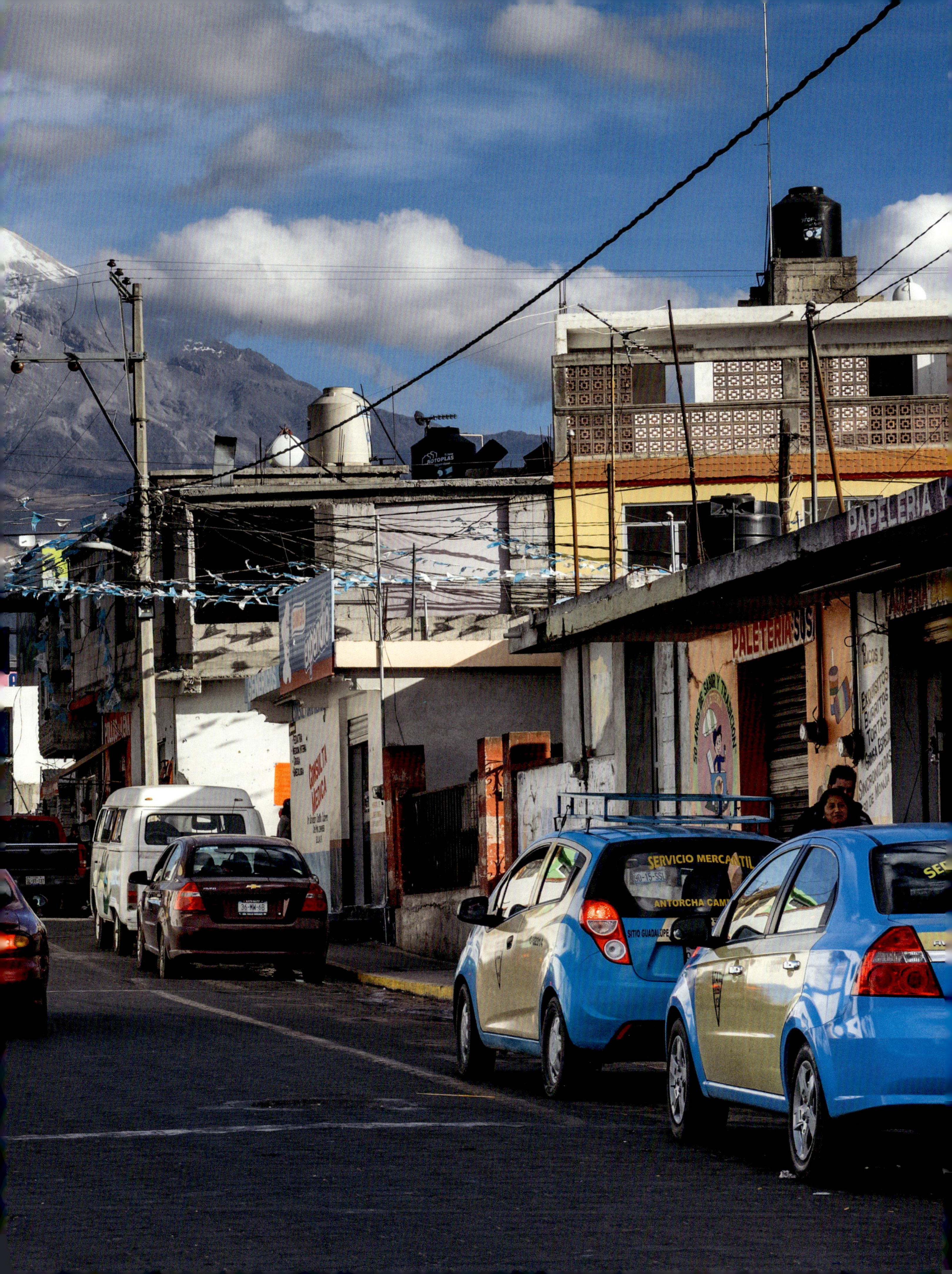

PAPELERIA Y
PALETERIA SUS
SERVICIO MERCANTIL
ANTORCHA CAMP
SITIO GUADALUPE
36-MW-68

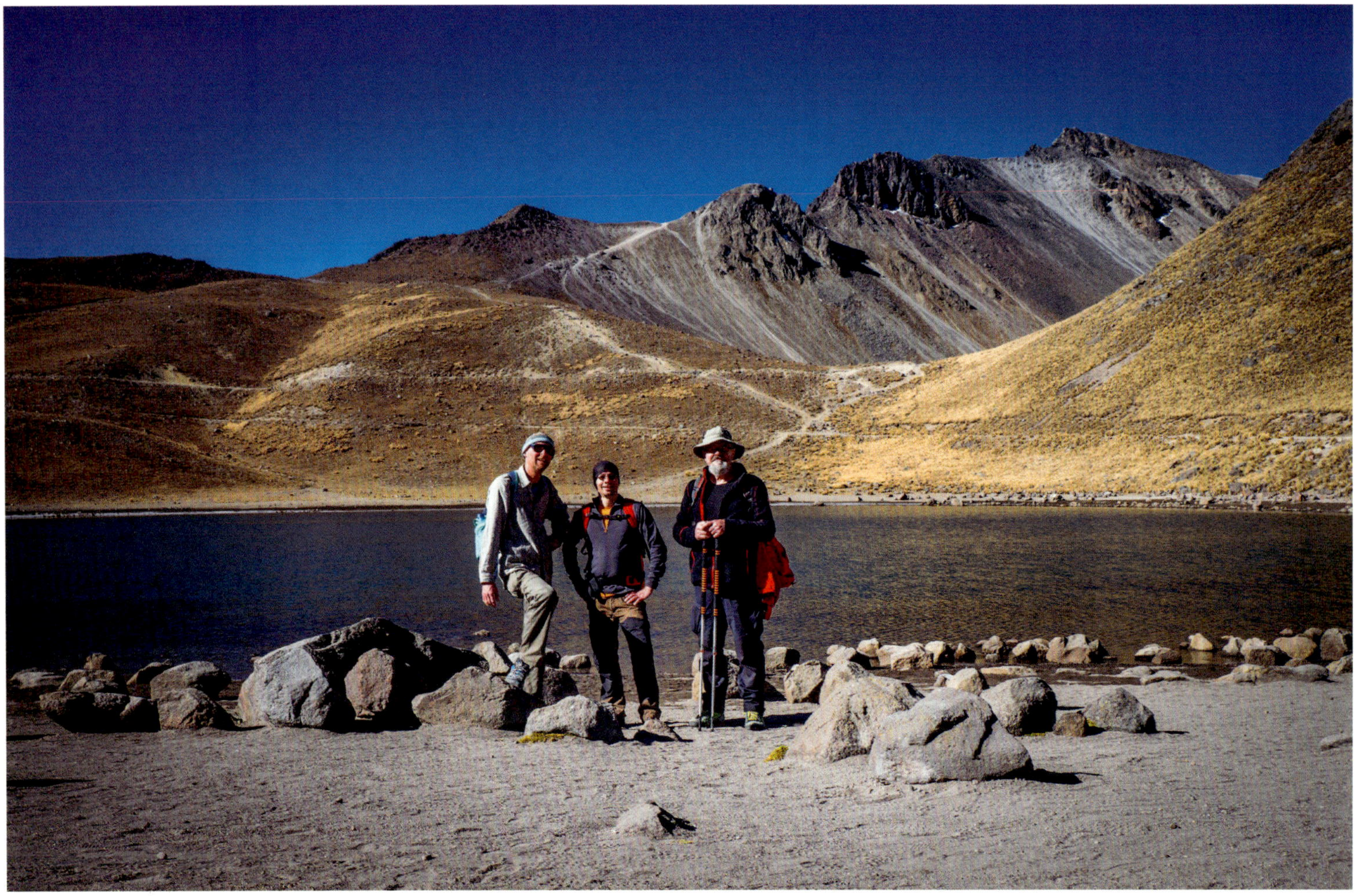

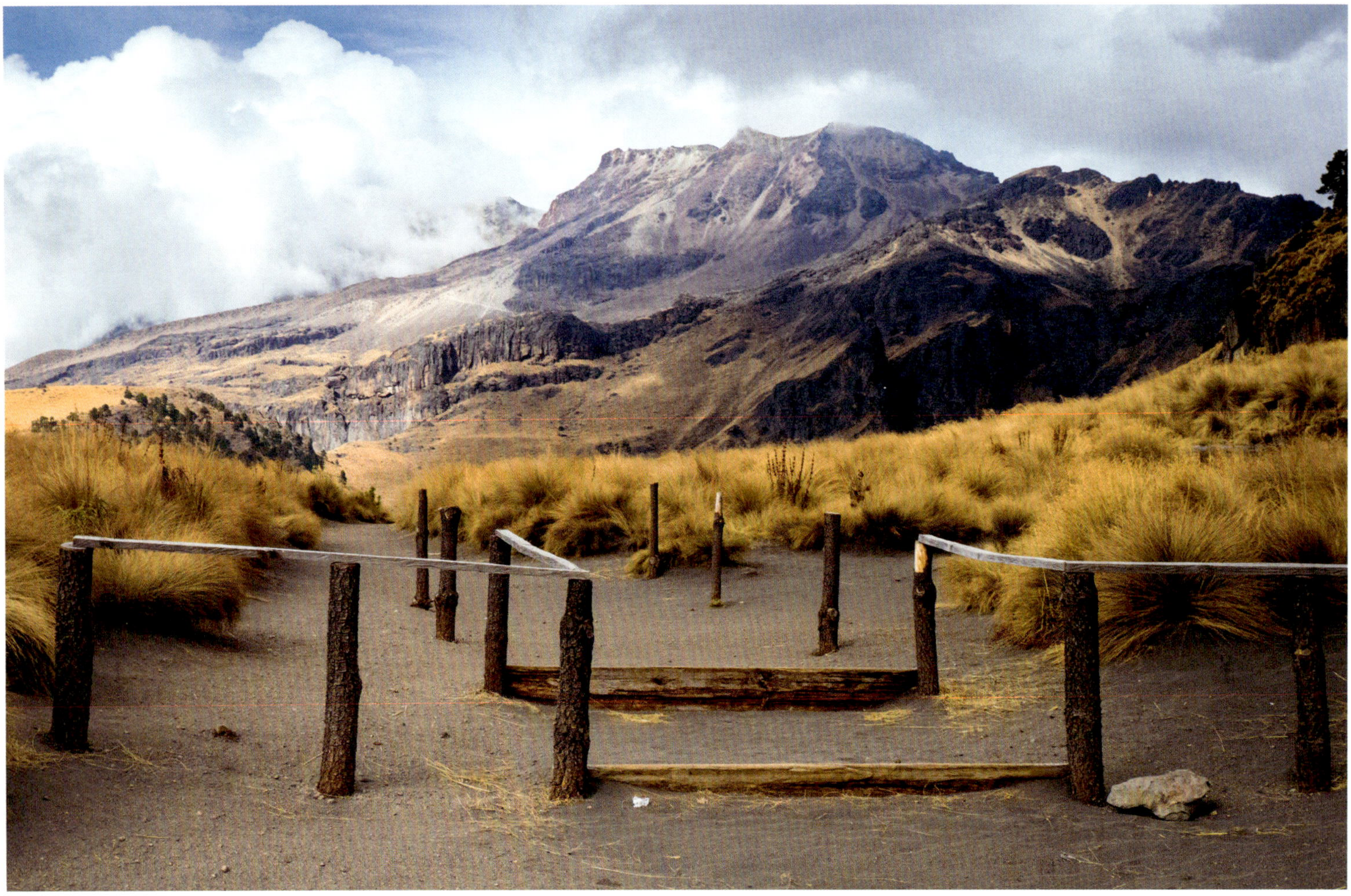

The Fire of Hope

Our overladen and underpowered rental van was struggling up a short slope when a broad sign announcing the "Ruta de Volcanoes" appeared above the road. "Looks like we've come to the right place," Karl-Heinz said dryly. And indeed, soon after we had passed the sign, we arrived at the parking lot in the Paso de Cortés, at an altitude of 11,150 feet.

Paso de Cortés is a mountain pass situated between the two volcanoes Popocatépetl and Iztaccíhuatl. Aside from offering excellent views of the surrounding landscapes, it is also a historic landmark. In 1519, the Spanish conqueror Hernán Cortés crossed this pass on his way to a meeting with the ruler of the Aztecs.

There was still some time left until the so-called "blue hour", which in my opinion is the perfect time to photograph volcanoes. We tried make the best of the delay by creating an improvised yet surprisingly delicious camping meal. We assembled slices of white bread with cheese on top and placed them on the van's hot roof. Then we all gathered around the open hood. We placed a packet of traditional Mexican refried beans on the engine which was still burning hot from the ascent. Chris grinned while our refried beans were slowly heating up: "A dual-purpose stove, this is camping 2.0!" Later, when we had finished making our sandwiches and were enjoying our food accompanied by the smell of gasoline, Chris joked again: "Saudi-Arabia, nice, south-facing oilfield with a view." Our own sandwiches à la Popo were delicious though.

And then it arrived: the blue hour! In the fading light, the surrounding landscape's structures and surfaces appeared sharper, clearer. Right now, the lava's red glow would be perfectly visible. The only thing that was missing from this image was the fire itself. Small clouds of gas and vapor were emerging from the crater.

"Come on, where are the fireworks?" I silently urged the volcano. But the clouds emerged and vanished while the sun was setting deeper and deeper beyond the horizon. Here, at over 13,000 feet, night was beginning to fall, and with it came the cold. I began to shiver, put on my jacket and my hat and pulled the sleeves over my hands—never letting go of the shutter release button, of course. Shaken by shivers, with my hands starting to become numb, still I felt I had to ask my friends for "five more minutes".

More gas clouds emerged—I pressed the shutter button. Still no fireworks though. After about a dozen times of begging for another "five minutes", I had to see reason. It was pitch black outside when we finally left the Paso de Cortés—I, with a sense of frustration, Chris and Karl-Heinz with a sense of relief.

I reminded Chris: "Do you remember, pretty much exactly five years ago we got pretty lucky at a volcano not that far from here." In 2011, Volcán de Fuego in Guatemala had gifted us a fantastic and unforgettable night of uninterrupted fireworks. "I can still feel the pressure waves that hit us back then," Chris agreed.

Picture-Perfect

Back here in Mexico City, we can only dream of the peace and quiet we had experienced at Popocatépetl. Planes are flying so low, it feels as though if you were to stretch out your hands, you could touch them. I take another gulp of my hoppy beer, wipe my wet fingers against my trousers and continue to look through the pictures. I find a photograph of the volcano Pico de Orizaba—at 18,491 feet the tallest volcano in North America, and the real destination of our journey.

I have a clear memory of the moment I took this picture. We had taken our usual positions and were driving towards the mountain. When I say "our usual positions", I mean: I was the driver, Karl-Heinz acted as navigator using Google Maps, and Chris was on the lookout for "topes"—speedbumps which occur at regular intervals. I was used to driving on roads with speedbumps; many countries use them to regulate driving speed. In my experience, however, they were normally relatively wide and flat. The Mexican topes were narrow and unusually high. Going even just a little bit faster than the speed limit would be enough to do serious damage to both car and tires. The bumps were often hidden, as they were the same color as the rest of the road, and most frequently found

Popocatépetl is considered one of the most active volcanoes in the world. The past 20 years alone have seen several eruptions, with eruption columns rising up to 2.5 miles into the air.

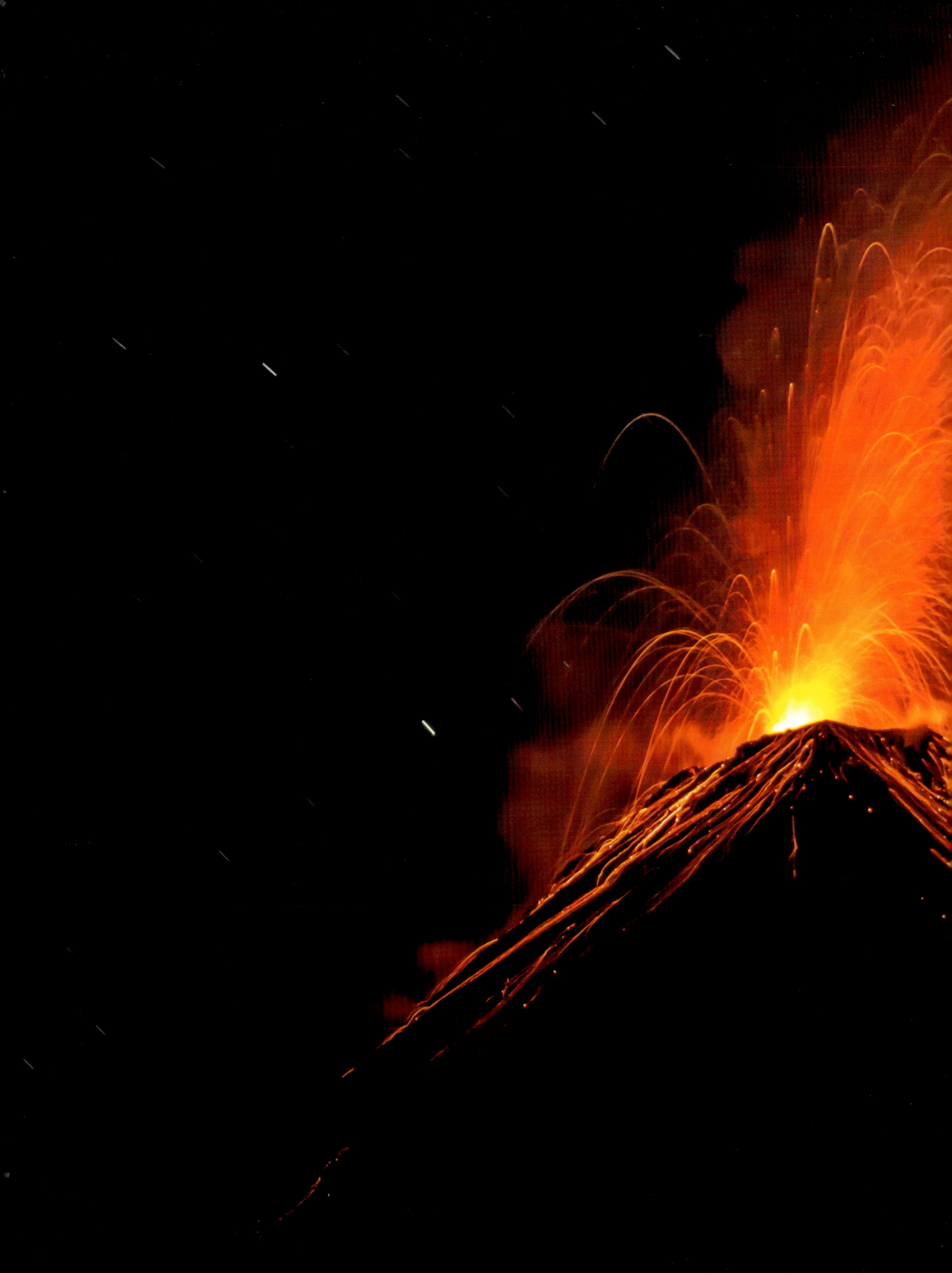

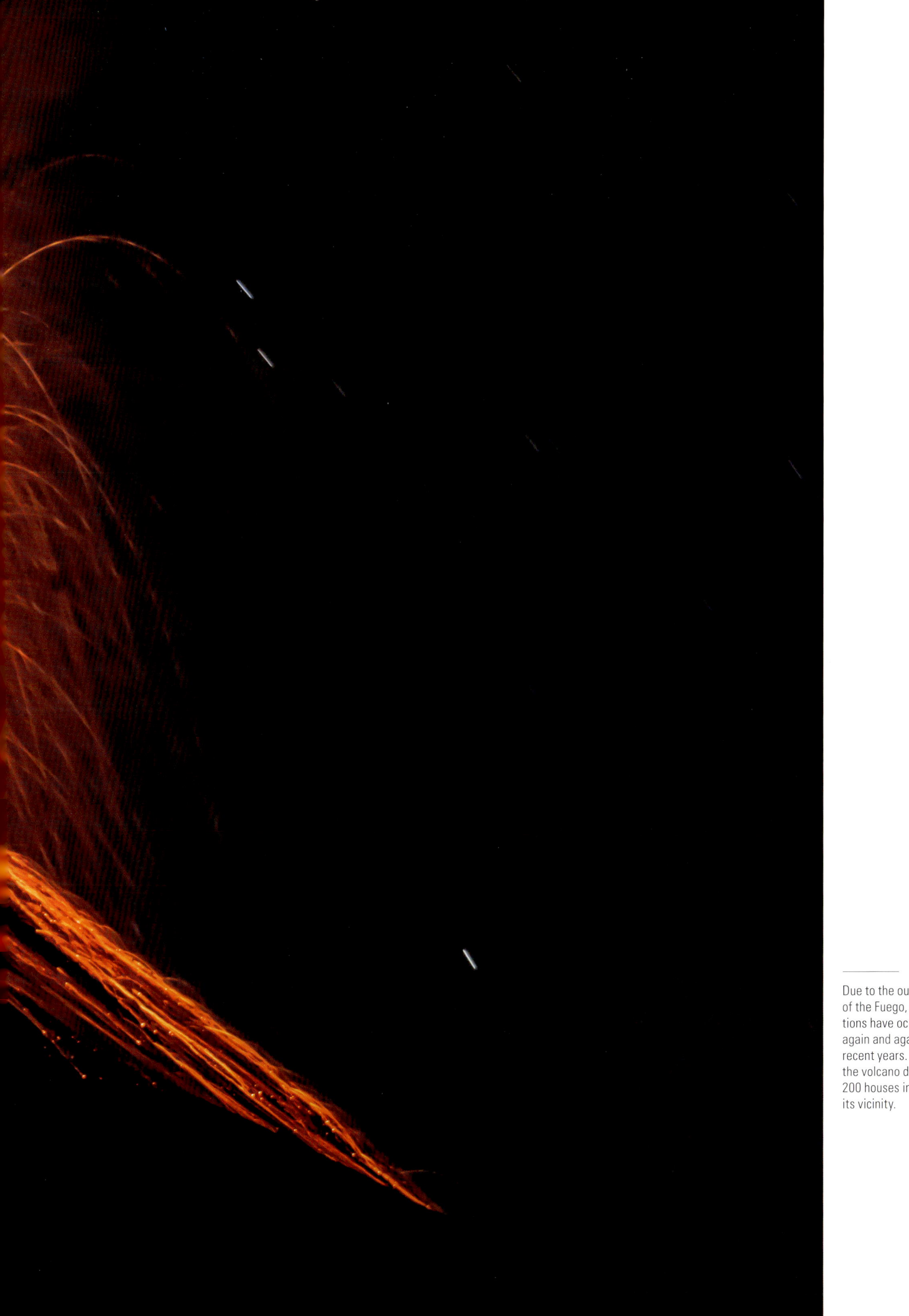

Due to the outbreaks of the Fuego, evacuations have occurred again and again in recent years. In 2018, the volcano destroyed 200 houses in its vicinity.

The spanish name
Volcán de Fuego
means "Volcano of Fire".

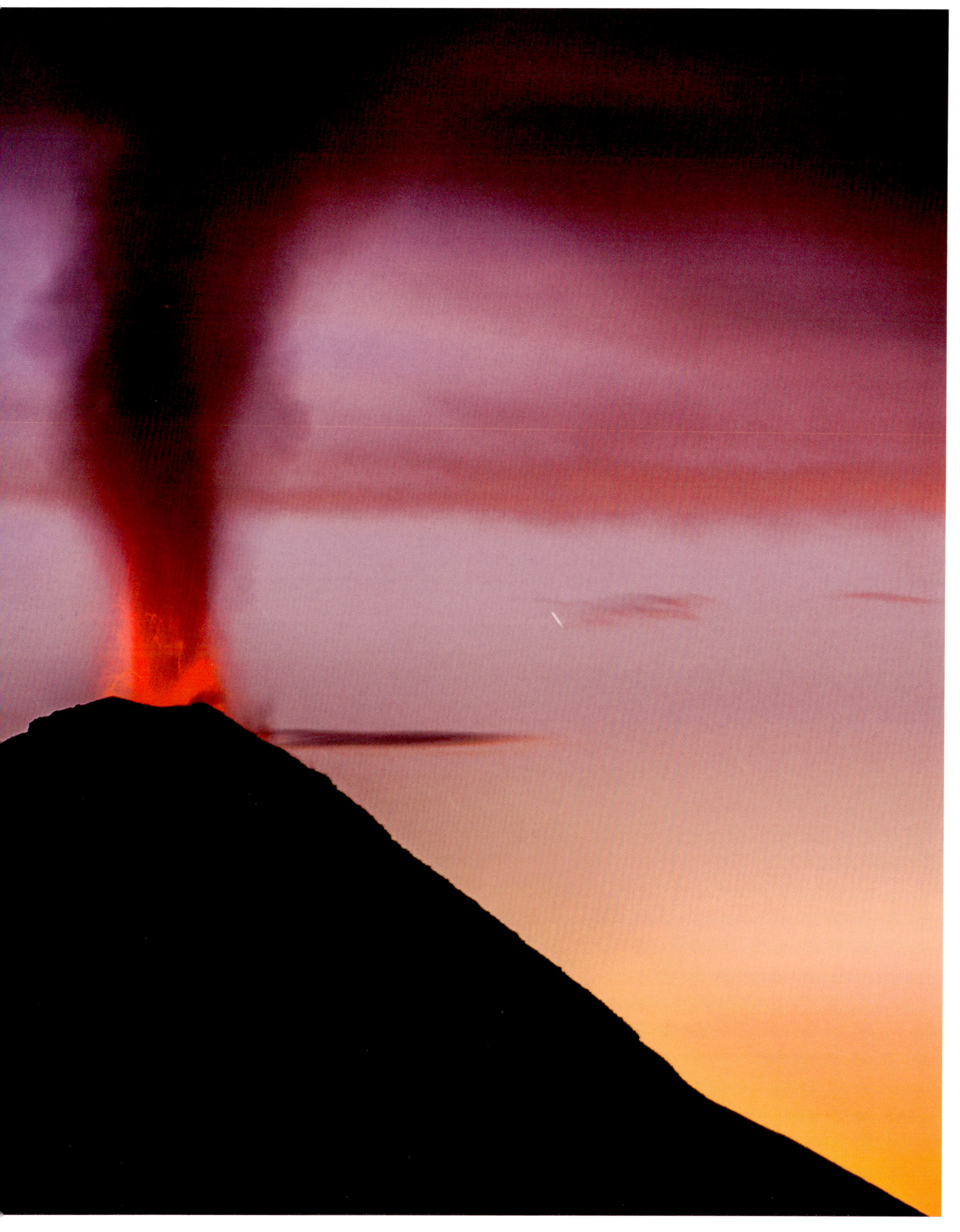

in residential areas. While I was driving, I was always keeping an eye out for my next shot—the photographer's condition, I fear.

And then I saw it—my next perfect shot. Pico de Orizaba looked just like I had imagined it when I was researching and preparing our journey. My heart was racing with excitement. By way of an explanation I shouted: "Picture perfect—literally!" and stopped the car, perhaps a bit too abruptly. I grabbed my camera from the back seat and sprinted away from the car to a better vantage point.

There it was in all its glory: North America's tallest volcano. Yellow bundles of straw and a row of green trees were in the foreground, blue skies and sunshine in the background. A few clouds had gathered just below the imposing, steep glacier at the summit, emphasising the mountain's impressive height. It was intimidating.

Yet even more intimidating were the extraordinary conditions at the summit at the time. Usually, the glacier is covered in snow and can be climbed fairly easily. Yet during my preparations I learned that this year, things were looking a bit different. Due to extreme cold and aridity, the glacier lay bare, as if it had been polished. The steep path to the summit lay across hard glacial ice—and during the days of our arrival in Mexico, this circumstance had a tragic outcome for two fellow mountaineers.

"To Freddy and Nathan"

Below us, Mexico City's carnival rages on but we no longer feel like celebrating. I open a second bottle of beer and raise it. "To Freddy and Nathan," I say. We all toast them and take a long silent gulp from our bottles. My lips feel very dry all of a sudden. Even several days later we can barely grasp and understand what really happened.

Our base camp was situated at an altitude of 14,000 feet. We reached the friendly little orange and red stone hut around noon. From here we had a fantastic view above the thin wisps of cloud drifting between the tree tops just below

us. We also had an unimpeded, clear view of our final destination: Pico de Orizaba's ice-covered summit. Yet we would not be able to enjoy this clear view for long.

Julio, one of our wiry local tour leaders, pressed his crackling radio unit against his ear. He received the shocking news that two mountaineers were missing. They had started their summit day just after midnight—16 hours ago, far too long. Less than 10 minutes later, the voice from the radio piped up again and confirmed our fears. A search helicopter had found a climber just below the summit, signalling SOS. They immediately prepared a small rescue party which comprised of several mountain guides. Our own guide Julio was one of them. Sending mountaineers rather than a rescue team on a search and rescue mission may seem improvised but there was no other choice: there is only one member of the Red Cross's official mountain rescue team at Pico de Orizaba, so there was no way of sending a search and rescue helicopter.

As fast and as thoroughly as possible, the small team assembled their gear: they prepared and distributed long ropes, carabiners, hooks, and ice screws. They stuffed blankets and bivouac tents into backpacks, and brewed some hot tea with which to full thermos flasks. Although the tension in the hut was palpable, the rescue team seemed to function as if they were running on autopilot.

We kept watching them as they disappeared in the distance, slowly making their way uphill towards the summit and towards the presumed location of the accident. What could have been going through their heads at that moment? They would probably reach the summit area long after nightfall, at temperatures of 5 degrees and lower. They would be peering through their pitch black surroundings with nothing but their small headlamps. They would be shouting and hoping for an answer, waiting for any reaction at all, then persevering with their searching and shouting until they were too exhausted to go on.

It was even more difficult to try and imagine how Nathan and Freddy, the two missing climbers, may have been feeling at that moment.

On clear days, ships in the Gulf of Mexico have good visibility of Pico de Orizaba's summit. At 18,491 feet, it is both the highest volcano and the most prominent point in Mexico.

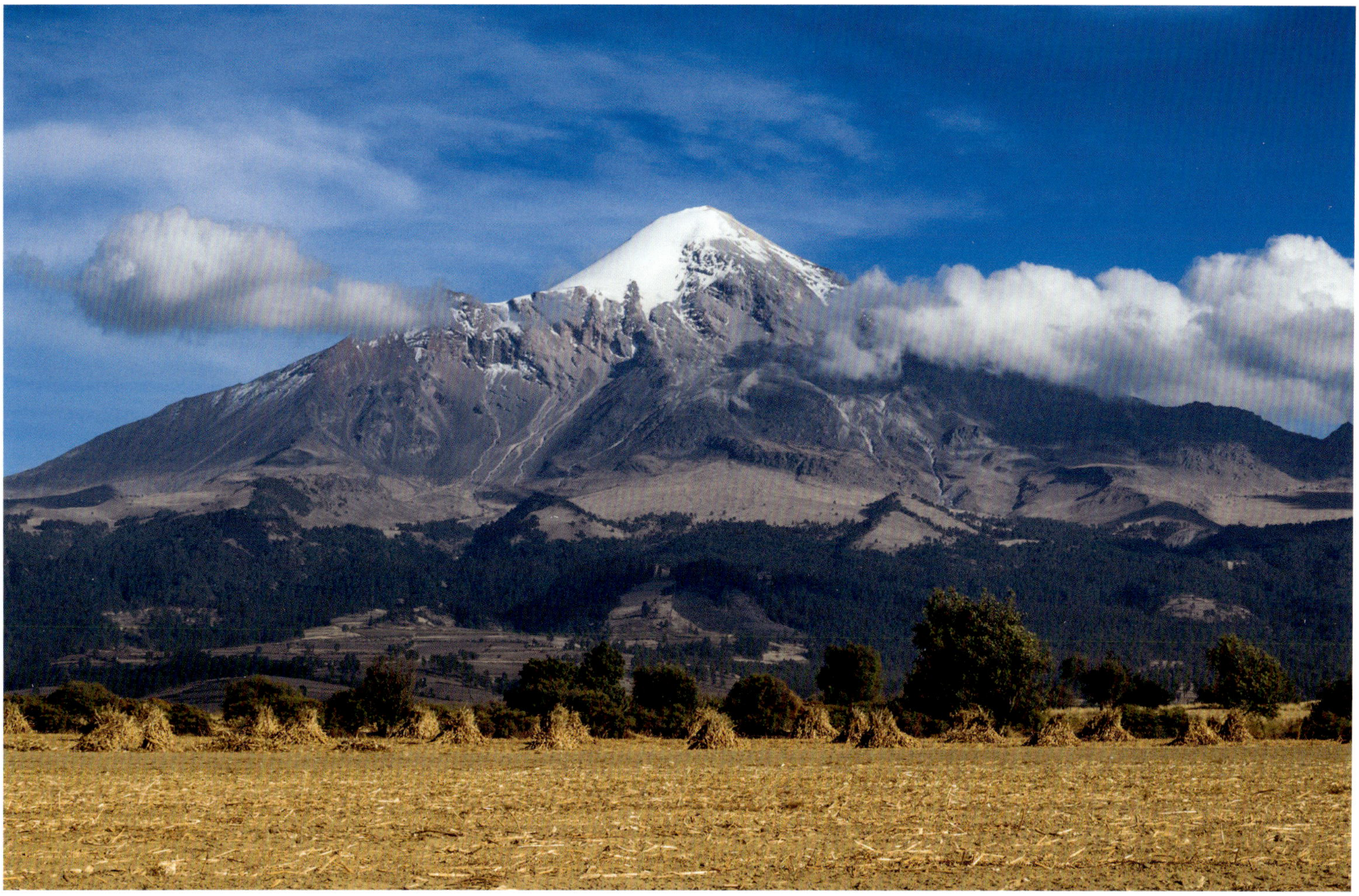

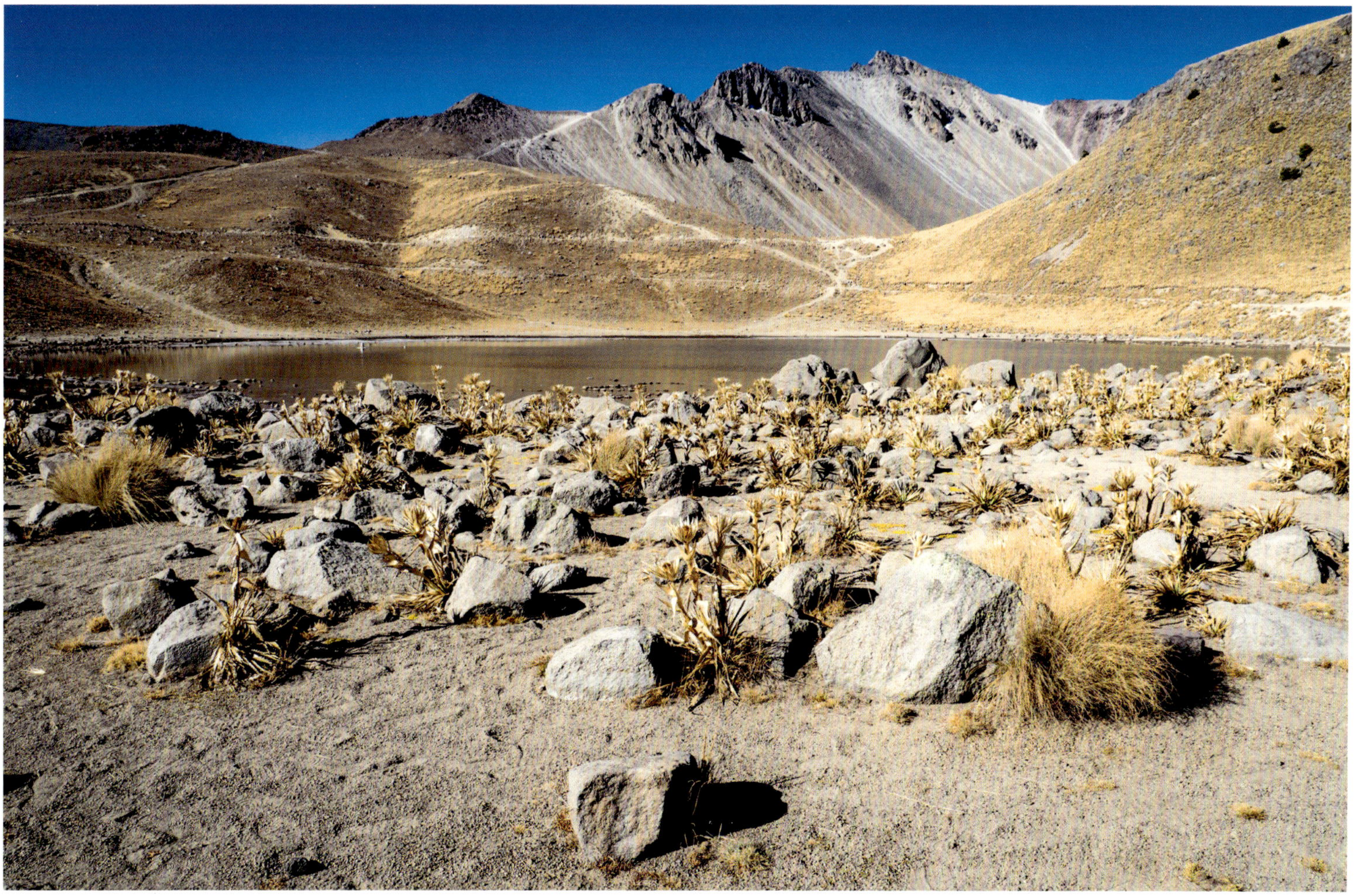

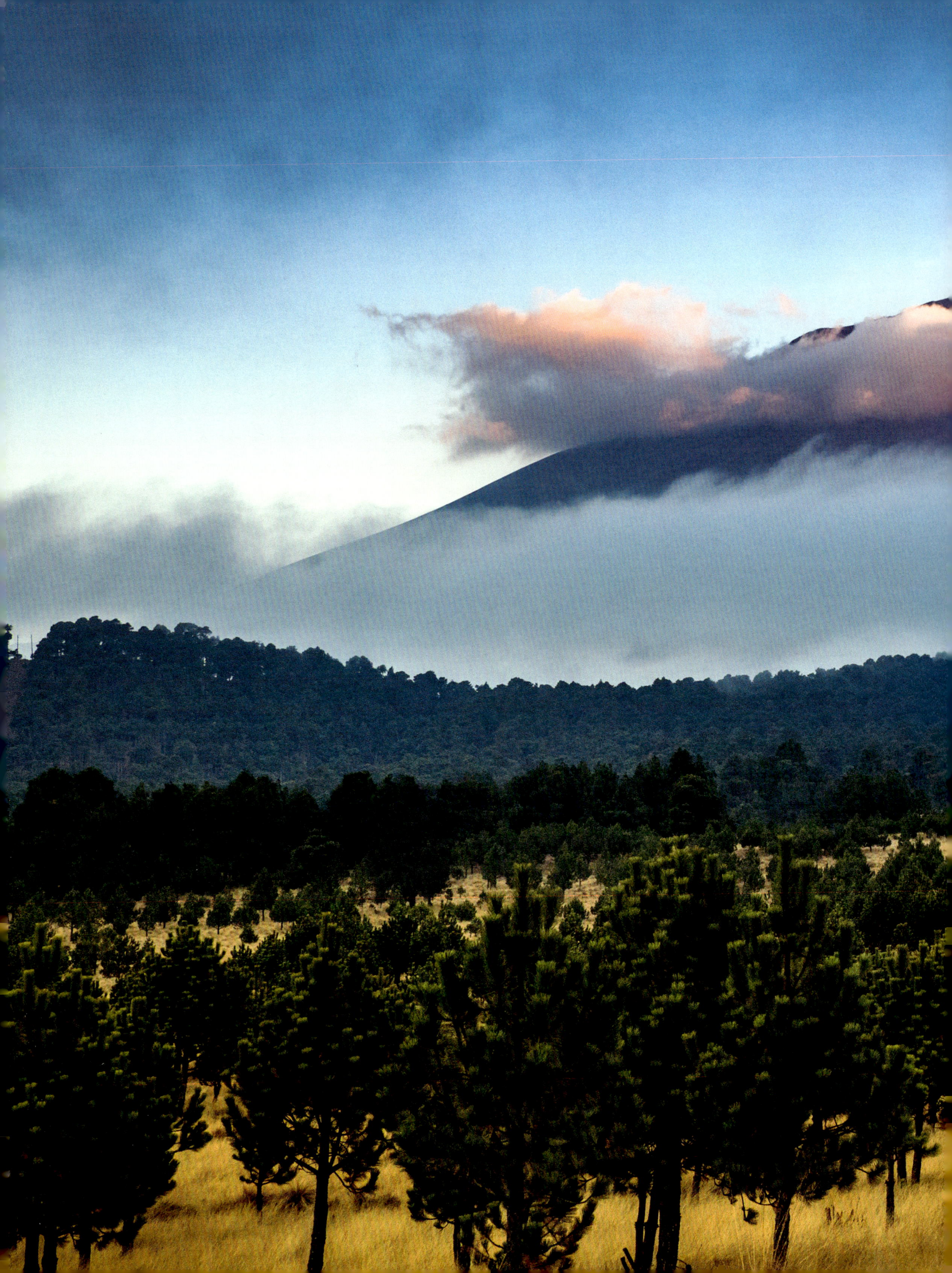

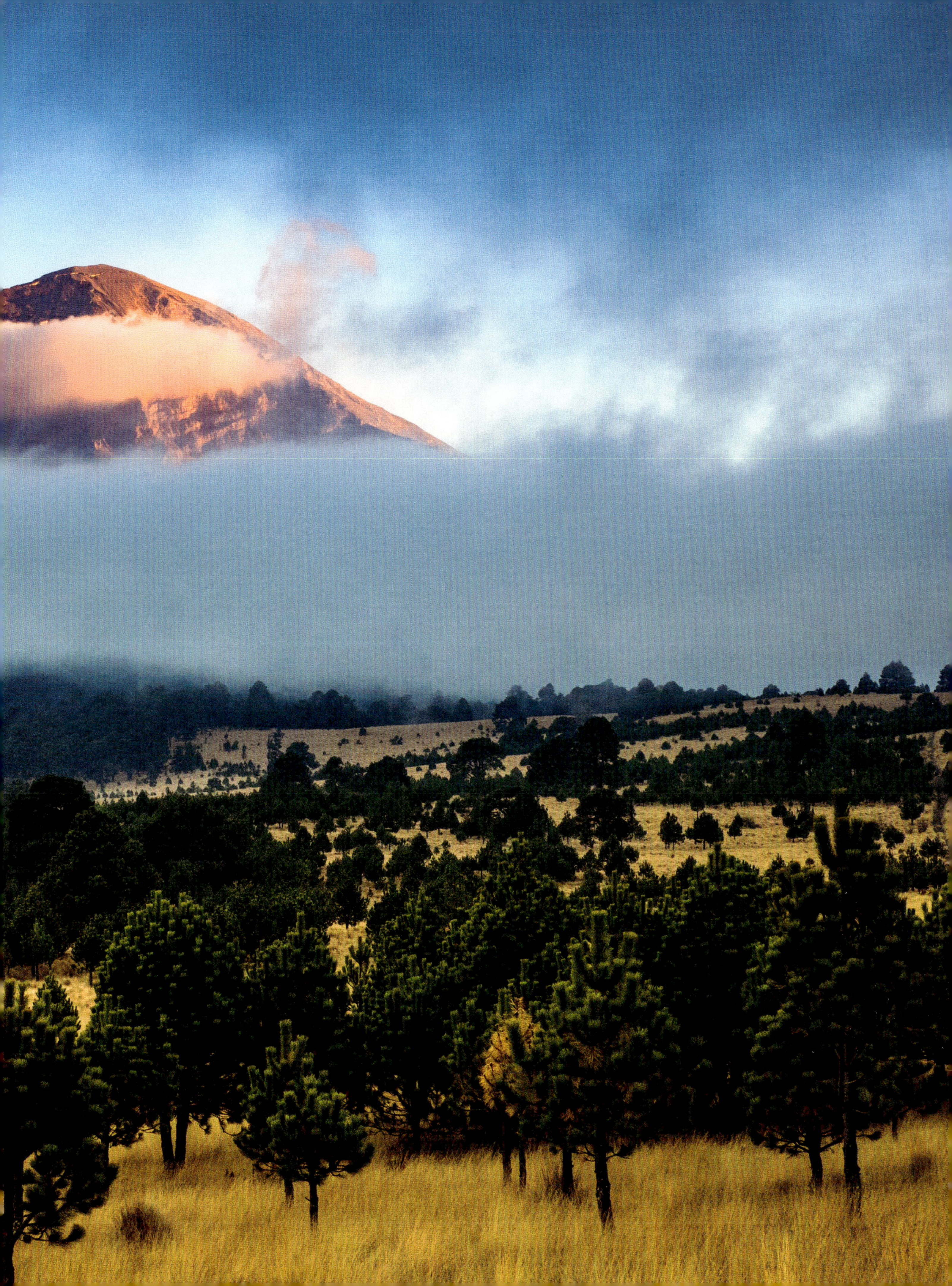

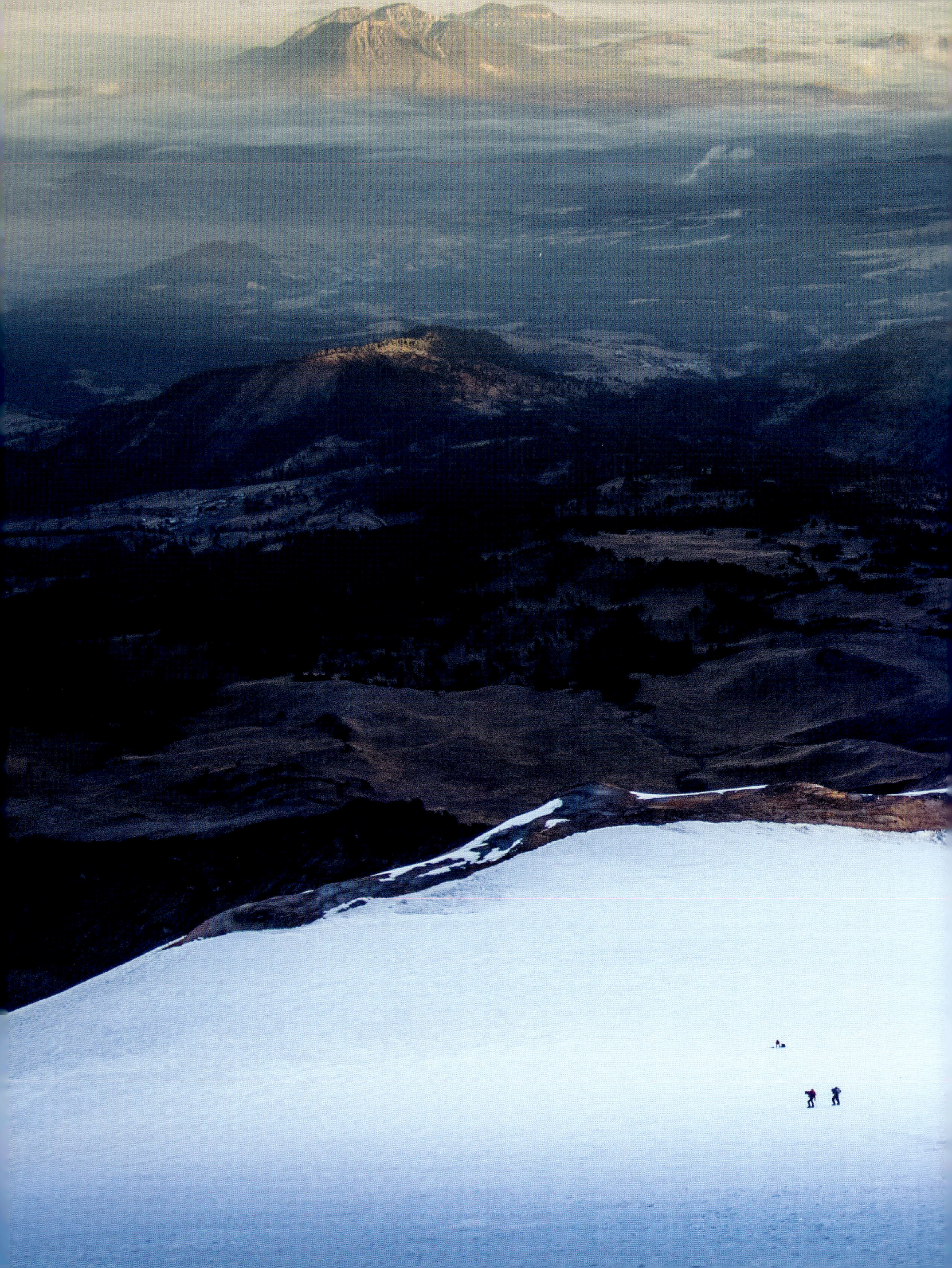

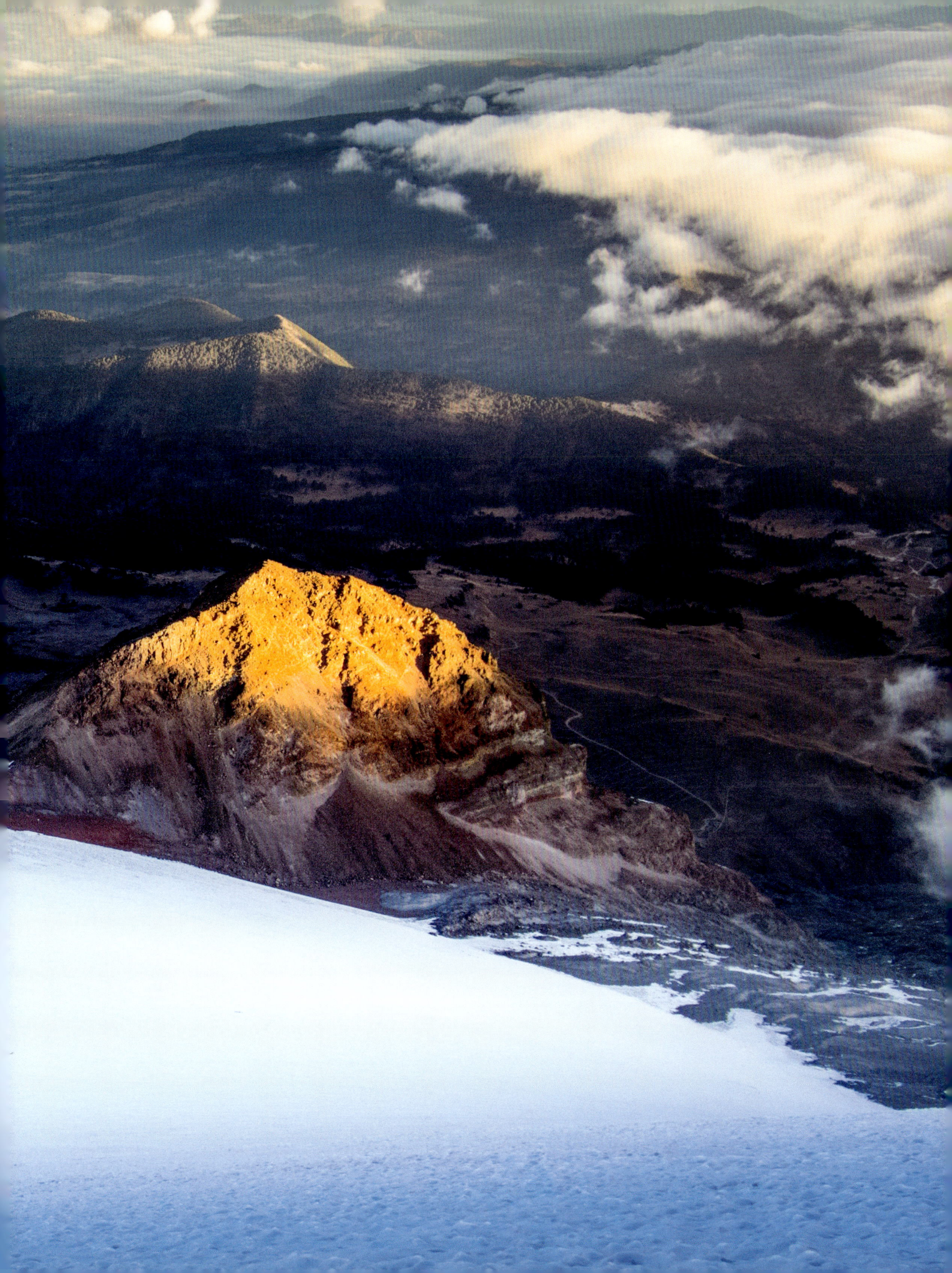

It may have been a constant assault of different emotions: fear, panic, hope, and resignation. Were they lying somewhere in between the rocks, with broken legs, unable to move? Falling asleep would mean certain death in this situation. They would have to force themselves to stay awake—if necessary they might have to shout at each other and quench their thirst with ice cold snow. Unable to stop the pain, they would not know when or if someone would come to their rescue.

That night, we kept waking up and twitching restlessly in our thick sleeping bags, always full of hope—and fear. We did not want to hear bad news, but at the same time, this uncertainty was equally nerve-wracking.

Yet the uncertainty was to continue until later the next morning. The rescue party had found one of the missing climbers, Nathan, and had managed to stabilize and support him in an emergency-bivouac. He miraculously had suffered nothing worse than a few scratches and mild hypothermia.

As we learned later, both climbers had lost their footing just below the summit. They tumbled down the ice-covered, 60 degree incline slope and fell 1600 feet—it was the tragic end of a daring expedition. Nathan's friend Freddy could not be rescued—only his body was recovered. In our small, crowded hut we had to witness Nathan receiving the news from the rescue team. It is still difficult for me to remember the shock on his face; for him, it must have been a trauma that defies all description and words. It was certainly the most awful moment I had to experience during my Volcanic Seven Summits project.

Decisions

We cannot at this point do anything to change Nathan and Freddy's fates, yet we can change our own. We could not imagine worse conditions for our preparations to climb the summit—both psychologically, and in terms of the weather. I kept having to stop myself from obsessing over images of stumbling, losing my footing, and slipping, panicking, fumbling for the ice pick, then sliding at a speed which even after just a few feet is so fast that actively stopping one's own fall is no longer an option. I kept conjuring up visions of my last thoughts during the increasingly rapid fall, of seconds stretching out to become hours—even now I dread to remember those fearful thoughts. It was a huge psychological strain for all of us.

"I'm definitely going back," Karl-Heinz declared. "I don't do well at high altitudes, so I doubt I'd be able to reach the summit anyway." Even Chris seemed hesitant. "I'd probably give it a go, but the final decision lies with our mountain guides." Julio tried to calm us down. "You can do it, no problem. We won't be taking the same route as Nathan and Freddy. And we'll use all the necessary safeguards and we'll be linked by ropes."

It seemed like we were going to make an attempt at the summit after all.

One False Step

"That's insane," I mumble more to myself than to Chris and Karl-Heinz as I look at the next photograph. Luckily, I have only just realised quite how steep the summit must have been. The photograph shows Julio concentrating as he stares down the steep, icy slope. Just behind him, the sheer summit's sharp edge with an incline of up to 65 degrees is just about visible. It is made of nothing but hard, bare ice. At that point, the steepest part of the ascent was still ahead of us—and we had already been climbing for six long, cold and exhausting hours. Our bodies were aching and screaming for a break.

To make the incline on the first half of the ascent a bit more manageable, Julio and I had walked in a tight zigzag. We crossed the slope, climbing only a little bit on the way, turned around almost 60 degrees and walked back in the opposite direction. With each slight diagonal climb across the summit's flank, with each turn at the end, we made slow progress.

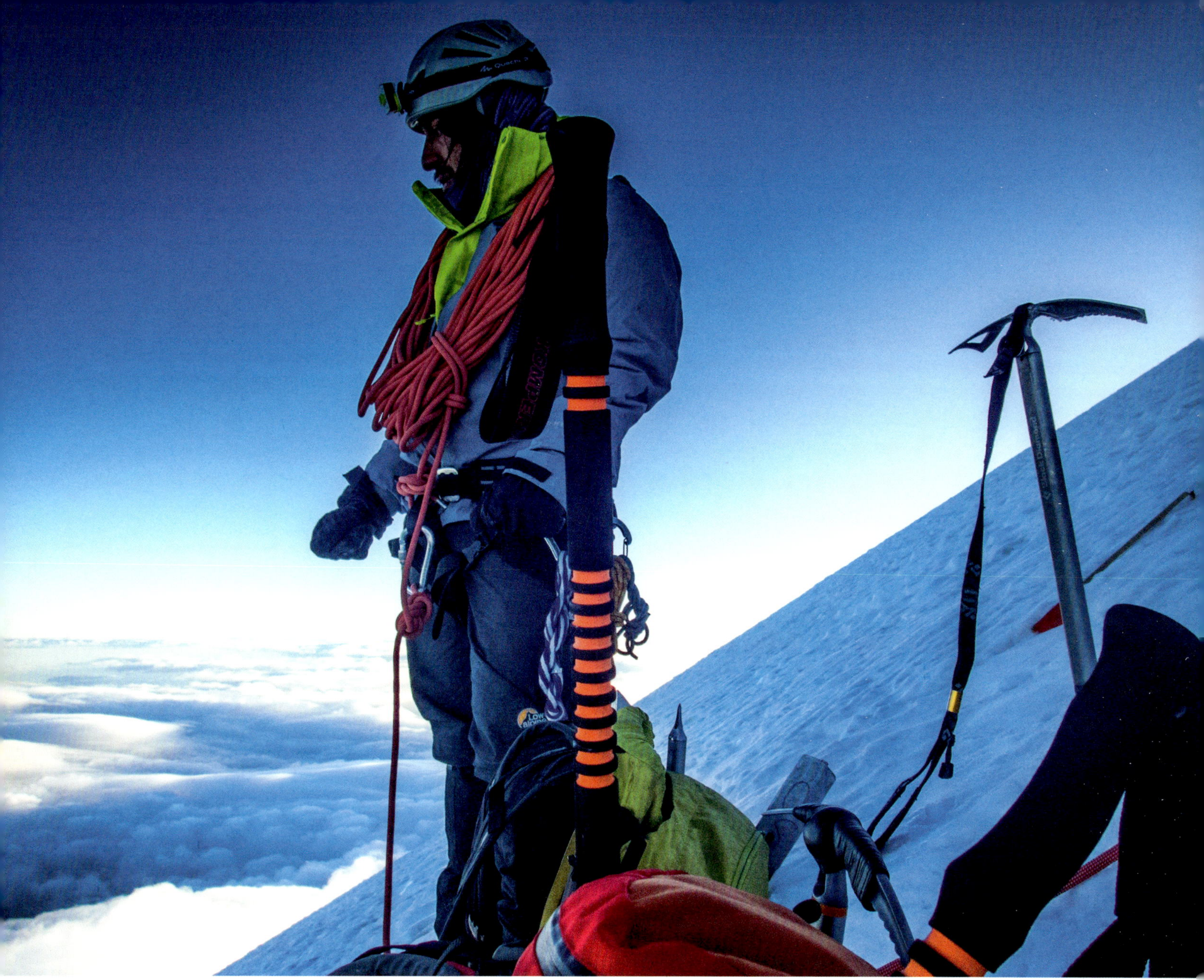

Pico de Orizaba's last recorded eruption dates back to 1846. Since 2010, new reports of fumarole —the emergence of vapor and sulphurous gases—have emerged. This may be a sign that the volcano is reawakening.

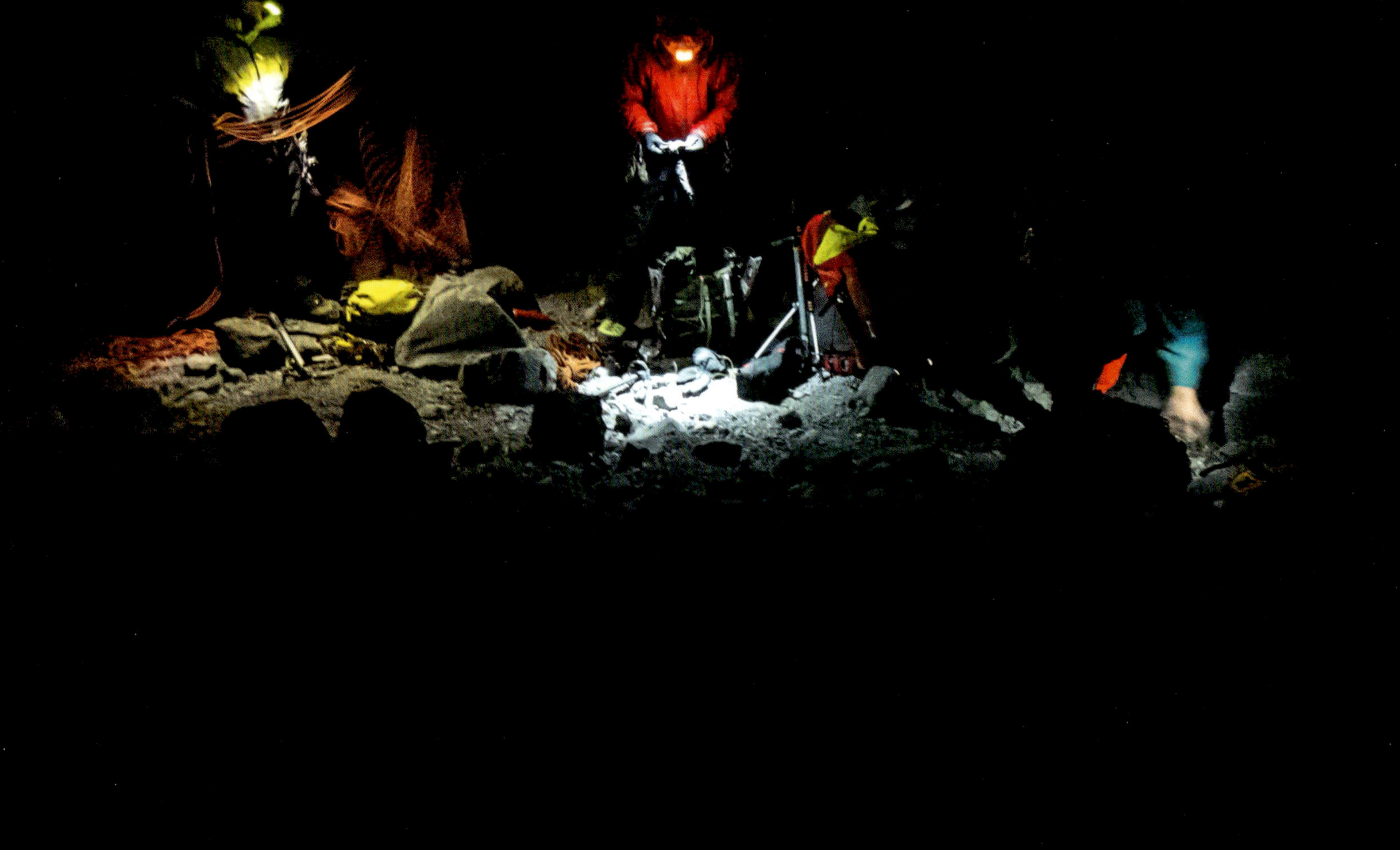

One of Pico de Orizaba's neighbouring summits, Sierra Negra, is home to the Large Millimeter Telescope, which was erected there in 2006 and is operated by Mexican and North American universities. It is one of the world's largest radio telescopes and is used to investigate the structure of cosmic background radiation.

The spread of our headlamps' cool blue light crawled through the pitch black darkness.

I had just arrived at another one of those turns when it happened. I twisted my foot, pushed my crampons down and into the ice, listened to the sharp teeth digging into the surface, and suddenly met unexpectedly hard resistance. Was it a stone? I was already moving forwards though, and so automatically I redistributed my weight onto this now rather unstable foot. The following fractions of a second felt like I was experiencing them in slow-motion. There was a shrill scraping noise as I lost my footing on the hard ground. As a result, I lost my balance and fell backwards, redistributing my weight again back onto the other, relatively stable foot, and noticed with shock that it, too, was beginning to slip. My heart skipped a beat and I felt like I was falling. I was picturing myself sliding down the slope towards the large rocks below, which seemed to be waiting for the impact of my body—sliding faster and faster …

But fortunately for me Julio had years of experience as a mountaineer and rescuer. He reacted instantly. In hindsight, his presence of mind seems all the more amazing considering that he had been out on a different rescue mission just the night before, and he surely must have felt it both mentally and physically.

His arm came shooting forward, more a reflex than a deliberate action, and he pulled on the short rope between us, interrupting my fall. The abrupt tug at the rope made me stumble forwards and my crampons finally dug into ice again.

Take a deep breath. Keep breathing. Calm down. Wait for your pulse to settle. Stand up straight. Look Julio in the eye. His gaze as he met mine was perfectly calm and full of confidence. Behind Julio, a natural phenomenon I will never tire of watching was unfolding—the sun's fireball was slowly emerging from beyond the horizon and climbing into the sky. Seeing all this gave me confidence for the remaining 1000 feet of altitude.

"You really are the luckiest man in the world," Karl-Heinz says and brings me back into the here and now. I keep leafing through the pictures and we look at the next photograph that shows me striking a triumphant pose at the summit. The sun is shining, and there are colourful flags tied around the summit's cross. To the right side of the picture, just below the summit, a few white clouds are nudging in and covering the wonderful view across Mexico's wide plains. Yet the image's crowning element is the rainbow glowing in rich colours right in the middle of the picture, just at the edge of the carpet of clouds. It is another picture-perfect moment and an extraordinary photograph—it felt as if nature were giving me a special, personal reward for having climbed this volcano.

I raise my bottle again and toast to my friends —this time, however, also I toast myself and my own summit day—probably my biggest to date.

We all finish our beers and we hope that the combination of alcohol and exhaustion will help us find sleep while, outside in the streets, the Mexican carnival is still in full swing with no sign of losing momentum. Although it will be a short night's sleep for us, for we have booked a taxi to take us to the airport at 5am the following morning.

Tomorrow morning, we will be saying "Hasta la vista Mexico" and "Hola Chile". In Chile, our next big challenge is waiting for us: Nevado Ojos del Salado, at 22,615 feet the highest volcano in the world.

> There was a shrill scraping noise as I lost my footing on the hard ground.

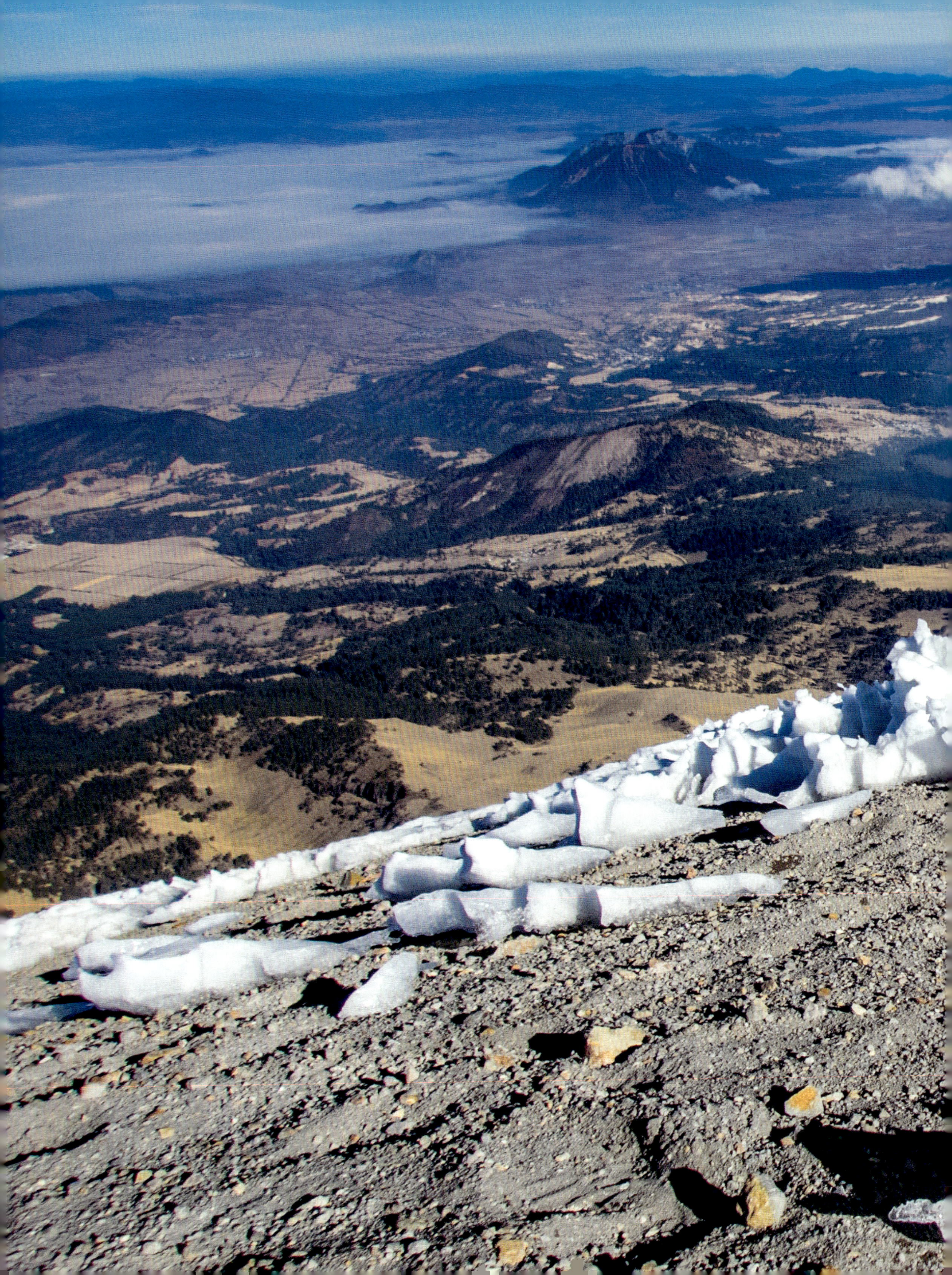

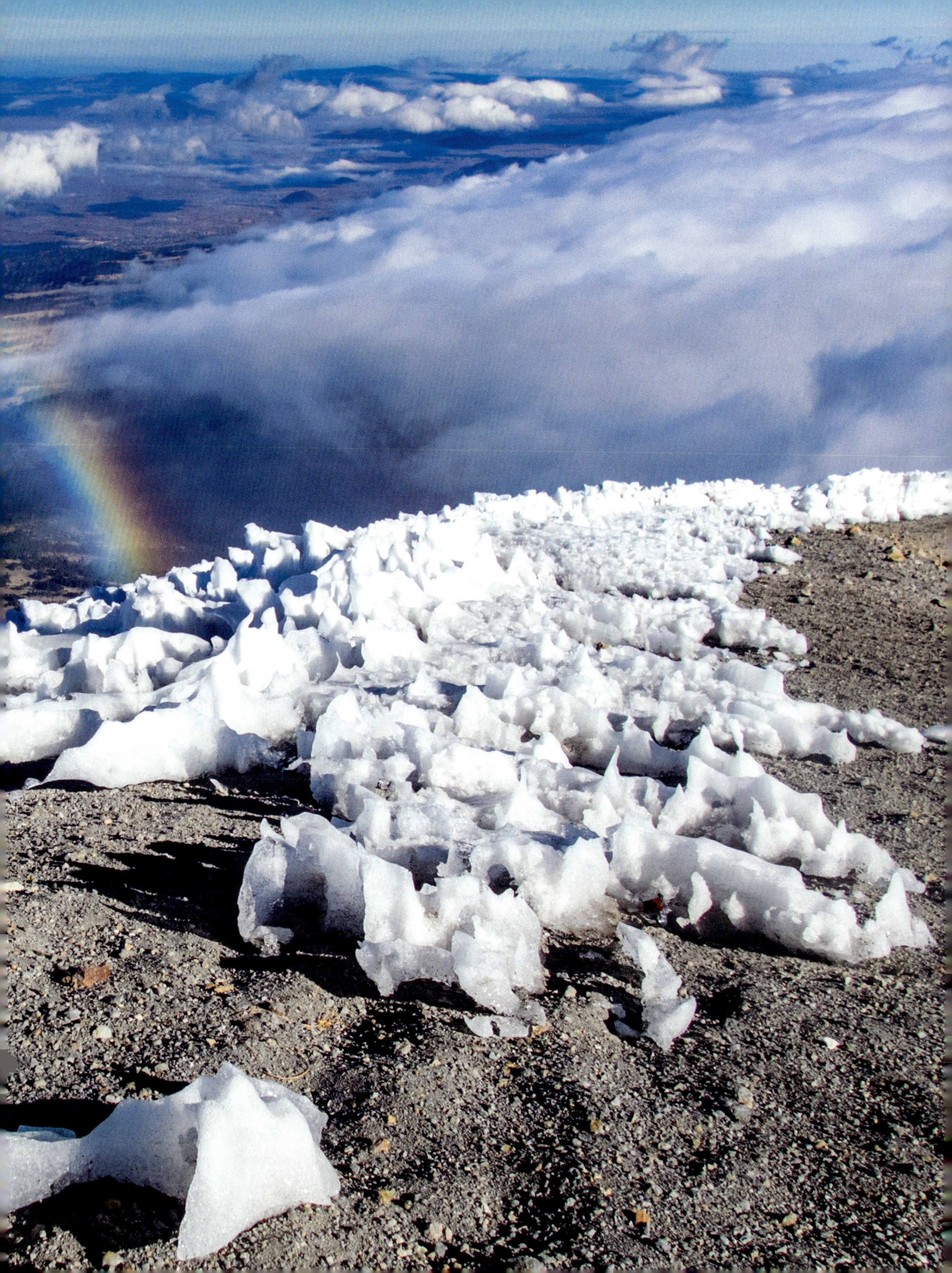

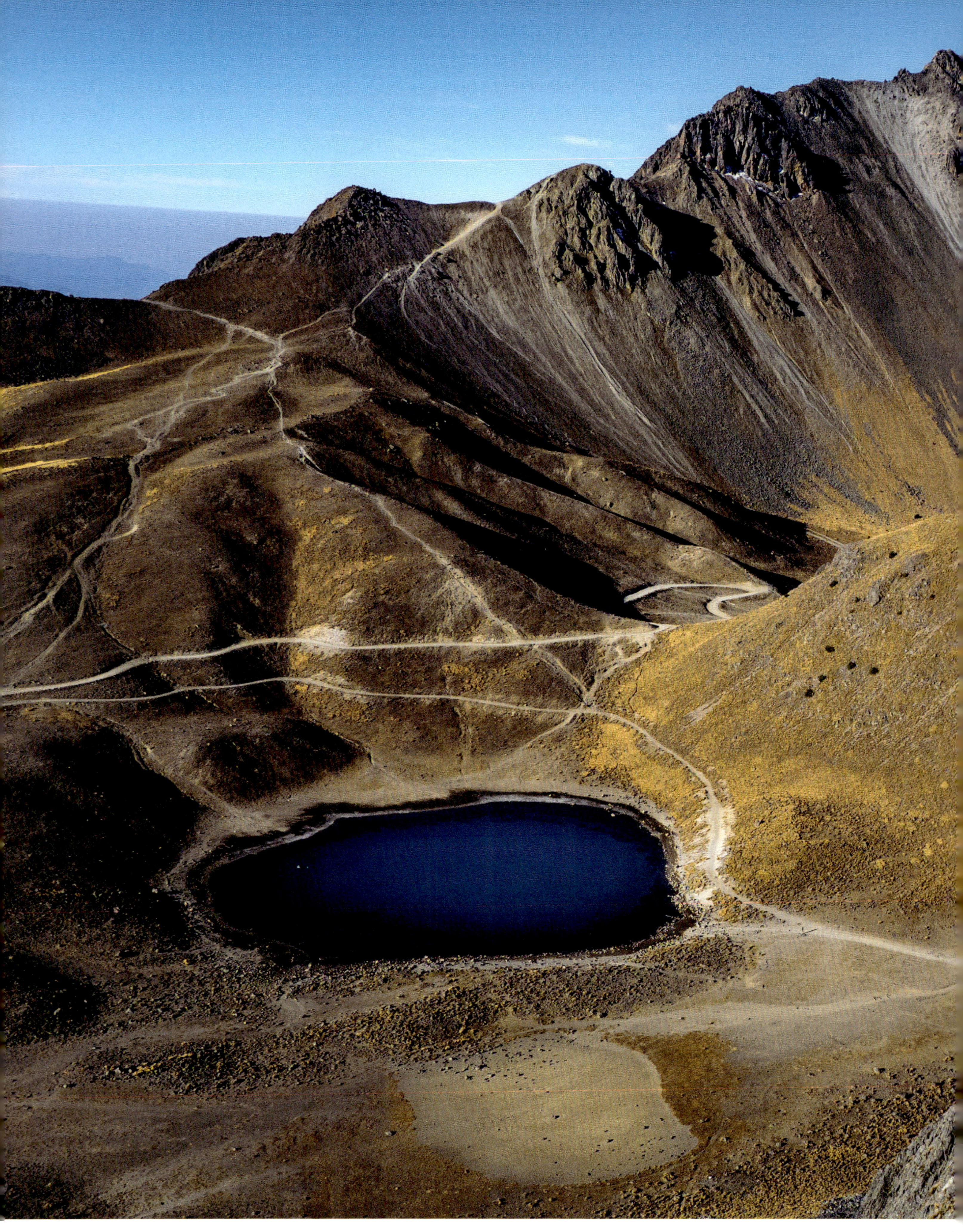

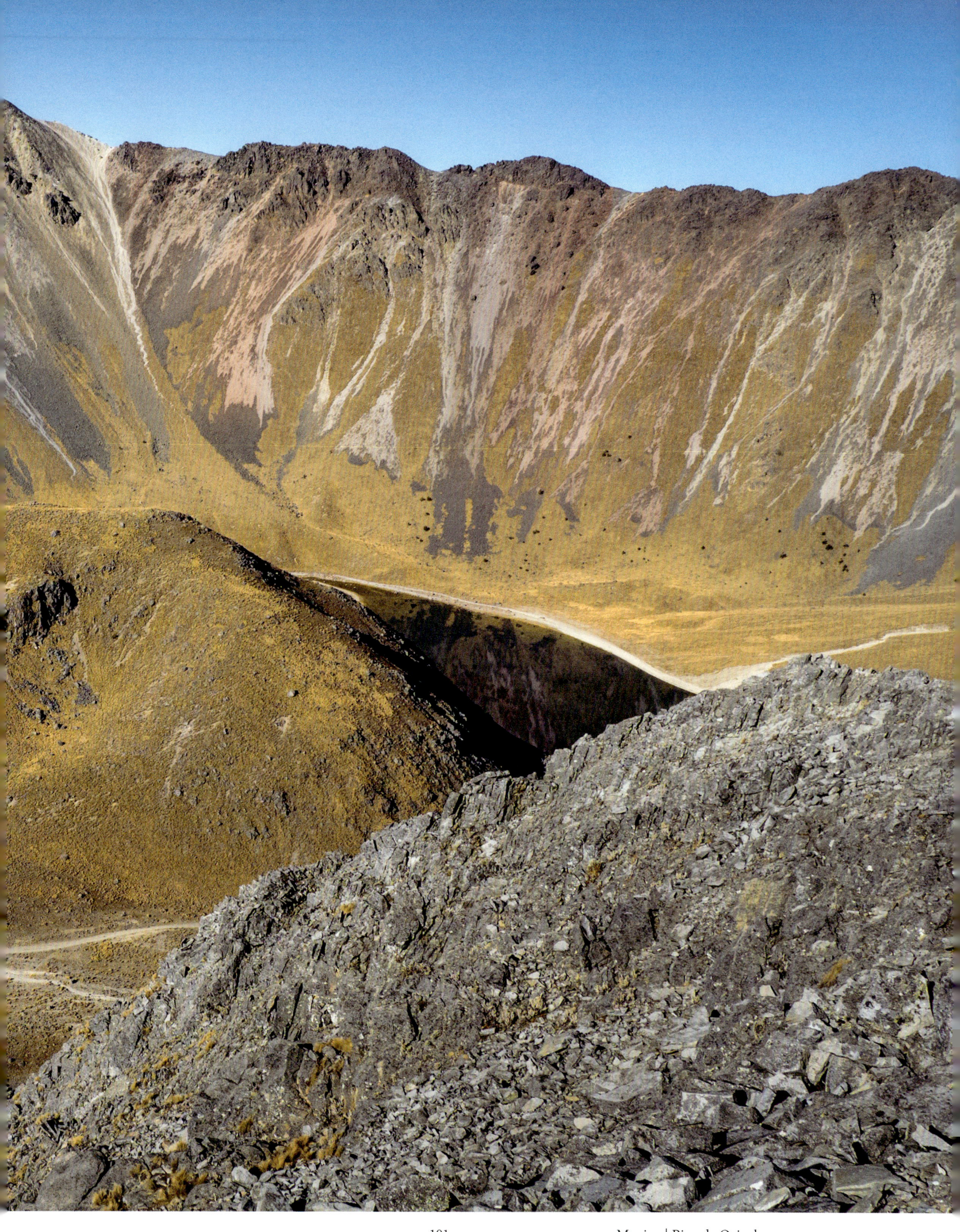

Thursday, February 15th,

Carnival in Mexico is incredible—such an infectious energy, such a colorful, fierce country. Luckily, "my" Mexico could not be further from the negative portrayals we often find in the media: drugs, gang wars, ruthless murder—I didn't encounter any of those.

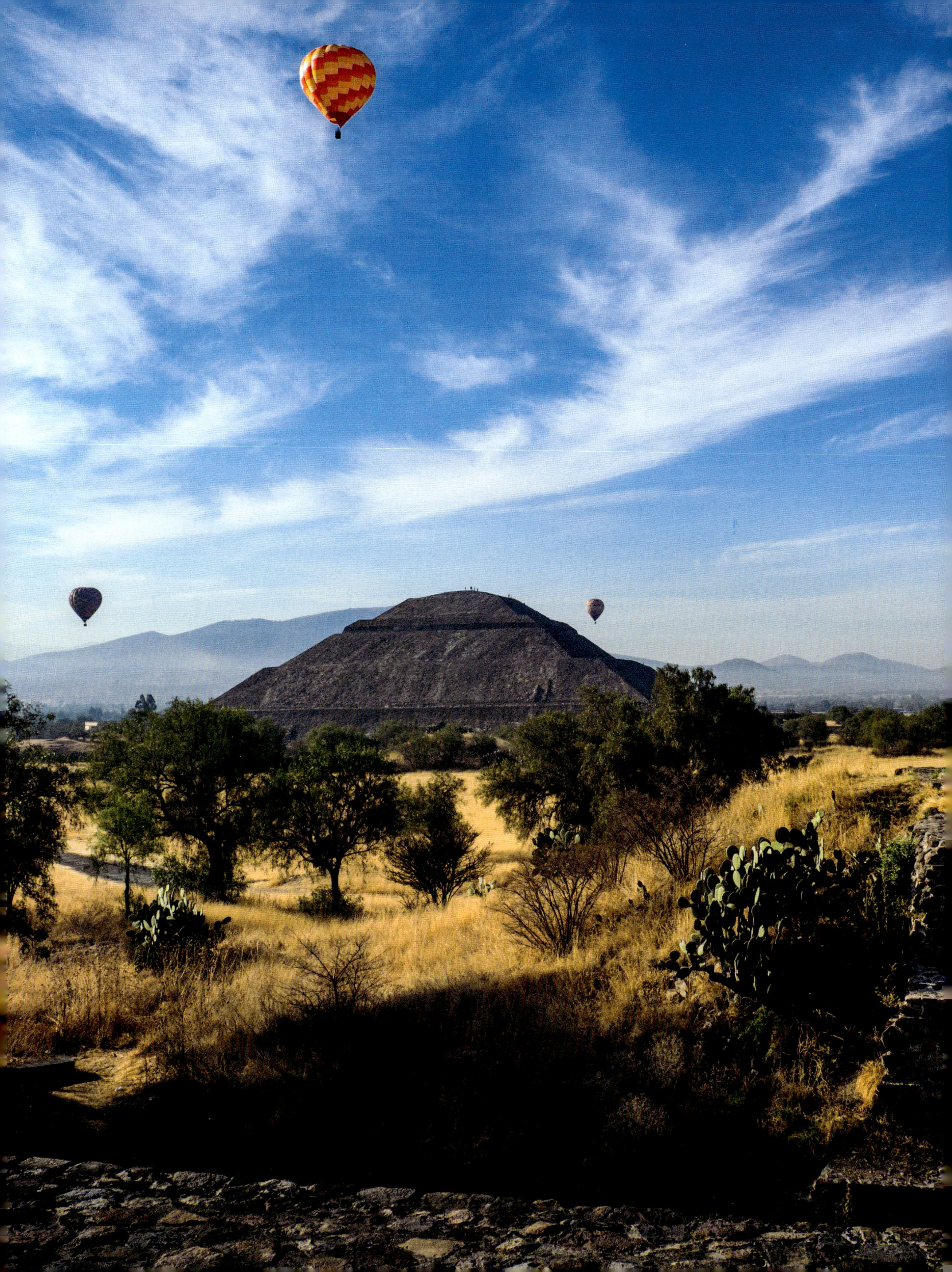

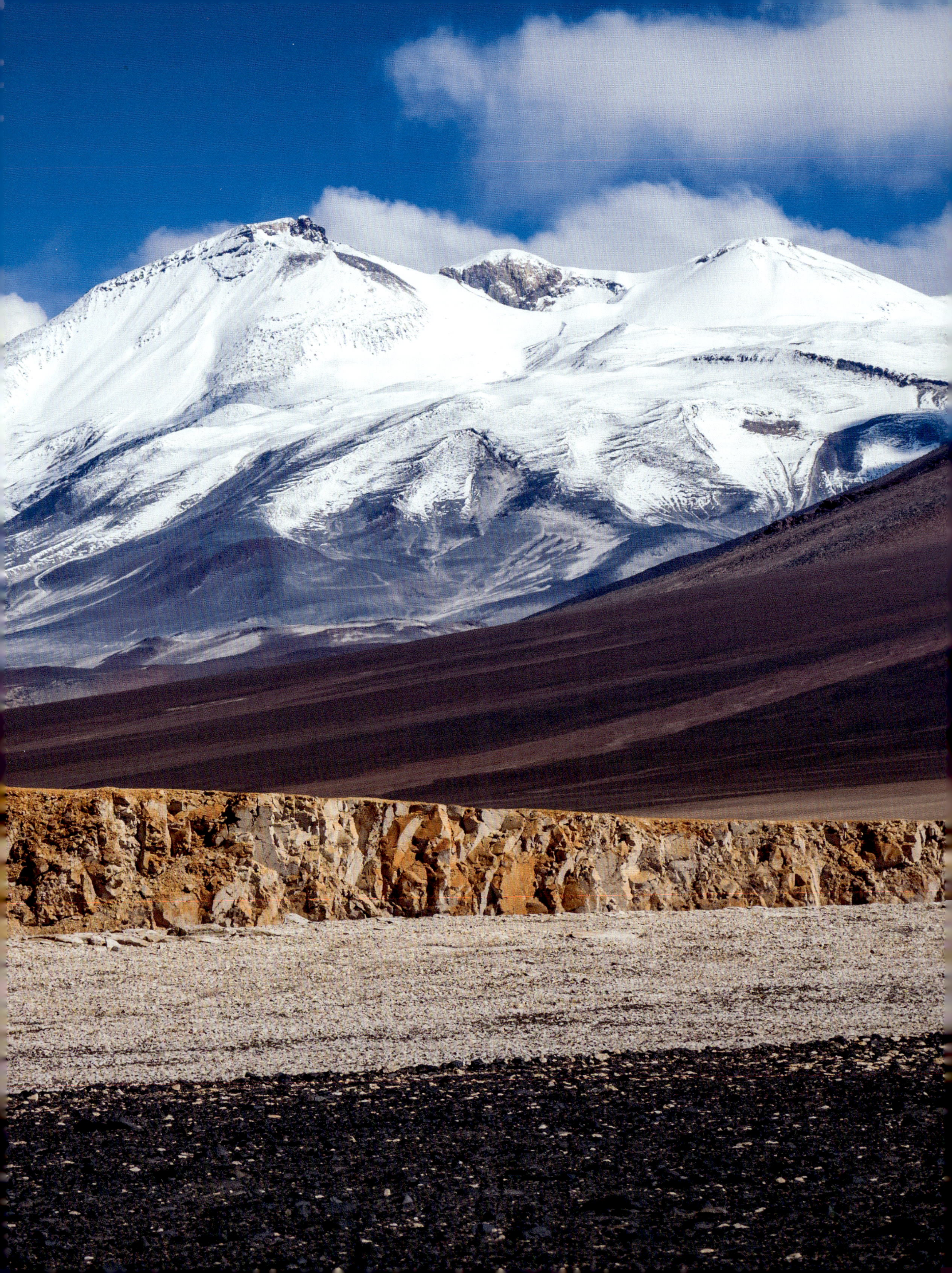

4

OJOS DEL SALADO

The Ultimate Desert
Chile

"These colors are incredible," I keep saying to my fellow passengers, who do not seem to care. In the car with me are still Chris and Karl-Heinz as well as our mountain guide with the comforting name Jesus—nicknamed Pica. We are traversing the Atacama Desert plateau in Chile on a dust road at about 60 mph—I am driving. Our rental four-wheel-drive pickup looks like a small fire engine: a crimson red finish with one bright yellow stripe across it. Our destination is Laguna Rosa, which is located just by the border to Argentina, and above which towers a volcano: Nevado Tres Cruces. We can already see one of its three summits, all of which sit at over 20,000 feet in elevation, as it appears behind the hills. There are all shades of red and brown to be found in the hills' rough sand, with waves and curved lines of white, beige, yellow, orange, and black cutting through. In the foreground, a few patches of yellow-green grass appear almost luminously. In the background, the snow-covered, pristine white summit stretches into the deep blue sky.

"Did you know," I ask my friends, "that the Atacama is the driest desert outside the polar region? There hasn't been any rain for hundreds of years in some of the areas around here." "That's right," says Karl-Heinz, "it's because the Andes block any potential rainfall. Any atmospheric humidity that comes from the east will come down as rainfall in the mountains. Nothing reaches this side of the mountains. Nothing but dry air reaches this area here. And it is a similar story in the west, at the Pacific coast. The cold Humboldt Current comes in from the Antarctic sea, and the cold water cools down the air, too. So, as a result, it is almost 50 degrees colder over there than anywhere else on the same latitude. Any humidity there falls as rain over the cold sea as the air cools down. And so, from the West as well, no rain can reach this desert." Due to its extreme altitude and dryness, conditions in the Atacama Desert are extreme; they are, in fact, close to the conditions found on Mars. For this reason, space agencies developing rovers to search for life on the red planet come here to test their machines. During the analysis of the gathered test data, an international research team discovered a wealth of microorganisms in the Atacama Desert. In moisture, they become active, yet they can also survive extended arid periods. They may have been living in the desert's deeper layers for millions of years. Even though conditions on Mars are much harsher due to UV-radiation, temperature, and even greater aridity than the Atacama Desert, there are also signs that water—one of the preconditions of life—used to be prevalent in the past. Even today, there still appears to be water on Mars, below and within the ice at the planet's poles. If indeed life on Mars really did exist at some point in the past, under more favorable environmental conditions, then there is a distinct possibility that it may still be there today, preserved just under the planet's surface.

Laguna Rosa

Up until now, there had been a constant fresh breeze accompanying us on our drive. At Laguna Rosa, though, the air is perfectly still. The lagoon's steel-blue water is perfectly even, and on it, the reflection of Nevado Tres Cruces' three white peaks appear almost identical to the original—except of course that it is upside-down. Pink flamingos are standing on one leg like pretty little ornaments in the lagoon that has been named after them. This place is a landscape photographer's dream come true.

As an interesting aside, flamingos have the ability to balance on one leg without much effort. They simply shift their body's center of gravity and gain additional stability through a "locking mechanism". They can even sleep while standing on one leg. For their habitat, flamingos prefer alkaline salt water lakes. As a result they are often found near areas with high

The Andes are the highest mountain range outside of Asia and are part of the Pacific "Ring of Fire", an area of high volcanic activity. They range from Venezuela in the north down to Chile in the very south, which makes it the world's longest continental mountain range.

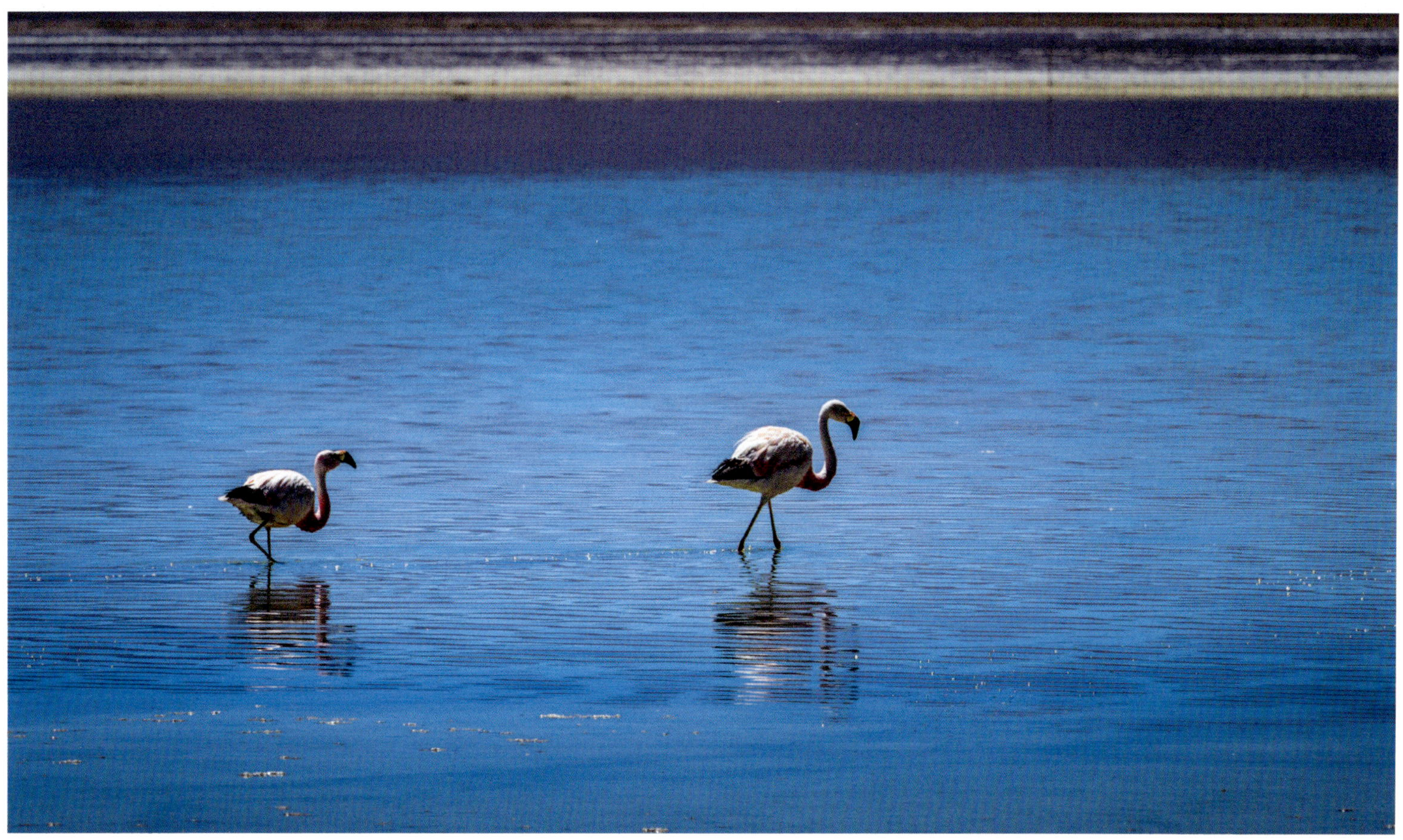

volcanic activity. Few other vertebrate animals manage to survive under these conditions, but flamingos can filter out the meagre amount of organisms from the water for sustenance. Even the Andes' rough winters—which can reach around -22 degrees—do not cause these tough birds to leave their habitat.

"I would never have thought that such a small bird can be so resilient," I ponder, but I am immediately distracted again, for I have rarely had the opportunity to capture a landscape as beautiful as this. I am pressing the shutter-release button as if in a trance. Frantically I run from one point to the next, searching for a new, better perspective, and switching lenses every other minute. "Had a bit too much coffee this morning?" Chris asks with a smirk. There is no time for me to reply, though, as I have already spotted my next subject. I rush over, not quite believing my luck.

Only once I am certain I have captured every conceivable image at least once onto my SD-card, I allow myself to stop and take in my surroundings with my own eyes rather than

There hasn't been any rain for hundreds of years in some of the areas around here.

through a lens. I put my camera aside and enjoy the unbelievable and incredibly peaceful scene. My gaze stops at the Nevado Tres Cruces' three peaks. Momentarily, my thoughts drift and I think of our travels a few days back—to our time at another volcano, Nevado Ojos del Salado.

A Sleeping Giant

At 22,615 feet, Nevado Ojos del Salado is the world's highest active volcano and the second highest summit in the Americas. Its name means something like "Eyes of Salt", which refers both to the snow and ice on top of the mountain and to the salt lakes in its vicinity. It is located almost 200 miles away from any inhabited area and due to its height, it takes some effort and preparation to reach and climb. This is probably why, despite being well-known as the world's tallest volcano, few mountaineers attempt the ascent.

We had come prepared. Our rental pickup featured four-wheel-drive and could navigate

The Atacama Desert is one of the world's most arid deserts. Precipitation in Death Valley in California, one of the most arid places in the northern hemisphere, is 50 times higher than in the Atacama Desert.

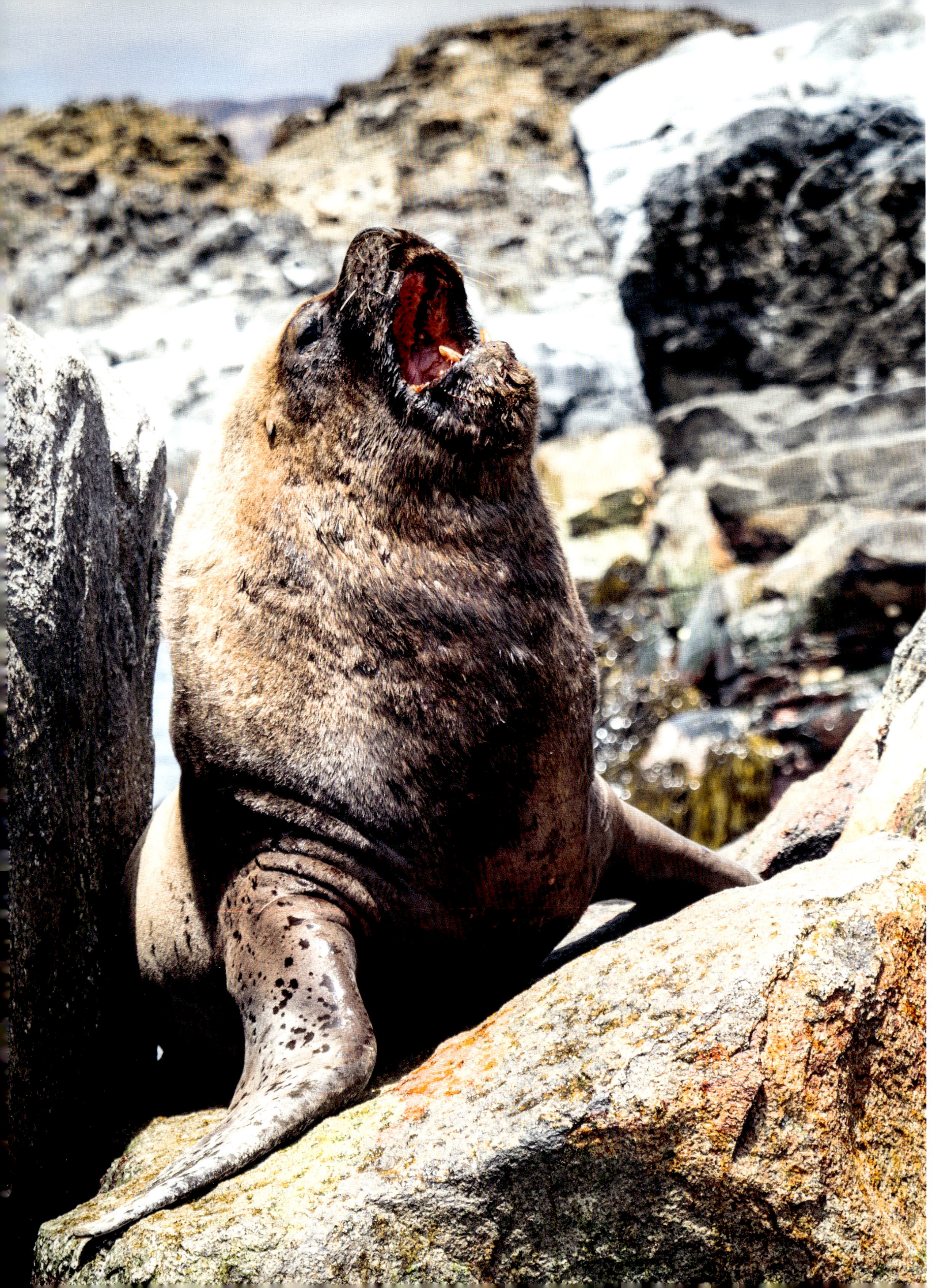

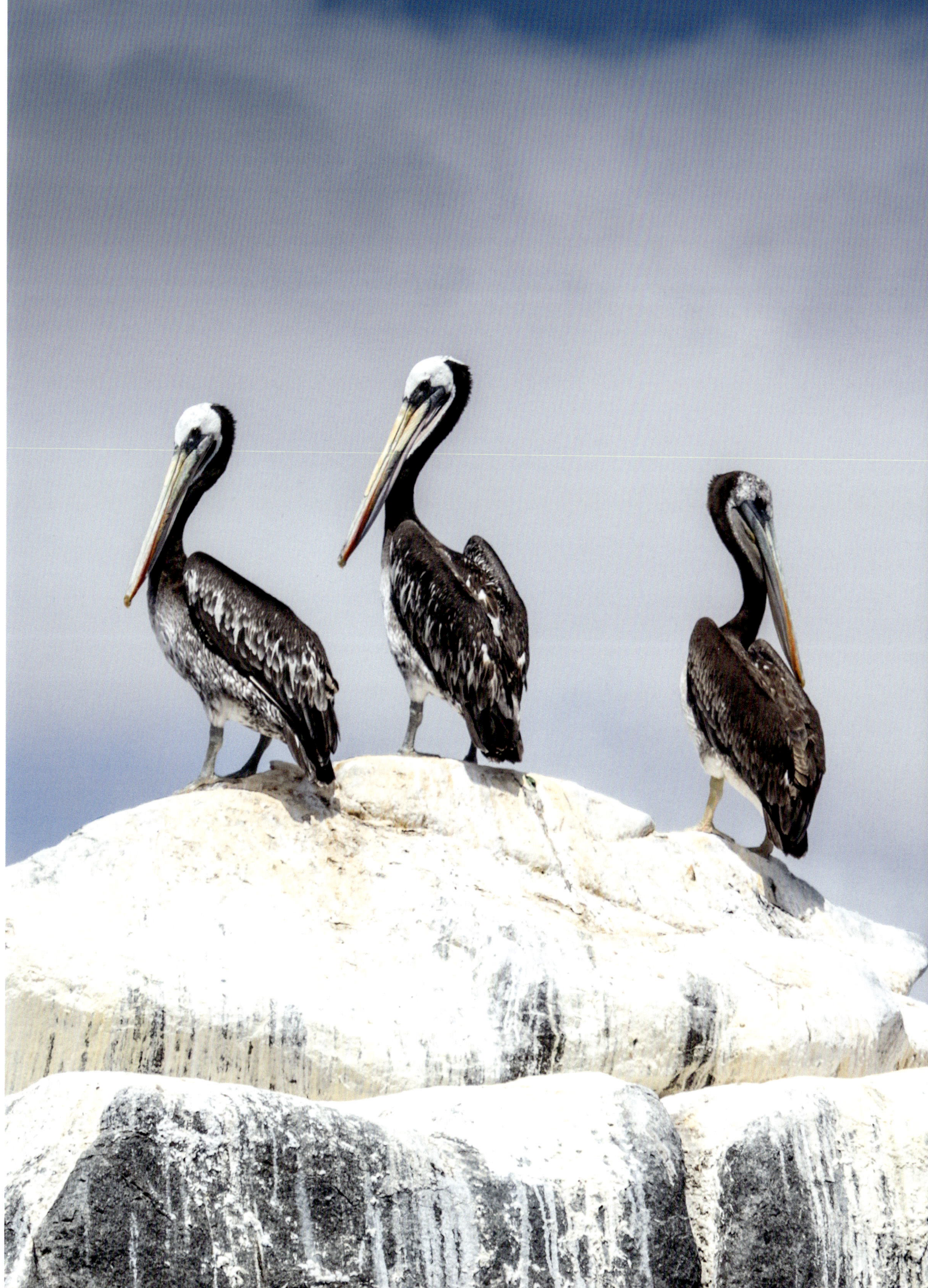

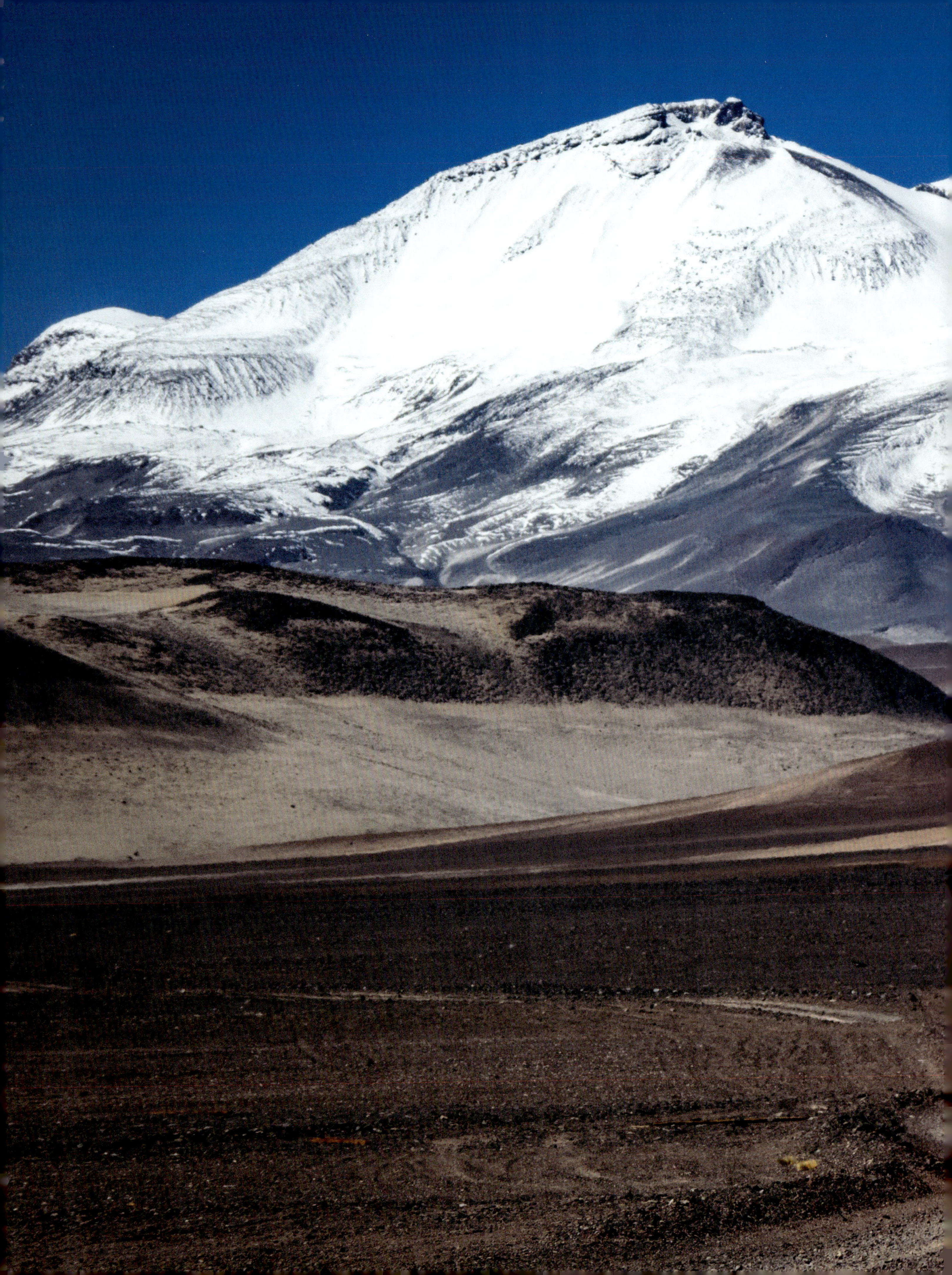

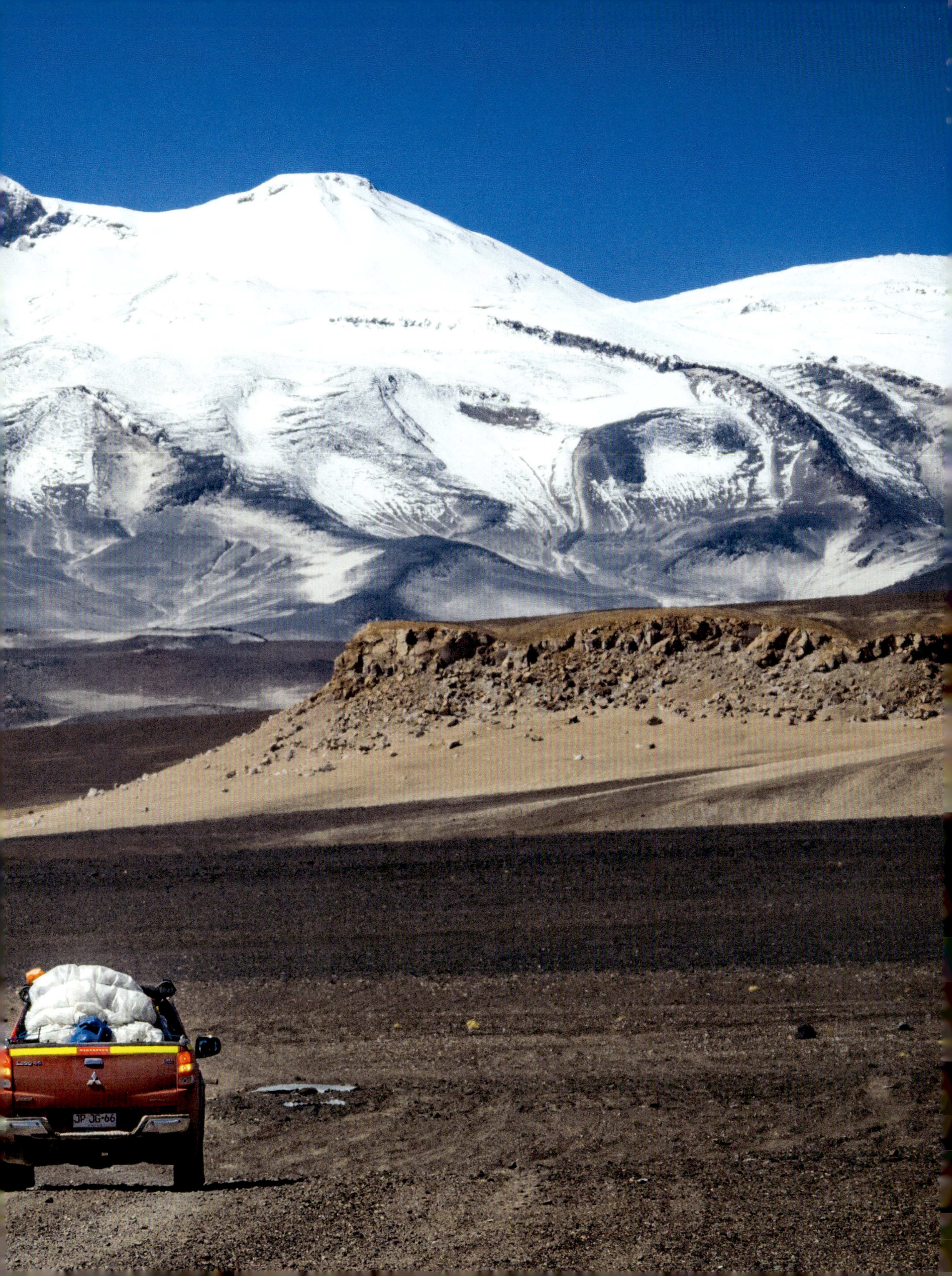

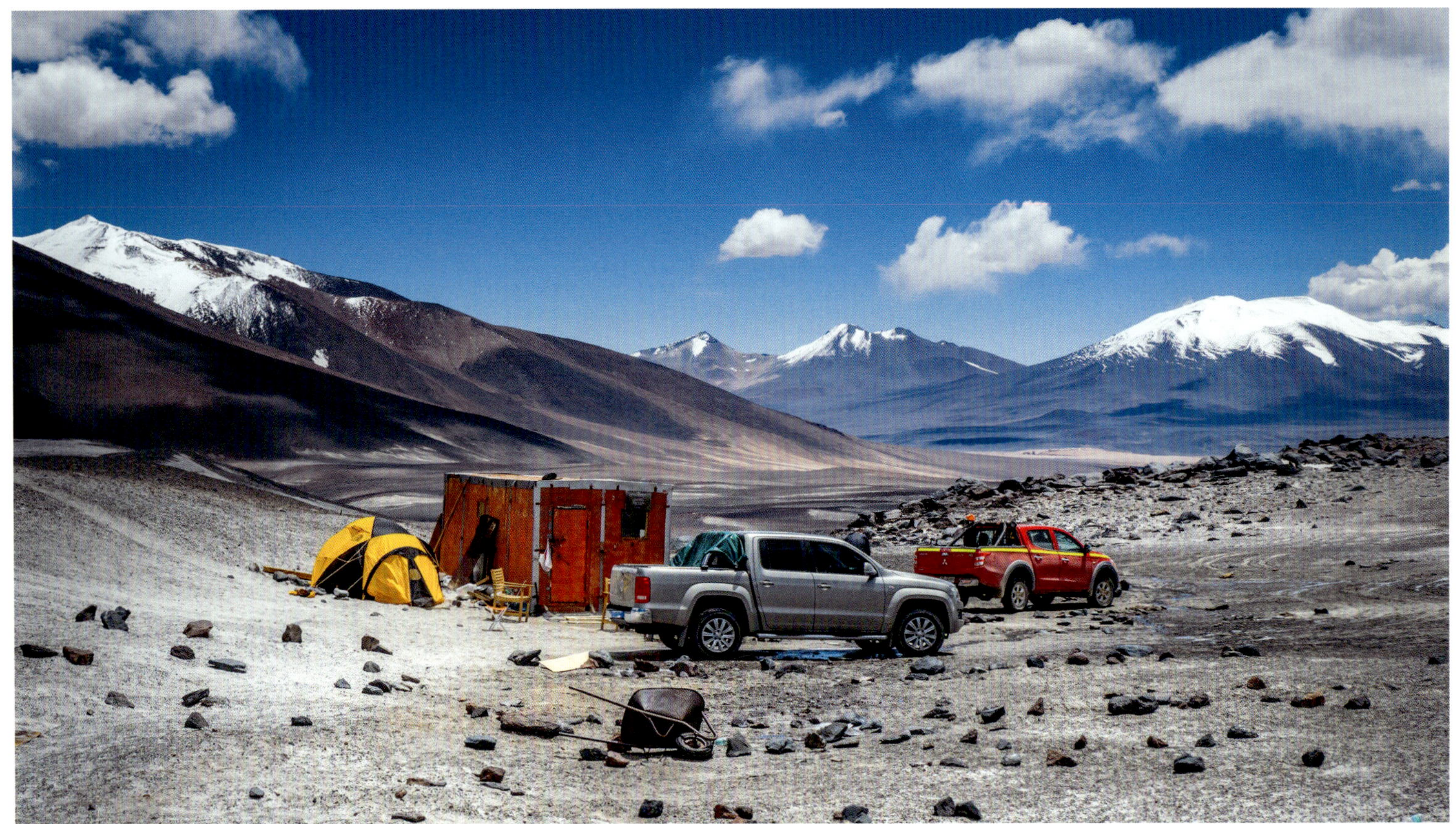

any terrain. Its loading area held our luggage in addition to several spare cans of petrol. Most importantly, we had brought plenty of drinking water. Some of our concerns were unfounded, however, as it turned out that the infrastructure around Nevado Ojos del Salado was well-developed and efficient. We had mobile network connections almost throughout and so we were able to use Google maps for navigation, which showed an impressive network of roads across the desert. The main thoroughfare was well-maintained, with occasional stretches of tarmac. Numerous roadworks encountered along the way showed us that the road was in the midst of being transformed into an actual highway across the desert.

Eventually we arrived at an area that was a little more difficult to traverse, where we had to cross some sand dunes and employed the four-wheel-drive for the first time. Other than that, we managed to reach the high camp at an altitude of over 17,000 feet without difficulty. Two fellow mountaineers we met at the camp had not been as lucky: some of the circuitry inside their pickup had frozen overnight, so in the morning, the engine would not start. For two hours they had been sitting outside in the cold,

kindling a small fire just beneath the engine, before the frozen parts had finally warmed up enough to use again and they could get back on the road.

The view from up there was breathtaking—and we had not even reached the summit yet! I stood in the midst of a wide, natural, volcanic-grey landscape. There were volcanic rocks scattered everywhere and every so often you could even find traces of solidified streams of lava. Looking up at the summit, the sky above the Nevado Ojos del Salado was a deep blue, speckled with white clouds. At this height, they appeared to take on more definition, more depth. It almost felt as though you could reach out and pluck them from the sky. There was a profound silence. Suddenly, it was interrupted by delicate paws padding over the rocky ground. A curious brown desert fox came over to watch us from a higher vantage point. It paused, surprised, and seemed to wonder, for a few seconds, what or who we were—and then vanished from sight.

I try to imagine what scenes would have unfolded here, the last time this giant volcano erupted. Streams of lava would have been spewed forth from the crater. Burning chunks

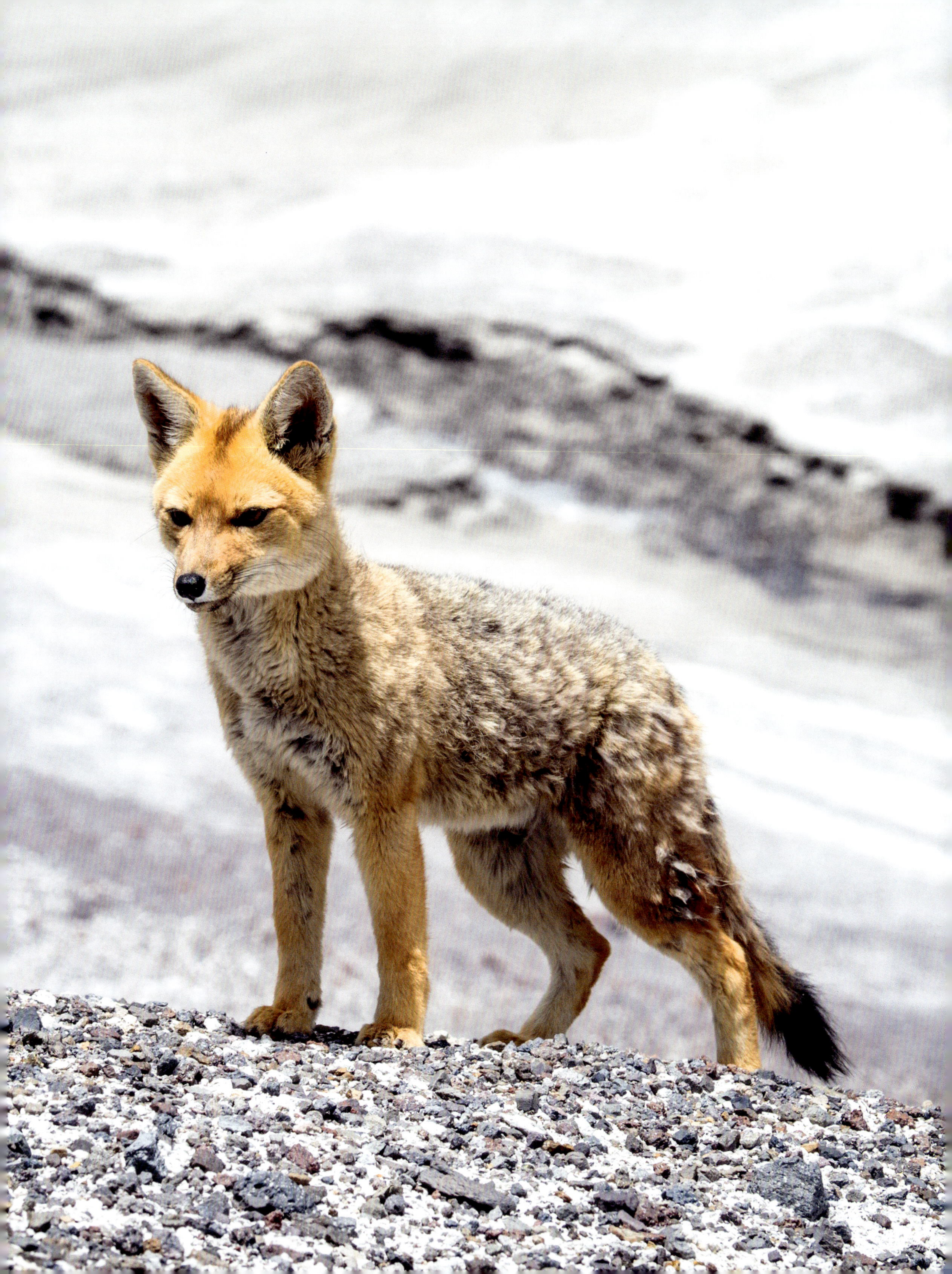

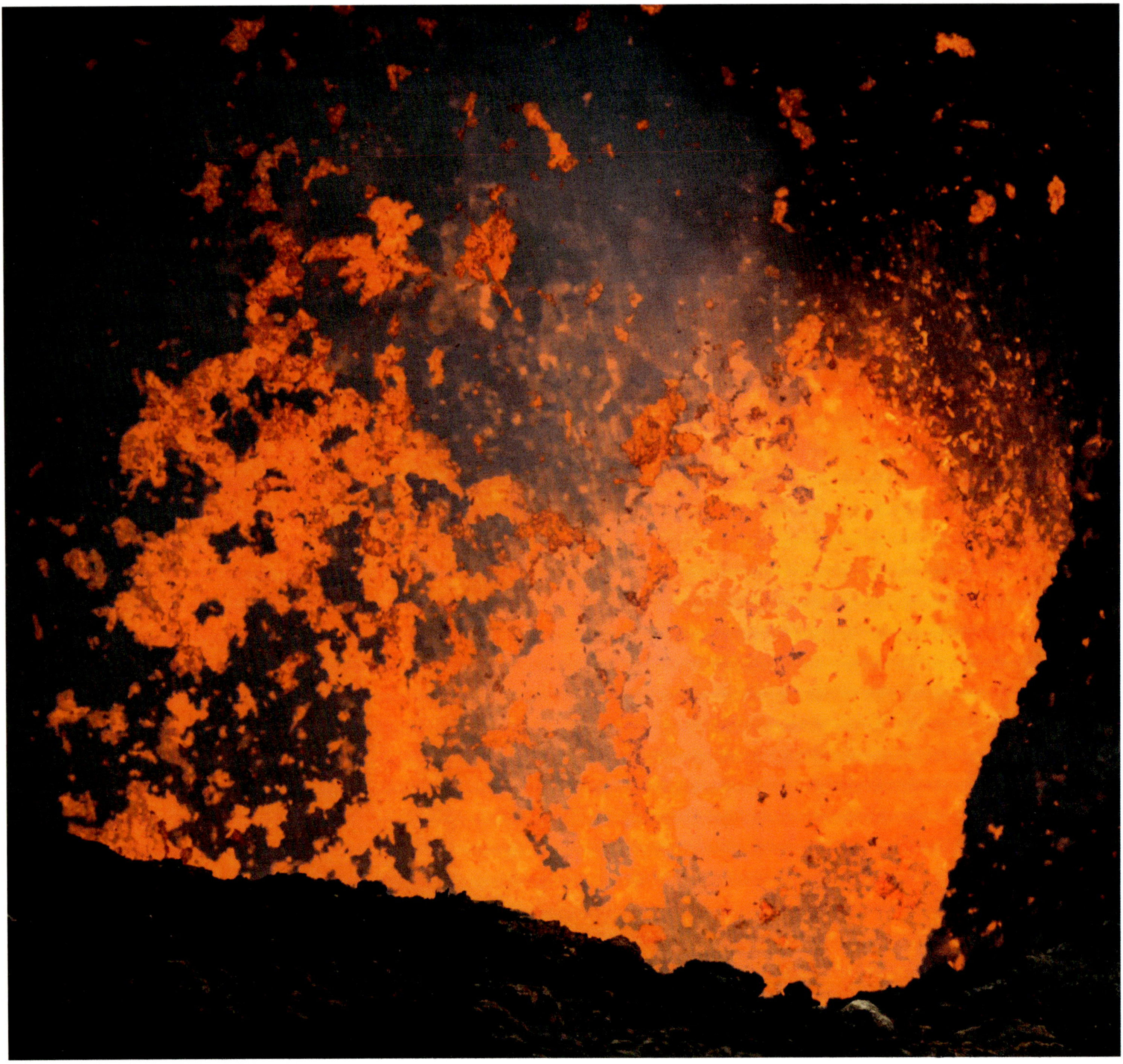

of molten stone the size of fridges would have been hitting the ground around me, smoking and sizzling. The singed smell of destruction, fire, and sulphur would be everywhere, making it hard to breathe. The volcano's deep, threatening, sustained growl would still be audible miles away. It would have felt like the apocalypse.

Luckily—though the photographer in me feels a twang of regret—the images I am trying to conjure belong to the past now. Nevado Ojos del Salado is a dignified old volcano, and it only occasionally shows signs of activity. Even then, all that remains of its power is to emit a few clouds of sulphurous vapor.

Breathtaking

Our intended resting point, a metal hut called Refugio Atacama, turned out to be smaller than we had hoped and only had enough space for three people. We had been planning to erect a small makeshift camp of tents up here anyway, and so we try to pitch our tents in a sheltered

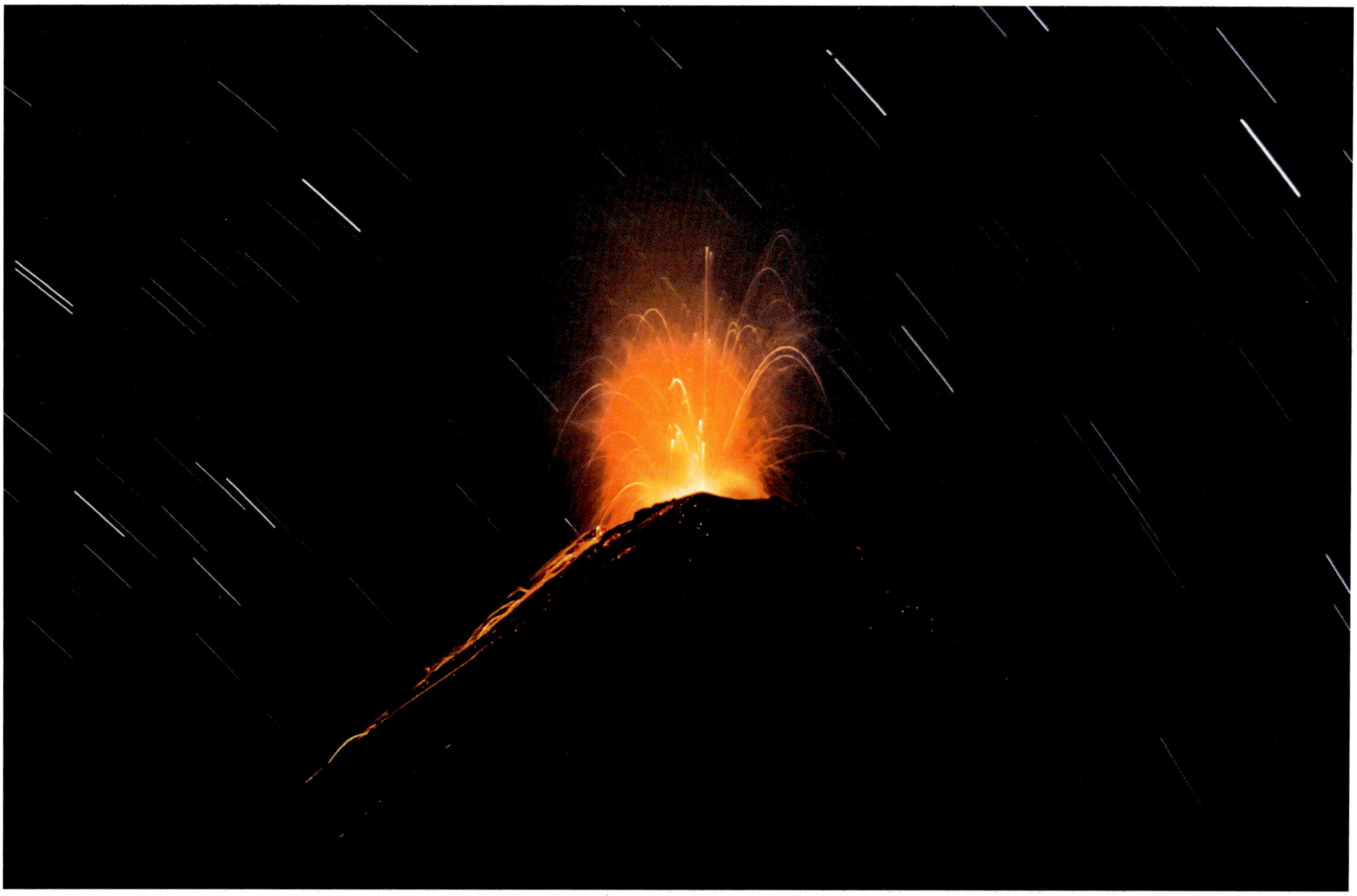

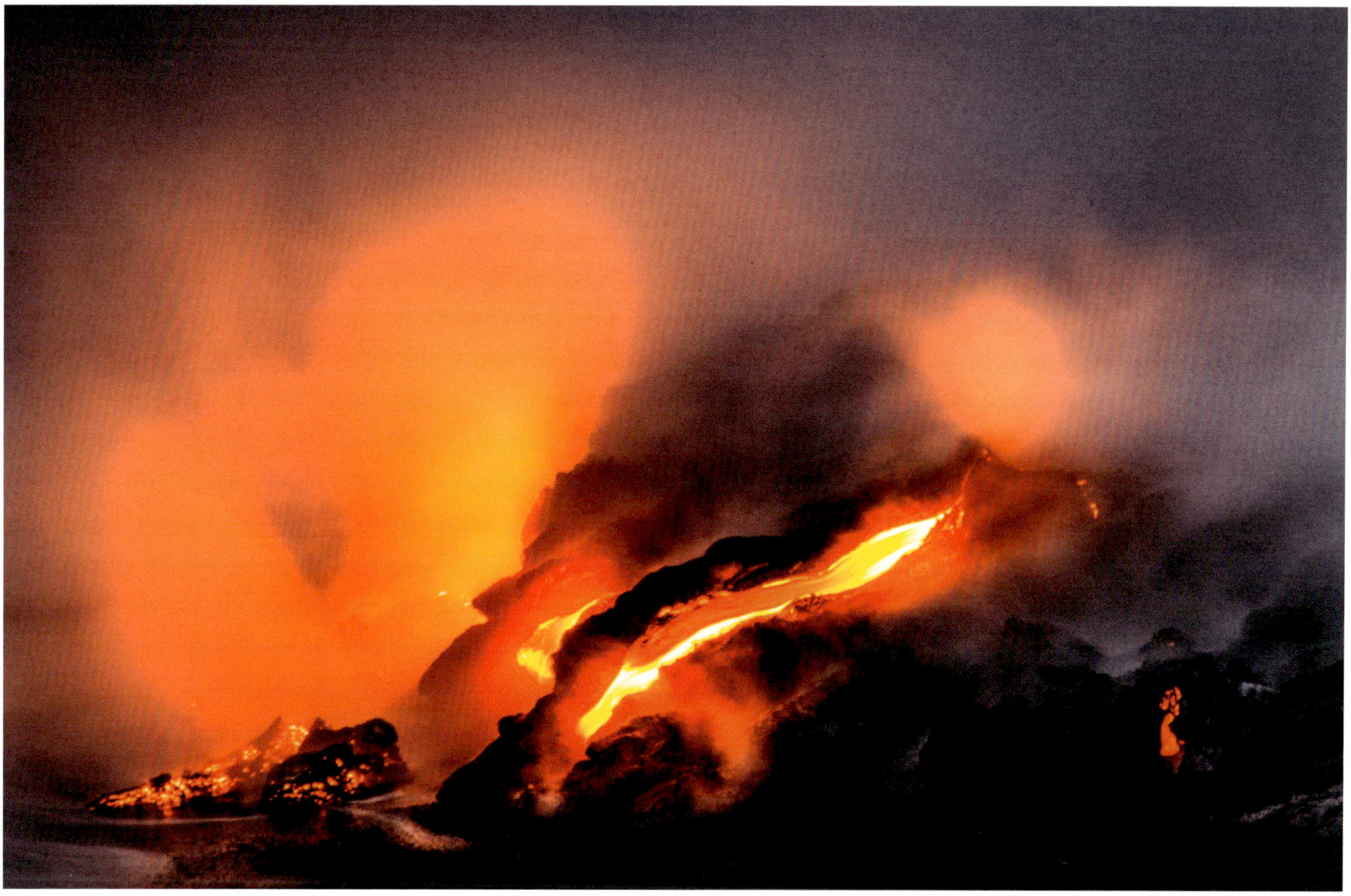

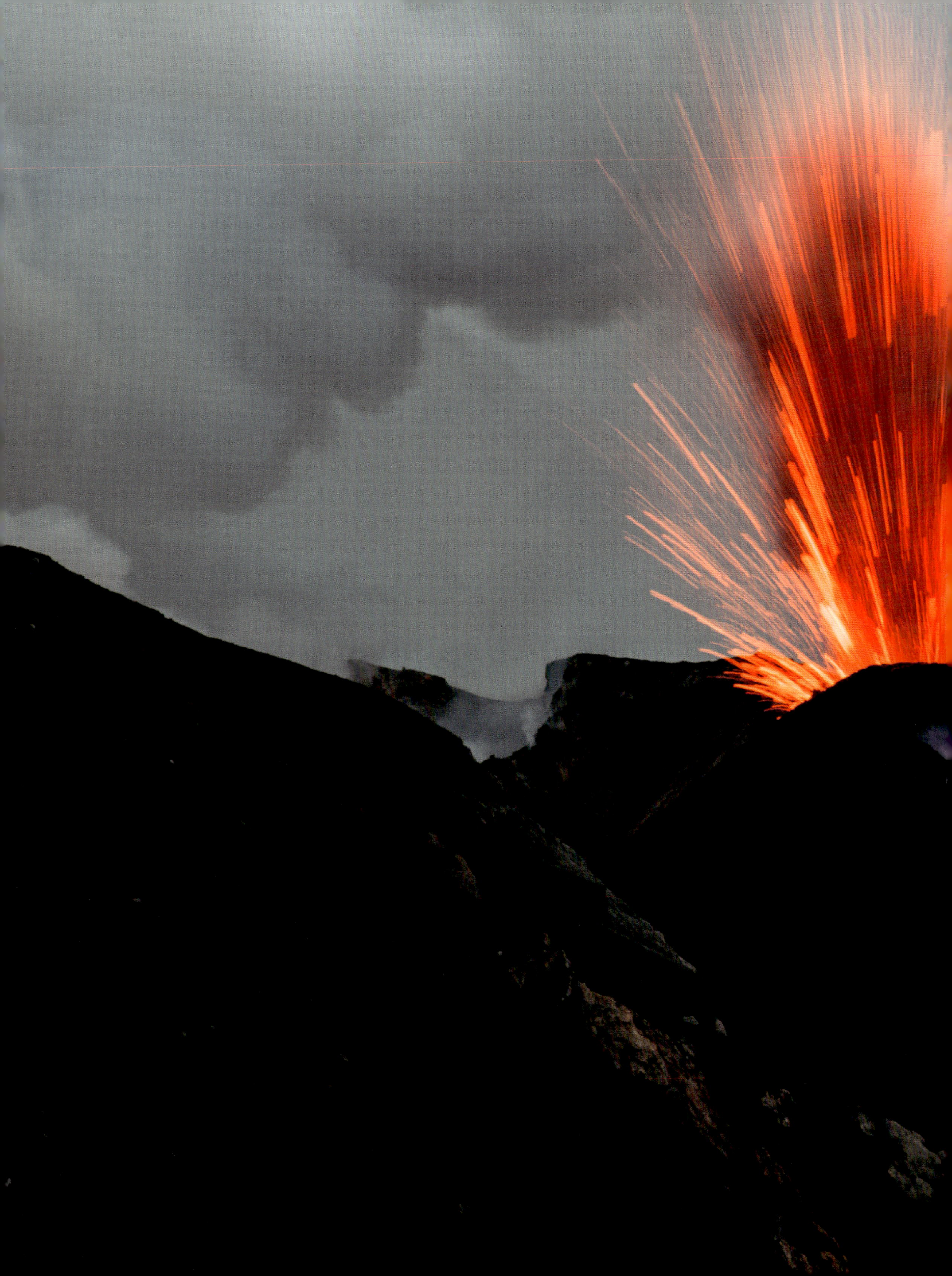

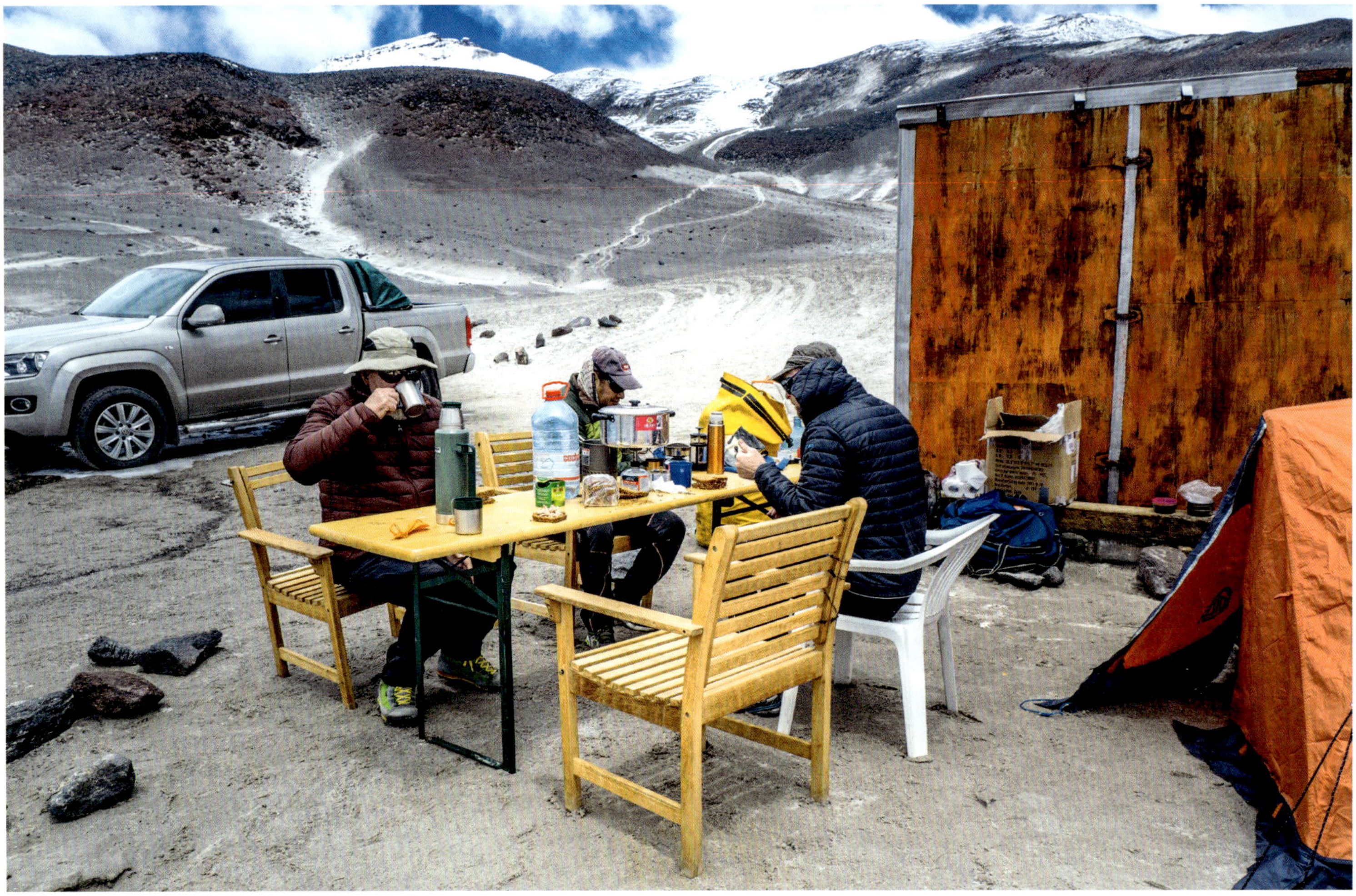

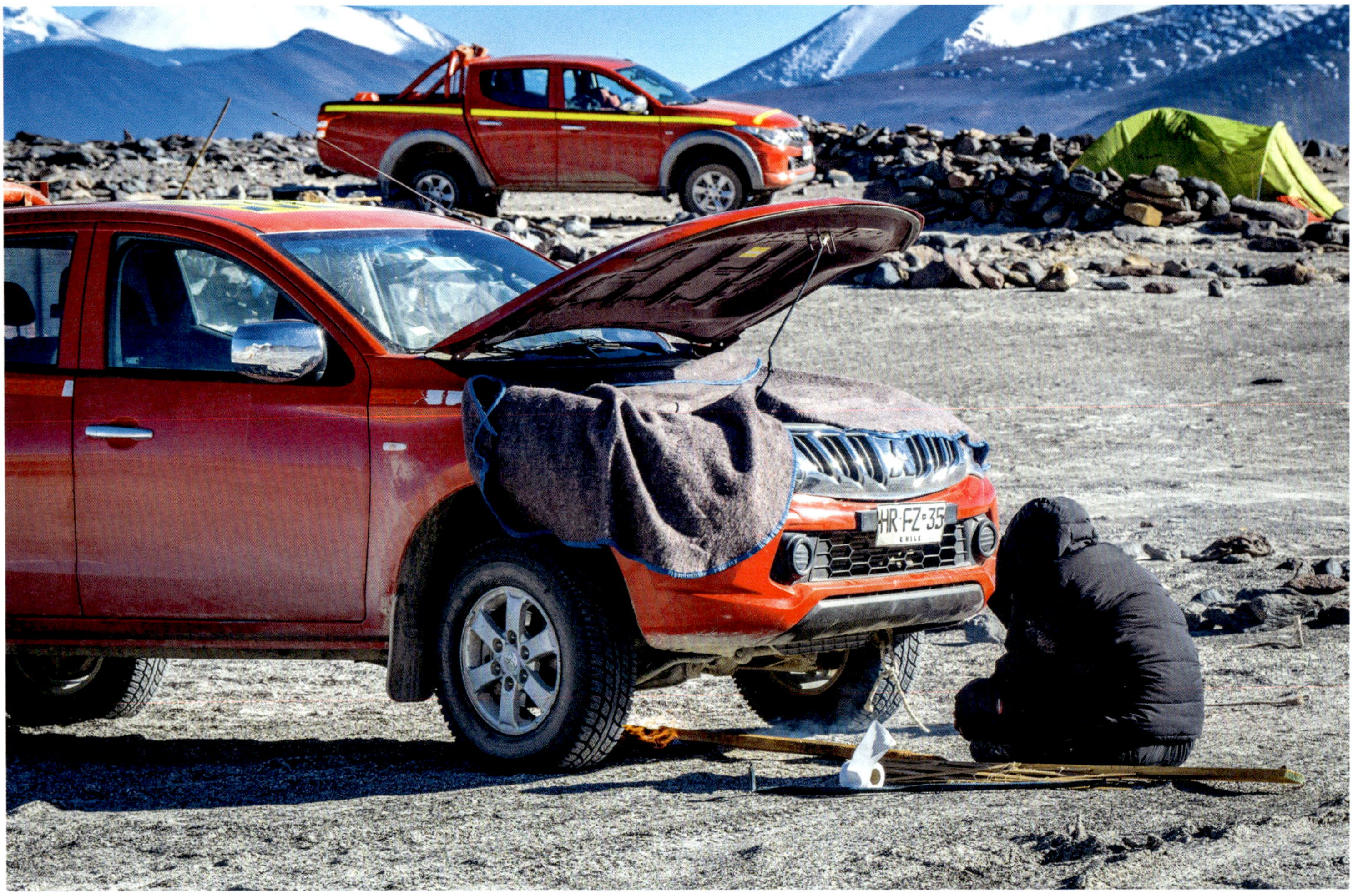

area. One of the biggest challenges here at Nevado Ojos del Salado is that the wind speeds can reach up to—and sometimes even exceed—60 mph. As a result, the wind chill temperatures can drop as low as -40 degrees. We are now at a truly breathtaking altitude of 23,000 feet.

"The problem is," Chris said one night as we were sitting around the fire, "that up here, the oxygen pressure is a lot lower than back home. That means that both the weight of the air and the amount of oxygen particles per volume are reduced." He took a few mouthfuls of his pasta with tuna, sat up straight and resumed his impromptu lecture. "Now, the body reacts accordingly. It tries to make sure the most important organ, the brain, still receives enough oxygen. Because of this stress reaction, your breathing and heartbeat speed up, and the percentage of water present in the bloodstream is reduced." "Really does sound breathtaking," I think to myself. "That's why it's so important to keep hydrated," Karl-Heinz joined the conversation. "I heard the recommendation is to drink one additional liter per day with every 3000 feet in elevation. Carbs are important, too. It's better to have pasta with tuna rather than food that has a high fat content. At this altitude, it's harder for the body to burn fat as that would consume even more oxygen."

Maybe I should have listened more closely, because looking back I realize that during those days of climbing the Nevado Ojos del Salado, I did not pay enough attention to my water intake. The following night I felt nauseated, had on and off headaches, and I constantly felt like I was suffocating. For every single breath I took, I had to make a deliberate effort, as if my lungs would only continue to work if I concentrated really hard. Which is why later, in bed, I had the terrifying feeling that I must not fall asleep. If I drifted off and stopped thinking about my breathing, I may just stop breathing altogether—or so it felt. It seems like an absurd idea now, but back then, during a sleepless night at 16,000 feet, where the air's oxygen levels are a lot lower than what I am used to, it seemed like a perfectly reasonable concern.

> For every single breath I took, I had to make a deliberate effort, as if my lungs would only continue to work if I concentrated really hard.

The next morning, Chris and Karl-Heinz also looked a bit worse for wear, so we decided to turn around for now and pitch our tents again at a lower point—at 14,000 feet, near Laguna Verde.

An Adventurer's Heart, a Photographer's Heart

After a short period of rest at Laguna Verde we were all beginning to feel a bit better. Yet our extreme reaction to the altitude did raise questions regarding our next steps. Several options were proposed. Pica suggested: "Let's stay here for one night and get some sleep. After that, we can make a new attempt at Refugio Atacama and then continue up to the summit, just like we said." Chris added: "We could also stay here for one night, then climb up to 20,000 feet to acclimatize, sleep here at the lagoon again for one night and then start the summit attempt." "Both sound good to me," I said, "but both of these options mean that we lose our reserve day and the day we were going to spend at Laguna Rosa, right?" "Right. Well, that's up to you to decide You're the one who wants to climb the Volcanic Seven Summits."

I retreated to my tent. I had to be on my own in order to make such a difficult decision. I took out my notebook and opened it to two empty pages. On top of the left side, I drew a big plus sign, on the right side, I drew a minus sign. Below them I wrote:

Minus:
- *Missed out on the world's tallest volcano*
- *Never reached 23,000 feet*
- *Didn't reach the summit of yet*
  another V7S

Plus:
+ *Kept my promise not to take risks*
+ *Ojos isn't going anywhere*
+ *More time for photography.*

On Ojos del Salado, a Chilean team set a record for the highest altitude ever reached by car. On April 21st 2007, Gonzalo Bravo and Eduardo Canales drove a Suzuki Samurai up the mountain, reaching a height of 21,942 feet—about 650 feet below the summit.

Minus:

– Missed out on the world's highest volcano
– Never reached an altitude of over 22,000 feet
– Didn't climb yet another one of the V7S

Plus:

+ Kept my promise not to take risks
+ Can always make another attempt
   at Ojos in the future
+ More time for photographs

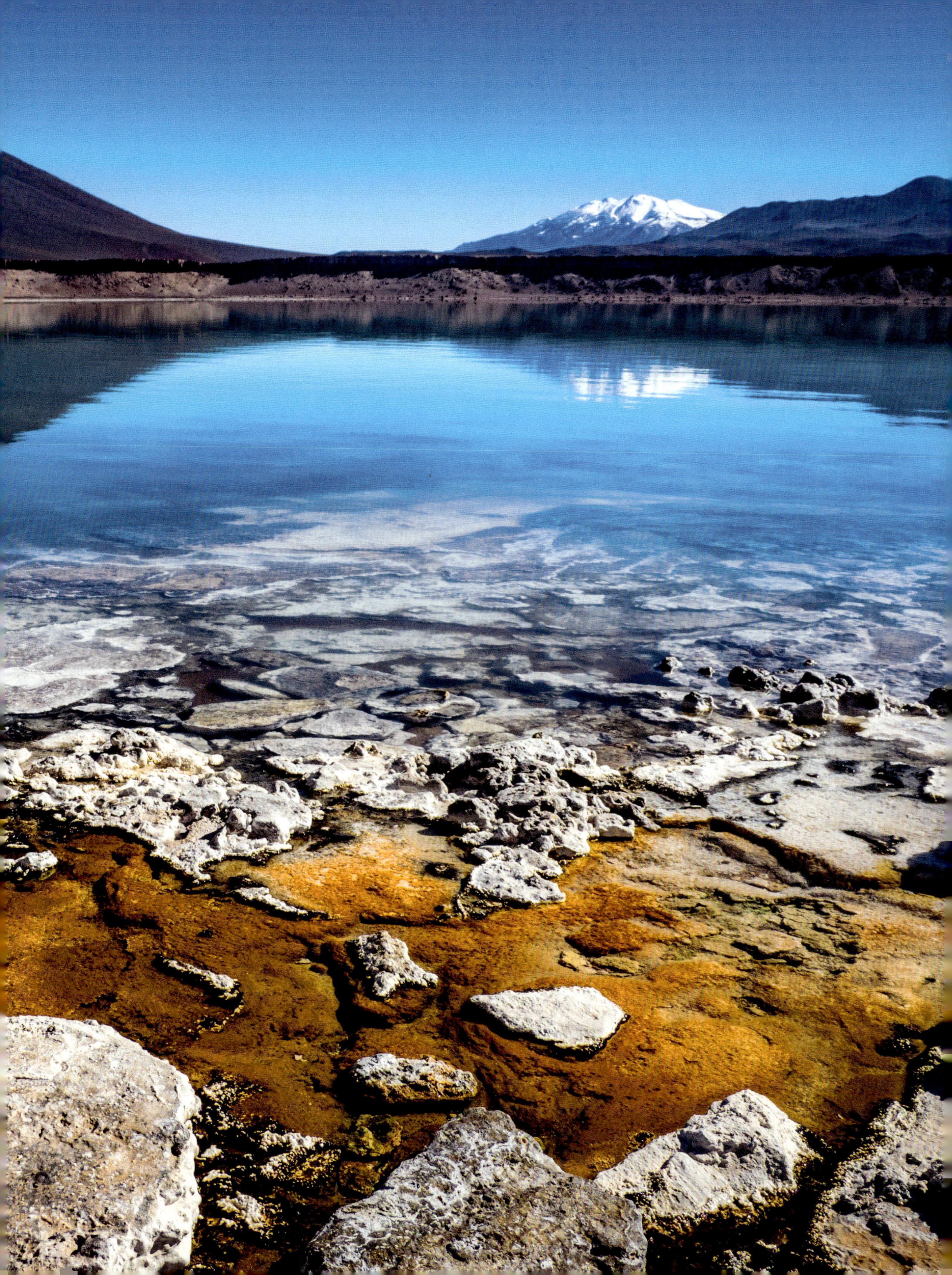

The score on my checklist was 3 vs 3. I hesitated for a moment, and then pulled down the tent's zipper. Right at that moment, the setting sun was illuminating the shore on the other side of the lagoon. What an arresting image. I quickly reached for my camera and at that moment, I made my decision. "The two main reasons why I wanted to see the Volcanic Seven Summits in the first place were to take photographs and to have new experiences. I'm a photographer through and through—I'm not a mountaineer."

Slowly I emerged from my tent and saw the relieved expressions on Chris and Karl-Heinz's faces. Without having to discuss it, we tacitly agreed not to continue with the ascent.

Tres Hombres

The words "Tres Hombres" interrupt my musings. "Tres Hombres—three men—are standing in front of Tres Cruces," Karl-Heinz jokes as he and Chris join me at Laguna Rosa's shore. "What a magical place," he adds. "You couldn't pay me enough to have the opportunity to be up there at the Ojos summit and miss out on all of this." "Same here," Chris agrees, "although I have already been up there once, back in my youth." I smile. "I'd also much rather be here right now. Although yesterday I had a great idea —I'll just wait for another 20 years before I try again with the Salado, and then I will break my personal altitude record and simultaneously also break the record for the oldest climber to have completed the Volcanic Seven Summits." Karl-Heinz and Chris burst out laughing. A flamboyance of flamingos is running and gathering momentum at the center of the shallow lagoon. Their wings disturb the water's tranquil surface, before they take flight and ascend in an elegant spiral of pink above the Laguna Rosa.

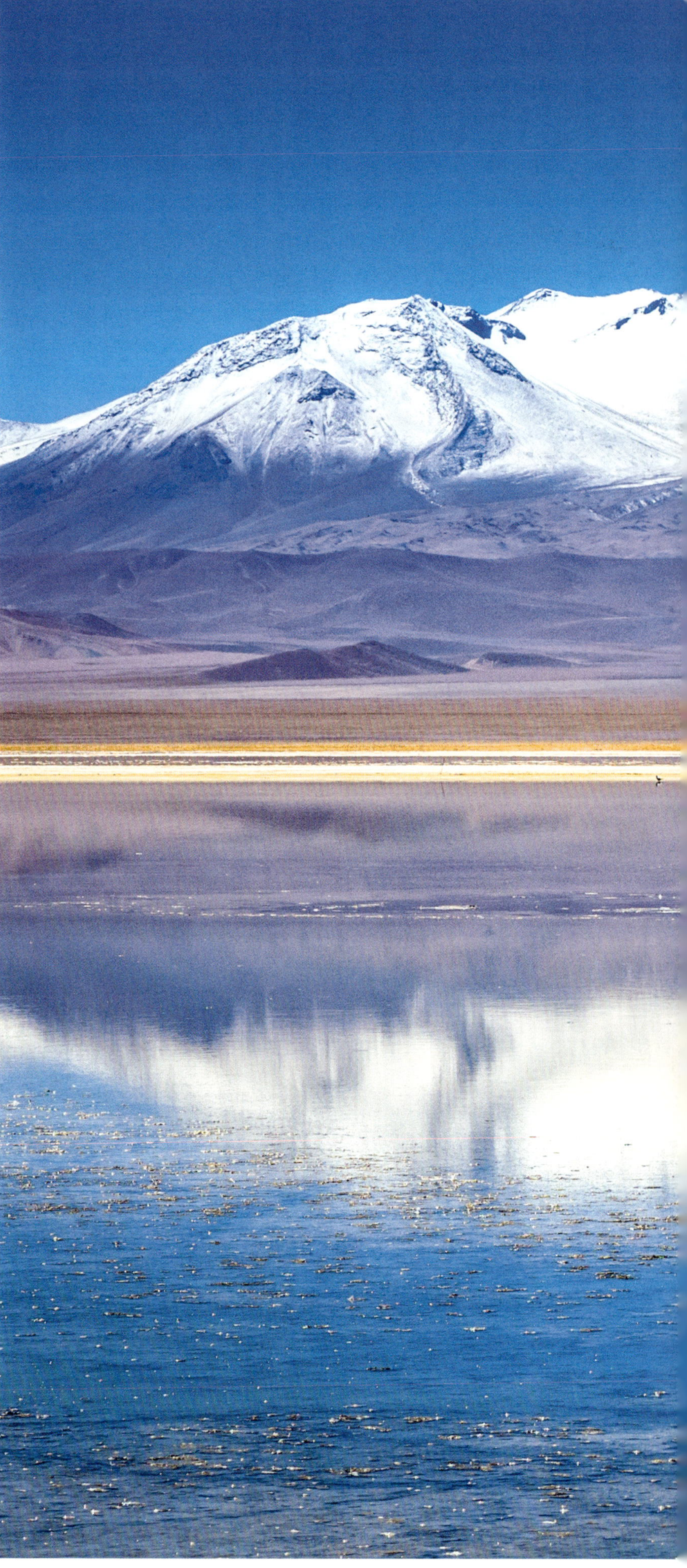

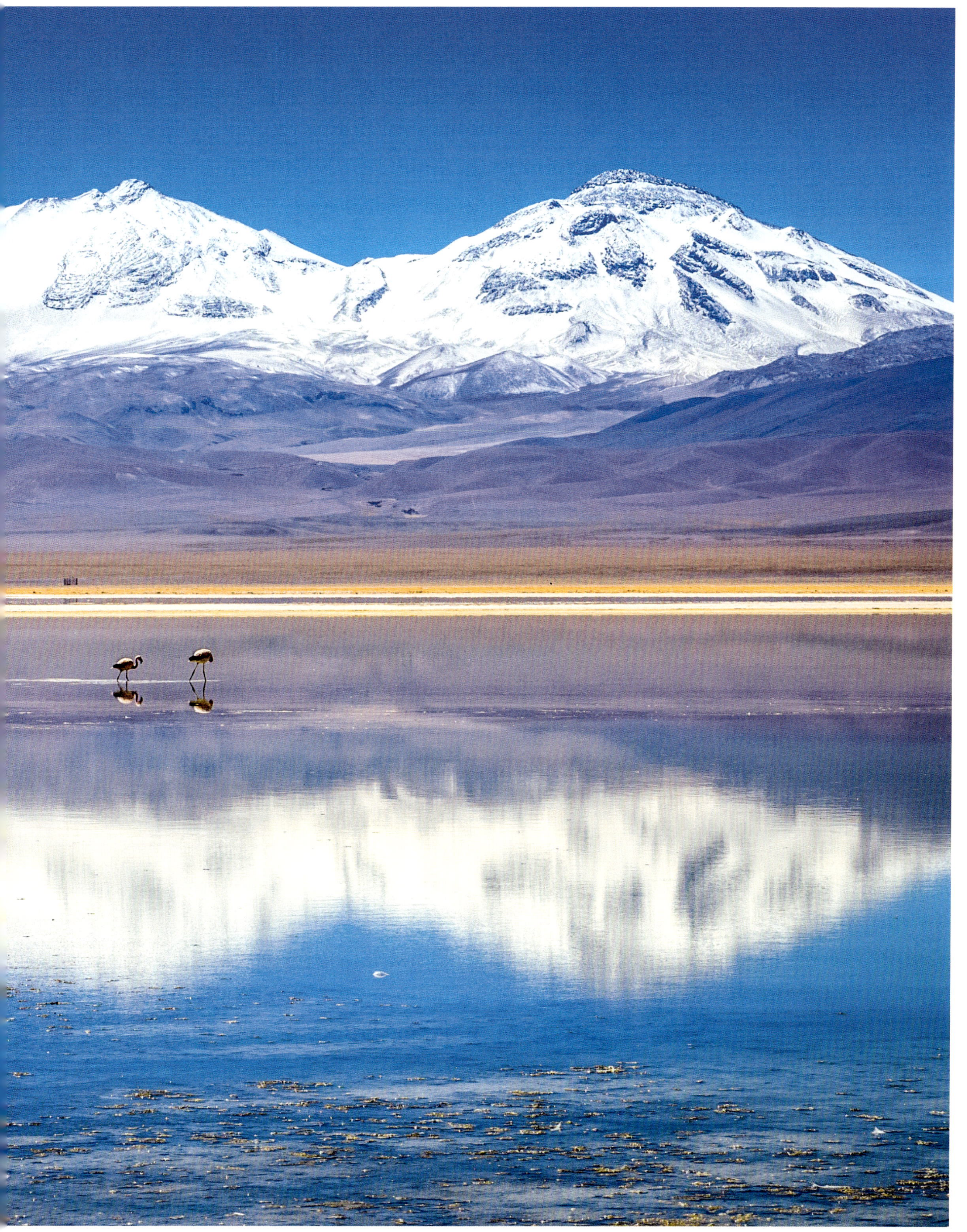

 Chile | Ojos del Salado

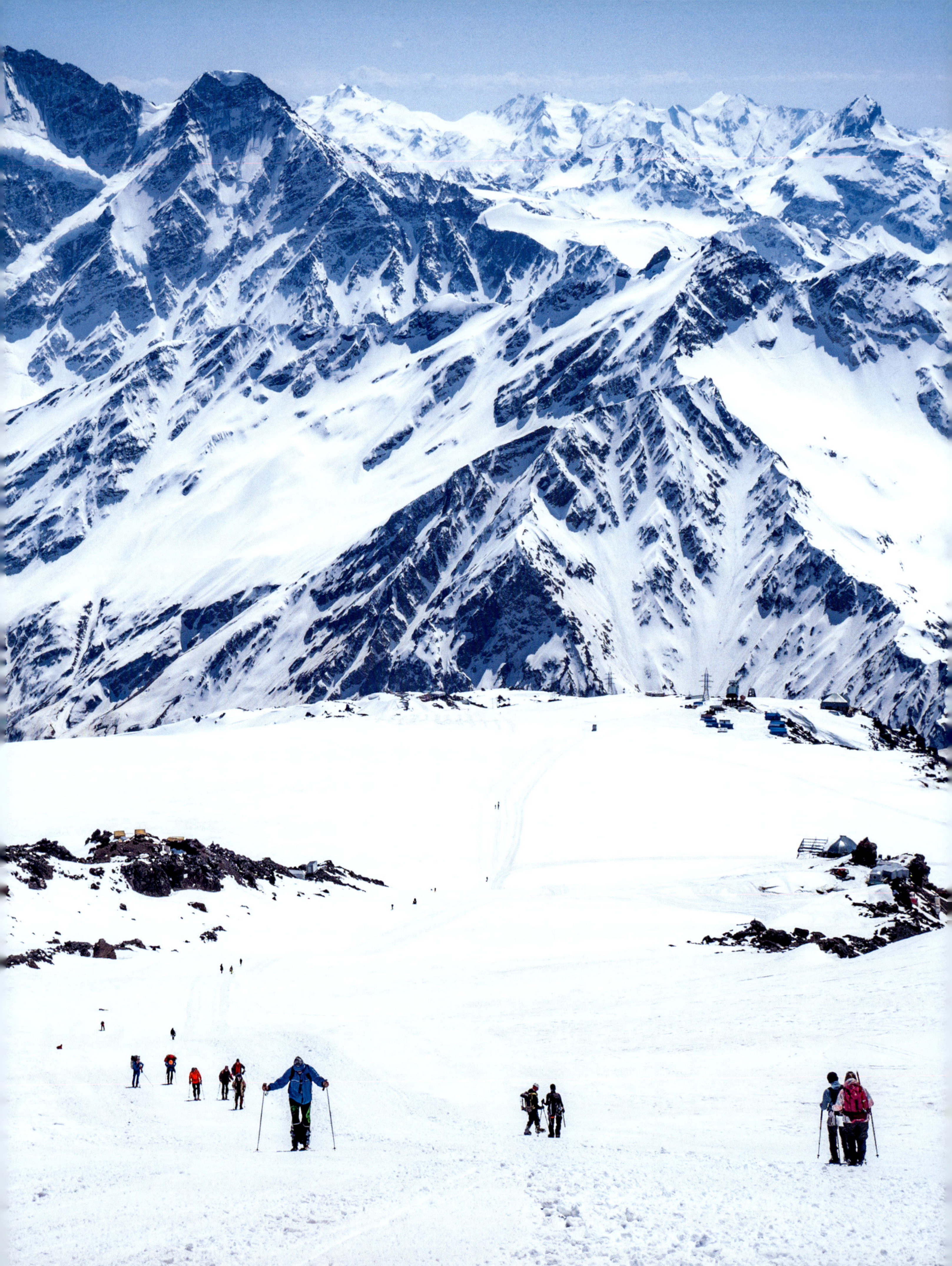

5

ELBRUS

A Photoshoot with Mother Earth

Russia

Back home in Germany: crisp, early spring weather. I am just back from my daily run when I receive a message from my friend Roman:

"Just checked weather could be ok but freezing cold at elbrus -18 deg!" His complete disrespect for grammar, punctuation, and capitalization in text messages never fails to amuse me. The content of his message is less amusing though, and so I reply: "Have I mentioned that I absolutely detest the cold? If you can arrange for sunshine and 70 degrees when we reach the summit, I'll buy you a beer."

At 18,510 feet, Mount Elbrus is the highest mountain and volcano in Europe; at its highest, it pushes Russia's rough climate to new extremes. The nickname, "Little Antarctica" has been given to it for a reason. It is located in southwest Russia, near the Georgian border. Those with an interest in Greek mythology will know it as the mountain to which Zeus chained Prometheus as punishment for having given fire to mankind—it seems as if I am not the only one who is attracted to the combination of fire and ice. Poor Prometheus…

"Well, won't that be fun," I think and in my head I am already picturing myself stomping up Elbrus sporting the astronaut outfit I had been wearing in Antarctica. Another trip into the eternal ice, it seems—or into the world of the Greek gods. It is still at least another three weeks until our departure; maybe I will be lucky and the meteorologists are wrong. In fact, Roman sends another, slightly more hopeful message just two days before my departure: "From tomorrow temp rising at elbrus from -17 to +1. Now wheres my beer?"

That Old Russian Charm

Over the next few days Roman, if indeed he has any hand in the weather and temperature, works extremely hard to earn his beer. A week of perfect hiking conditions, bright sunshine, and what feel like summer temperatures lies ahead of us. Viktor, a Russian mountaineer, greets us as we arrive at our simple hotel in Azau, a small ski resort.

The words "That old Russian charm" pop into my head as we stroll through the narrow, gently sloping streets. We see slightly dishevelled, stone-built hotels, corrugated iron roofs in various colours, clothes drying and dancing in the wind. There are sun-bleached, blurred skiing adverts on every corner. A few lonely sausages are charring on rusty barbecues, cloaked in clouds of smoke and waiting for a hungry passer-by. The streets and paths are covered in a thick dirty, sludge of snow, water, and mud; a smattering of souvenir stalls is braving the low season. The village seems like a ghost town.

Despite these solemn first impressions, we are in a well-known skiing resort. Every year, about 350,000 tourists visit Mount Elbrus. It is May, though, and the skiing season is nearly over. Most hotels in Azau are already closed. It seems as if the whole village has retreated into its comfortable den to wait out the summer and return in winter—a kind of reverse hibernation, so to speak.

Personally, I don't even enjoy skiing all that much, nor am I a particularly skilful skier. If I give it my all, I may just be able to get down a blue run but it most certainly would not be pretty, and falls would be inevitable. Even my eight-year old-daughter is a more competent skier than I am. I much prefer skiing uphill, but even here I often reach my limits, for no matter how high I climb, I will then have to traverse the same distance downhill—on two terribly slim pieces of wood. Despite this fact—or maybe because of it—I will try to use my skis here at Mount Elbrus: another new experience.

Another trip into the eternal ice, it seems—or into the world of the Greek gods.

Mount Elbrus is a mostly dormant volcano with an altitude of 18,510 feet. Its last eruption is said to have taken place more than 2000 years ago. Yet there are natural hot springs near the summit which are a sign of ongoing volcanic activity deep inside the mountain.

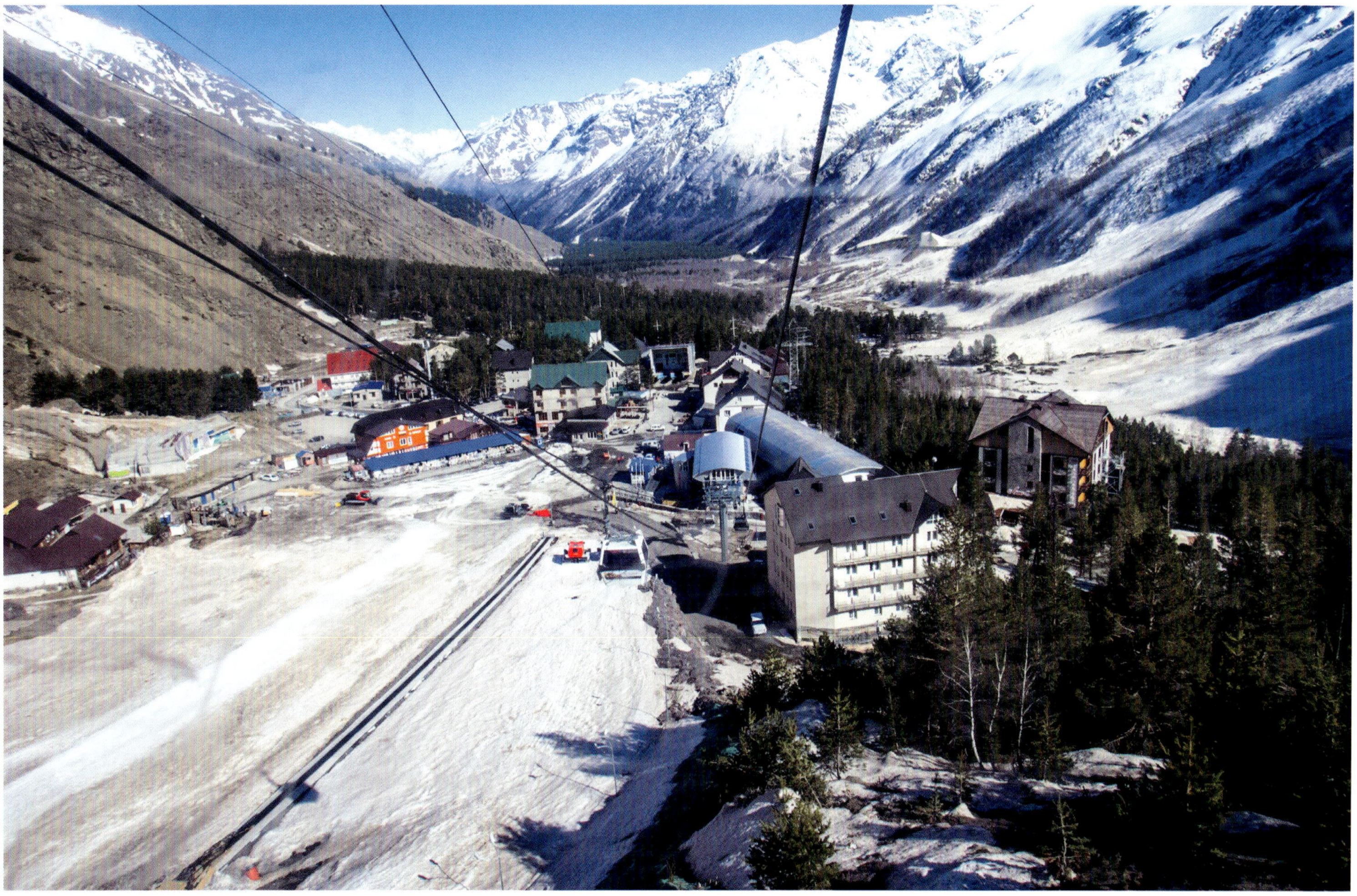

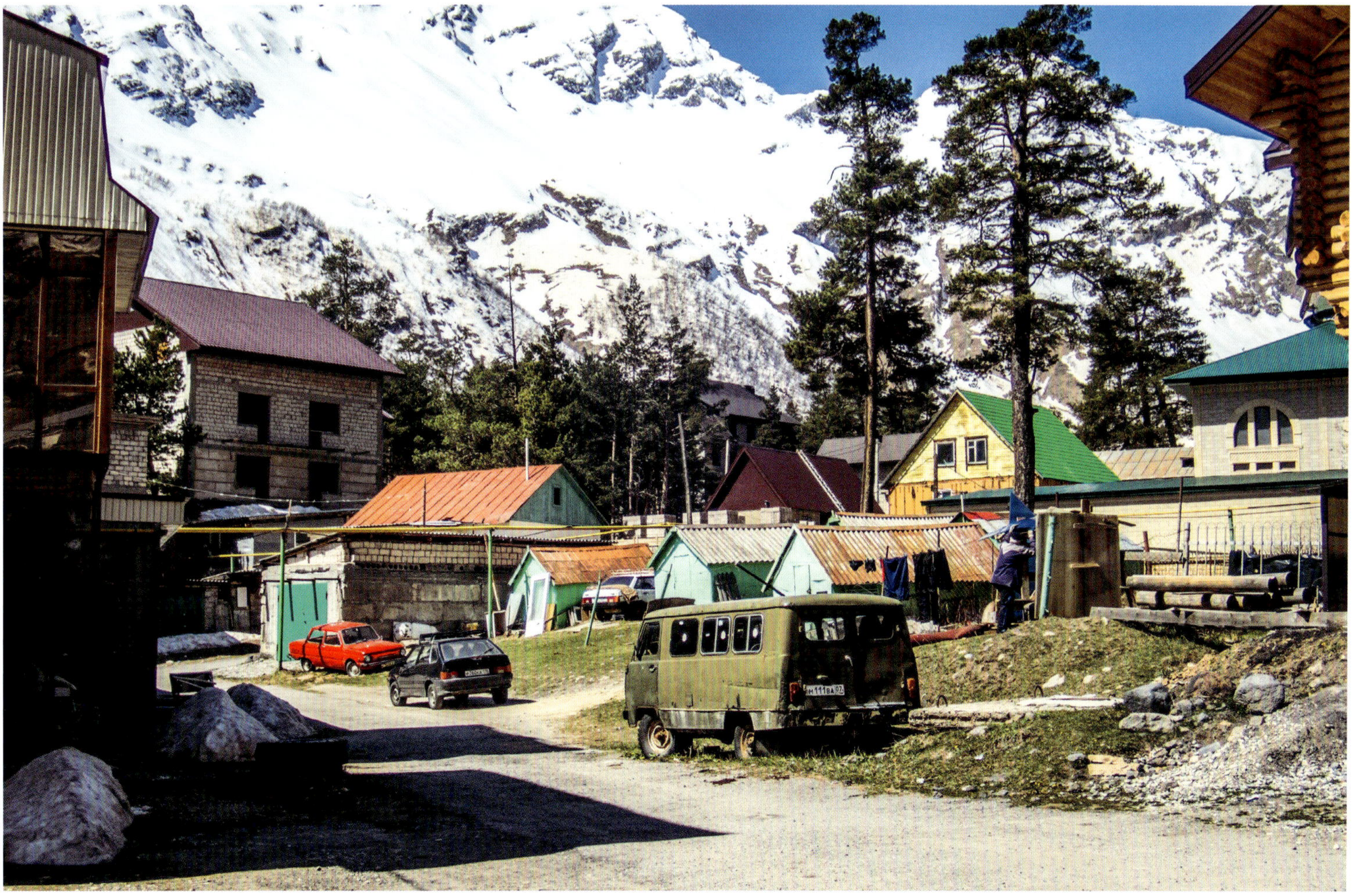

Russia | Elbrus

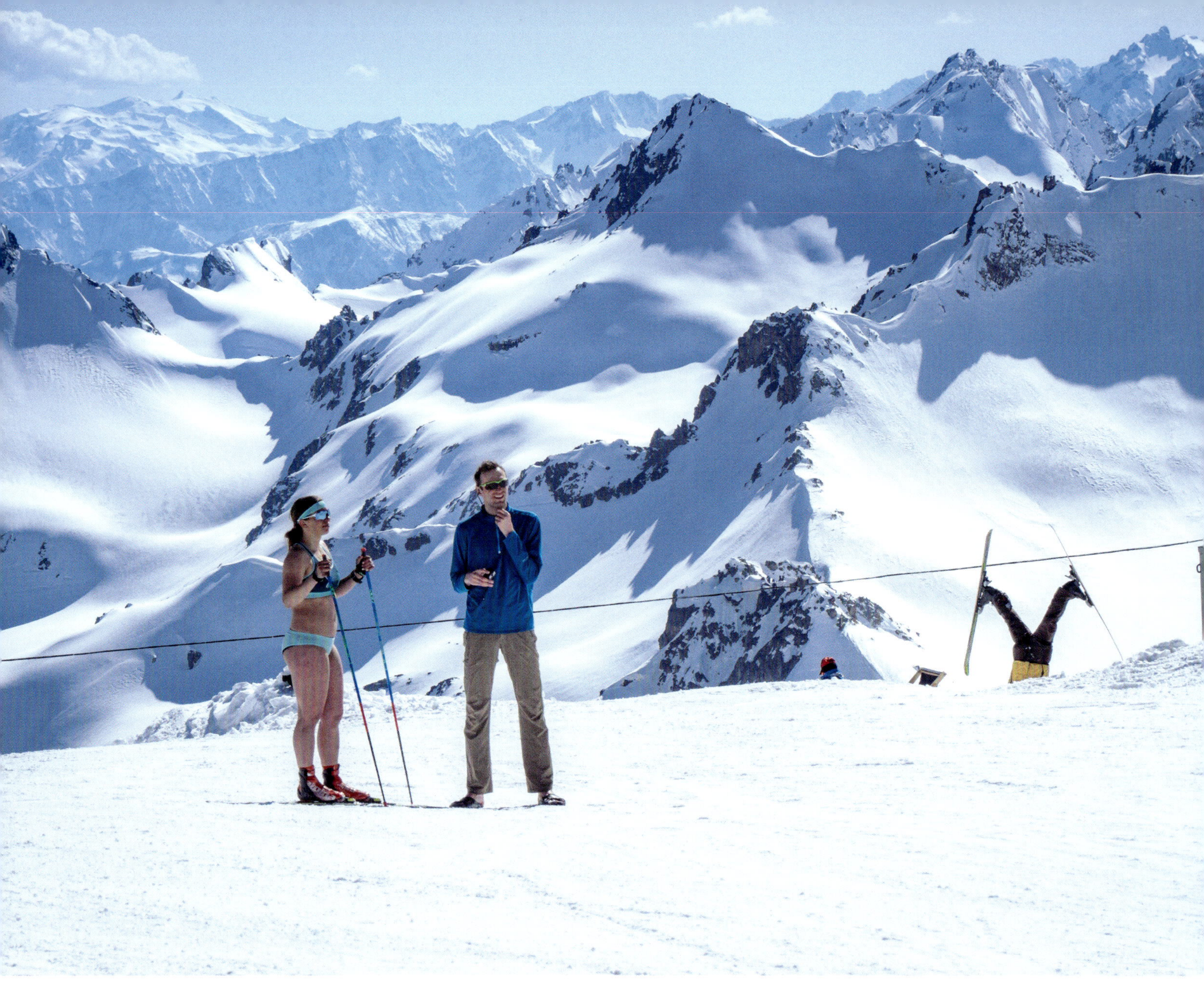

Mount Elbrus is the highest mountain in the Caucasus Mountains, a mountain range located in south-western Russia, between the Black Sea and the Caspian Sea. It is also the highest mountain and volcano in both Russia and Europe.

The next morning, Roman and I get into the "brand new and modern" ski lift, as my friend describes it sarcastically. It is nothing but a cableway with two cable cars, both of which have recently been painted bright red, have scratched windows and enough space for 20 passengers. They are a far cry from the giant high-speed cars that are being used in Austria and Switzerland, although Viktor proudly declares that this cable car "was previously used in Kitzbühel". We are not sure whether this piece of information is trustworthy. Maybe 70 years ago? Not that we really care, for this cable car fits perfectly with this quiet village. We make our way up to the first station at little more than walking speed. From there we start our acclimatization tour up the ski slope, along the bright red snow fence; following the very edge of the piste of course. Ahead of us, Mount Elbrus' two summits are clearly visible in the distance. The east summit sits at 18,442 feet. The west summit—our destination—is slightly higher at 18,510 feet.

Bare Facts

Not every volcano enthusiast will agree that Mount Elbrus is the highest volcano in Europe. This is because the location of the border between Europe and Asia is an age-old dispute that has not yet been settled with any finality. Both continents are located on the same continental plate, and so tectonically speaking, the question of where the geographical border is located cannot be answered. Nowadays, most people will agree that the border between Europe and Asia runs along the Ural Mountains in northern Russia and across the Caucasus Mountains between the Black Sea and the Caspian Sea. Mount Elbrus is the highest summit in the Caucasus Mountains and according to the definition given above, it is located in Europe—thus it is the European contribution to the Volcanic Seven Summits.

"Otherwise, Mont Blanc would be the highest mountain and Mount Etna in Sicily would be the highest volcano in Europe, right?" Roman asks me as I am discussing the issue with him. "You've probably climbed that one already, right?" I wait and let a group of screaming snowboarders pass before I answer. "Yes, Mount Etna would be the highest volcano in Europe if it wasn't for Mount Elbrus. And no, I haven't climbed it yet. A few years ago I was going to but then bad weather and an engine failure got in the way. It might be a future project though."

We resume our silent ascent under the blinding midday sun and the bright blue sky. I notice that Roman's weather forecast seems particularly accurate. Despite actual temperatures of roughly zero, the warm sun allows us to hike wearing only sweaters and thin headbands. "Tomorrow I'll be skiing in my swimming trunks," I joke—having no idea what this hike still has in store for us.

Minutes later, Roman points at the ski slope and shouts: "You have to see this!" A young, athletic woman with very toned thighs is racing down the piste at a frightening speed. Next to her there is a young man who seems to be filming her with a small camera—so far, so ordinary. The curious part of this scene is the clothing the young female skier has chosen to wear: a pair of red skiing boots, a light blue bikini—and nothing else. It is a pretty cool spectacle, in more than one sense.

Yet it will not be the last time we get to witness something like this. Here at Mount Elbrus, unusually light or a near total lack of skiwear seems to be nothing out of the ordinary, despite the sub-zero temperatures. With a sense of disbelief we see another three similar incidents—at almost 15,000 feet of altitude, entire tour groups tear off their clothes, take pictures, get dressed again, and start skiing. We appear to have reached an unlikely tourist hub for nude selfies.

We, being the weaklings that we are, do not even try to compete with these daring skiers, and so despite the agreeable temperatures, we keep on our clothes throughout the following days. Though I do get rid of two things: my skis.

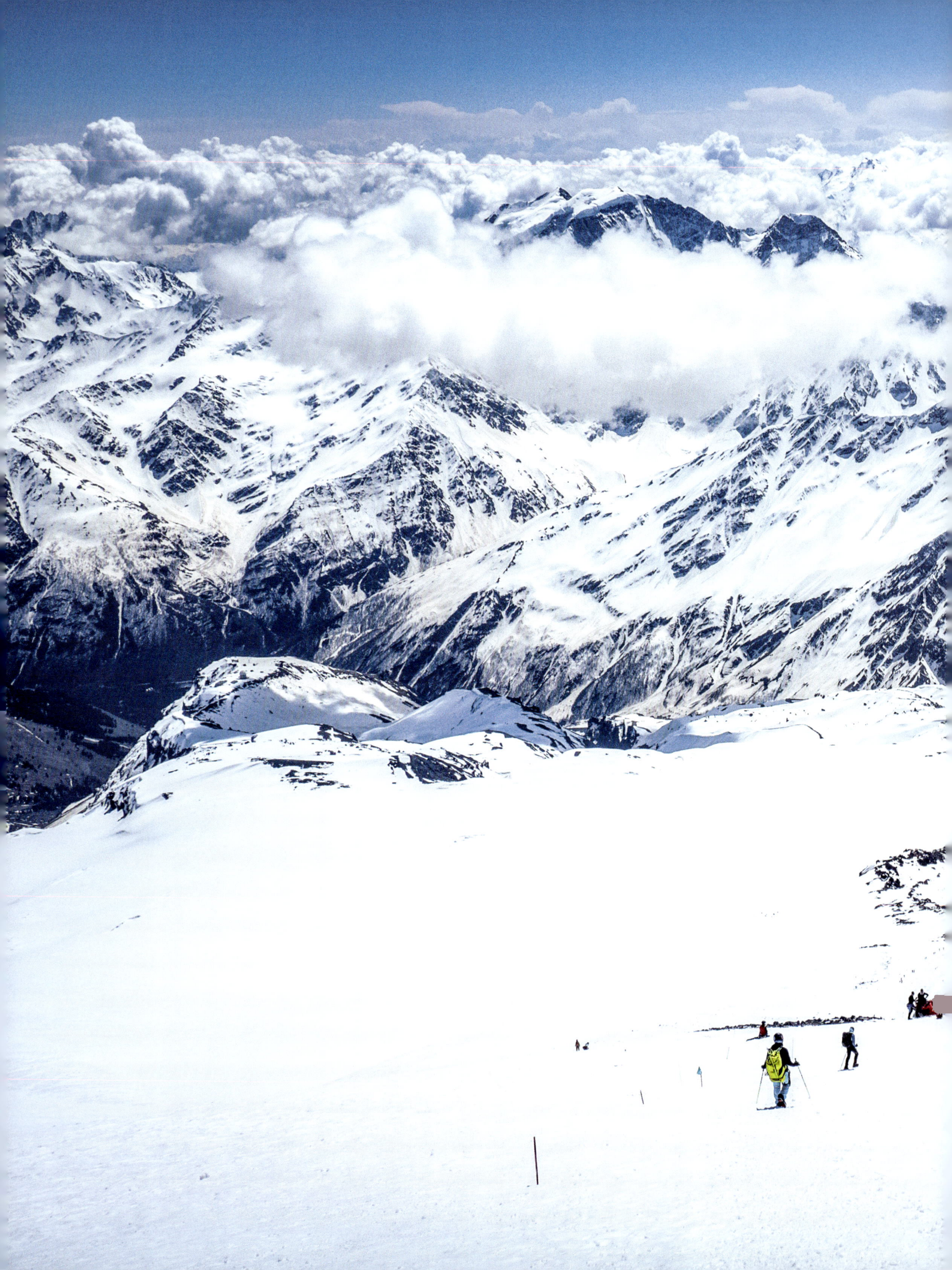

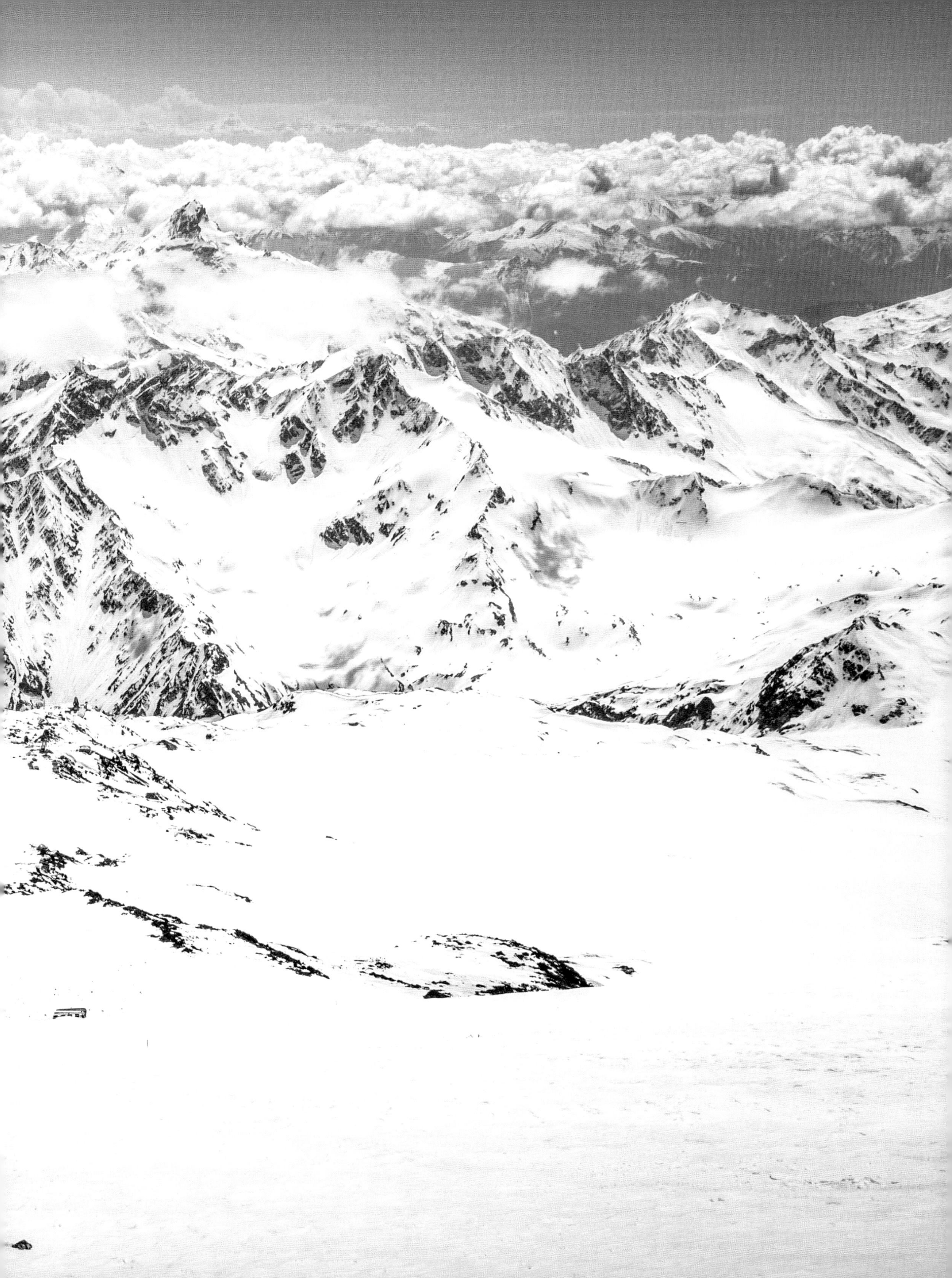

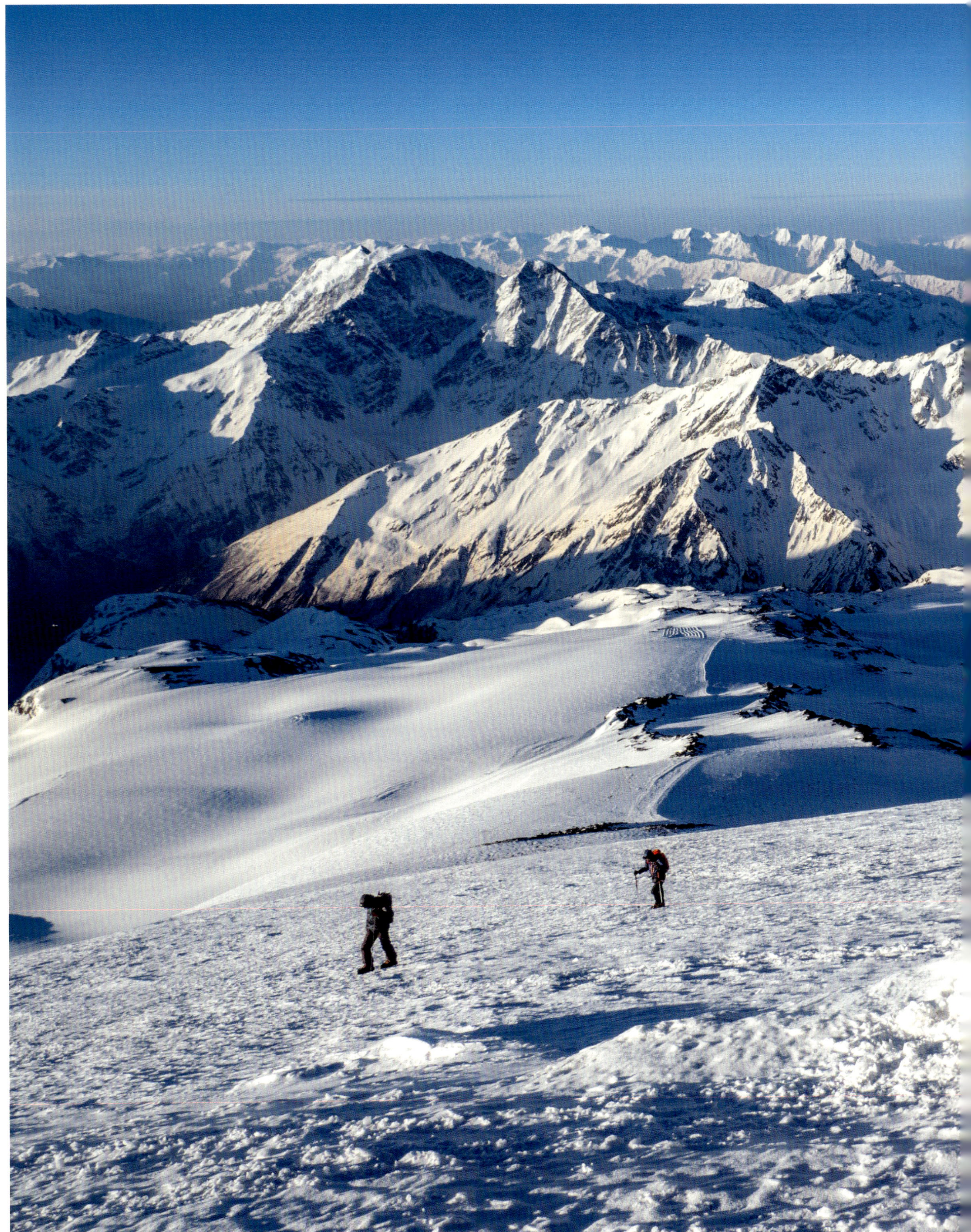

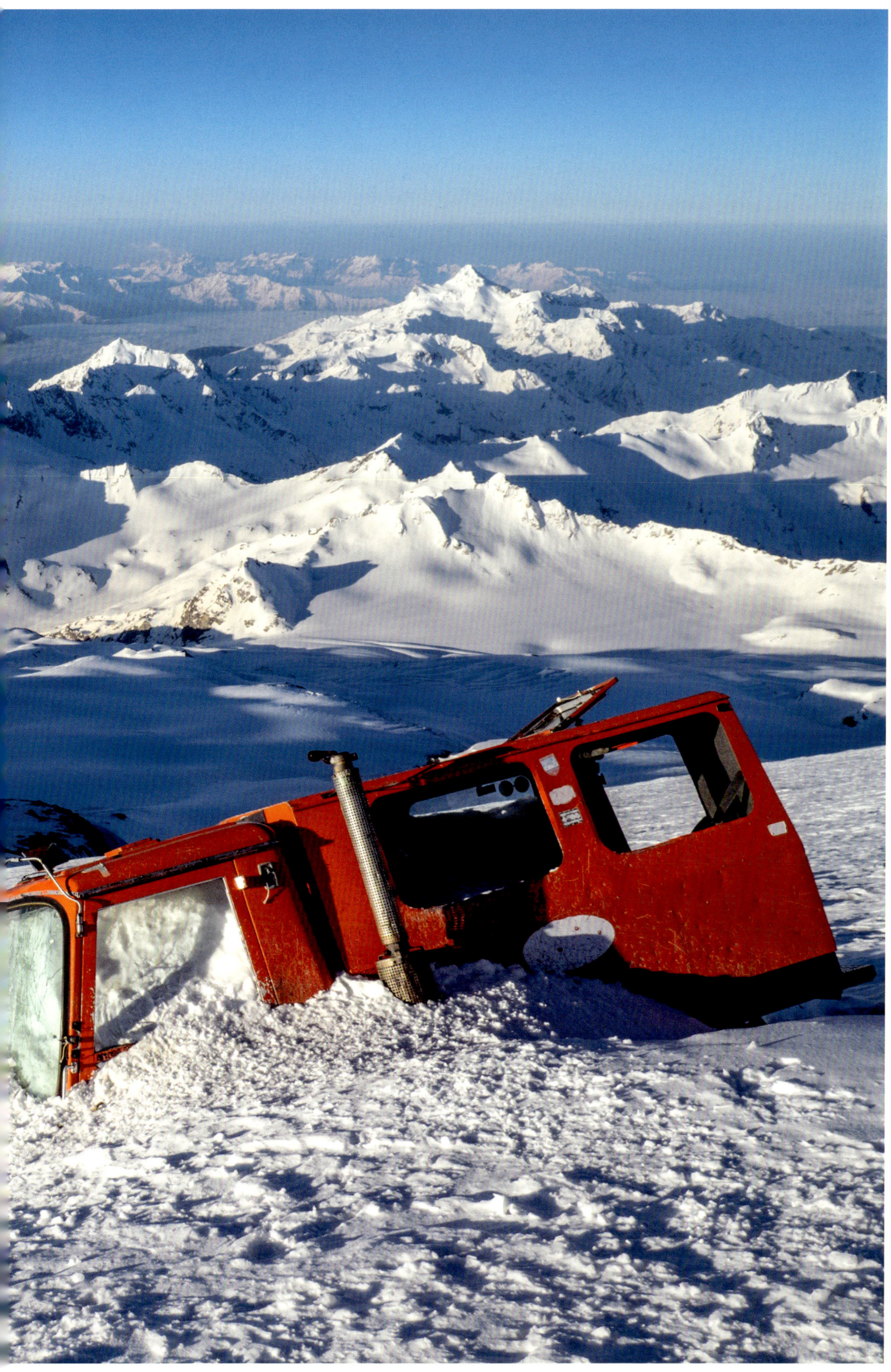

On a clear day, Mount
Elbrus' summit offers
an excellent view of
neighbouring Georgia.
Its border runs just
a few miles south of
the mountain.

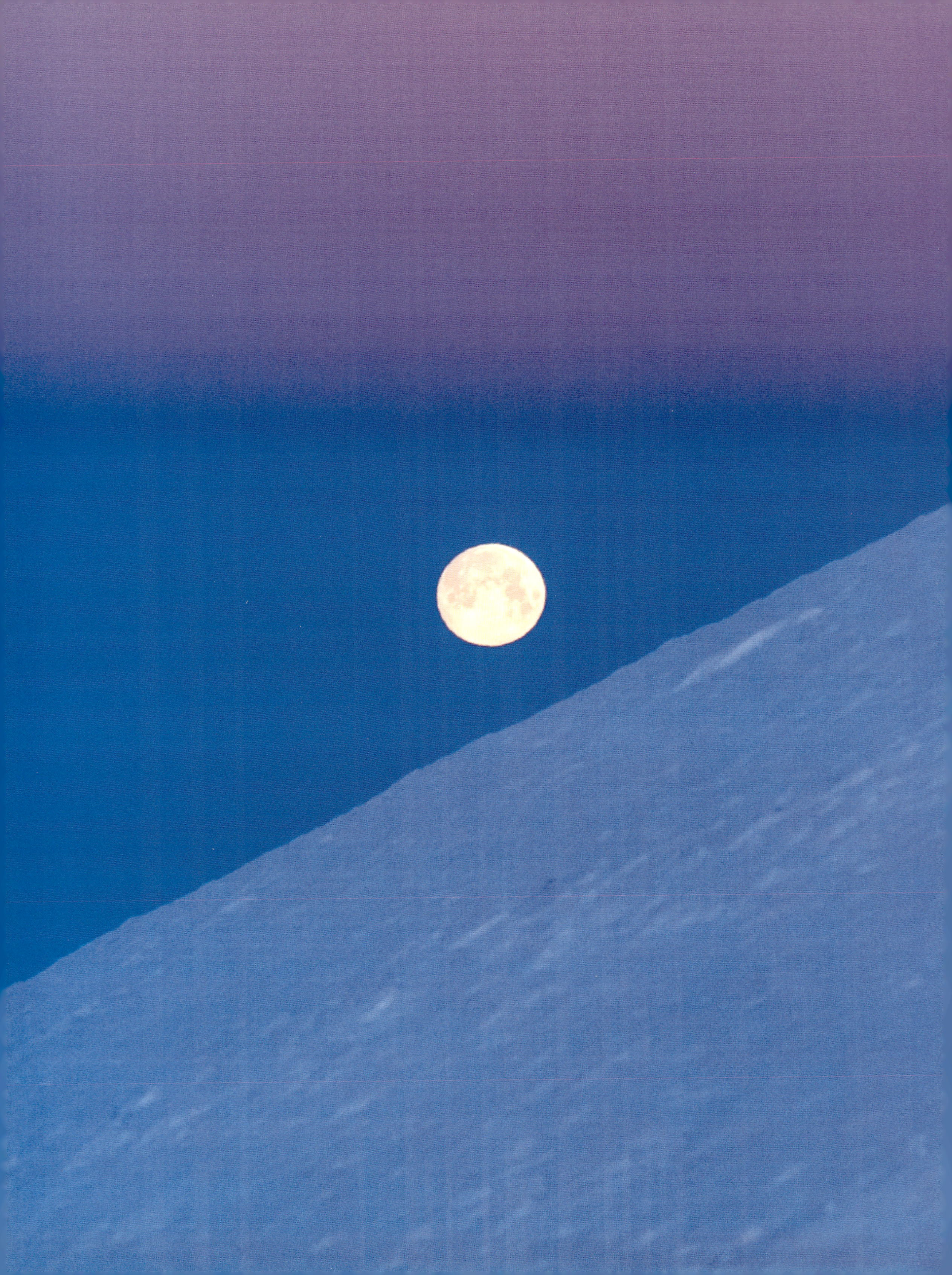

As was to be expected in the increasingly steep terrain, I quickly reach the limit of my abilities as a skier, which, as mentioned above, were never impressive. Up here on the mountain, false pride may all too quickly have serious consequences. For the last few acclimatization tours and on summit day I rely on my comfortable hiking boots and thick socks.

Photographer's Paradise

On summit day, I feel as if nature herself got dressed up just for me and then sent me an exclusive invitation for a very special photoshoot. After a roughly two hour hike in the early morning darkness, our photography-rendezvous begins with a thin line of pale lilac light on the horizon. The night air is freezing cold, but I must nevertheless take off my outdoor gloves in order to be able to operate the camera unencumbered by thick cotton. The first image I capture is of the full moon just as it sets behind the summit's steep flank. The moon emits a friendly light. The pastel yellow and orange that envelop it stand in beautiful contrast to the deep blue landscape and the first morning light that creeps across the horizon in a pale purple.

I silently bid my goodbye to the moon as it sets slowly behind the sheer slope. Almost simultaneously, I greet the rising sun behind us. It has not yet made an actual appearance. So far, all it is willing to reveal is Mount Elbrus' deep blue shadow that appears against the sky beyond—yet the sun itself still remains hidden. In the skies, the colours are steadily changing to shades of red and orange.

Treading carefully on the icy slope I turn left and look down into the valley. I have caught just the right moment. "You have to see this!" I enthusiastically try to get Roman's attention. In the light of the sunrise, a few of the Caucasus Mountains' snowy peaks begin to glow bright red. As if spellbound, I admire this explosion of colour. The sun's steady ascent illuminates more and more summits and crags.

The colours are in flux, changing rapidly, until at last they drench the entire mountain range in a bright ocean of colour, ranging from bright yellow to the dark, rich red of blood oranges.

Being a night owl, I often struggle to rise early and leave my comfortable bed in order to catch the so-called "Golden Hour" in time. This, along with the "Blue Hour" just before sunset, is my preferred time for photography work. Today the red, soft light of early rays tint the sky a golden hue. The long, low sunbeams hitting the mountain range before me from the side, almost horizontally, give the landscape a special sense of depth, a feeling of three-dimensionality.

I am awestruck and find it impossible to put down my camera until at some point the sun packs up and calls off the photoshoot. Almost abruptly, the colourful spectacle comes to an end. In its place appears plain daylight—far too bright for photography.

It is time to move on.

Summit Day with Obstacles

The final climb on summit day proves to be very strenuous. We have to climb up and along a sheer slope covered in ice and snow. One mistake, one misplaced step and I would tumble hundreds of feet into the deep abyss below. Despite the fact that several hours of climbing are already behind me and my body aches accordingly, there is no room for error—I cannot lose my focus at any time. And yet I do.

Suddenly, memories of my terrible accident at Pico de Orizaba are flooding my brain. In my head, I see myself lose my footing and slipping down. In reality, my body begins to shut down and for a fraction of a second I feel like I am actually tumbling, falling. "Roman, I don't think I can do this," I hear myself say. Roman quickly spins around, ready to catch me if he has to. "Hey, don't panic, you'll be fine," he tries to soothe me. "It's just a few dozen feet to the next fixed rope. Once we're there, we'll just click in your carabiner. That's a walk in the park for you!" I take a deep breath. The cold air in my lungs finally makes the dizziness go away. He is right, of course. The safety of the long, black fixed rope is just about 30 feet away. Again, Pico de Orizaba appears in my head, but this time I remember the moment I finally reach the summit. This memory cheers me up and gives me renewed hope and energy. Slowly and carefully,

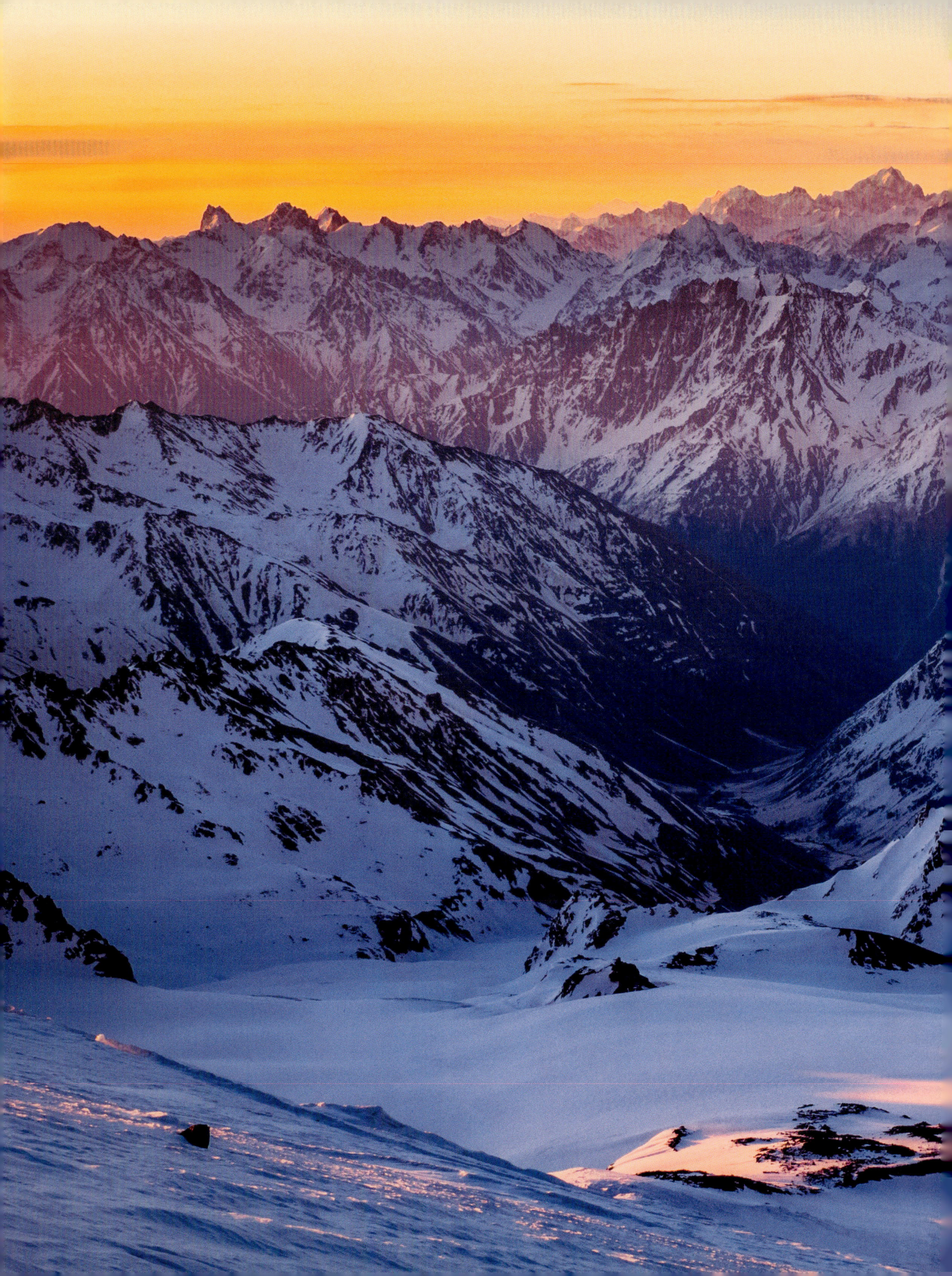

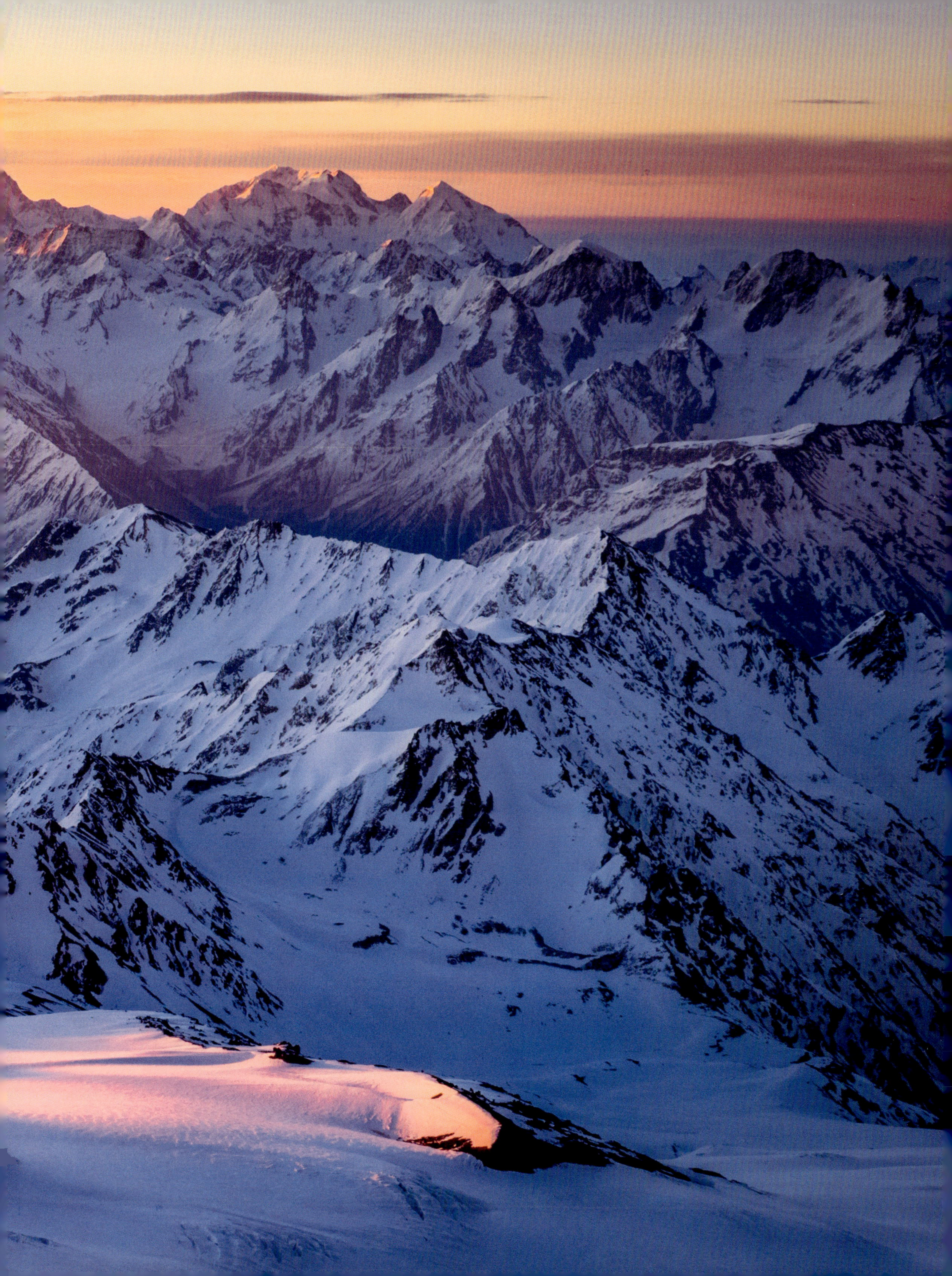

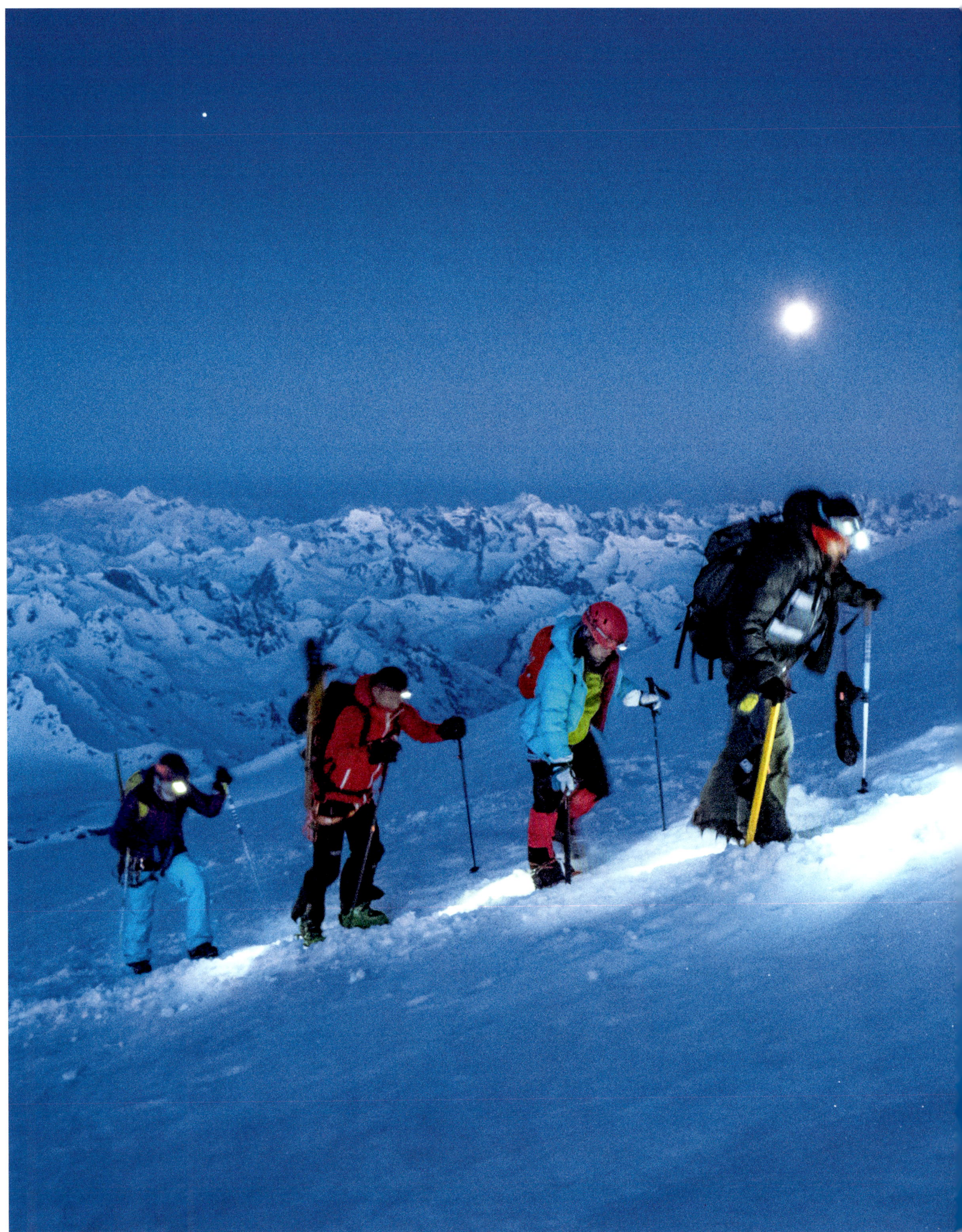

Saturday, May 28th,

   People in Russia really seem to have their own way of doing things. At Kamchatka, they were casually running along the Tolbachik volcano's rim, dodging falling lumps of lava, not a hint of fear. Here at the Caucasus Mountains, they are skiing almost naked at an altitude of over 13,000 feet and freezing temperatures. Insane—yet you can't help but like them.

I keep going. I take the terrifying slope one step at a time. My crampons are digging unnecessarily deep into the icy ground, and I try to stay steady by shifting some of my weight away from my legs—away from the deep—and onto my left hand, leaning against the mountain. Trying to gauge the terrain and the earth beneath me, I forget all about my fear of falling. Two more steps and I will be at the rope. My body relaxes immediately and I attach myself to the rope.

For a moment, I am euphoric. I even allow myself to think that from now on, it will be easy. "Not so fast!" I immediately try and rein in my thoughts. For mountaineers, being overly confident can be just as deadly as giving in to panic. From now on though, everything really does get easier. I climb the remaining steep 650 feet of altitude with renewed energy and enthusiasm. At that point, we reach a large plateau. From here, we can already see the cross at the summit of Mount Elbrus which lies behind a slight bend in the path leading up. Now I am certain that I will reach the summit, and I allow myself a little air punch of triumph. Roman, who overtakes me with his skis, shouts: "See you up there in five minutes!" Even though we are already at over 18,000 feet of altitude, I feel as if I am floating as I follow him. The snow beneath my feet is bright white and pristine. At these heights I am often overcome by fascination and an almost childish disbelief of the purity of the deep blue of the sky as it appears so far beyond the reach of human pollution. I am enjoying every step. The snow between the crags around me is almost blindingly white. At last, just a few more feet—and we are standing side by side on the summit. After the Roof of Africa, Roman and I have now reached the Roof of Europe.

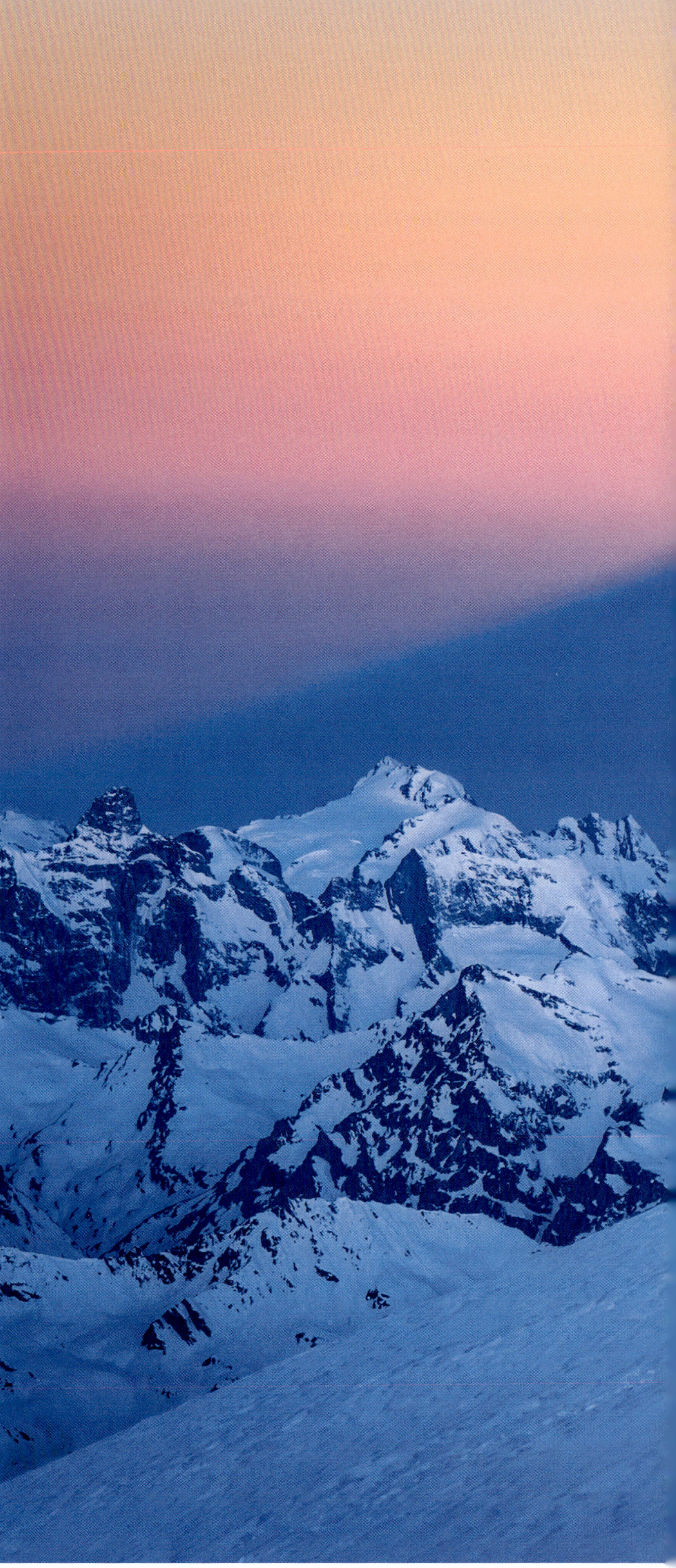

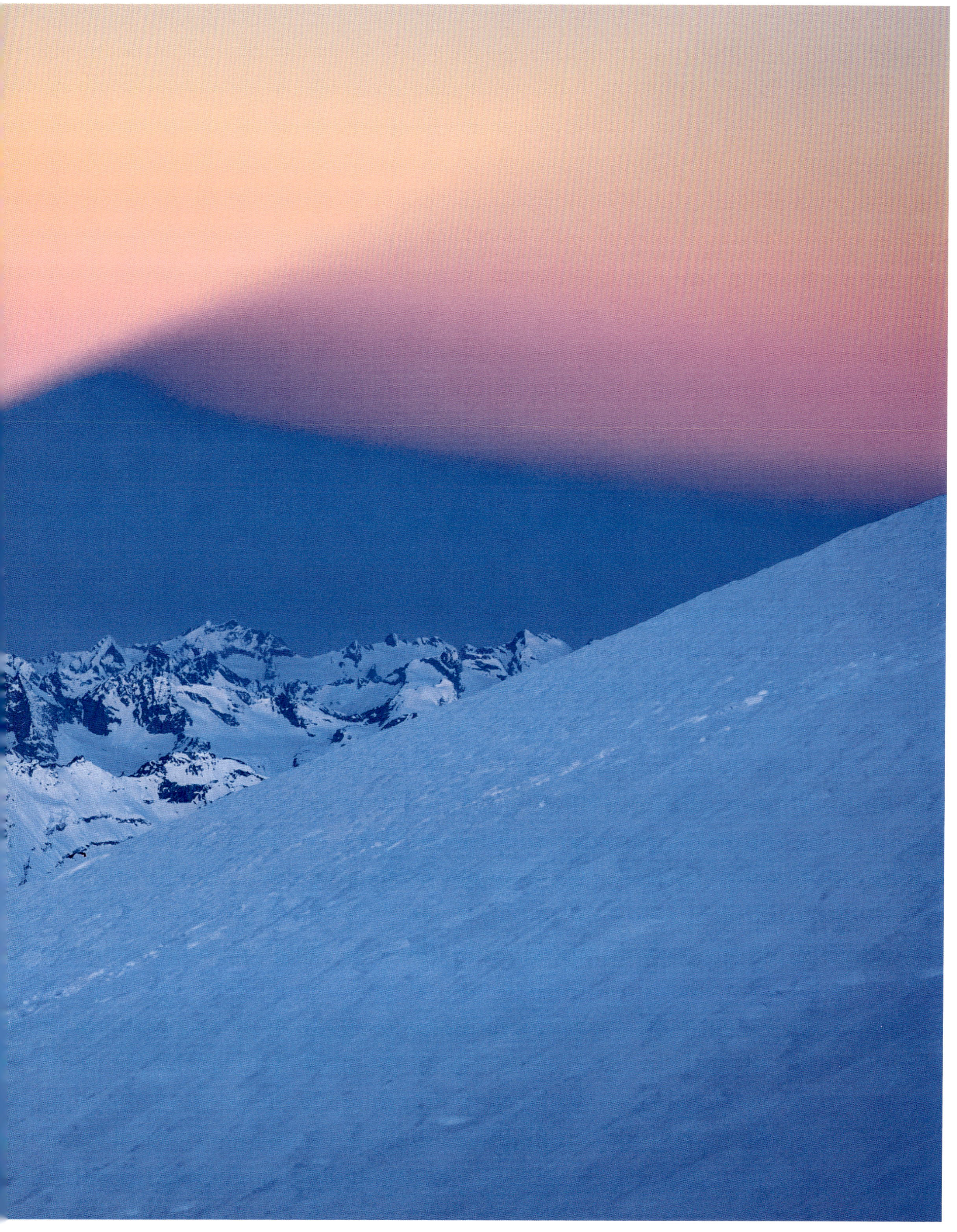

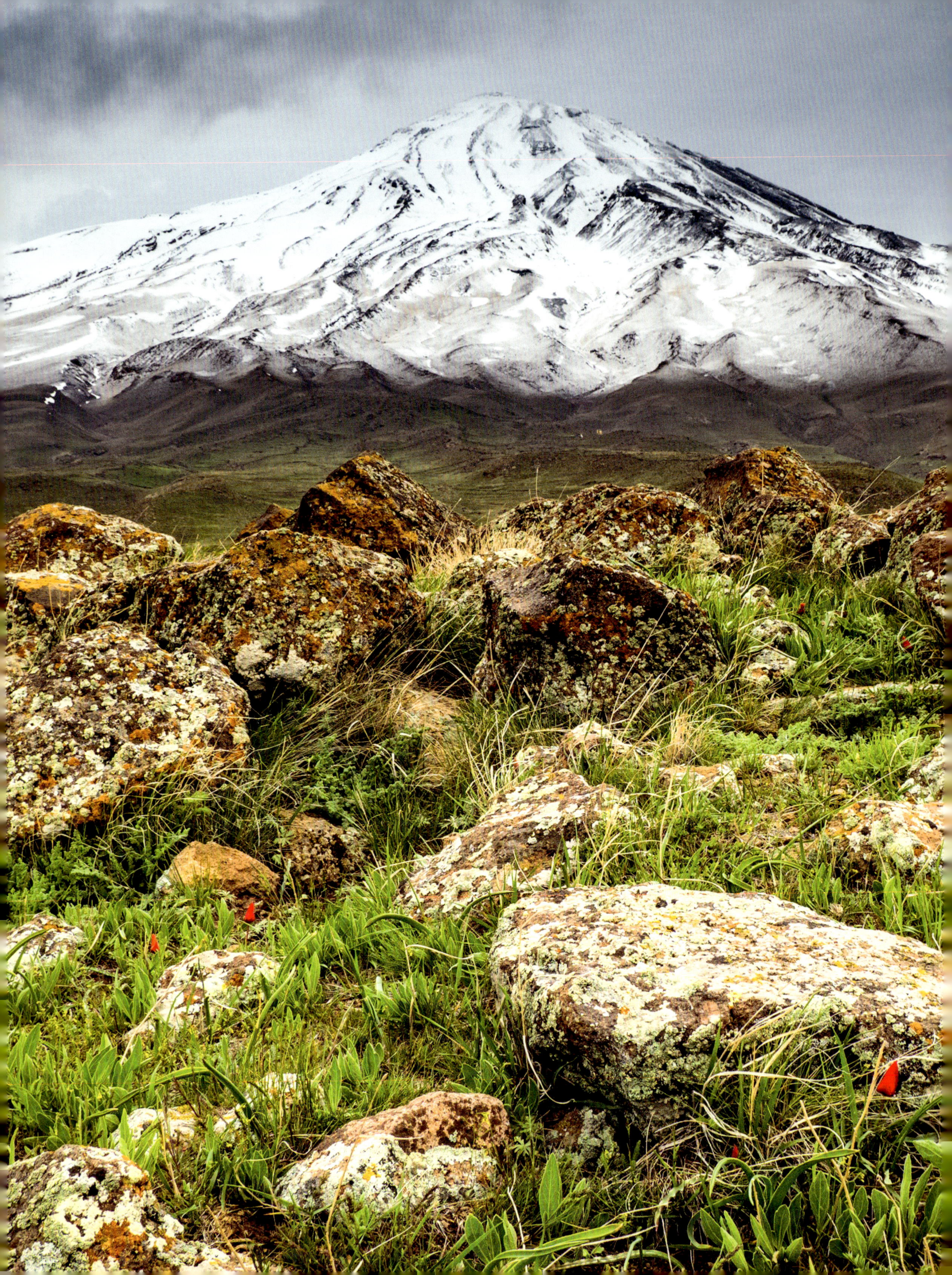

6

DAMAVAND

A Fairy Tale from One Thousand and One Nights

Iran

Iran had been the destination I had anticipated most eagerly during my travel preparations for the Volcanic Seven Summits. Mount Damavand, at 18,403 feet the highest volcano in Asia, was only a secondary priority for me. I wanted to get to know the country, its culture and its people. I had heard and read so much about Iranian hospitality and the friendly welcome the country extended to visitors, and was eager to experience it myself.

Iranian landscapes are famous for their beauty; they look stunning in photographs. I was impatient to get an opportunity to shoot Iran's deserts and mountains myself. Yet the discrepancy between my own eager anticipation and the reactions I received when I told people I was going to Iran could not have been greater. I heard the same things over and over again. "That's supposed to be really dangerous!" "Aren't you worried you'll get kidnapped?" "Have you lost your mind?" On top of this, at the time of my preparations, headlines describing Iran as the axis of evil were dominating the press. Nuclear threats, dangerous mullahs, and terrorists who are lying in wait for unprepared European tourists who they can pull out of their cars at night, rob, and then make disappear—that is the image of Iran that has been promulgated in our society for years now. In one way, the rumors are true: Iran is in fact a very dangerous country—in terms of traffic.

Courage at the Zebra Crossing

According to my personal rough estimates, about 98 percent of all cars in Iran are white—and our minivan is no exception. Our driver overtakes on the left, brakes, swerves to the right with screeching tires, accelerates and undertakes another car, accelerates again, then abruptly slams on the brake again to pull back to the left. Throughout these operations, each car drives bumper to bumper. Whenever we overtake on either side, there is barely enough space to put a sheet of paper in between our van and the next car. How our minivan is still in possession of both of its side mirrors is beyond me. "Those should have gone long ago," I whisper to my friend Christophe, staring in awe at the intact mirrors. "I can't believe that we haven't even touched another car yet today." What makes this feat even more incredible is the fact that the two lane road has four lines of cars on it. In between the cars, scooters and motorbikes squeeze through impossibly narrow spaces. Most bikers do not seem to care about wearing helmets or other protective clothing —nobody seems concerned for their own safety or for that of fellow drivers. "This is suicidal," I mumble and sigh. Christophe nods. "Did you know that Iran has the world's highest rate of fatalities due to traffic accidents? And from what I hear, Iranians are actually proud of that record." The scenes that are unfolding here in front of me make that statement very easy to believe. Having learned about this record, I am even more nervous. Something occurs to me though, and I cannot help but chuckle. "And to think, people keep asking me if it isn't dangerous to be climbing active volcanos for a living." Even though that does not make the traffic any less dangerous, it is a comforting thought.

What Christophe and I did not know at that moment is that our biggest and most dangerous adventure in Iranian traffic was yet to come, a few days later in Tehran. The sprawling metropolis has a population of nine million inhabitants. At the time of the accident, we are strolling through its streets on foot, surrounded by a screaming symphony of car horns, screeching brakes, gurgling motorbike engines, muezzins'

In one way, the rumors are true: Iran is in fact a very dangerous country —in terms of traffic.

Tehran's air pollution index is one of the highest worldwide. According to recent estimates, an average of 27 people die every day from air pollution-related diseases in Tehran.

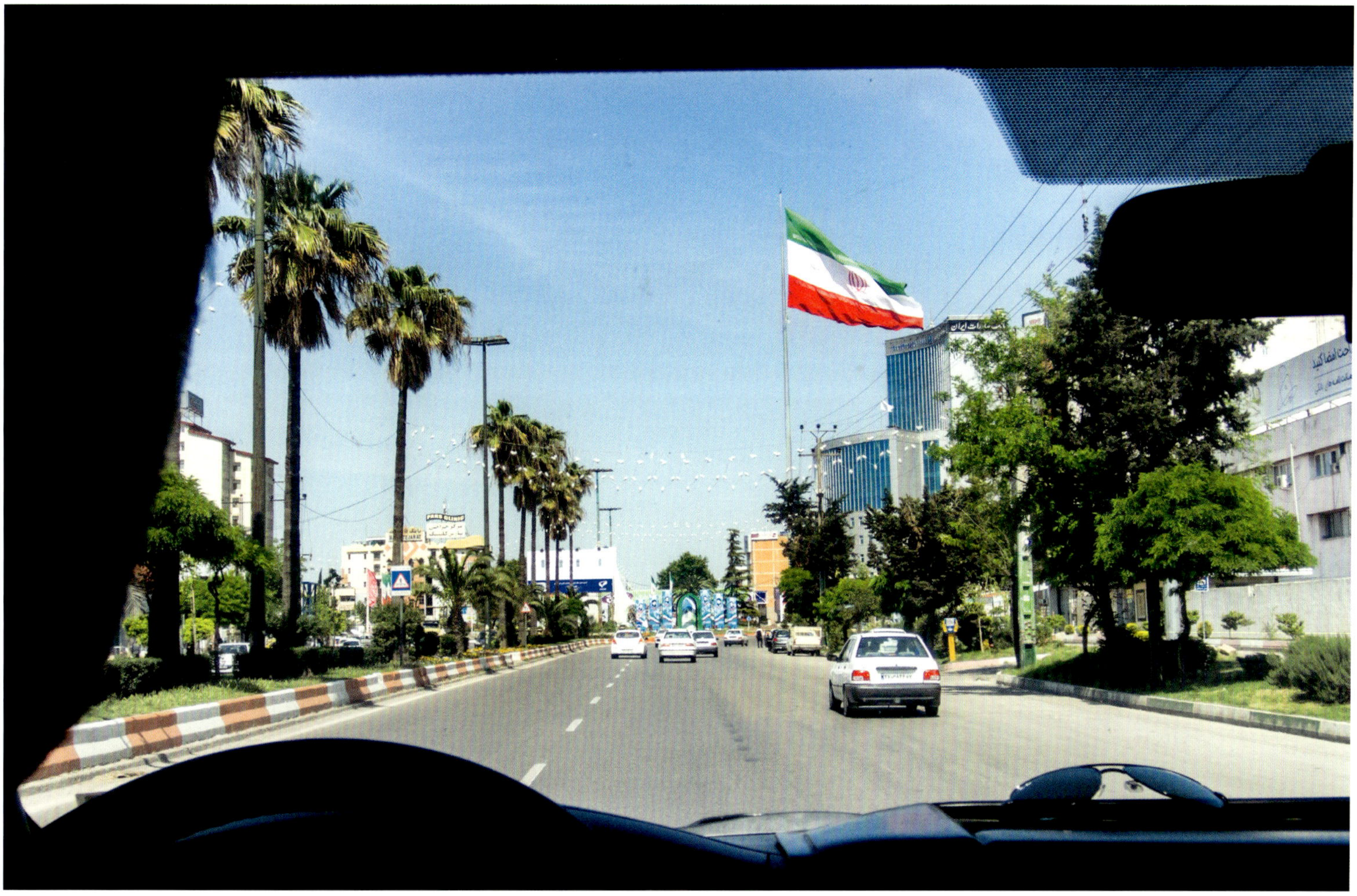

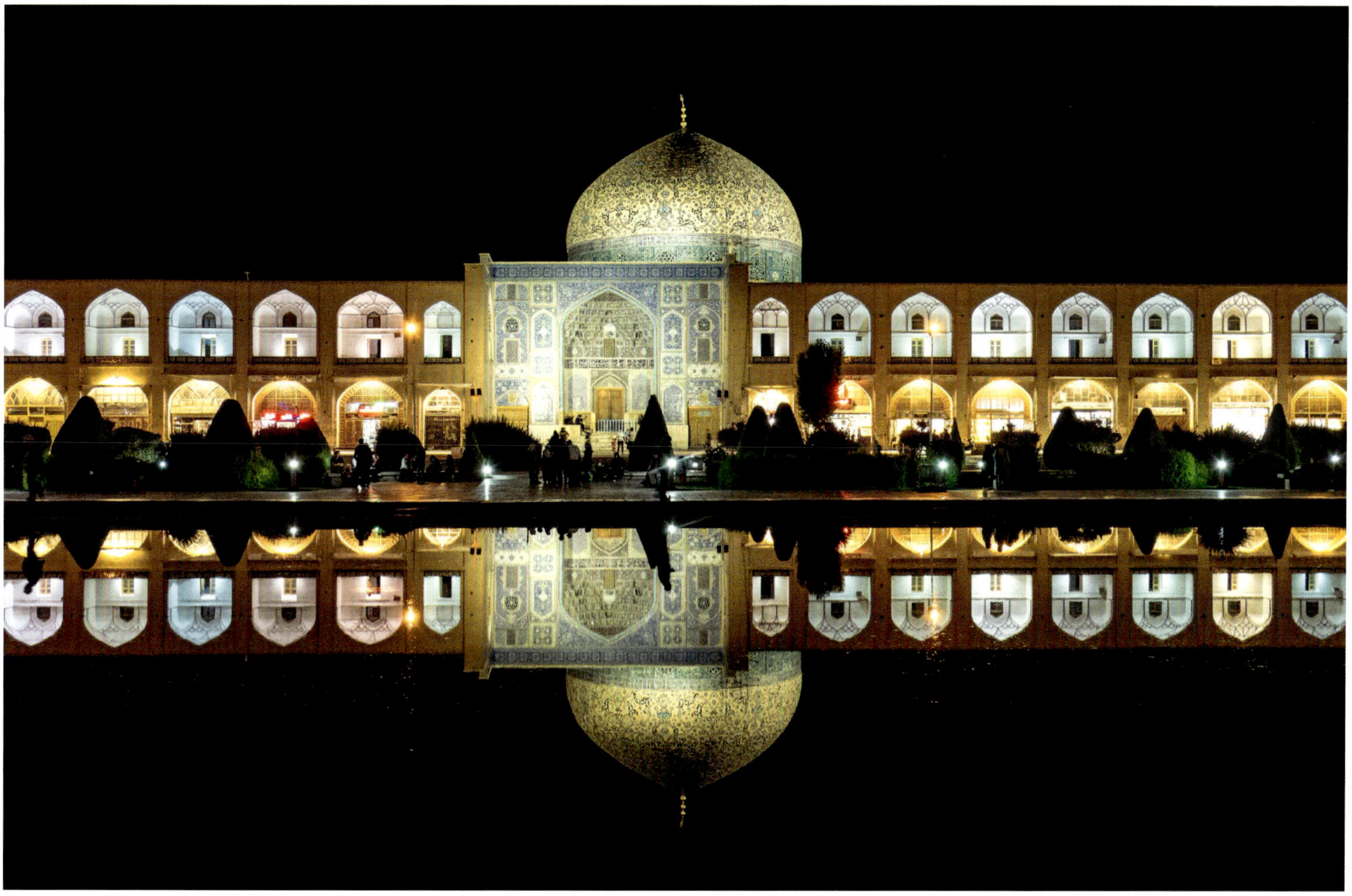

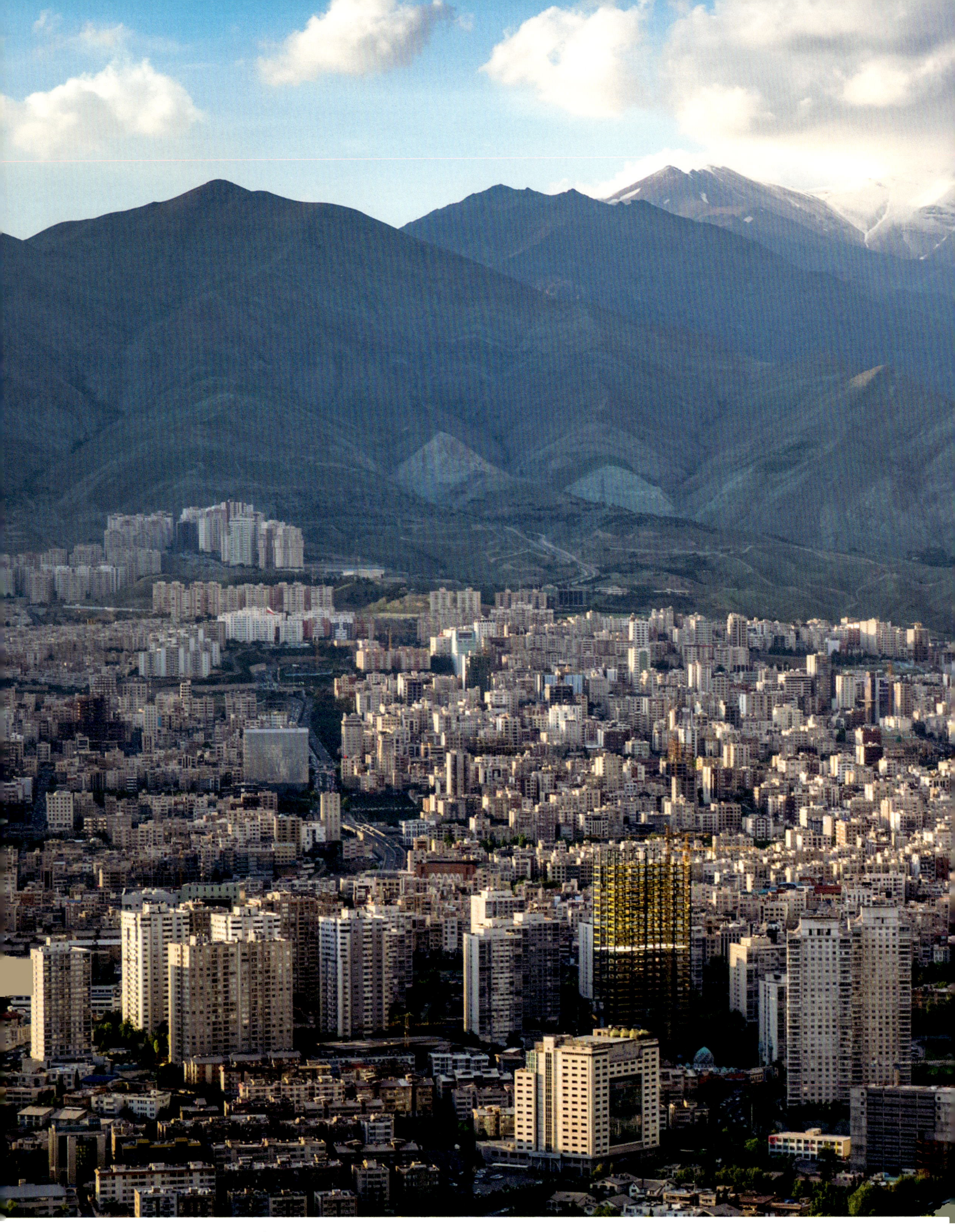

Damavand | Iran _________________________ 148

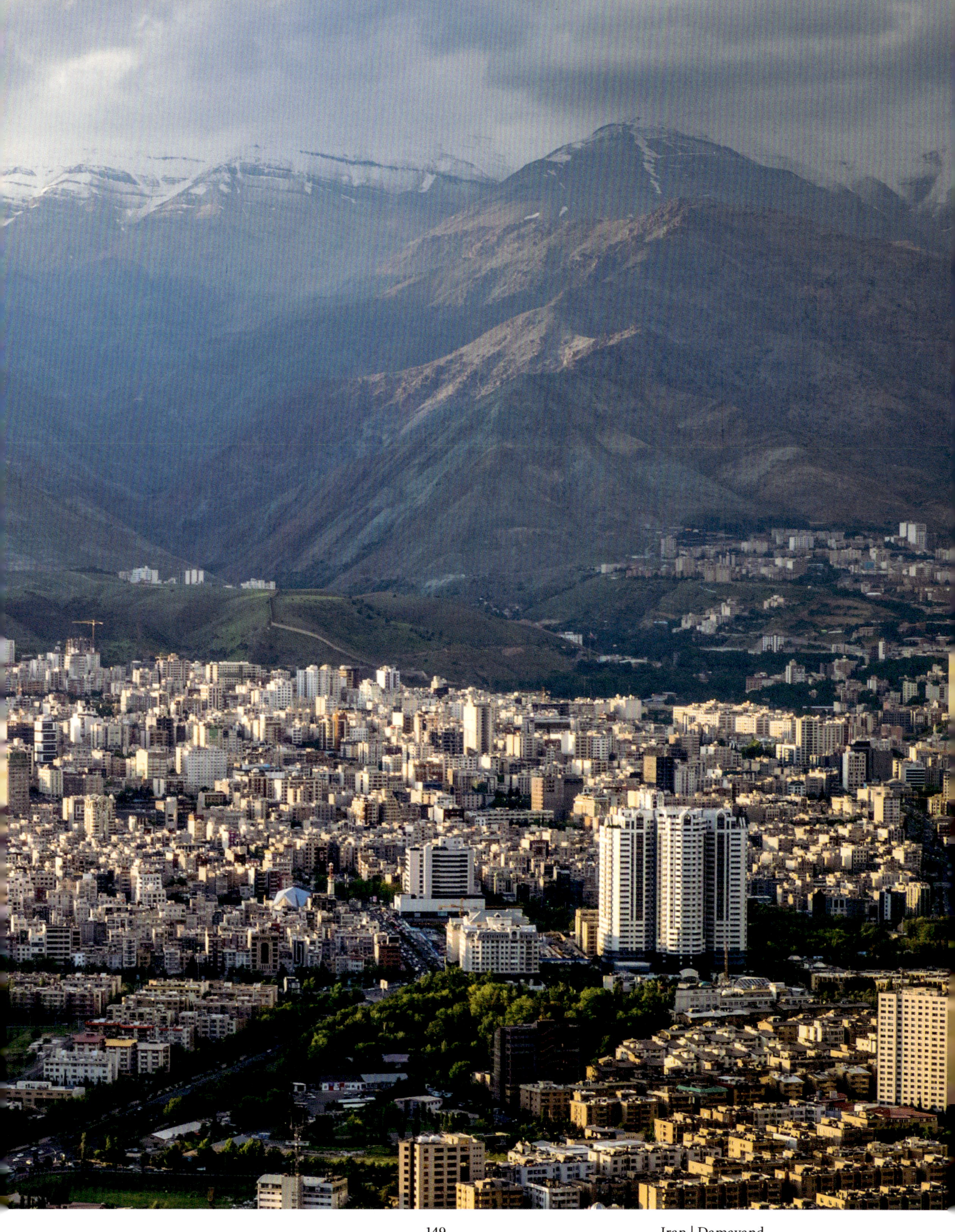

 Iran | Damavand

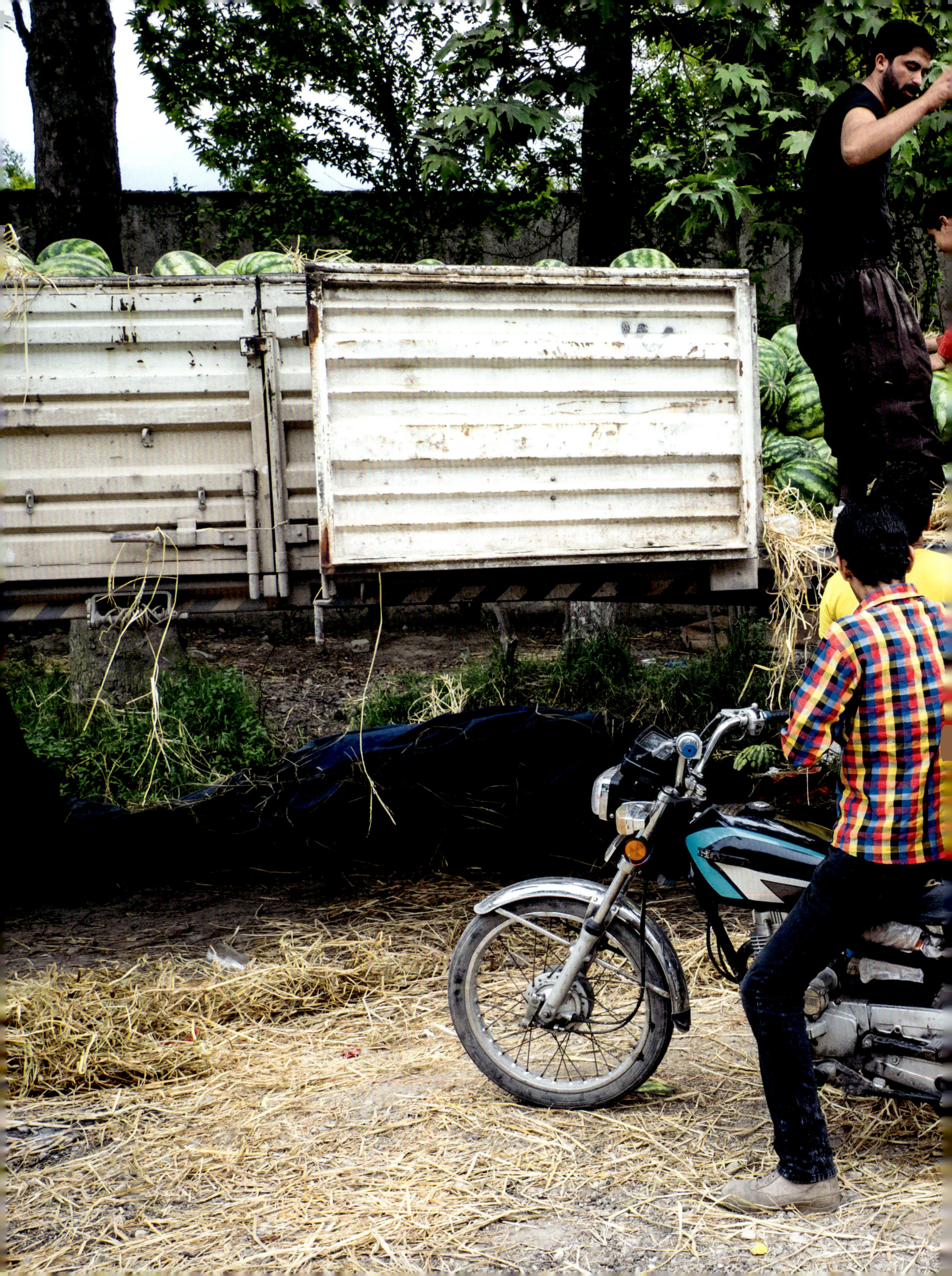

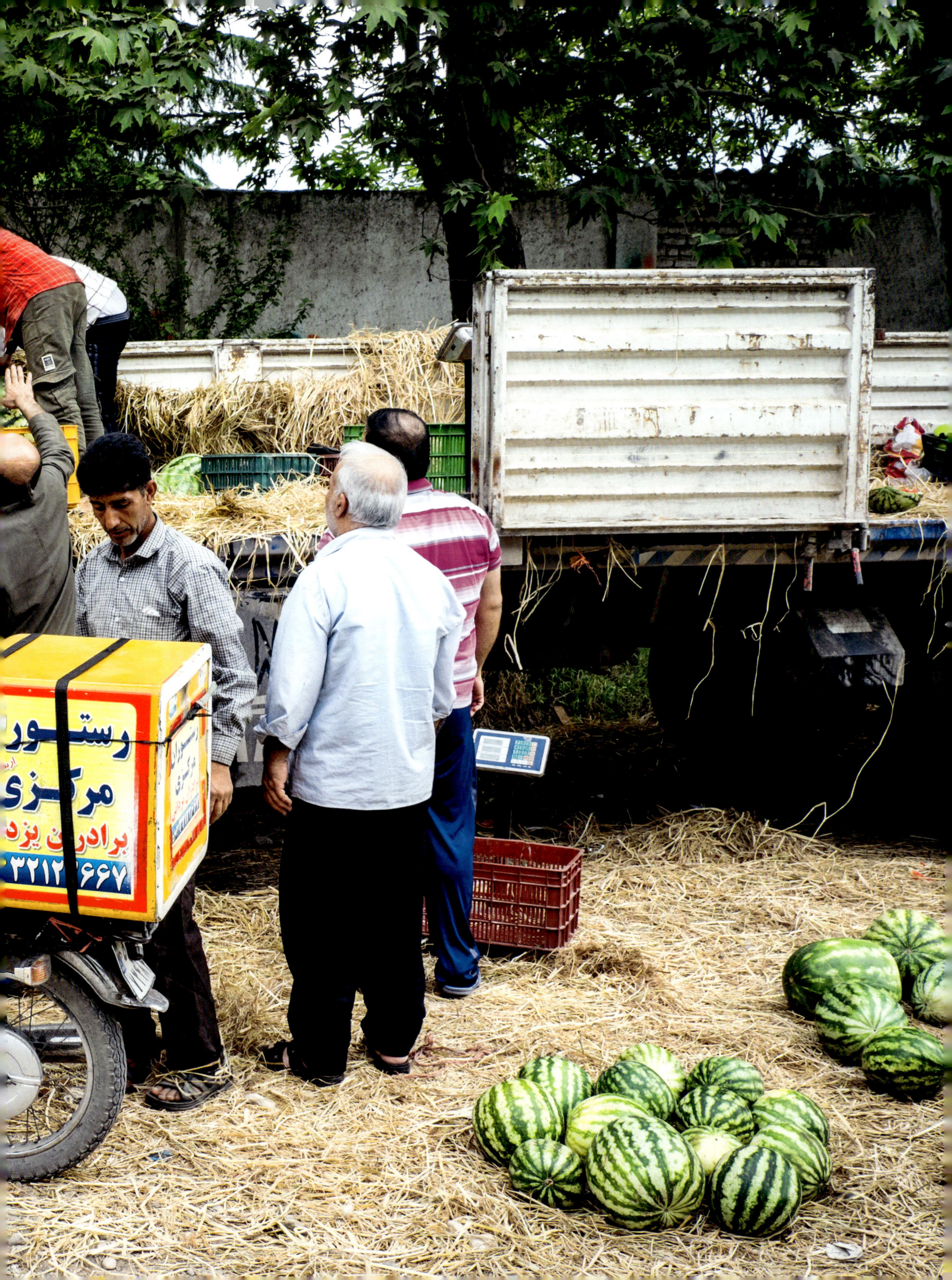
رستور
مرکزی
برادرن یزد
۳۲۱۲ ۶۶۷

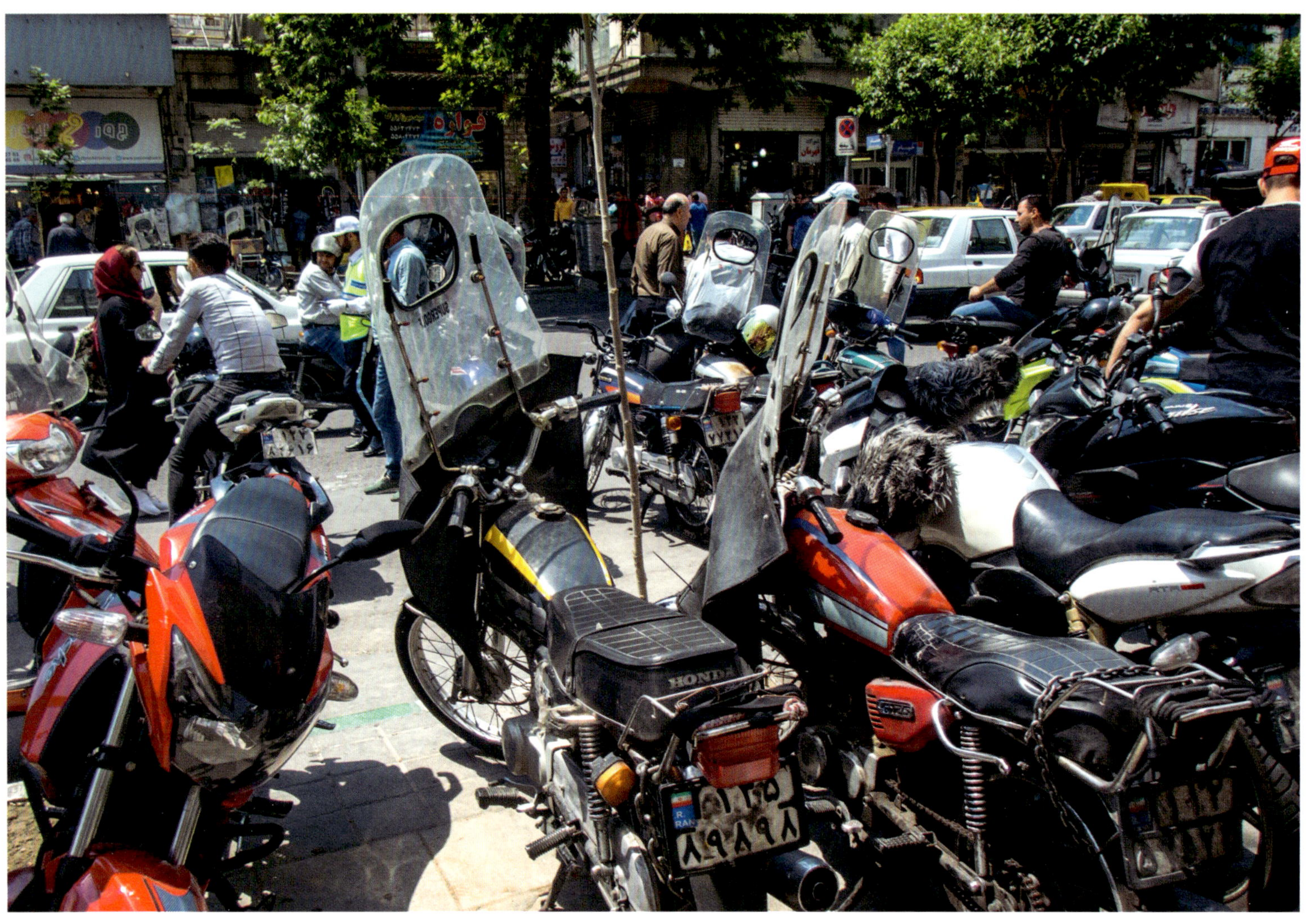

prayer calls, street vendors advertising their goods, and much more. The air is heavy with the smell of exhaust smoke, gasoline, and rancid oil. Here in the city center, German air pollution limits would probably be exceeded by a hundredfold. In between the overwhelming smells of pollution, there is a faint whiff of the more traditional scents that I had expected: freshly roasted pistachios, cinnamon, coriander, cardamom, a mix as if from a fairy tale in One Thousand and One Nights—but I fear that not even this can save our suffering lungs at this point.

All we had set out to do was to cross the street at a zebra crossing. Yet zebra crossings, much like traffic lights, seem to be purely ornamental rather than having any function or meaning here in Iran. Nobody thinks to stop or even just slow down as they approach one. Suddenly there is a motorbike racing past us—against the direction of traffic. I can still feel the blast from the change in air pressure when I am yet again overwhelmed by the biting smell of gasoline. I am beginning to wonder if the trick is to wait for One Thousand and One Nights before crossing the road. "Do you still remember that old computer game called Frogger?" I ask Christophe. "Sure," he says and I have to lean over a bit in order to hear his reply over the street noise. "Isn't that the one where you're a frog and you have to try and cross a busy five lane street to get to the other side?" He begins to laugh. So we gather all our courage and try to learn from Frogger. A short sprint, stop, wait for a new opportunity—we end up crossing the street as if we were playing a computer game. Once we arrive safely on the other side, we look back on our small adventure at the zebra crossing with relief. I feel like after this experience, whatever challenges Mount Damavand holds in store for us will be child's play by comparison.

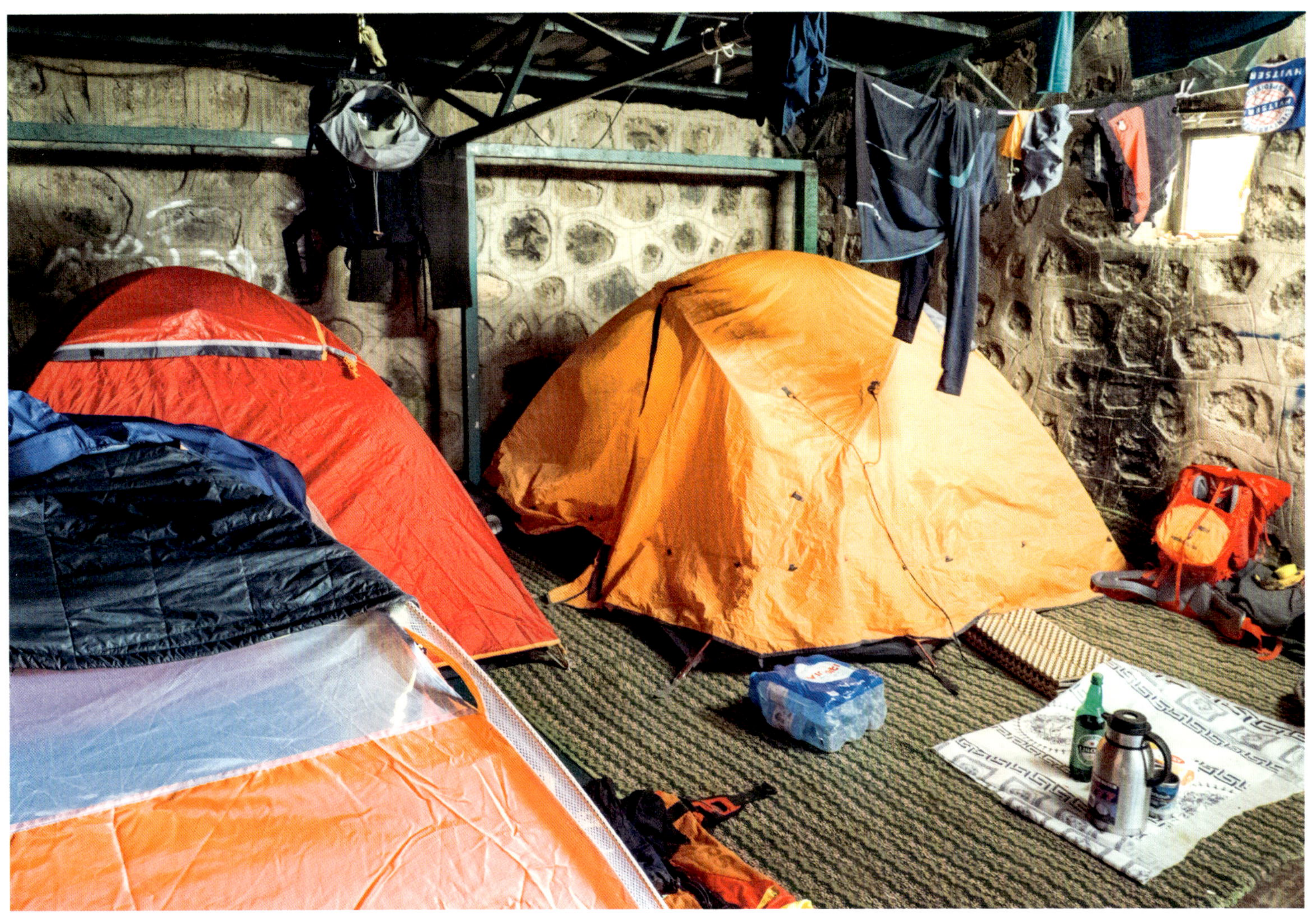

An Unusual Campsite

Less than two weeks have passed since my recent "summer holiday" trip in swimming trunks at Mount Albroz, and the unexpected sunshine I found there has spoiled me somewhat in my expectations regarding the weather. So here at Mount Damavand I hope for similarly good conditions. One look at the ten day weather forecast already tells me that this hope is overly optimistic. Predictions vary between bad, very bad, and extremely bad: it is a mixed bag of rain, wind, snow, and freezing temperatures. According to the forecast, there is not a single afternoon of sunshine, blue skies, and mild temperatures coming up in the following ten days. Christophe and I do not give up so easily though, for the weather can change quickly in the mountains. Current conditions aside, Iran's climate is almost as colorful and varied as the country itself. It is located at similar latitude to northern Africa, and so has large, arid desert regions. Then there are the snow-covered Albroz Mountains whose peaks reach up to 18,000 feet with an impressive 30 miles of ski slopes. Yet what took me completely by surprise was the lush vegetation in the low mountain ranges north-east of Tehran. Its meadows and forests make European travelers feel as though they had never left their home countries. The colorful roofs of the village of Polour can be seen at the foot of Mount Damavand, about two hours' drive east of Tehran. Here, too, the surrounding vegetation reminds me of the Alps. Our accommodation for the night is a no-frills building that belongs to the Iranian Mountaineering Association. From here, we have an excellent view of the summit—in theory. Actually, we end up sitting at a large plastic table, our spoons rattling against the cheap metal plates and hastily swallowing warming vegetable soup, while outside the window a storm is raging that makes us feel as if a new ice age was about to begin. There is zero visibility. On top of that, the raindrops

At 18,386 feet, Mount Damavand is both the highest mountain and volcano in Iran and in all of the Middle East. Literally translated, its name means "the mountain that contains vapor"— and even today, it often emits steam.

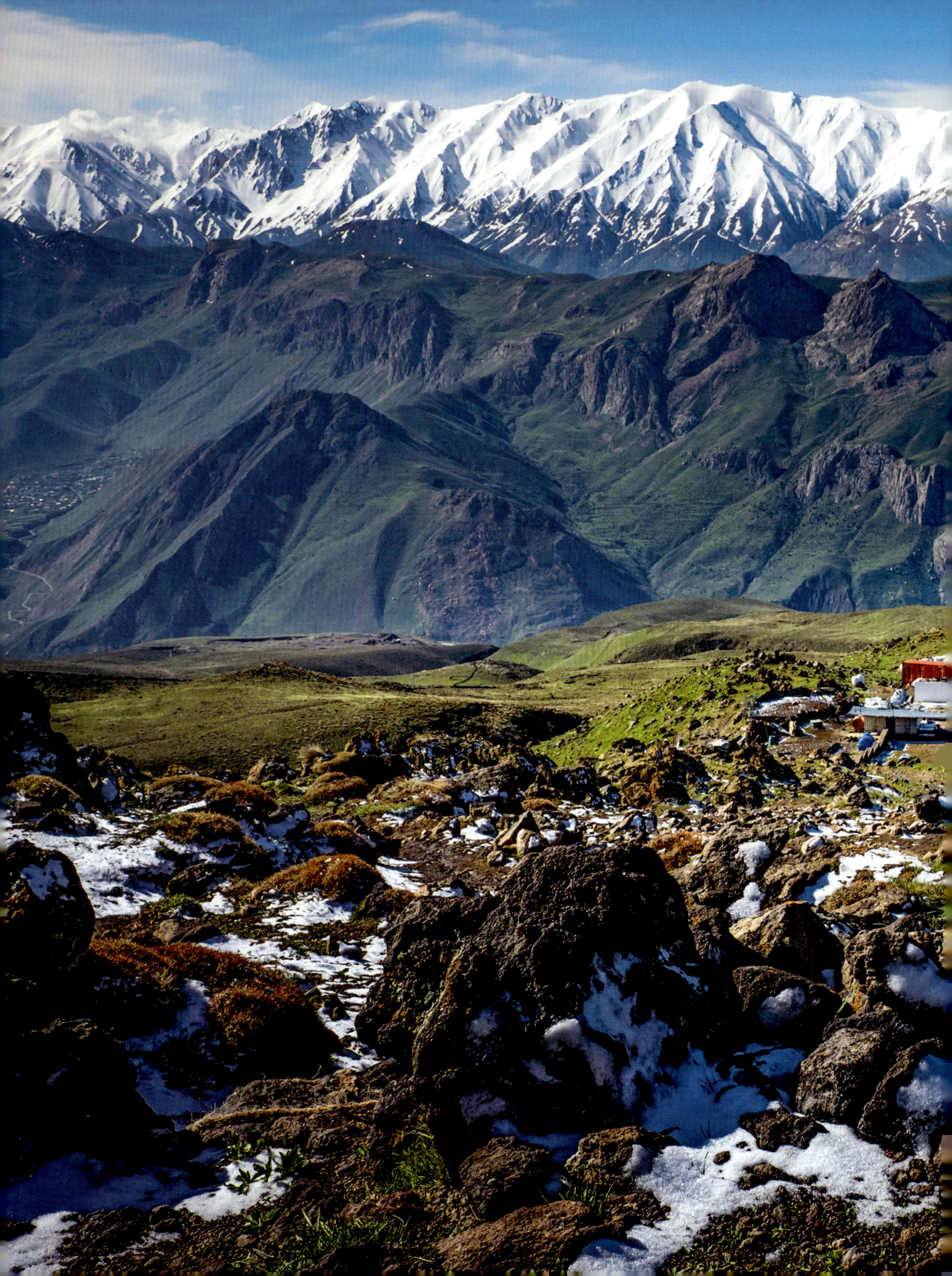

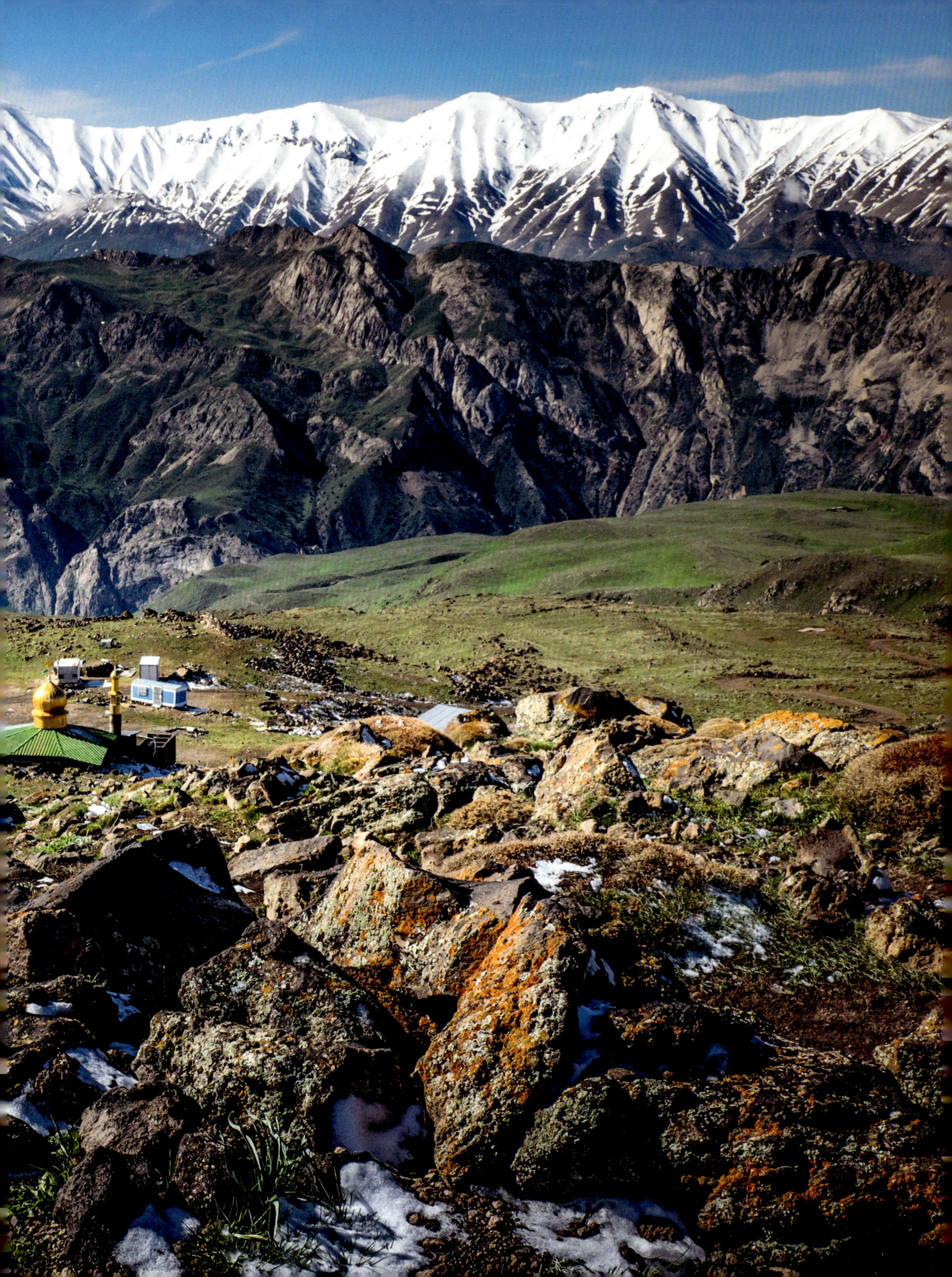

hitting the building's metal awning sound as hard as stones. As it turns out, it is hail—swiftly followed by an almost monsoon-like period of rainfall. Frustrated, I try and catch a glimpse of our environs. Mount Damavand is nowhere to be seen—instead, I stare at a grey blanket of clouds which is suddenly torn in two by lightning. The sound of thunder makes us jump out of our seats. "I would like my money back," I say jokingly to our tour leader Babak. His brown eyes blink, then he gives me a cheeky smile, exposing a large gap between his upper teeth. "Don't worry, I promise the weather will get better—all part of the job."

In the morning, the summit peeks through a thick yet slightly less ominously dark layer of clouds, so we optimistically begin loading our SUV. Looking at the car and its heavy cargo, I am beginning to feel that we may have brought a bit too much gear. Six mountaineers, each of us with a hefty backpack, squeeze into the rusty Nissan. Our near-toothless driver starts the car and we begin to make our way to base camp. Luckily for us—and for the poor SUV which is audibly struggling with its cargo—the windy ascent is soon over. Yet the first stop holds another surprise for us: our base camp is a mosque. It is made of stone, with a green roof and golden dome which glistens in the—equally unexpected—sunshine. The golden rays it reflects creates a beautiful contrast to the blue sky and the snow-covered summit beyond. "Did I promise too much?" Babak asks with a contented smile. He did not.

Within a short period of time, the small dark room inside the mosque is transformed into the kind of chaotic camp mountaineers are wont to produce: three multicolored tents, backpacks of different colors and shapes, clunky hiking boots, water bottles, trekking poles, two boxes of supplies, gas cookers, mats, blankets—all of this spread out everywhere, until the carpet inside the mosque is covered almost completely. Jackets, jumpers, and towels dangle off clothes lines above our heads. We are impatient now and eager to start hiking. The sky is still blue and clear when we leave and begin our ascent

of Mount Damavand, chatting away happily. Babak points at a herd of donkeys grazing contentedly in the rich green meadows. "They will carry our luggage to the upper hut for us," he explains. After about half an hour we allow ourselves a short rest and look back at what we have achieved so far. The view both above and below us is amazing. The snow line below the jagged summits looks as if it has been drawn with a ruler. Below it lies a landscape of dark brown boulders, light brown lichens, and rich, green vegetation—it offers a stunning contrast to the untouched snow's perfectly even white. Right in the middle of this composition, as if buckets of varnish had toppled over and spilled, our mosque glows in the sunshine, and beside it sit the two red-and-blue containers which serve as accommodation for the donkey herders. All of this is illuminated by bright blue skies. "It seems as though the weather gods have taken pity on us after all."

Maybe it was this last thought of mine that jinxed our expedition. Soon after I thought these words, fog begins to rise all around us. Slowly, our clear view of the summit begins to fade, until finally it disappears completely behind thick, ominous clouds. Below us, even the mosque's golden glow is no longer vivid, but tired and dim like colors in a sun-bleached picture. Eventually, it also disappears from our view, just like the summit before it. "Come on, Babak, do something!" I jokingly urge our tour guide. But it seems as though Babak's cheerful mood has turned as quickly as the weather. He urges us to descend again. Up here in the mountains, bad weather and poor visibility are a real danger.

Time for Dreams

Back at our camp at the mosque, Babak prepares fragrant hot tea which helps to make up for the lost day. With it he offers traditional Persian rock candy sticks as well as freshly roasted pistachios, flavored with saffron. Babak embodies the qualities that I had been most looking forward to on this journey. Despite the disbelief

In ancient Persian folklore, Azi Dahaka is a demonic dragon with three heads and six eyes. As punishment, the demon is chained to Mount Damavand. Dragon slayer Garshasp later throws it into a river of fire which, according to legend, runs underneath the volcano.

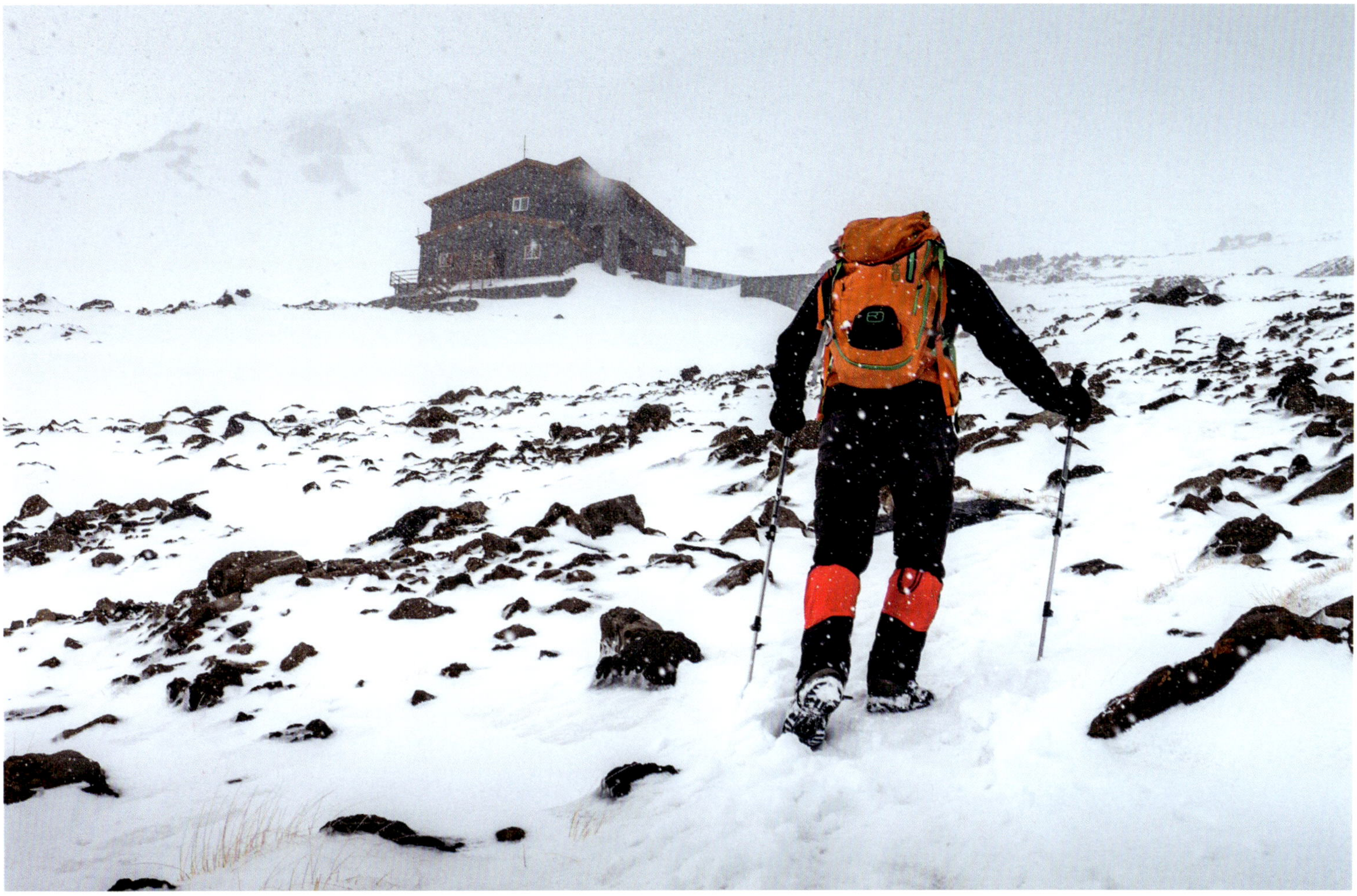

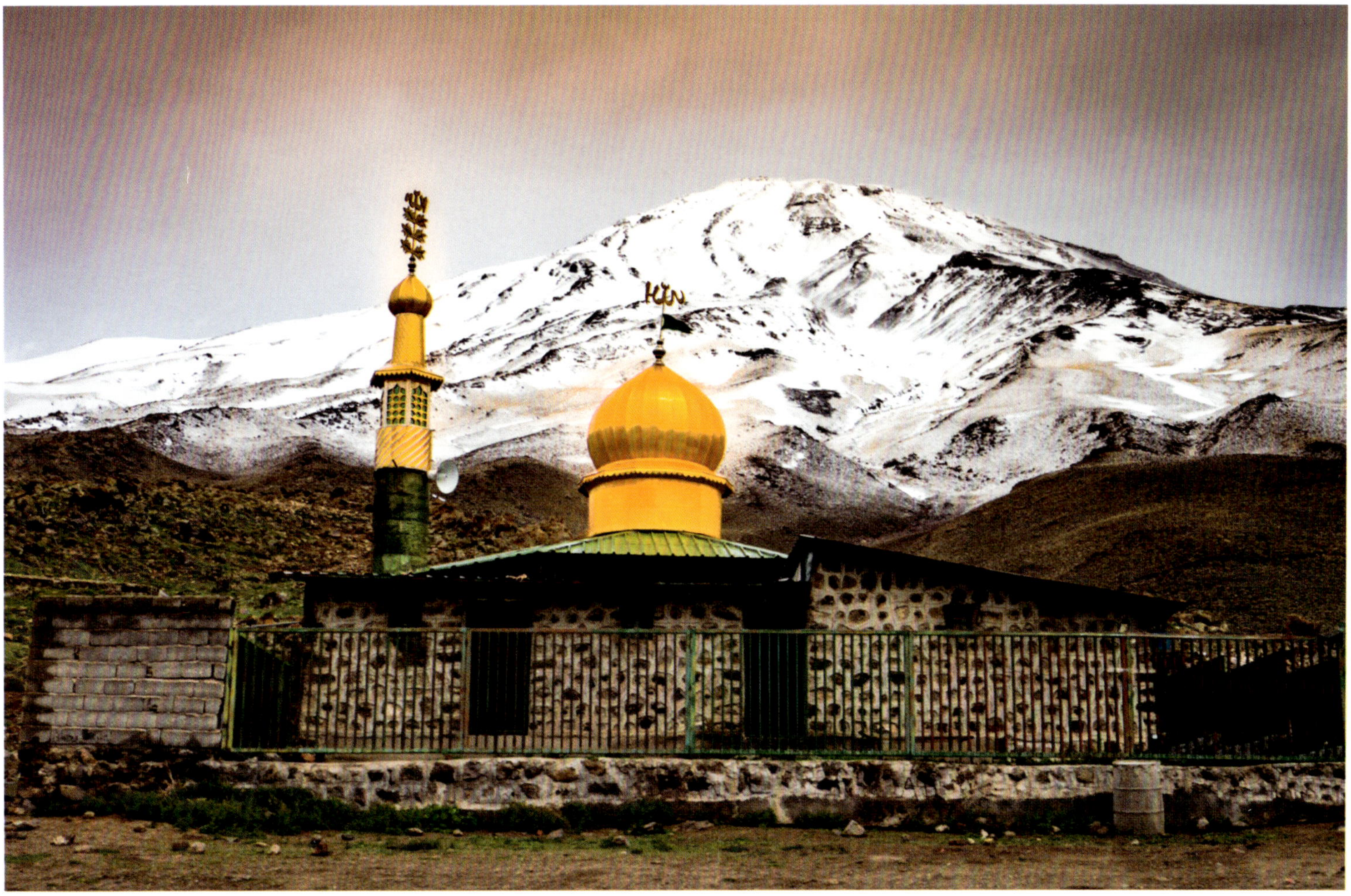

 Iran | Damavand

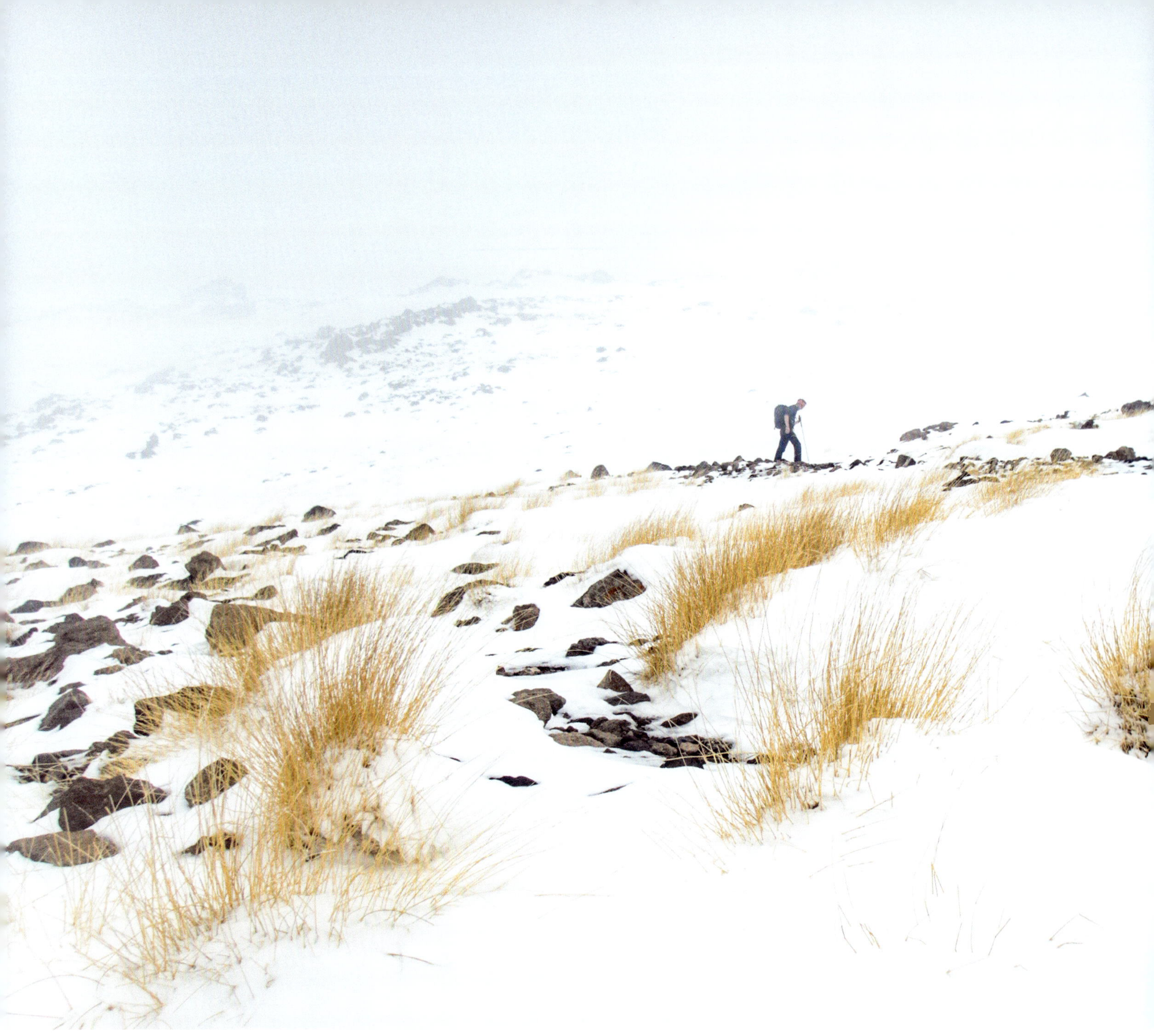

Deserts with very little rainfall cover almost half of the Iranian state territory. Extremely hot summers with temperatures of up to 120 degrees are followed by freezing winters and relentless sub-zero temperatures.

and doubt I had encountered from other people during my preparations for my trip to Iran, the country and its people have offered me their famous hospitality. In the streets, in cafes, in small villages, and in the metropolises—wherever we go, Christophe and I are invited to join people to drink tea, eat lunch, or have a picnic. Hospitality, as well as helping anyone in need, appears almost like a primal urge for the Iranians. Babak explains: "If a stranger were to ask me for help, I would have no other choice but to sell everything I own if that means I can help that person."

While we continue to shell and nibble our pistachios, Babak tells us about the electronic goods store in Tehran he used to have. He admits: "One day I simply couldn't take it any longer. The bad air, the lengthy commute on the subway every day. So I rented out my store and my flat and moved to the countryside with my family." He shells a pistachio and continues. "Ever since then, I have worked as a tour leader up here in the mountains. I couldn't think of a better way to make a living."

For a moment we are all silent, taking some time to think about Babak's story and his life. I can understand how he felt: three years ago I also decided to swap my tie for trekking trousers and my camera. From banker to globetrotter—it was a huge step for me. One thing I knew from the beginning: I would never be able to make as much money from travel photography as I had made during my banking days. But is life not more about contentment and self-realization than money? I was lucky enough to have a family that supported me every step of the way, and without them, all this would have been impossible. Another sign that showed me that I had made the right decision was that during my three years working as a photographer, I had made more good friends than I had in the previous 20 years. To me, each one of them is worth more than a Porsche. For that is what life is about, after all: trying, within our means, to make the best of what we are given, and finding personal fulfilment. For me, that means leading an independent, interesting, and mindful life, and living rather than dreaming my dreams. In the end, I want to be able to leave this world in peace and take many wonderful memories with me when I go.

We sit like this all afternoon, philosophizing about our lives, our goals, and our dreams. I am determined to live my dream of climbing Mount Damavand, and so we continue to check the weather forecast. Babak believes that there may soon be a very small weather window we could try and use for our ascent.

The weather will prove him wrong.

Snowed In

The next day we arrive at the high camp at 14,000 feet around midday. The ascent is hindered by thick snow and poor visibility, but we make it. Inside the dark communal room with its bare stone floor, it is so cold that we cannot afford to take off our thick down jackets for a second. Even the hot tea from our thermos flasks fails to warm us up, and for a while I wonder what I might have done to incense our weather gods on this tour. "First we had sunshine and high temperatures at Mount Albroz, now ice cold wind here at Mount Damavand, surely something's up here," I try to cheer my friends up. "It's got to be fire and ice with me, there's just no way around it."

Needless to say, the joke does not really go down well. When we look outside, the weather appears relentless: the snow is falling faster and thicker than ever. Far away we can already hear thunder. Again we have to abandon our ascent, turn around, and try and get back to base camp while the option remains.

We quickly pack our bags, pull down our gaiters to cover our boots, and rush out of the door—only find ourselves standing in fresh, knee-high snow. We cannot afford to get snowed in here, so we choose the shortest route, a steep snowy slope leading straight down the mountain. With every step I sink deeper and deeper into the snow. The descent is increasingly strenuous. We increase our pace so we are almost running, vaulting tree trunks and leaping across fissures in the rocks. Half an hour later,

But is life not more about contentment and self-realization than money?

Tehran, Wednesday, May 3rd,

I can't believe myself—I came ill-prepared, and now I'm here in Tehran and I have no money. I didn't bring enough cash and European credit cards don't seem to work here. Luckily, this isn't an issue when you're in Iran. A complete stranger helps me and lends me a large sum of money. Iran's hospitality is overwhelming.

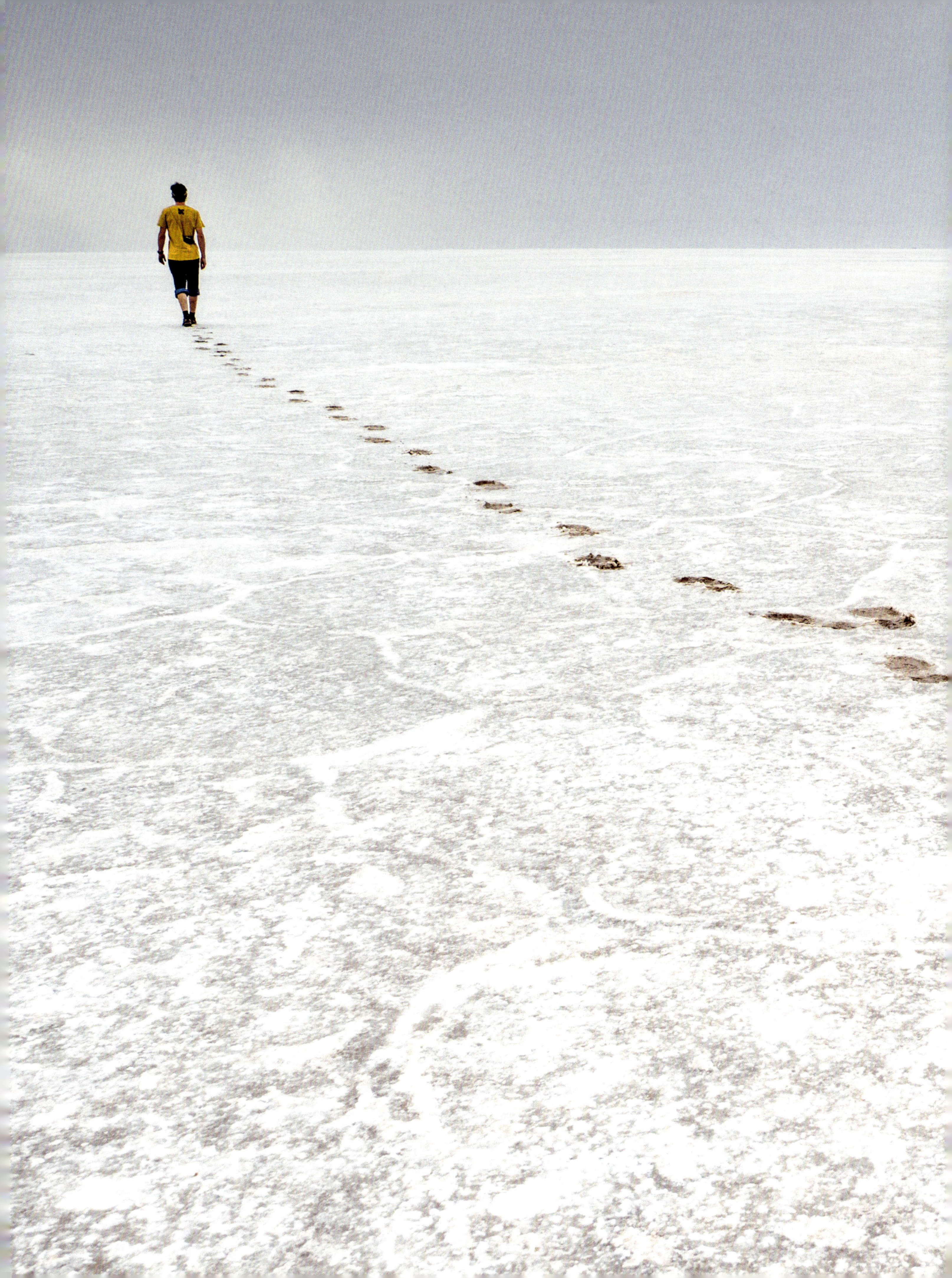

we can finally feel solid, stony ground under our boots again. After a short break to recover, we continue our fast-paced walk back to the mosque. All we can do is hope that the weather gods will treat us more kindly the following day.

No such luck—if anything, they appear even angrier the following morning. The snow line sinks until it reaches our accommodation. The wind speeds continue to increase and eventually the hut's owner calls to inform us that the high camp is now completely inaccessible due to snow. The weather forecast is getting worse again and reports temperatures as low as -4 degrees in the days to come. We briefly discuss our options. Babak advises that the best thing to do at this point would be to start looking for a "warm place", and there is no alternative that we can see. Over the following days, several mountaineers who made futile summit attempts at Mount Damavand tell us that we made the right decision in giving up our ascent.

One Thousand and One Nights

Sachertorte and Christmas carols in Tehran? Nobody is going to believe me.

We are back at the capital, having left the mountain, its snow storms and towering clouds behind us. It is sunny here in Tehran and we visit the park outside Golestan Palace, the former royal seat of the Shah (King) of Persia. Here we come across several colourful tables. They are heavily laden with delicacies and small artefacts from various countries. People in traditional dress are hurrying past us. It would appear that this is a small international cultural festival of some sort—of course we must go and take a closer look. I can see tables which introduce the countries and cultures of China, Norway, Italy, and India, when suddenly a familiar smell makes me turn around. "Coffee!" I almost squeal with delight. Iran had turned out to be a country of tea aficionados, and over the past few days, the only form of coffee we could find was instant Nescafé—which we only tolerated because it gave us the caffeine we craved. I am a coffee addict, and the past few days had felt like going cold turkey.

I follow the smell and find myself in roasted coffee bean heaven. A large blackboard next to one of the tables reads the following words in cursive handwriting: "grosse braune" (large black), "espresso", "caffee latte", as well as "Strudel" and "Suchertorte"—probably meant to read Sachertorte, a Viennese specialty. I run towards it, almost knocking over another man on my way, and order coffee with milk—and, of course, a slice of "Suchertorte".

"I can't believe this," Christophe mumbles. We sit down on the ground and enjoy every sip of coffee and every bite of cake. It really is authentic Austrian Sachertorte. The coffee is the first real coffee brewed from freshly roasted beans we have had in two and a half weeks. From the corner of my eyes I see a school choir getting ready for a performance, not knowing that soon I am about to experience the biggest surprise of my entire, rather adventurous life. The children's choir begins to sing. I am pretty sure my disbelief must have been written all over my face: with a strong, charming Iranian accent, the children begin to sing the unmistakable German Christmas carol "O du Fröhliche" —in German. In Tehran, in May, right inside the alleged axis of evil, I am eating Sachertorte and listening to German Christmas carols. Never before have I felt so at home in such a foreign situation. And never before has any country exceeded my expectations the way Iran has— just like in a fairy tale from One Thousand and One Nights.

Iran's remote, uninhabited territories serve as habitats for rare animals such as cheetahs, leopards, lynx, and brown bears. In the west, an island in Lake Urmia is home to the Persian fallow deer – everywhere else it used to roam, the Persian fallow deer is now considered extinct.

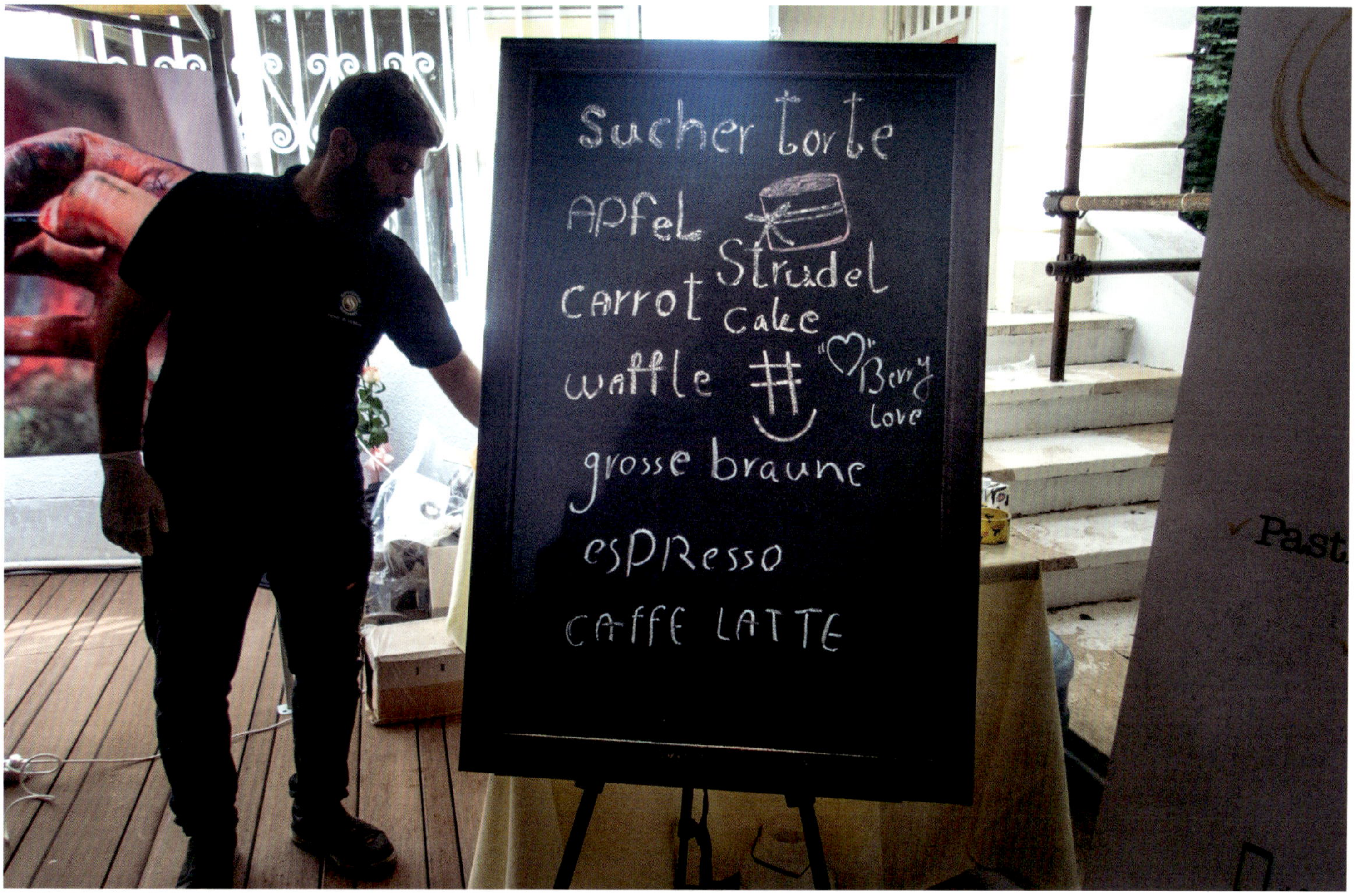

 Iran | Damavand

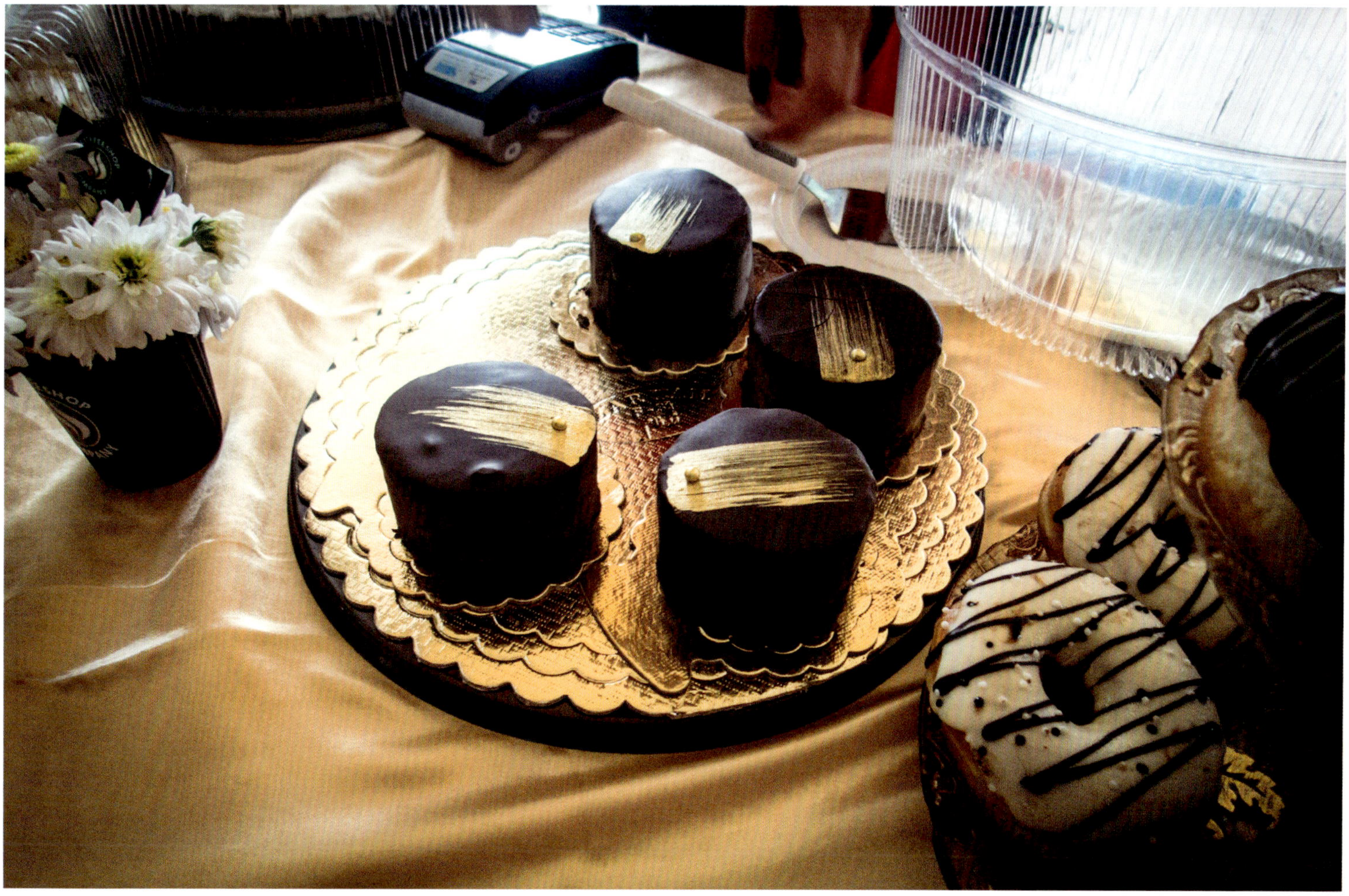

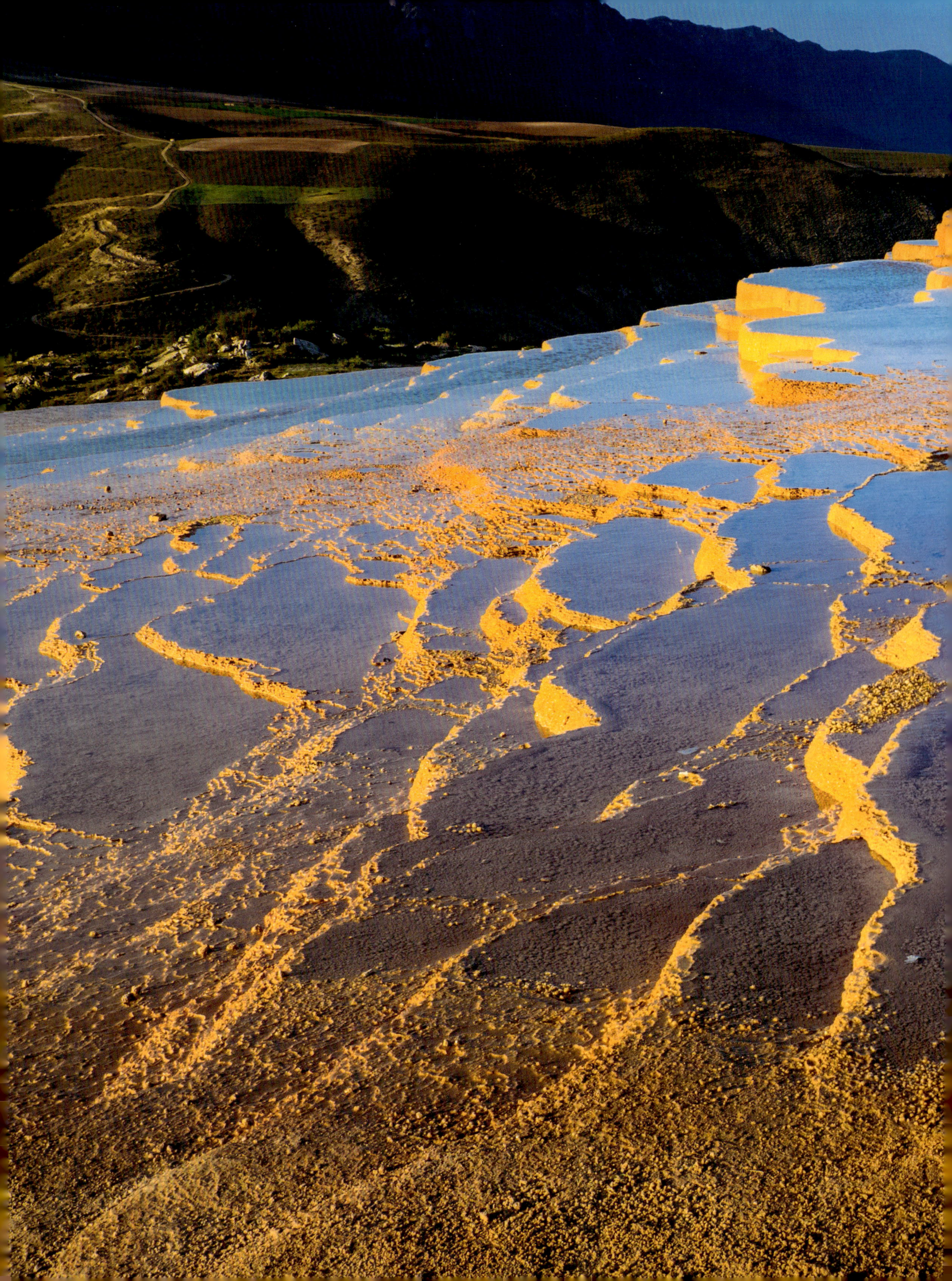

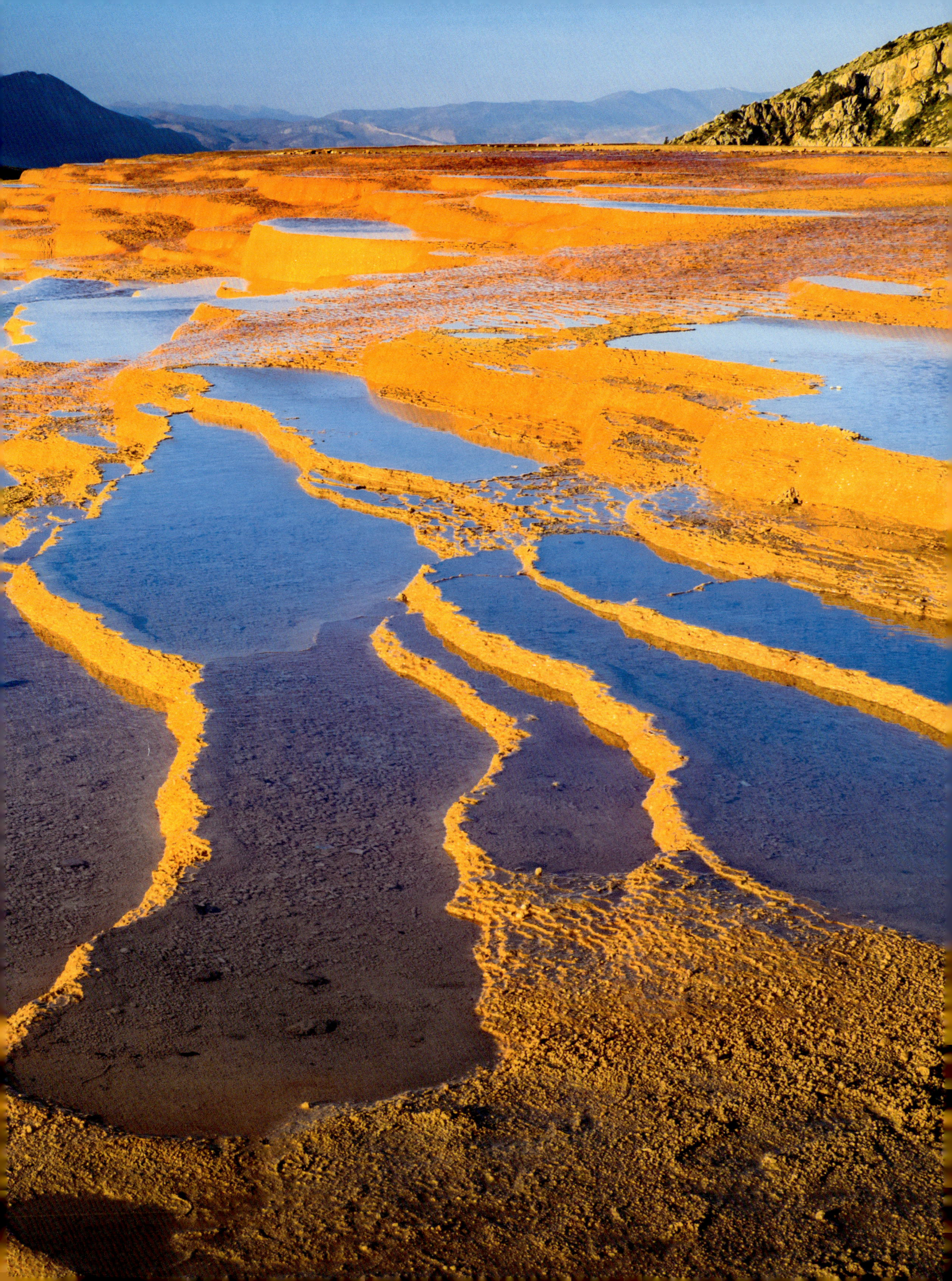

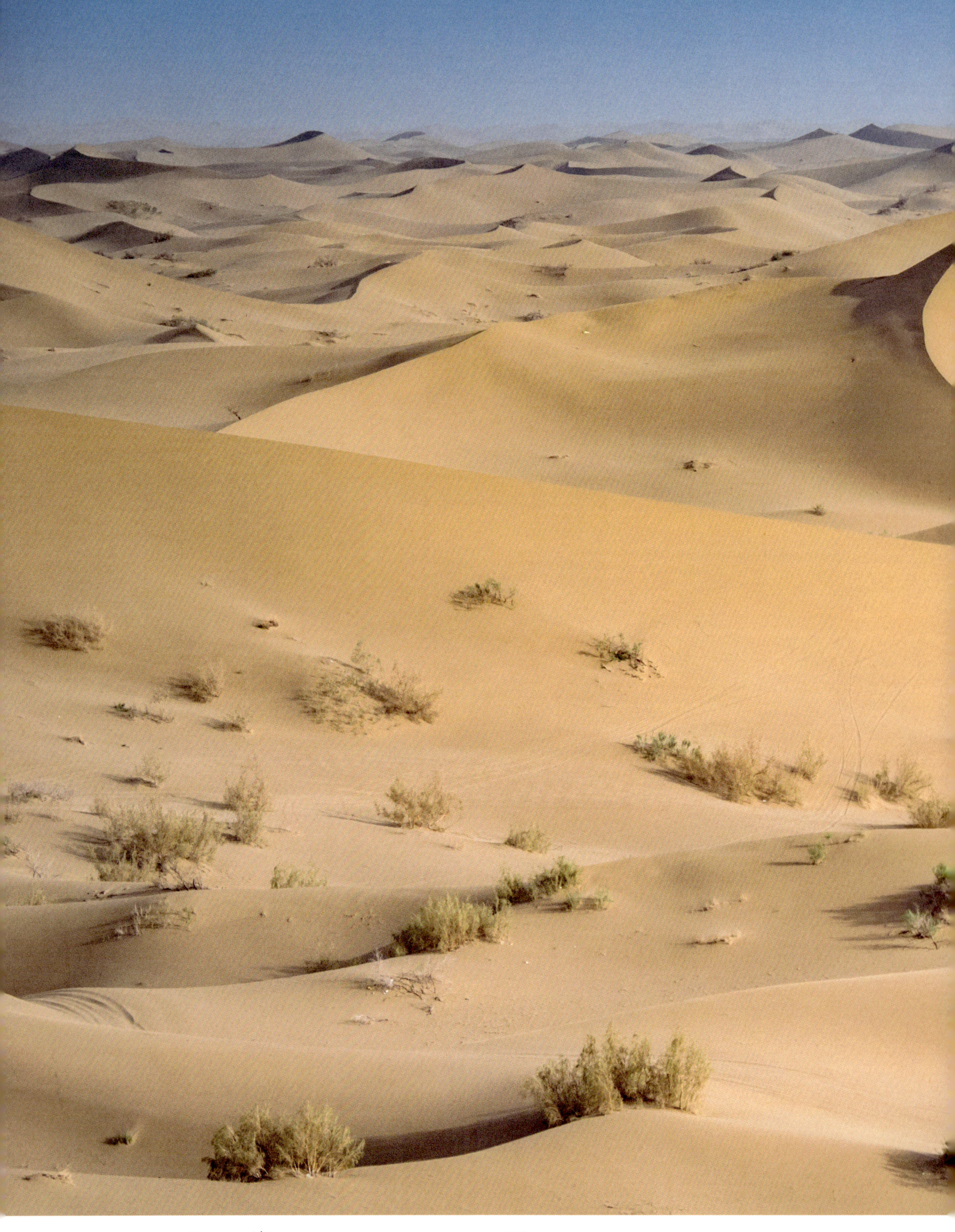

Damavand | Iran ___________________ 166

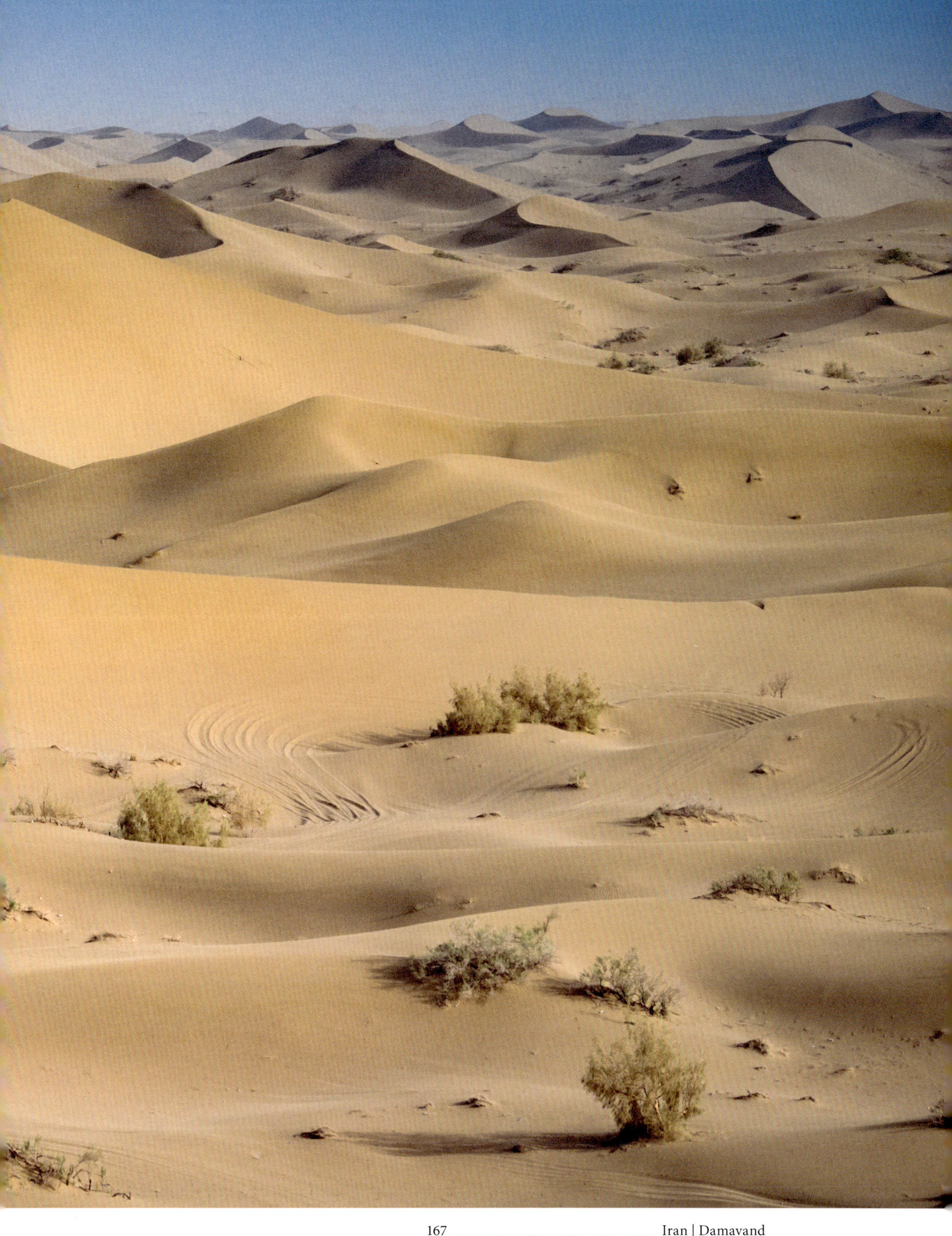

 Iran | Damavand

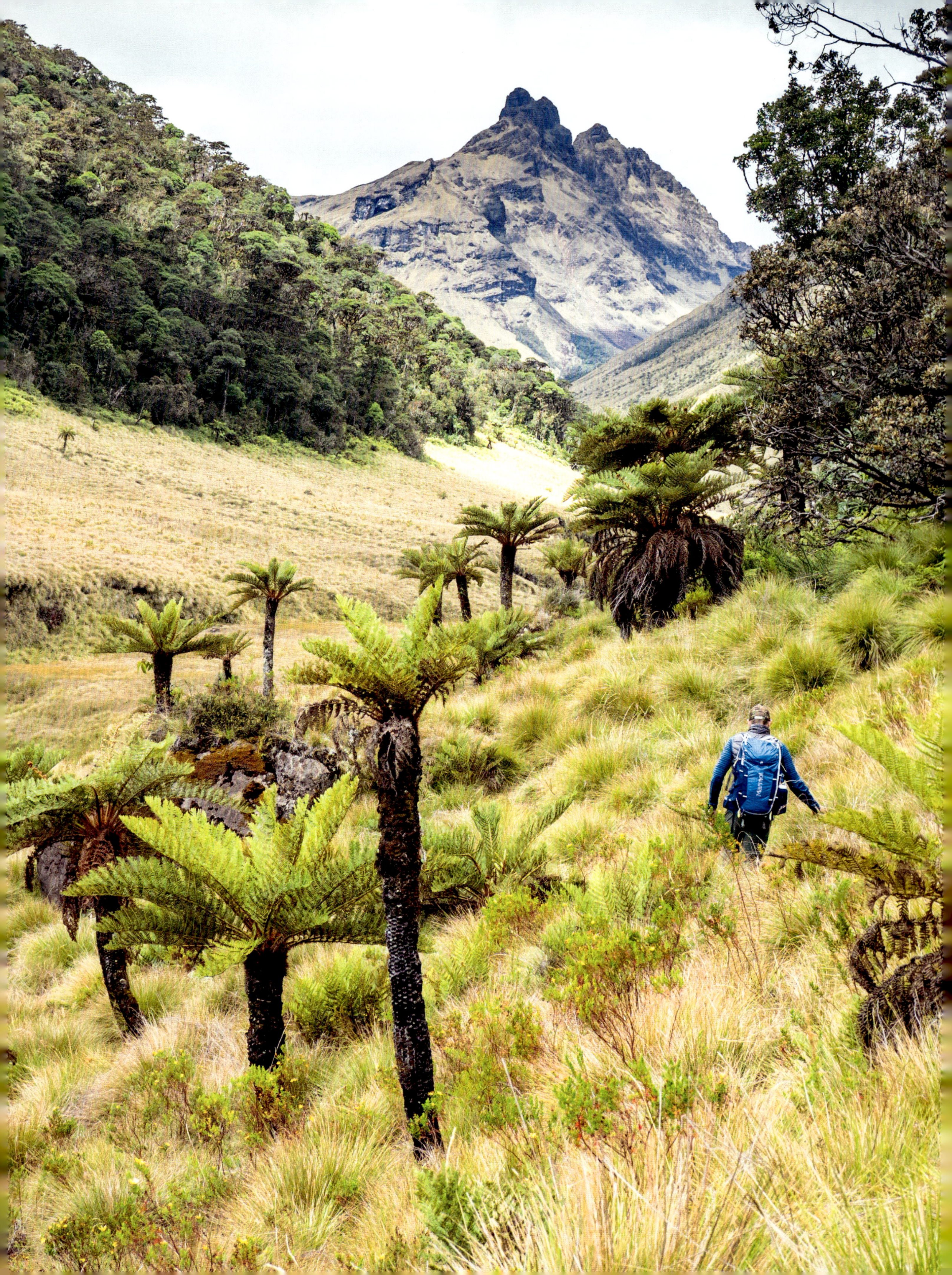

7

MOUNT GILUWE

"Black Magic Exists"

Papua New Guinea

"Action! Action! Sing!" Peter does an uncanny Schwarzenegger impression. We are standing on the peak of Mount Giluwe in Papua New Guinea, the seventh and final volcano of my Volcanic Seven Summits. I grin straight into the camera Peter is pointing at me and scream with joy: "Yeah, Mount Giluwe, the last stop on my tour!"

"I really did it," I think, and I cannot quite believe it. In the past two years I have travelled each of the seven continents and visited each of their highest volcanos. Unfortunately, I was not lucky enough to reach each summit but that had never been my primary goal. I struggle to find the right words to express my feelings. "Incredible—seven continents," my mind is spinning. "What a project. What an adventure. And now—what a grand finale."

I pause for a moment, walk away from the summit cross and enjoy the wonderful view of the expansive green grassland below and the dense jungle beyond. I would love to capture this moment, to somehow immortalize it. I close my eyes and in my mind repeat the names of the seven volcanoes: "Mount Sidley, Mount Kilimanjaro, Orizaba, Nevado Ojos del Salado, Mount Albroz, Mount Damawand, and Mount Giluwe."

I open my eyes again and nothing has changed. The scenery is just as vibrant as it had been before. At first, it felt almost strange to be looking at a landscape so full of life. During my photography practice, especially over the past two years, I have travelled in much harsher conditions and rougher regions, surrounded by ash, volcanic dust, desert, snow, and ice. Usually, there is an almost complete lack of habitation and vegetation. But at 14,327 feet, Mount Giluwe is a comparatively small mountain, relative to the Nevado Ojos del Salado's 22,615 feet, for example. Yet it is still the tallest volcano in

New Guinea Island is the world's second largest island—after Greenland and before Borneo. The island is divided in the middle: its eastern half is the independent state of Papua New Guinea; the western half is Indonesian territory.

Oceania and the second-tallest mountain in Papua New Guinea. Prior to this journey, I'd had my reservations. Would I even be able to take good pictures in this kind of unfamiliar environment?

Jurassic World

All my concerns were put to rest before I had even laid eyes on the volcano itself. When I was still on the plane, I caught an initial glimpse of Papua New Guinea's natural, fertile land, and I immediately fell in love: its rich, thick, deep green rainforest—the third largest rainforest in the world—sprawled over gently rolling hills, which stretched as far as the eye could see. The forest seemed to be waiting for me to come and take its portrait, and I was only too happy to oblige.

We left the capital, Port Moresby, and entered the wilderness. Around our jeep, the jungle was closing in. The more impenetrable it seemed, the more it intrigued me—I was impatient to explore it more. We got out of the jeep and proceeded on foot. As the rainforest began to swallow us, I still clearly remember my very first, admittedly not very poetic, thought: "I can't believe this is happening." At that point, we had been walking for about five minutes, and already the rainforest had captivated me.

The narrow path through the jungle was just about visible. Our local guide William was hacking away at plants left and right; his impressive machete was "Made in Brazil," of course. Despite his best efforts, I still had to push aside ferns, lianas, tendrils, and other foliage. All around us, there was nothing but thick, impenetrable greenery. For some stretches of the path, the few gaps between the leaves and tree trunks became so narrow that they all

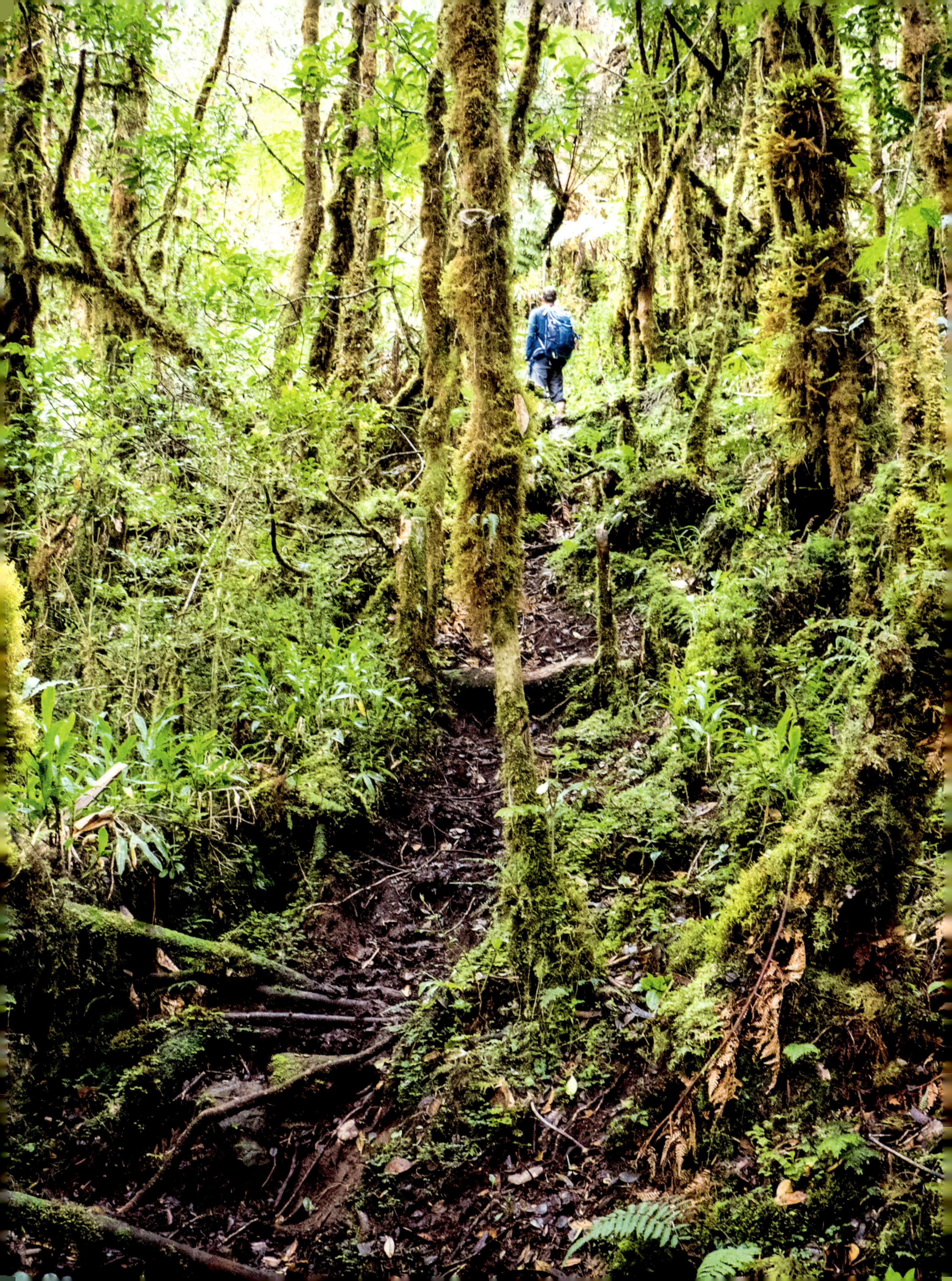

Just over 2000 miles to the west of New Guinea, the Indonesian island Sumatra may have seen the biggest volcanic eruption in human history. According to a theory, the eruption of Toba some 74,000 years ago may have brought humanity to the brink of extinction.

but blocked out the sunlight altogether. Only the most daring sunbeam would make its way through the morass above us and pick out a fern, a bit of rough tree bark or a patch of moss, as if to give them an opportunity to show off their exceptional beauty. None of this seemed familiar—the woods I had come to know in Germany were so well-planned and maintained, they almost looked like a spotless, tidy apartment in comparison. Spellbound, I continued to admire the thick moss that covered almost every tree like a soft cloak. "Softer than a unicorn, my daughter would say," I mused. "Or should that be: softer than a large, hairy spider?"

Of course, spiders are indeed a common occurrence here in the jungle, but at our current height of 6500 feet, there were no poisonous animals or predators—nor were there mosquitoes which could spread malaria. The same cannot be said for the Sepik River in the lowlands, however. It has one of the highest water discharges in the world—second only to the Amazon and the Congo. In the swamp and jungle regions around the Sepik River, the risk of contracting malaria is the highest in the world. Yet malaria is not the only danger looming in the lowlands: the cone snail produces a neurotoxin which in large doses can be lethal for humans. In smaller doses, it is used as a painkiller which is stronger than morphine. Furthermore, the taipan, a snake which can reach two to three metres in length, produces a toxin which is considered to be one of the most powerful found in nature. Once bitten, there is almost no chance of survival without the antivenom. Due to the jungle's overgrown paths and impenetrable growth, it can take hours or days for the victim to reach a doctor. The bite itself is swift and painless; often the victims do not realize they have been bitten until paralysis begins to set in. At that point, it is usually too late.

"At any rate, it is far softer than a poisonous snake," I finish my musings about the moss. Our current altitude has another advantage: earlier, in the lowlands, our damp clothes had been sticking to our moist skin, but up here on the mountain, even heavy tropical rain felt like a fresh, pleasant shower.

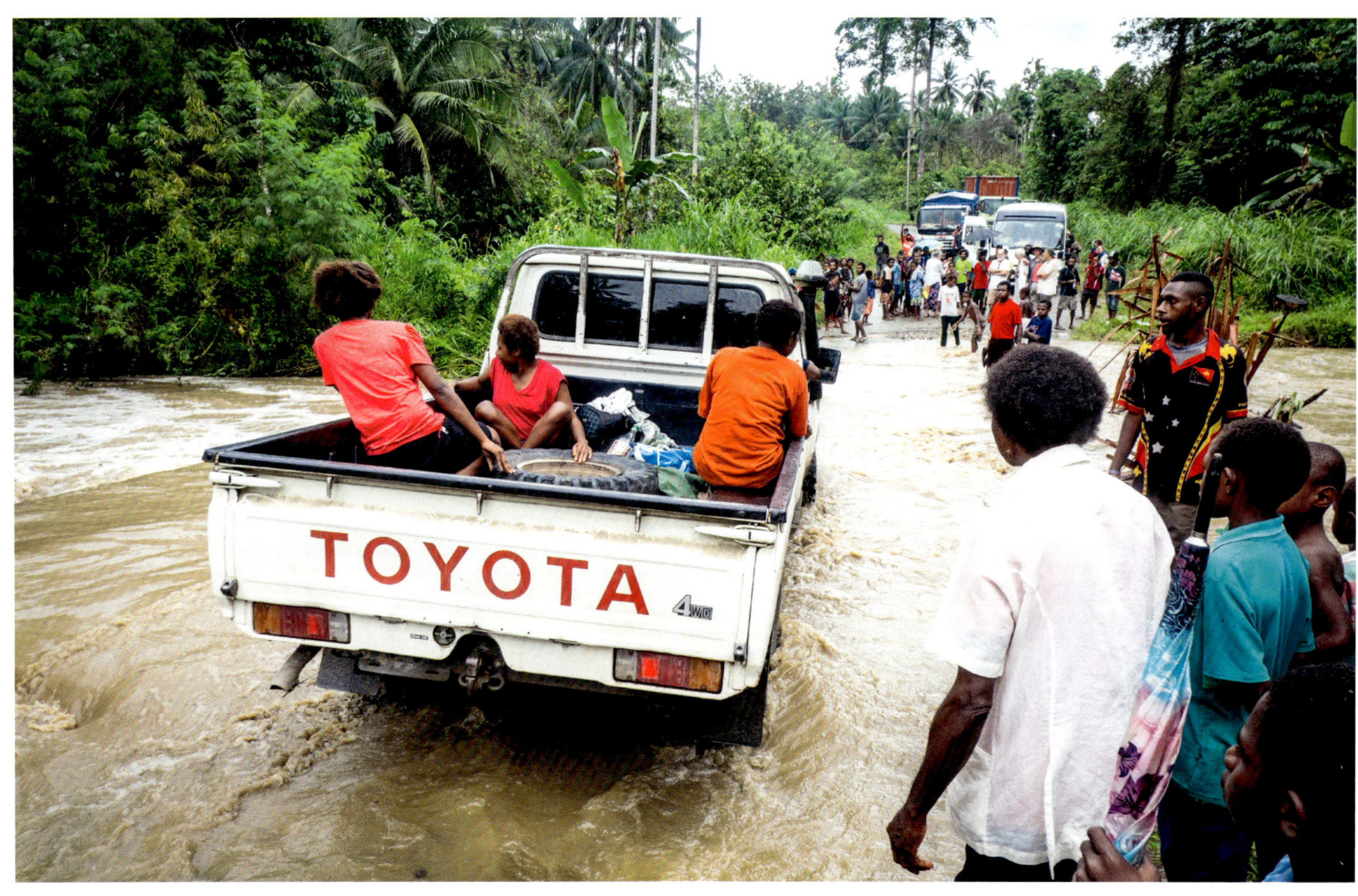

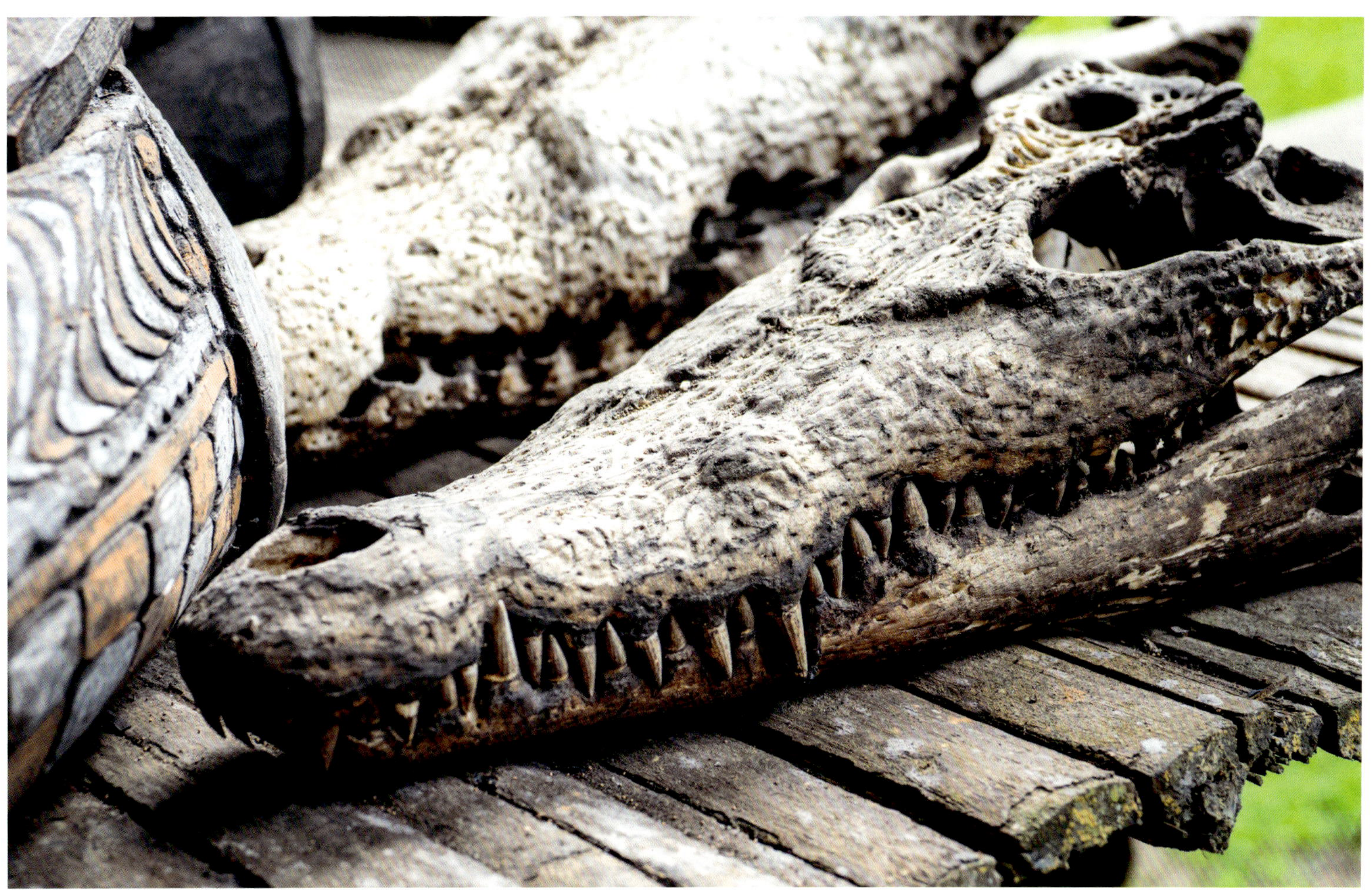

I walked through this unfamiliar world gaping at everything with a child's sense of wonder. I could not get enough of this lush vegetation, the countless shades of green that kept shifting and changing. Yet it was not merely the colors and the shapes that captivated me—I felt like I was breathing in life, evolution, diversity.

"Jurassic World," I mumbled to myself when I heard a sudden, shrill bird call. "Probably a velociraptor," I said jokingly, but one of our guides whispered: "That's a bird-of-paradise. If we keep quiet and don't move, it might come close enough for us to catch a glimpse." The bird-of-paradise is the national bird of Papua New Guinea, which became an independent state in 1975 and lies on the eastern half of New Guinea Island, the second largest island in the world. The western half of the island, Papua, is a province of Indonesia.

During my preparations for the journey to Mount Giluwe, I had read many accounts of this beautiful and extraordinary bird. Its golden plumage is said to make jewels pale in comparison. The feathers around its neck have a dark, metallic shine, and its long, cascading red tail feathers burn like fire in the jungle's darkness.

Yet only the males of the species are this attractive. Over thousands of years, evolution has given them an increasingly beautiful plumage with which to impress potential mates. To date, 39 species of this skittish bird that prefers to hide deep in the jungle, have been found. They are so well-hidden that the ornithologist Edwin Scholes and the photographer Tim Laman undertook a total of 18 expeditions, spent over 2000 hours spent in camouflage tents, and it took more than 39,000 photographs to find and document each individual species. Of course, we do not have as much time as they did. We stop for a moment and wait for the bird to appear—but after a while, we have to give up and continue our journey.

> I walked through this unfamiliar world gaping at everything with a child's sense of wonder.

The theory goes on to state that during Toba's supervolcanic eruption, an amount of energy equivalent to the explosion of one gigaton of TNT was released, and the Indian subcontinent was covered in eight inches of ash. Subsequently, the earth's surface temperature dropped by over 5.4 degrees.

"They're really beautiful, and very tasty," my local guide informs us, which gives me a bit of a start. "Tasty?" I double check if I heard right. "I thought they were a protected species?" He shrugs and continues to describe in detail how to hunt for this bird with bow and arrow as well as how to gut and fillet it, and which parts are edible. He is pretty sure it is not illegal.

"Black Magic Exists"

Many guidebooks describe Papua New Guinea as one of the last frontiers of the known world. In the past, some writers have described its rudimentary infrastructure, and painted its inhabitants as wild, uncivilized, and dangerous. Myths and customs have been kept alive here for hundreds of years.

More than 50,000 years ago, people began to settle in New Guinea. In the 16th century, European explorers arrived on the island. Yet the climate, the wildlife, and the local customs—at the time, cannibalism was widespread—slowed and ultimately stopped any attempts to explore the heart of the island.

First contact between the inland tribes and the outer world was established in the 1930s. It is assumed that even today, in some parts of the island that are difficult to access, there may be groups of people and tribes who have never been in contact with the outside world. As a result of this isolation, the traditional way of life has been preserved on the island. Even the most zealous of missionaries have not been able to change that.

As William's machete came down on soft lianas and hard tree bark, he explained: "About 96 percent of people in Papua New Guinea are Christians but over time, Christian rituals and traditional religious or magic rites all merged into one." We continued on our path, climbing over fallen tree trunks and ducking under mossy branches. "Here on New Guinea we have about 1000 different tribes speaking about 800 different languages. And of course, black magic exists here, too." He opens his eyes wide and stares at me for effect.

"Black magic exists," he repeated several times. His father had taught him how to defend himself against it, he said. "I believe my father, I believe in black magic."

There was fascination mixed with resolution and a hint of fear in his eyes. We had stopped and he continued to look at me. His eyes were so dark, I could barely make out his pupils, and I found it difficult to hold his gaze. His look was piercing—I felt like he could see right through me, and in turn I felt like I could see into his soul, into the soul of the age-old, uncompromised culture of his people.

"Black magic exists," he murmured one last time. At that moment, I was completely convinced that there are many things in this world which we in our Western culture, that puts so much emphasis on analytical, scientific knowledge, will never be able to truly understand. "Black magic exists."

A Symphony in the Grasslands

We had been hiking for more than four hours. While the rainforest had lost nothing of its fascination, the trekking had lost most of its fun. I felt as if I had slipped on a million wet roots and landed on my back at least a dozen times. Our guides were trekking in sandals or simply barefoot. I found this strange at first, but the longer we had been hiking, the more sense it made to me: the sandal's soft soles were much better suited to walking on the uneven, moist and often slippery ground. The soles of my hard hiking boots kept slipping in such conditions.

"I wouldn't mind if we got out of this jungle soon," I whispered to Peter after I stumbled and nearly fell over yet again. "Two hours ago they said we'd be reaching the grasslands soon."

Yet we were not to reach them for another hour. When we did reach the grasslands, the transition happened abruptly: almost without noticing it, we stepped out of the jungle and into a broad valley. In front of us, ground covered in yellow mounds of grass stretched as far as the eye could see. Of course, the grass here had little in common with the lawns we knew from back home in Germany. It grew up to our knees or sometimes as far as our hips, was lighter in color, and thicker than what we were used to. Later, as we started our summit ascent, we used it to

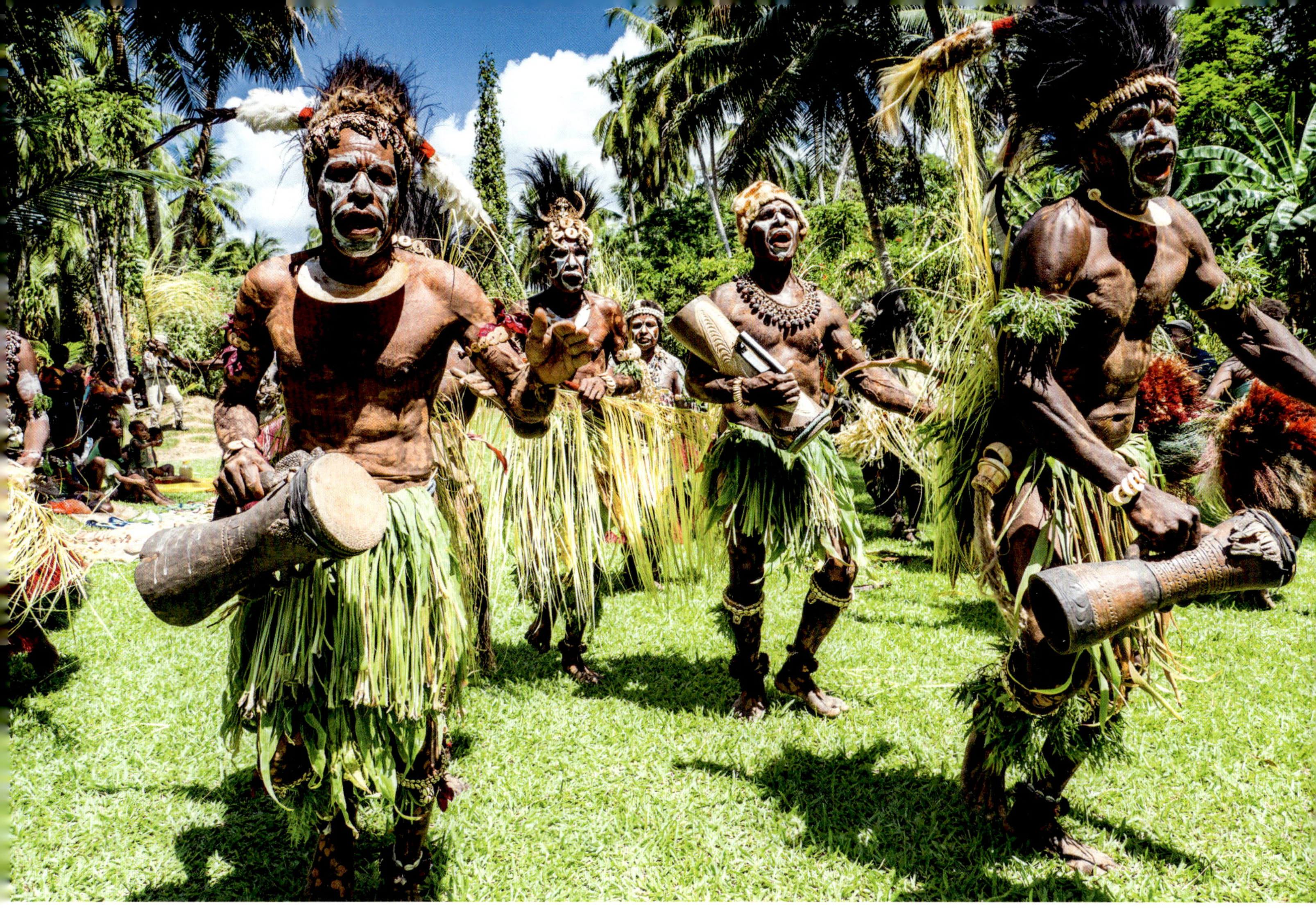

pull ourselves up the steeper slopes. Each of the clumps had the diameter of a large tractor tire. The plain looked as if it were covered in giant molehills. Thus, unfortunately, we were disappointed to find that the terrain was no easier on our feet than the jungle floor. The ground was just as uneven as it had been in the jungle, and our progress was interrupted by twisted ankles, stumbling, and boots getting caught in grass.

We made our way through the valley towards an imposing mountain flanked by hills and jungle. Occasionally, we came across ferns which were taller than us, and huge palm trees. The path led us to a small river which was burbling happily in this beautiful countryside. I felt like nature was playing a symphony just for me: the river's murmur, the grassland's whisper, and the sound of the wind. We had been invited to a festival for all the senses, or so it felt.

> Each of the clumps had the diameter of a large tractor tire.

"Isn't this wonderful?" I asked Peter. I was overcome by a deep sense of quiet and calm. After another three hours of hiking, a mountain could be seen from behind several palm trees. It was clouded in mist and the only part of it that was clearly visible was its craggy summit. It almost felt as if we were in a ghost story. The grassland made me think of ancient myths and tales.

"See the mountain up there?" William asked me, suddenly alert and nervous. His voice was shaking. "It's called Dog Living Stone and it's forbidden ground," he continued, his voice now lowered almost to a whisper. "You mustn't get too close to it. A large dog lives there. Half of it is a dog, the other half of it has been burnt by Mount Giluwe a long time ago. If you can hear its bark, your family will experience great misfortune. If you see it, you will drop dead immediately."

Even though the Papuan people only constitute about 0.1 percent of the world's population, roughly 15 percent of the world's languages are Papuan languages.

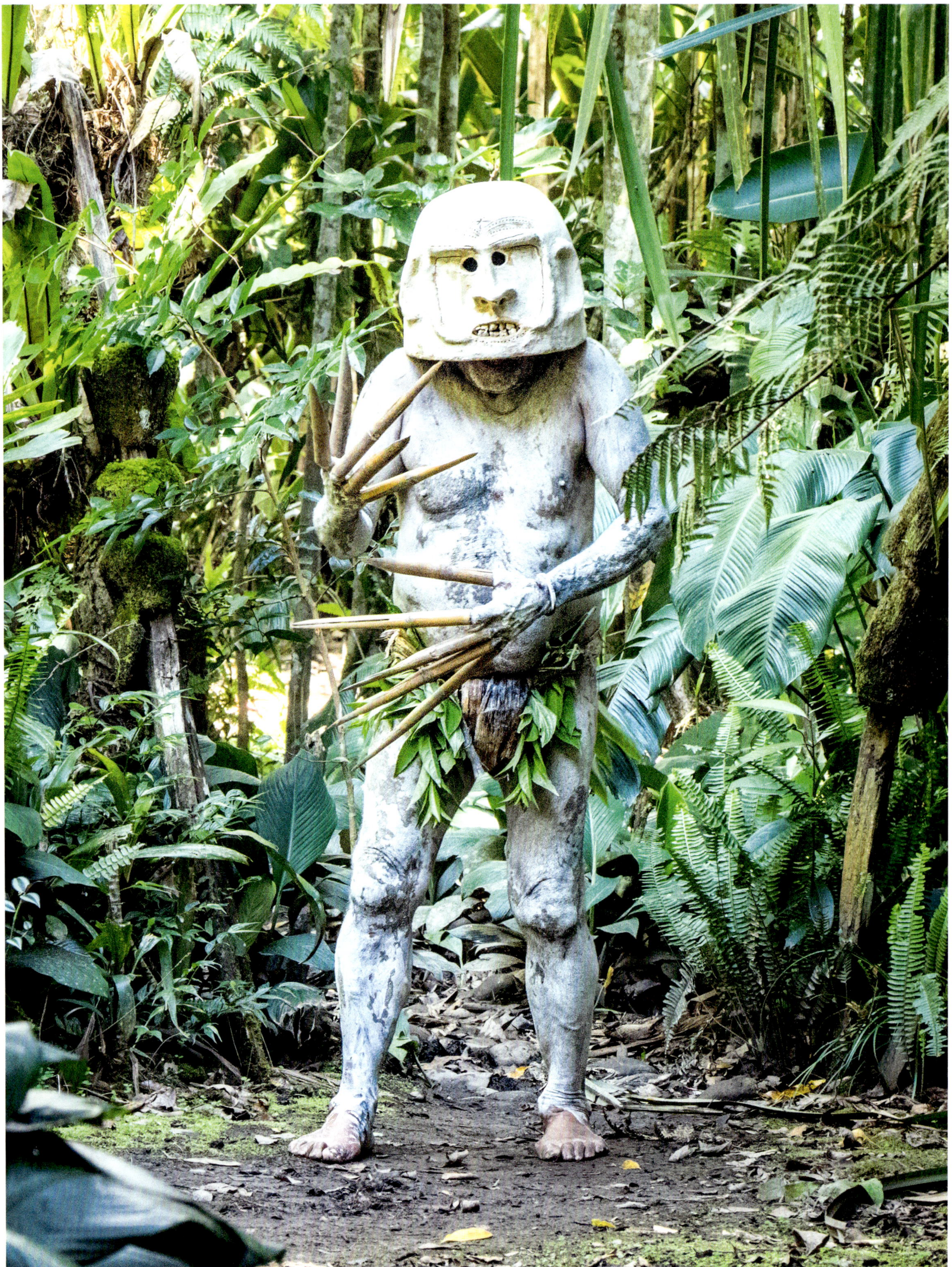

Friday, August 10th,

For me, this dazzling green country was love at
first sight. I'm beginning to realize one thing:
Our Western society is increasingly dependent on
technology—a dangerous obsession. Actually,
I believe that cultures and societies that live
closer to nature than we do have a kind of knowledge
we can only dream of acquiring: they respect the
environment and treat it with humility; they live
in harmony with nature rather than trying
to conquer it. It is just as the volcanoes have
taught us: In the history of the universe,
human history is but a wink.

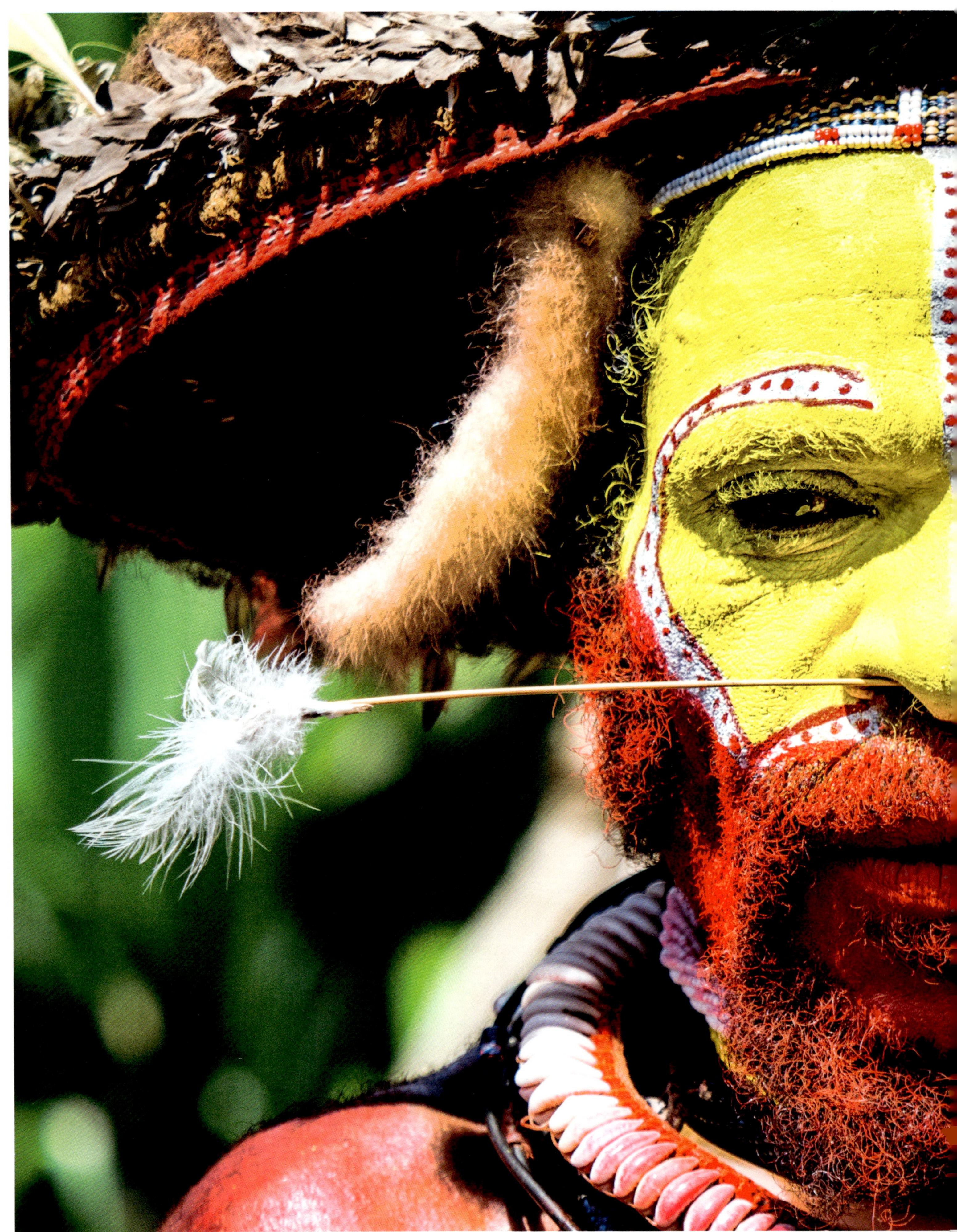

Mount Giluwe | Papua New Guinea _________ 178

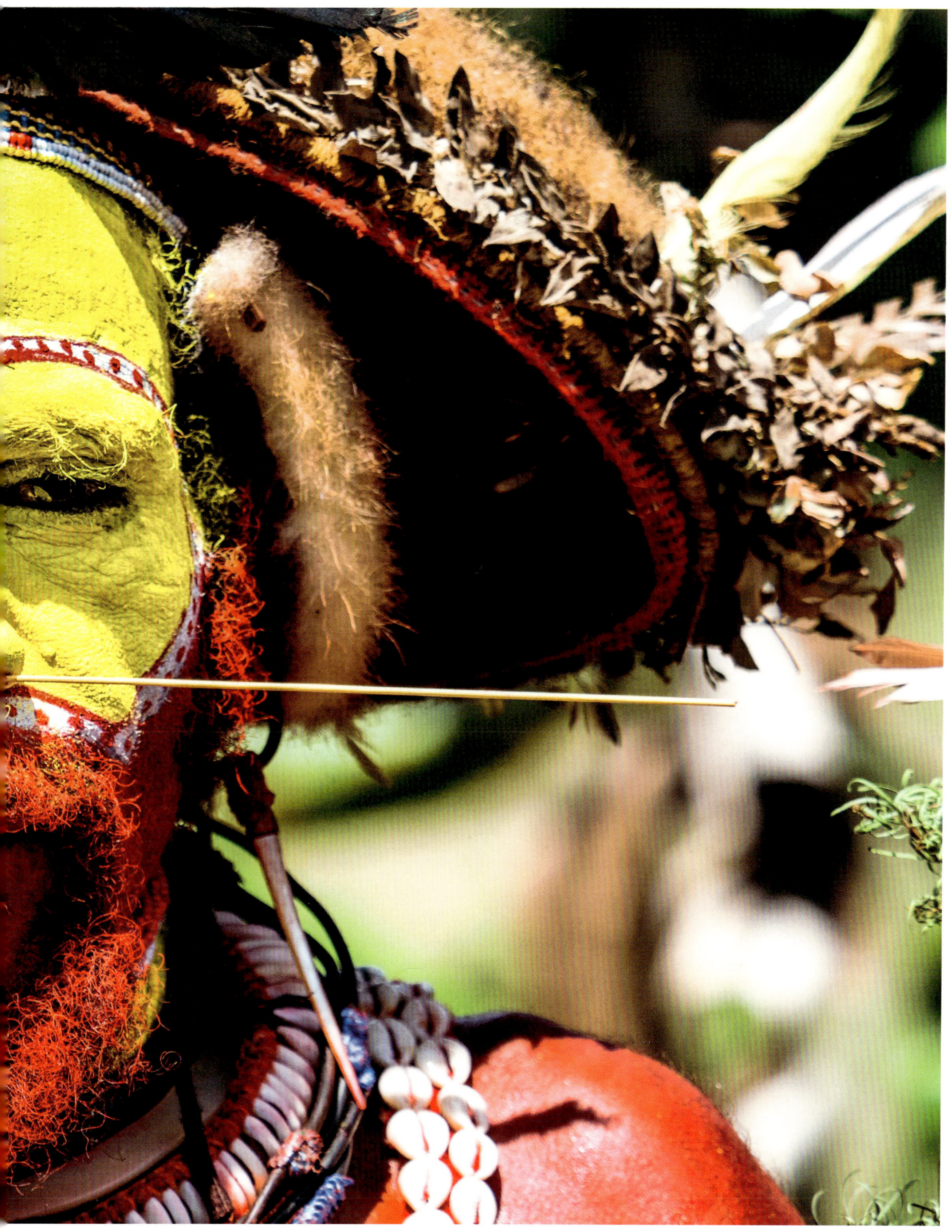

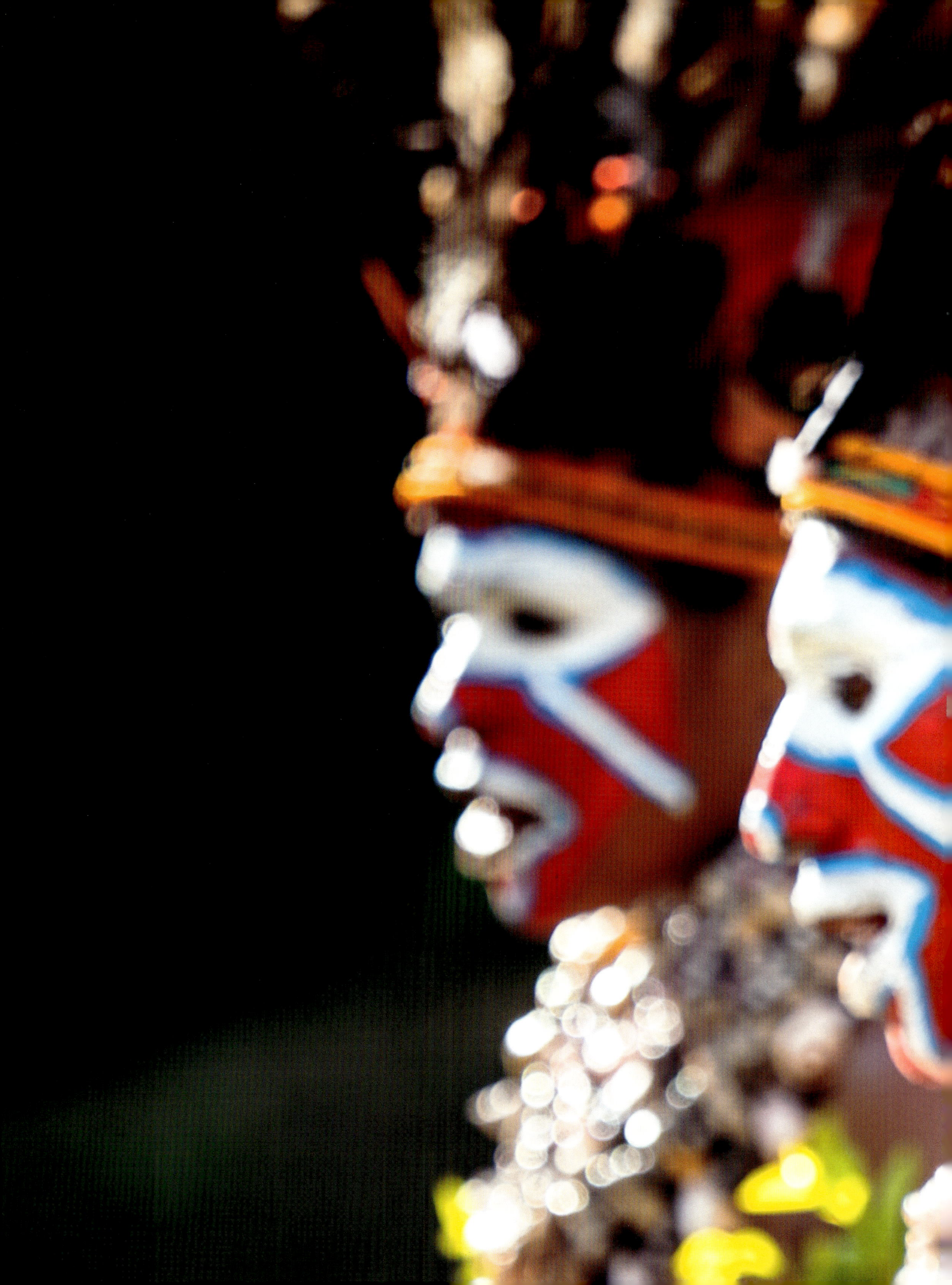

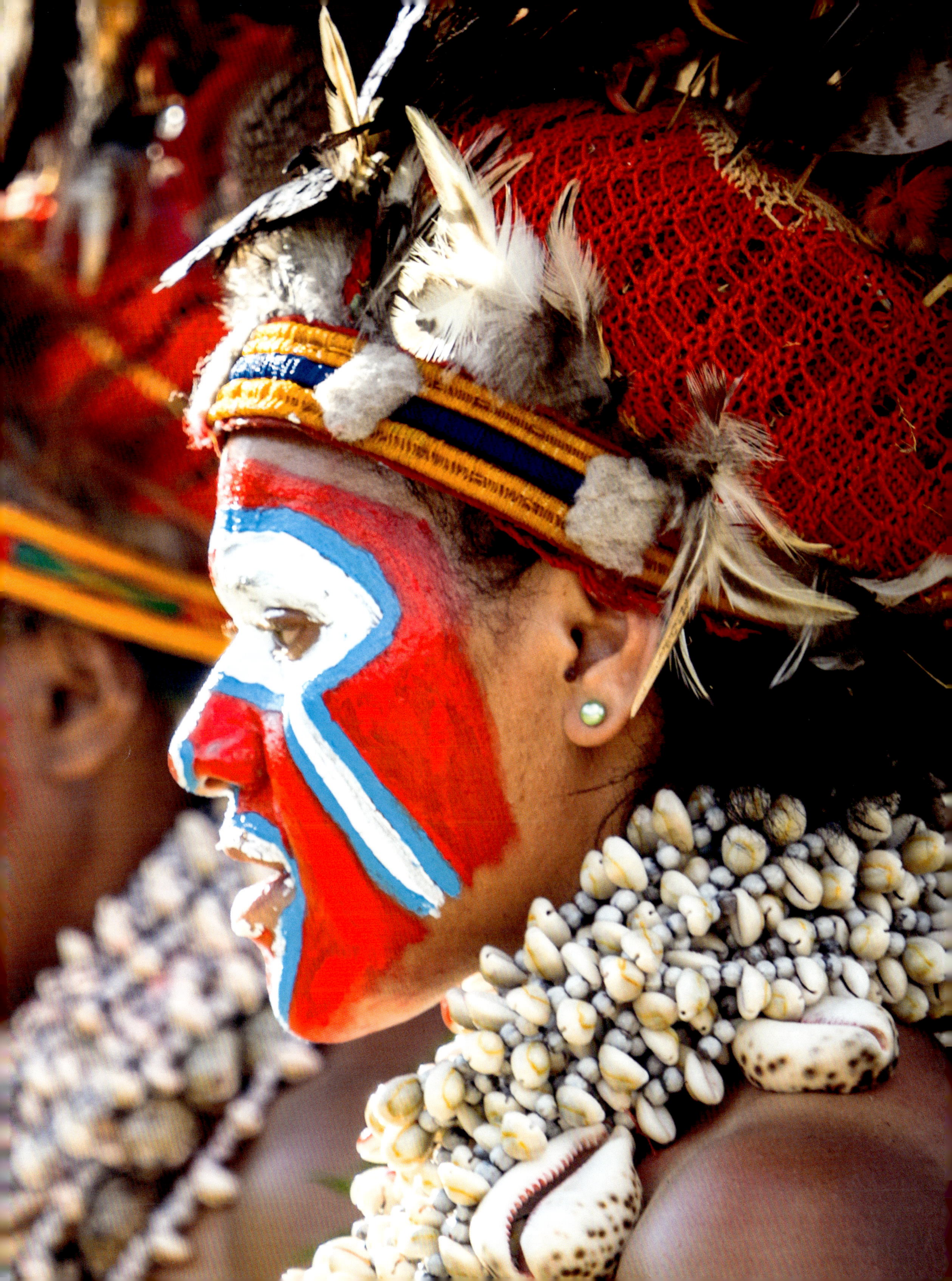

Much as this story sounded strange and out of this world, I felt a cold shiver run down my spine as soon as William finished his tale. I averted my gaze from the mountain.

I was burning to hear more about the story of Dog Living Stone, but William had already turned around and marched on, one hand against the side of his face to block his view of the mountain. I, too, did not dare to cast more than a fleeting glance over to Dog Living Stone and was strangely relieved when it disappeared behind a wall of clouds.

Generally speaking, I am a very analytical person, but here, in these surroundings, even I felt like anything was possible—even a tale as foreign-sounding as this might contain a grain of truth.

There is in fact a type of dingo that is native to the highlands around Mount Giluwe about which little information exists. Its exact habitat is not known—in fact, even proof of its existence in the wild is scarce. If I ever return to Mount Giluwe, I will be sure to bring camera traps and try to capture one of those elusive creatures on film.

"Wind of Change"

That night, we set up our small camp not far from the foot of Mount Giluwe. What a view it offered! Lit by the setting sun, it was the perfect image. I could not believe my luck. And even better—the glowing summit was reflected in a small pond amidst the tall grass. It was truly magical. No wonder this was the birthplace of so many myths and legends.

Slowly the shadows came creeping towards us from the mountains and over to our tents —and with them came the cold. At an altitude of roughly 12,000 feet, the nights here can get extremely cold, even in a country that is as close to the equator as Papua New Guinea. During the day I had been enjoying the mild temperatures and could not imagine the nights would get as cold as I'd been led to believe. I had not thought it possible during the daytime, but now I was glad I had brought my hat,

The world's third largest expanse of continuous rainforest is in New Guinea —only the Amazon and the Congo rainforests are larger. It is home to several isolated native tribes who do not seek contact with the outside world.

gloves, and thick down jacket to wear at night. Our guides had been constructing a makeshift kitchen tent from several tree trunks and a large tarpaulin. Over the past few hours they had been gathering large amounts of firewood in a nearby forest. And so, when all was prepared we sat together around a large fire. The mood was relaxed; the fire's red and yellow flames were dancing in the dark and casting strange shapes on the tarpaulin. The firewood was crackling so loudly, it sounded like the small explosions of popcorn kernels in a hot kettle.

Our cook was heaving another large, black cast iron pot full of water onto the fire to make more tea for the party. I began chatting to Augustine, one of our local guides. Throughout our conversation he was chewing on a betel nut. His black, pointed teeth and his dark red lips confirmed to me that he consumed this drug, which is popular and widespread in large parts of Asia, with some regularity. Just like tobacco, the nut has a stimulating yet simultaneously numbing effect. While he was still chewing, he lit a cigarette which he had rolled himself, using tobacco and a page from an old newspaper. It was difficult to say what would be the unhealthiest element of this indulgence: the tobacco, the burning ink, or the betel nut?

He was still chewing and exhaling smoke as he told me he was worried about the future of his country. "Each year, over 70,000 tourists visit our country. How can we preserve and practice our tradition and rites? How can we prevent them from turning into nothing but a cheap show for tourists?" He looked at me questioningly. "How can we stop rural depopulation, and solve the larger cities' many issues—alcohol, drugs, violence?" I was still pondering what he had just told me when he added: "I haven't given up hope though. Do you know what I see as the symbol for hope—hope for my country's future and its freedom?" I did not know what he meant and was very surprised when it was revealed to me. For instead of explaining it, Augustine began to sing the chorus to *Wind of Change* by the Scorpions:

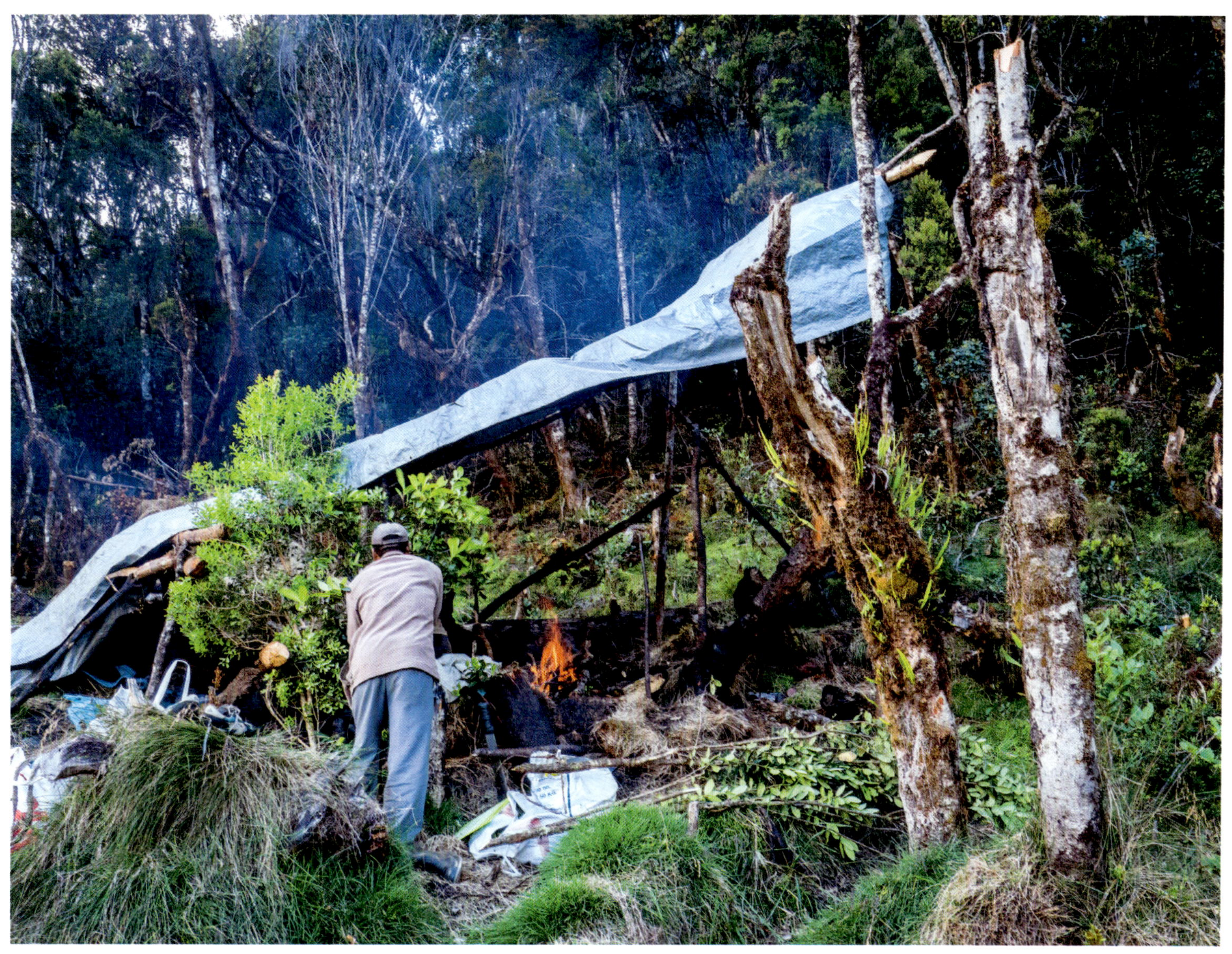

His voice resounded over the dark grasslands. It was strange yet comforting.

That night, it took me a long time to fall asleep in my sleeping bag. For one, our local tour guides were telling each other stories and laughing loudly, as if they were determined to make enough noise to scare away the Living Dog which could pounce from the darkness at any point. But yet another reason kept me awake: the lines Augustine had sung from the *Wind of Change* were stuck in my head.

Due to lack of accessibility and the resulting isolation, many ethnic groups in Papua New Guinea have been able to maintain their historic traditions, beliefs, and rituals to this day. Few other places in the world have succeeded in supporting the preservation of indigenous culture to a similar extent.

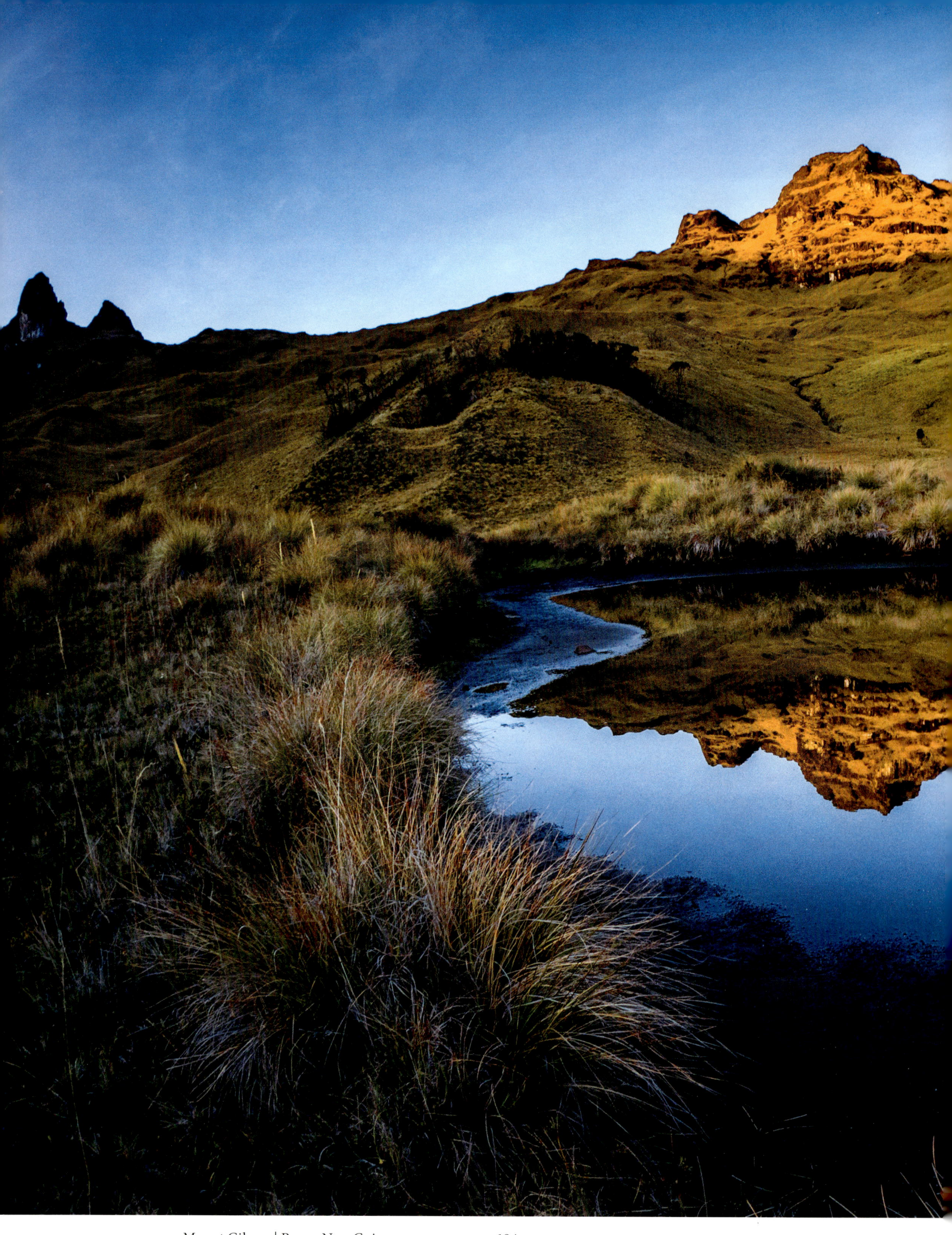

Mount Giluwe | Papua New Guinea _____________ 184

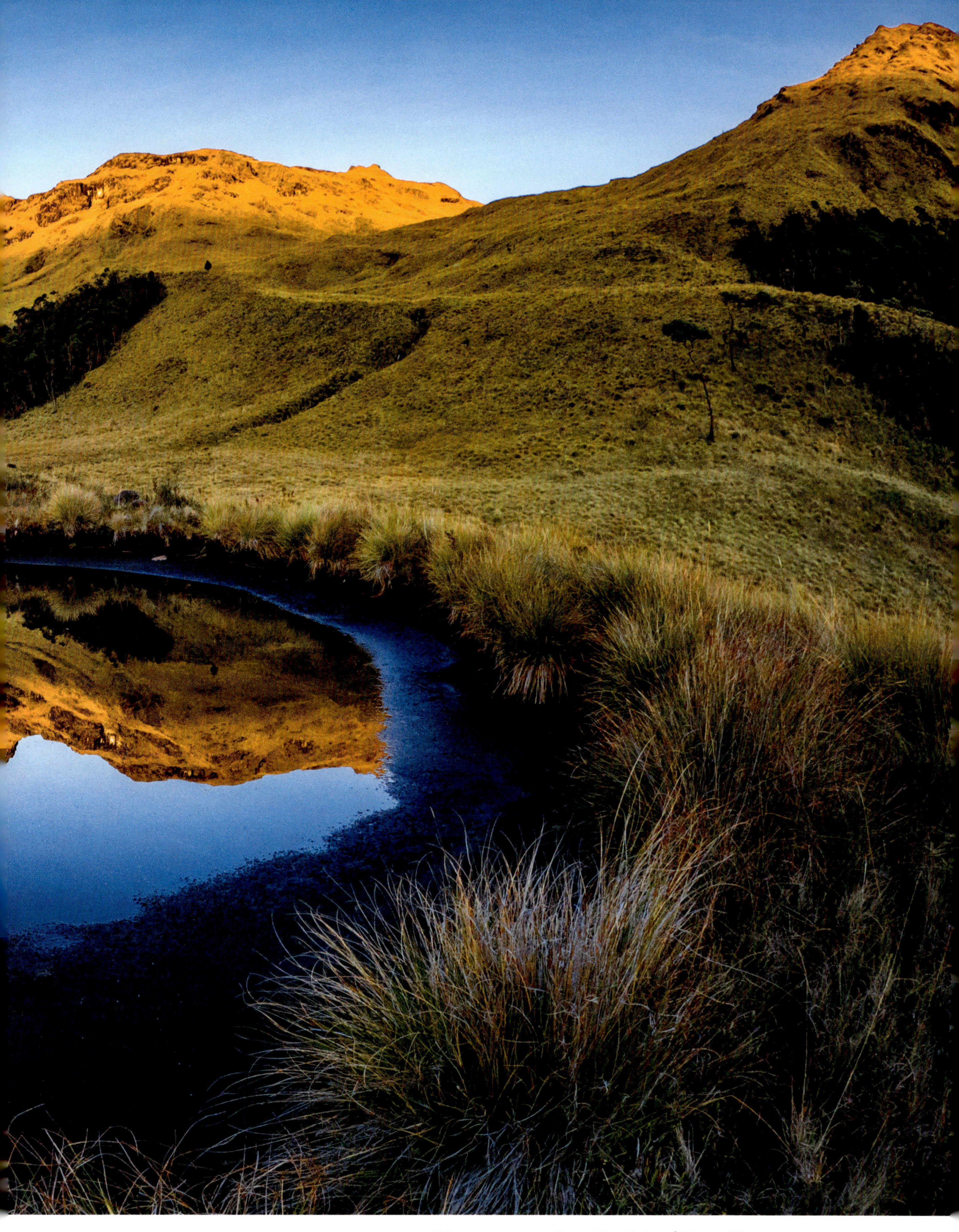

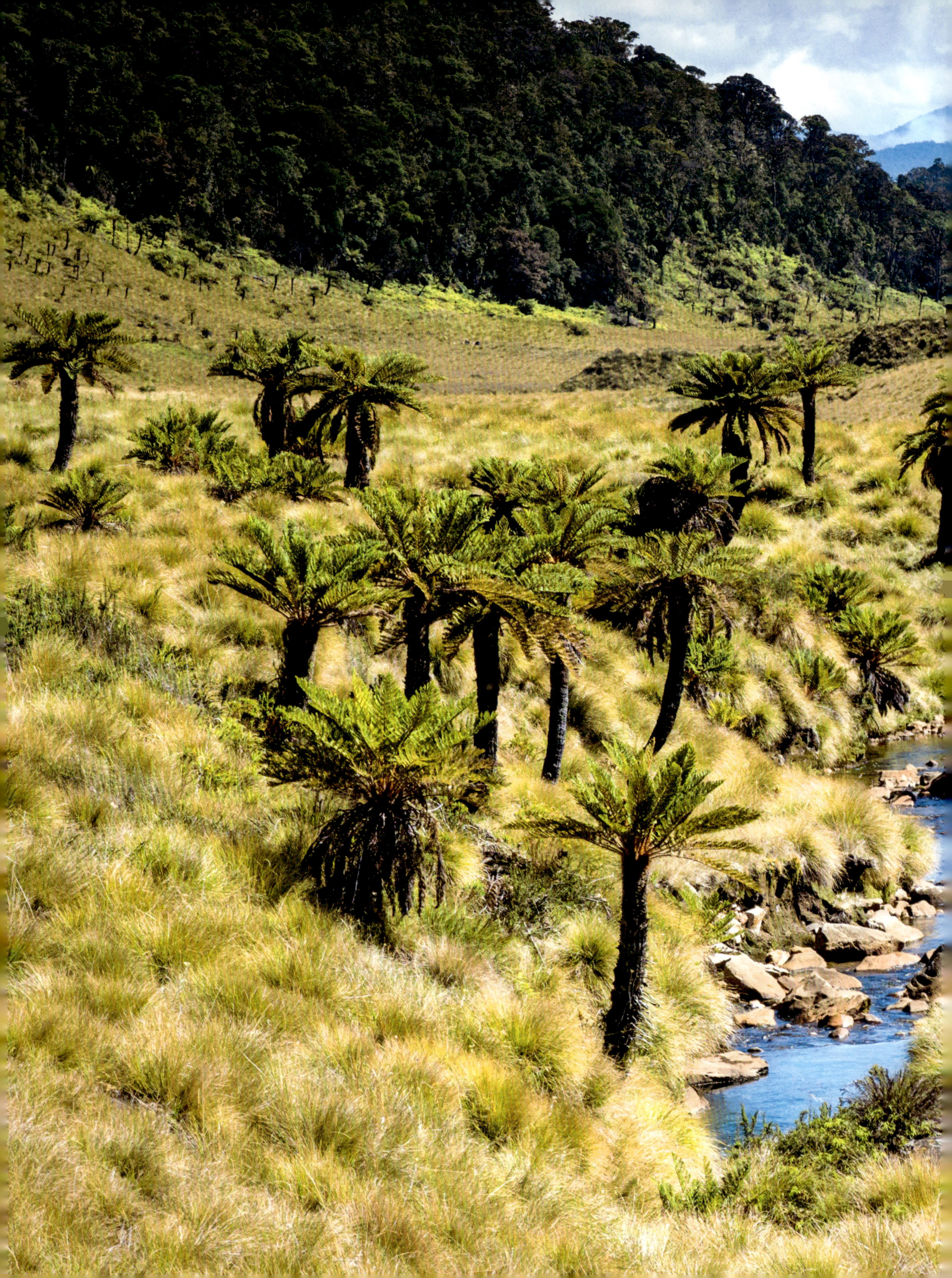

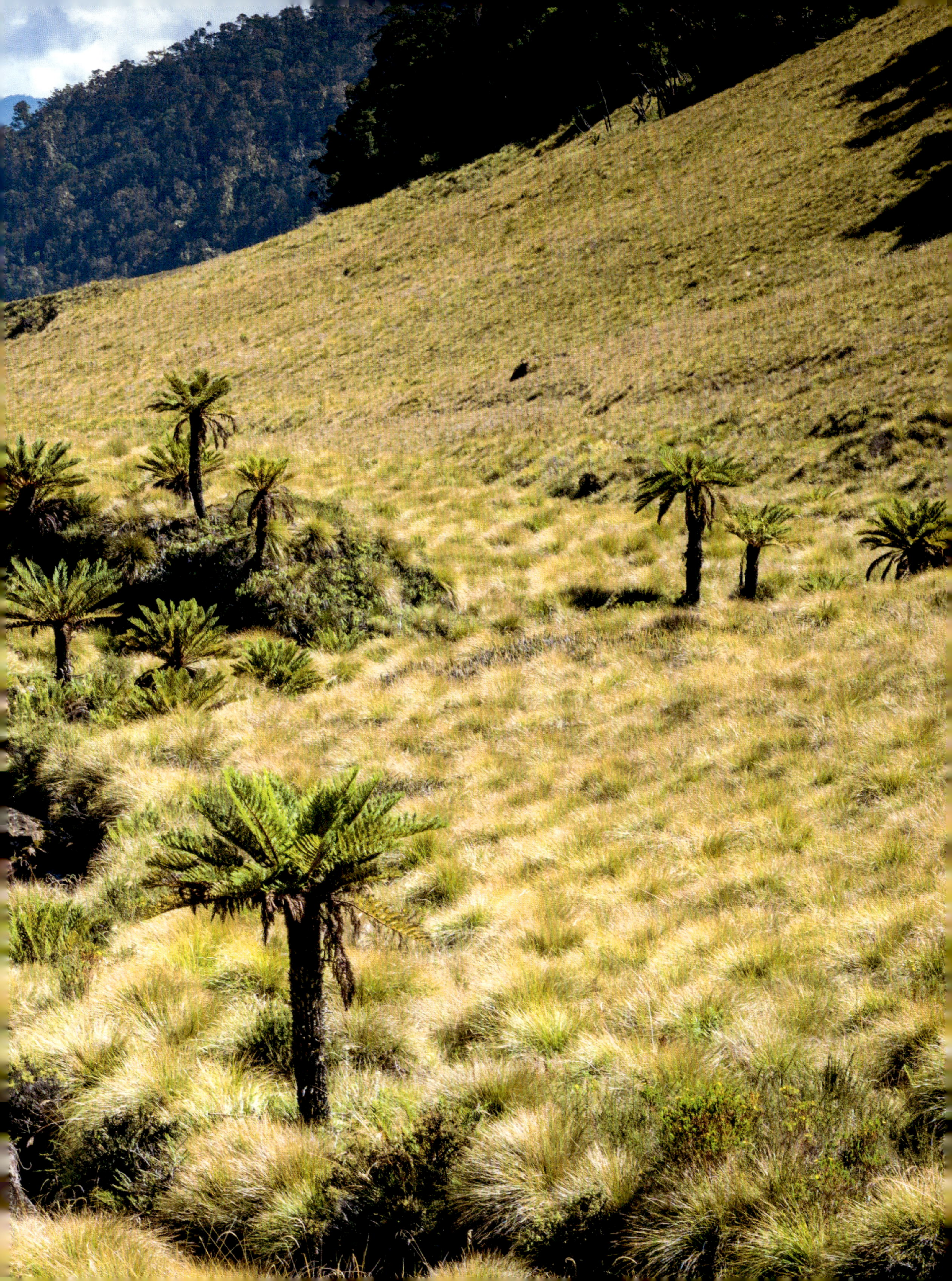

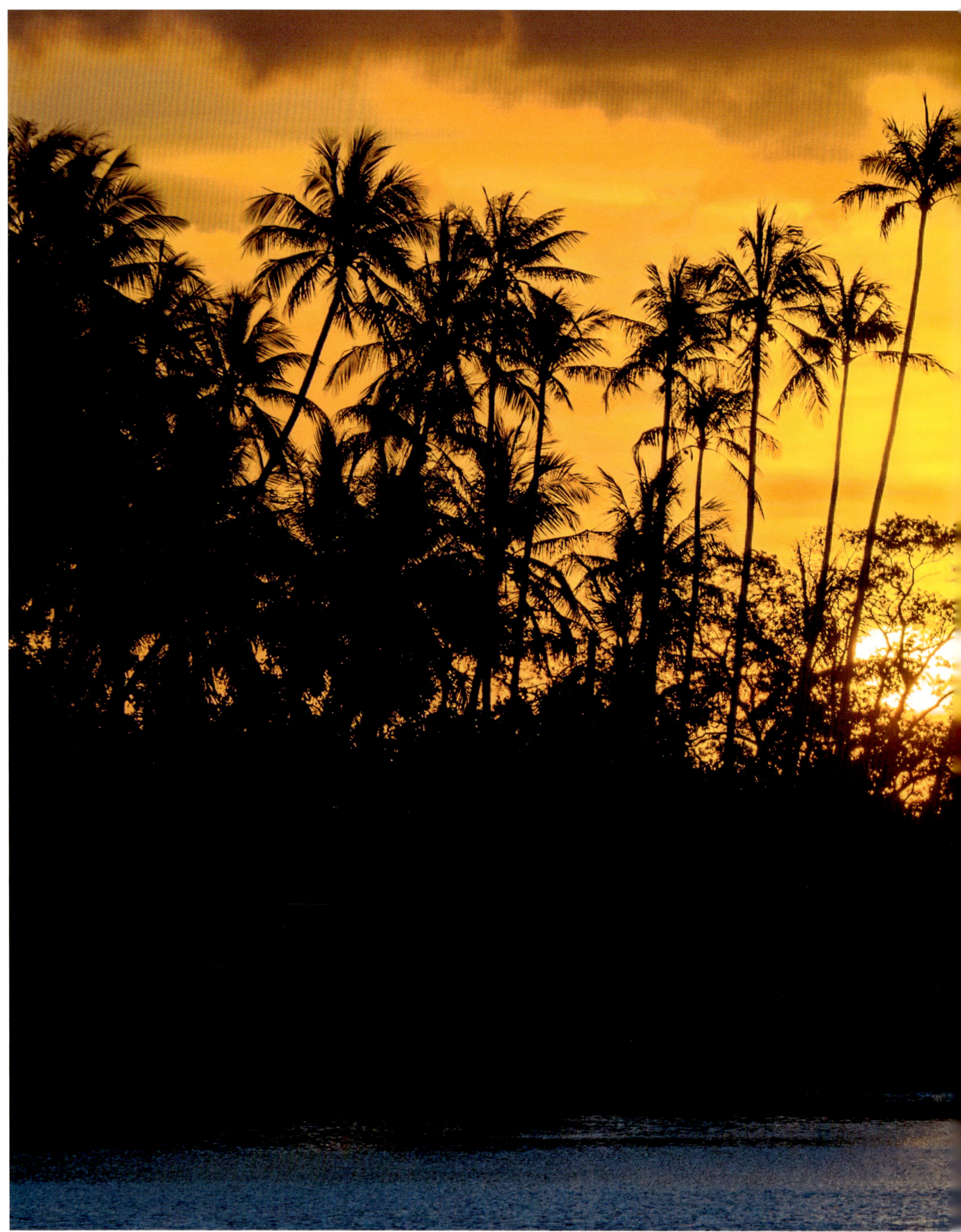

Mount Giluwe | Papua New Guinea _____________ 188

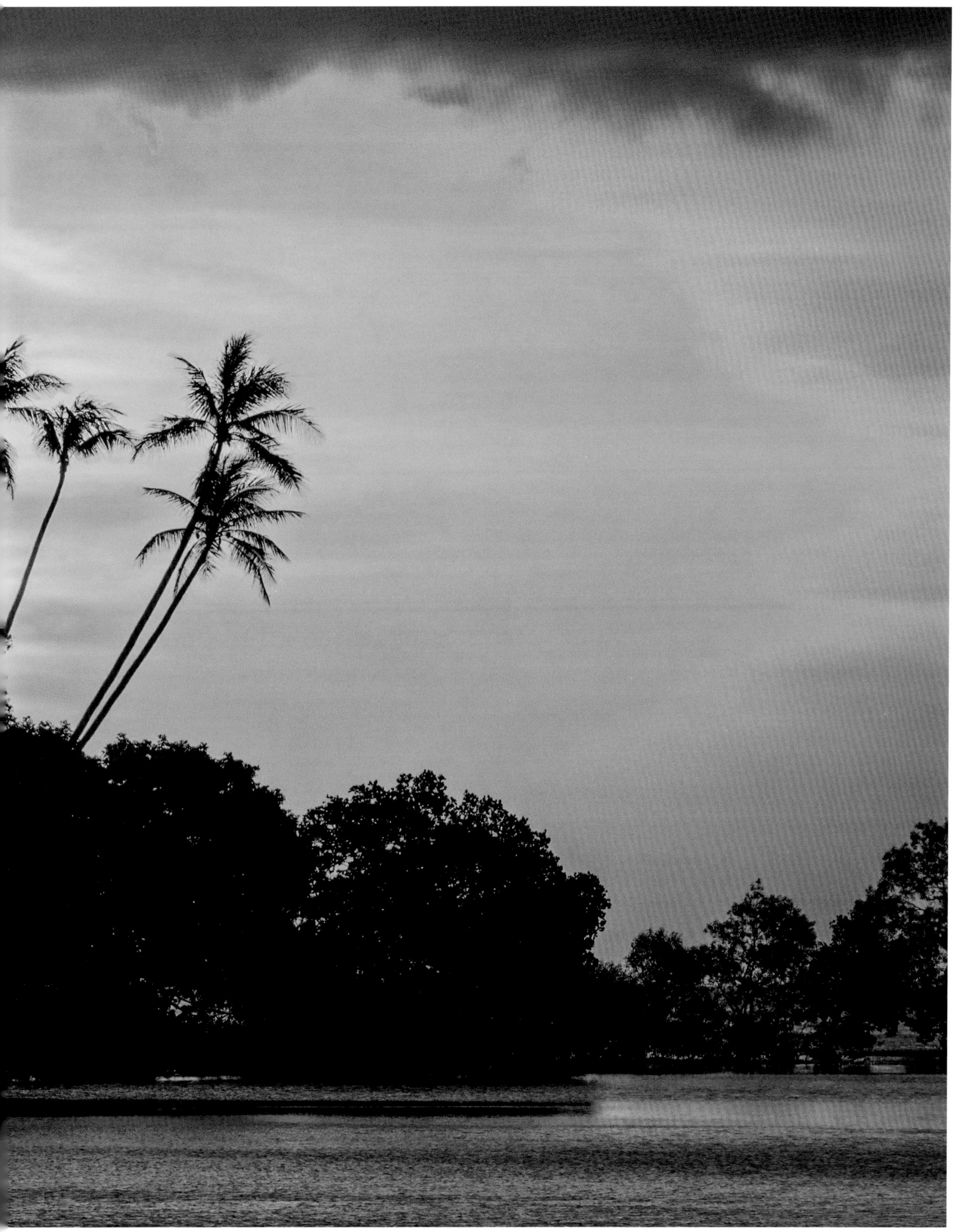

"Immortal"

Seven months prior to my trip to Antarctica, I had been standing on top of Mount Fuji in Japan. While I was taking the obligatory selfies at the silver summit beside the crater's wide gaping mouth, I met a Japanese mountaineer, Saito-san, and we struck up a conversation. Although we were at almost 12,400 feet of altitude, he was wearing a thin, brown-checkered shirt, dark sunglasses and an oversized safari hat. Yet Saito-san was anything but inexperienced; on the contrary, he was perfectly acclimatized: in his broken English, he told me that he had climbed Mount Fuji 650 times. I could hardly believe it, but he told me he was going to come back and climb it again the following day. What was even more incredible, though, was the fact that—as he went on to explain—having climbed the holy mountain, he was to become immortal. He did not grace my jovial question about whether he would now become immortal 650 times with a reply.

My own mortality was put to the test just a few days later when a Japanese friend of mine invited me to try Fugu, the poisonous pufferfish that is a famous delicacy in Japan. The round little fish looks rather cute, and it really is very delicious, but it can also be deadly—prepared wrong, its poison can permeate the entire dish and rapidly kill the person eating it. It is so difficult to prepare that even in famous Fugu-serving restaurants, accidents are not unheard of. We were lucky, though, and we got to enjoy a fantastic non-poisonous five course Fugu meal – the fact that I had the opportunity to write these lines should serve as proof. I lived to tell the tale, so to speak.

So I was to be immortal now. That may have worked to my advantage during the adventures that were, at the time, still lying ahead of me, for they were going to take me to my personal limits and beyond—the Volcanic Seven Summits. It may be the only way to embark on such a project:

Fugu, a type of pufferfish, produces one of the most lethal poisons in the animal kingdom. One microgram of this toxin is enough to kill a human. The toxin leads to complete paralysis of all muscles—while the victim is still conscious.

That may have worked to my advantage during the adventures that were, at the time, still lying ahead of me, for they were going to take me to my personal limits and beyond.

Five journeys in 16 weeks.

Seven continents and cultures.

Enough air miles to take me around the entire globe.

More than 65,500 feet of altitude in cars, on skis, by foot, or on e-bikes.

Entering unchartered territory several times.

Making the memories of a lifetime.

I still struggle to grasp the incredibly magical moments that I was lucky enough to experience over the last two years. I travelled to a far away, alien planet in Antarctica; I did something nobody had done before me in Africa; I met my limits in Mexico; I conquered a landscape photographer's paradise in the Atacama Desert; I had an exclusive photoshoot with Mother Nature at Mount Elbrus; had Sachertorte in Tehran; and gained deep insights into true magic in the jungle in Papua New Guinea.

Time and again, people ask me about the single most impressive memory of the past two years—and time and again, I find this question extremely easy to answer. That single highlight, that single answer does not exist. It is much simpler than that: the answer to this question is the sum of all possible answers. It is the extraordinary variety of experiences I was lucky enough to have had on my travels: icy-white no-man's-land, a humid, green sea of plants, the ash-grey surface of the moon, born out of fire, the desert glowing with all the colors of the rainbow, the rolling hills and the craggy, sharp mountain ranges. The fascinating and thought-provoking range of cultures and individuals is just as memorable as

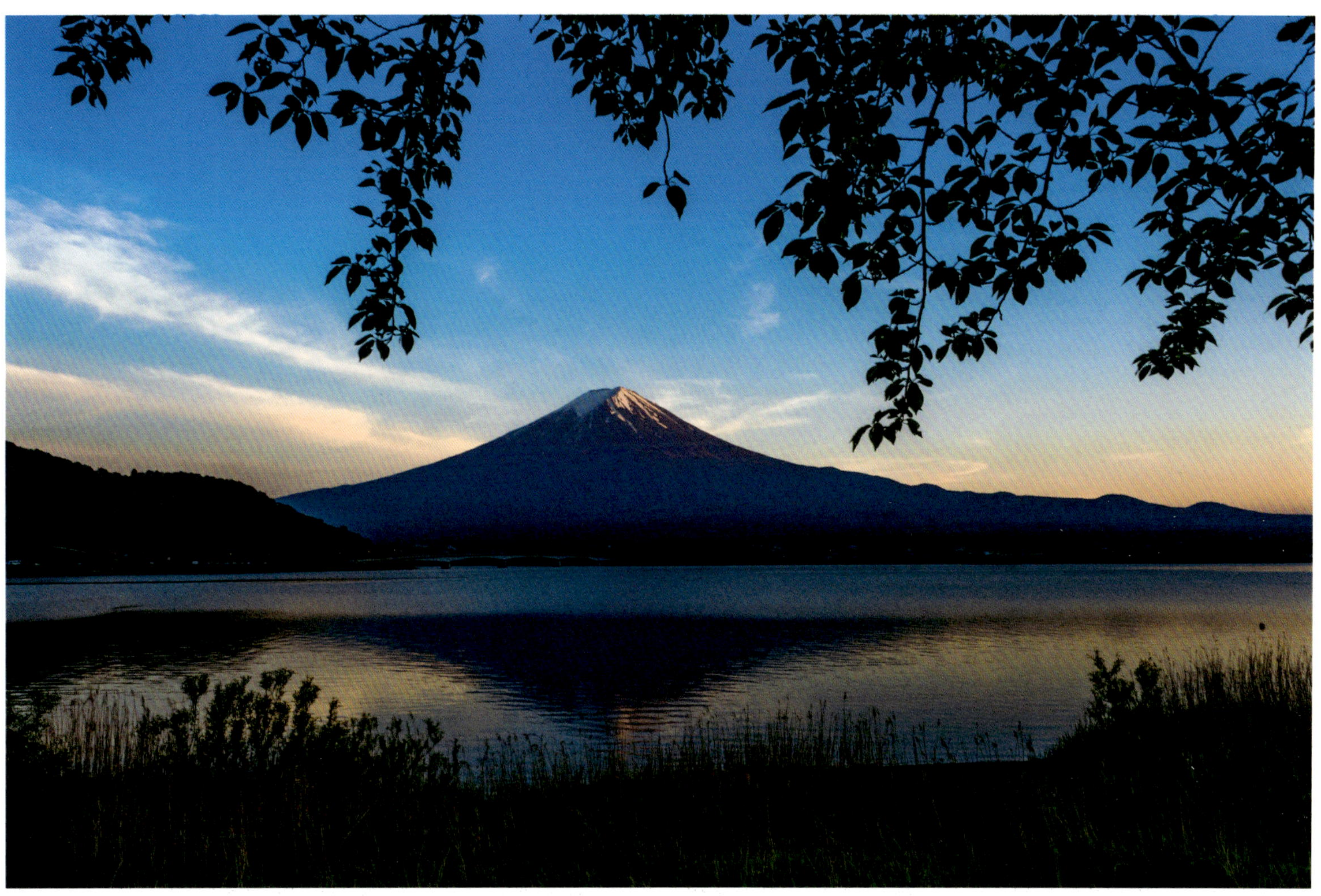

the landscapes: the magical, friendly locals, the Middle East which values hospitality above all else, Africa living resolutely in the moment, and fearless Russians who seem immune to the cold.

According to one scientific theory, we owe this variety of cultures and landscapes to volcanoes. The theory runs as follows: about 3.8 billion years ago, our planet was nothing but a huge ball of fire. On its surface, countless volcanoes were "sweating" out the primordial earth's atmosphere: vapor, carbon dioxide, hydrogen sulfide, ammonia, and methane. Through the addition of energy in the form of volcanic lightning, the first molecules were created in the midst of this primordial soup. Later, deep below the surface of the first oceans, these molecules turned into the first proteins, which are an essential part of every cell, from single-cell organisms to animals and plants. These, in turn, are the basis of the variety of landscapes and cultures I was able to experience on the seven continents. It has taught me two things: humility and caution.

We must be humble and respectful in the face of this miracle of nature. We must treat nature with care—for all we know, we only have this one planet. We must urgently start to protect and care for it. It is crucial that we learn to understand different cultures as an enriching, not a threatening experience. After all, I hope that my children, your children, and the generation after them will have the opportunity to experience our planet in all its glory, and that they, too, may get to live their dreams of exploration.

I may not be immortal but my love for this planet, our extraordinary earth, certainly is.

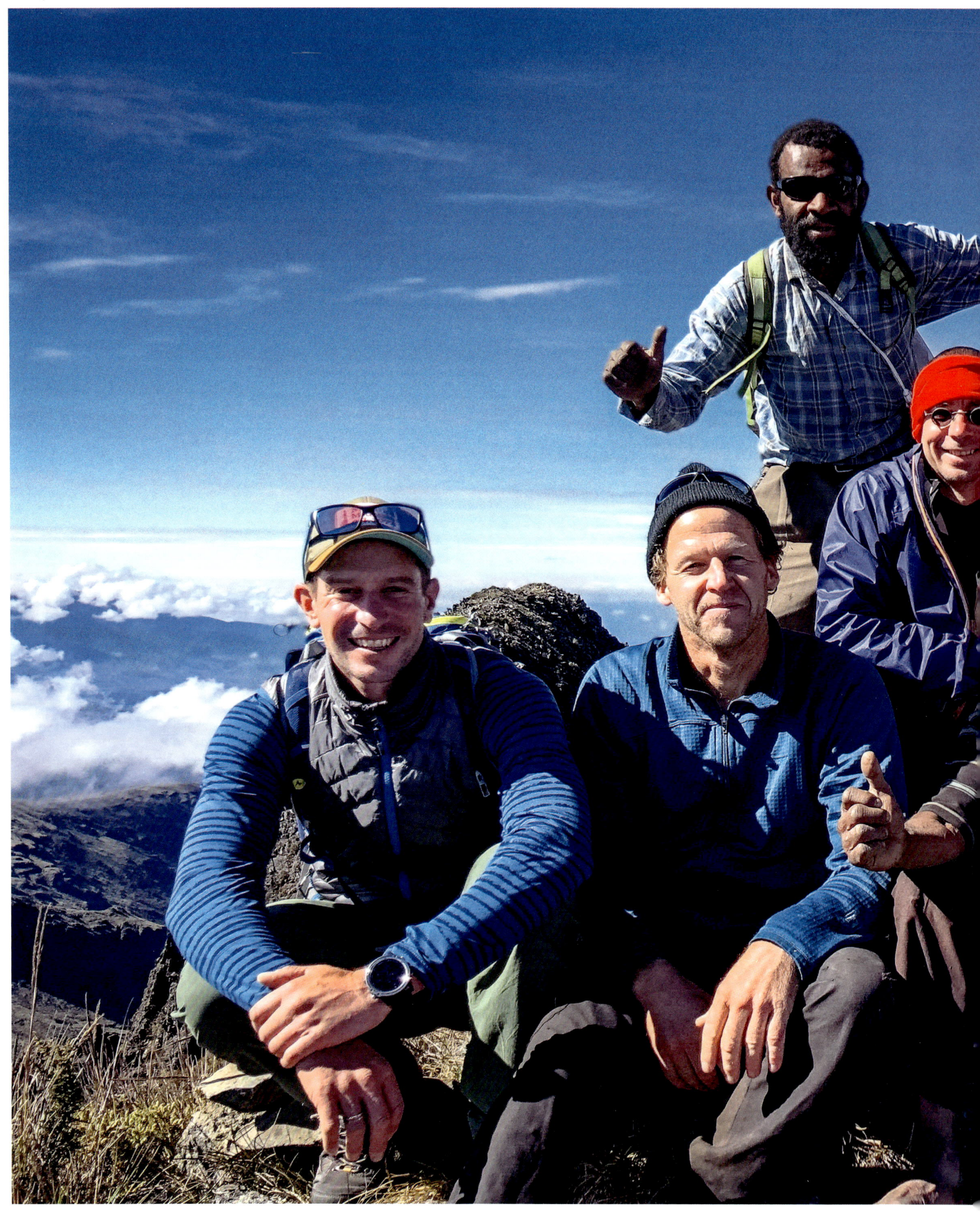

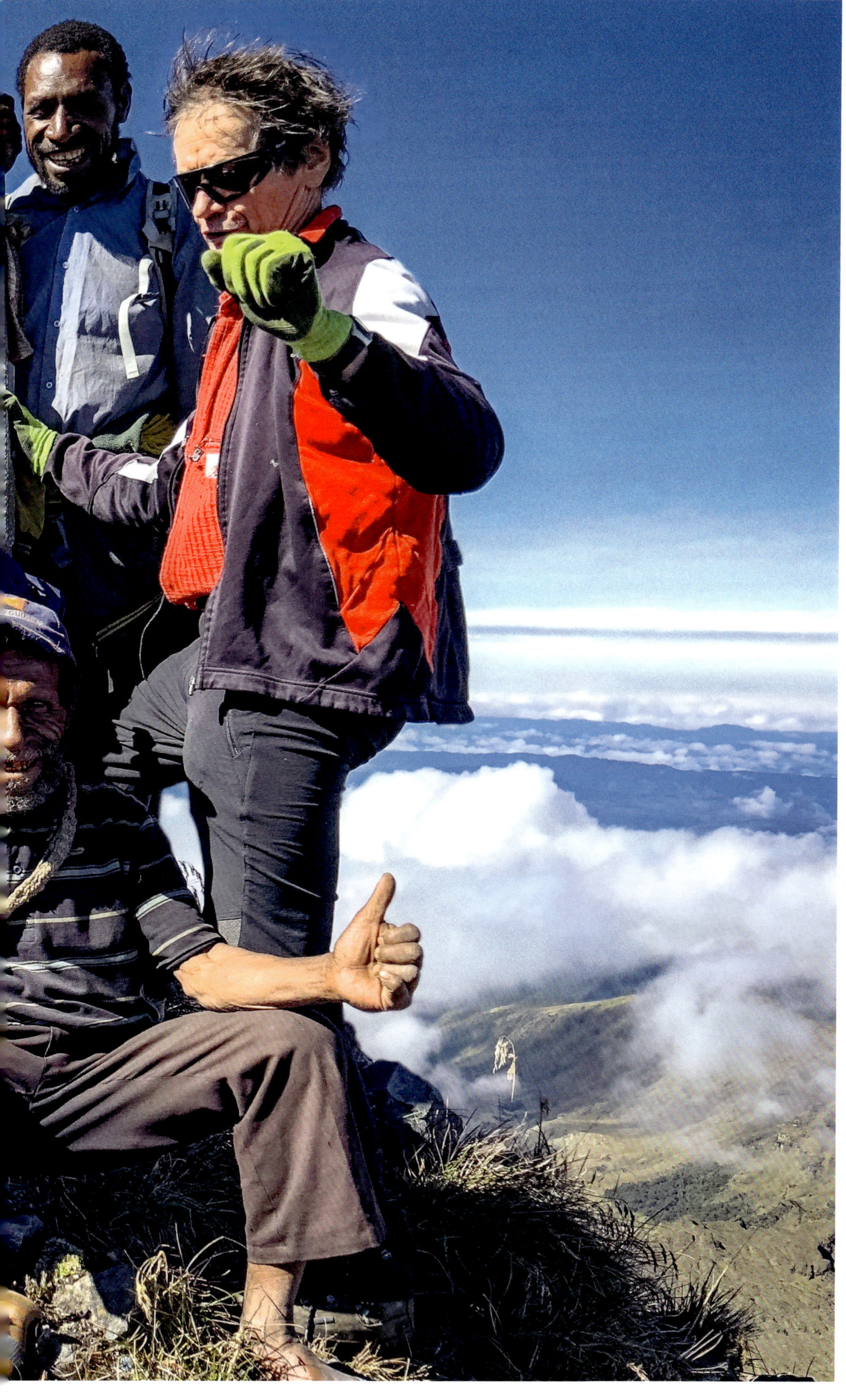

 "Immortal"

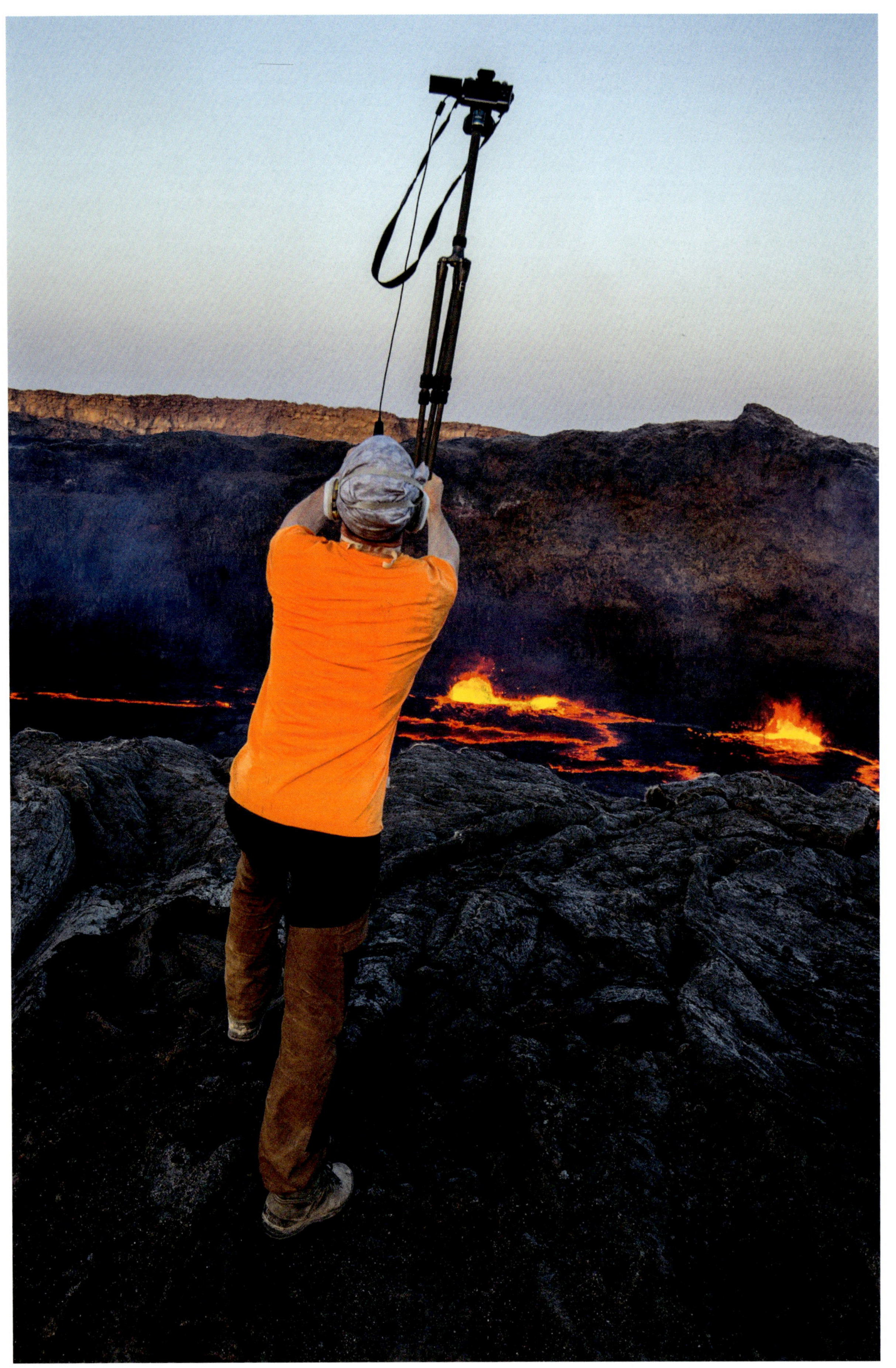

As it was going to be used in extremely cold temperatures, enveloped by clouds of volcanic ash, or during a tropical downpour, the camera had to be extremely robust.

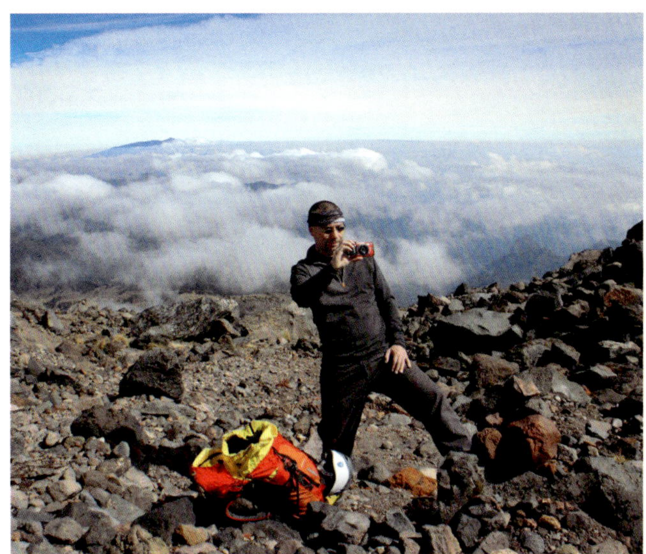

One of the biggest challenges I had to face on my Volcanic Seven Summits tour was that as a photographer-cum-adventurer was that I often had to navigate difficult terrain—carrying photography equipment and all. Due to my very limited experience as a mountaineer, I often had to concentrate almost exclusively on the climbing part of the experience. Only rarely did I have time and energy to stop and dedicate an extended amount of time to photography. Thus it quickly became a priority to find a camera and equipment that was lightweight and easy to handle so that I could have it at hand at all times, while at the same time not compromising on image quality. I was to take this equipment hiking, cycling, and skiing—all at dizzying heights and often in difficult weather conditions. As it was going to be used in extremely cold temperatures, enveloped by clouds of volcanic ash, or during a tropical downpour, the camera had to be extremely robust—it had to work no matter the conditions.

In the end, the camera that met all my conditions was the mirrorless Olympus OMD E-M1 Mark II and its PRO lenses. My most frequently used lens was the 12 – 100mm lens (extensive zoom range of 24 – 200mm). Its versatility made this lens perfect for my requirements: at wide-angle range, it was fantastic for landscape photography, and its telephoto reach allowed for great action shots—all without having to switch between lenses. This improved my speed and protected the sensor against dust and volcanic debris.

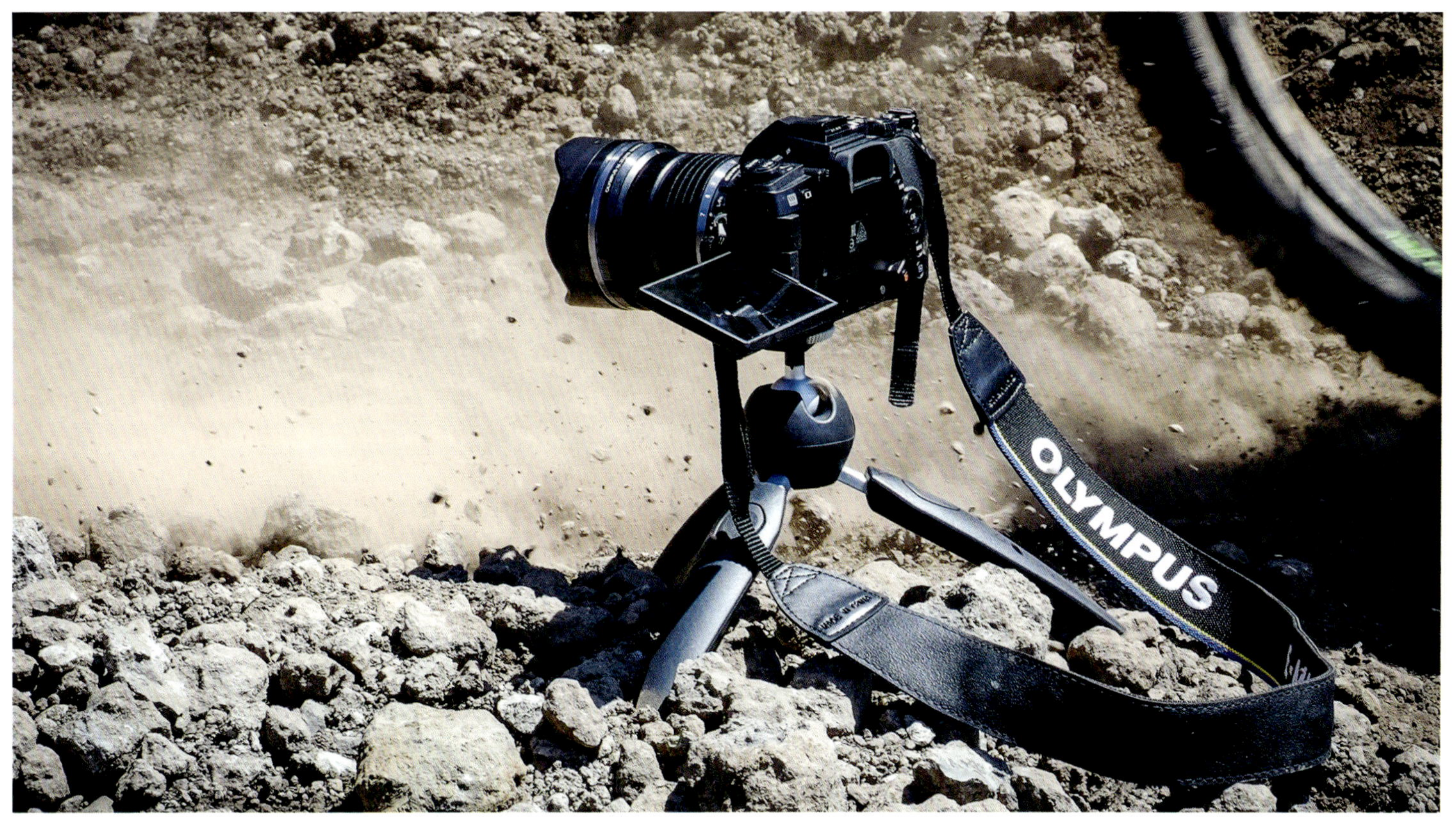

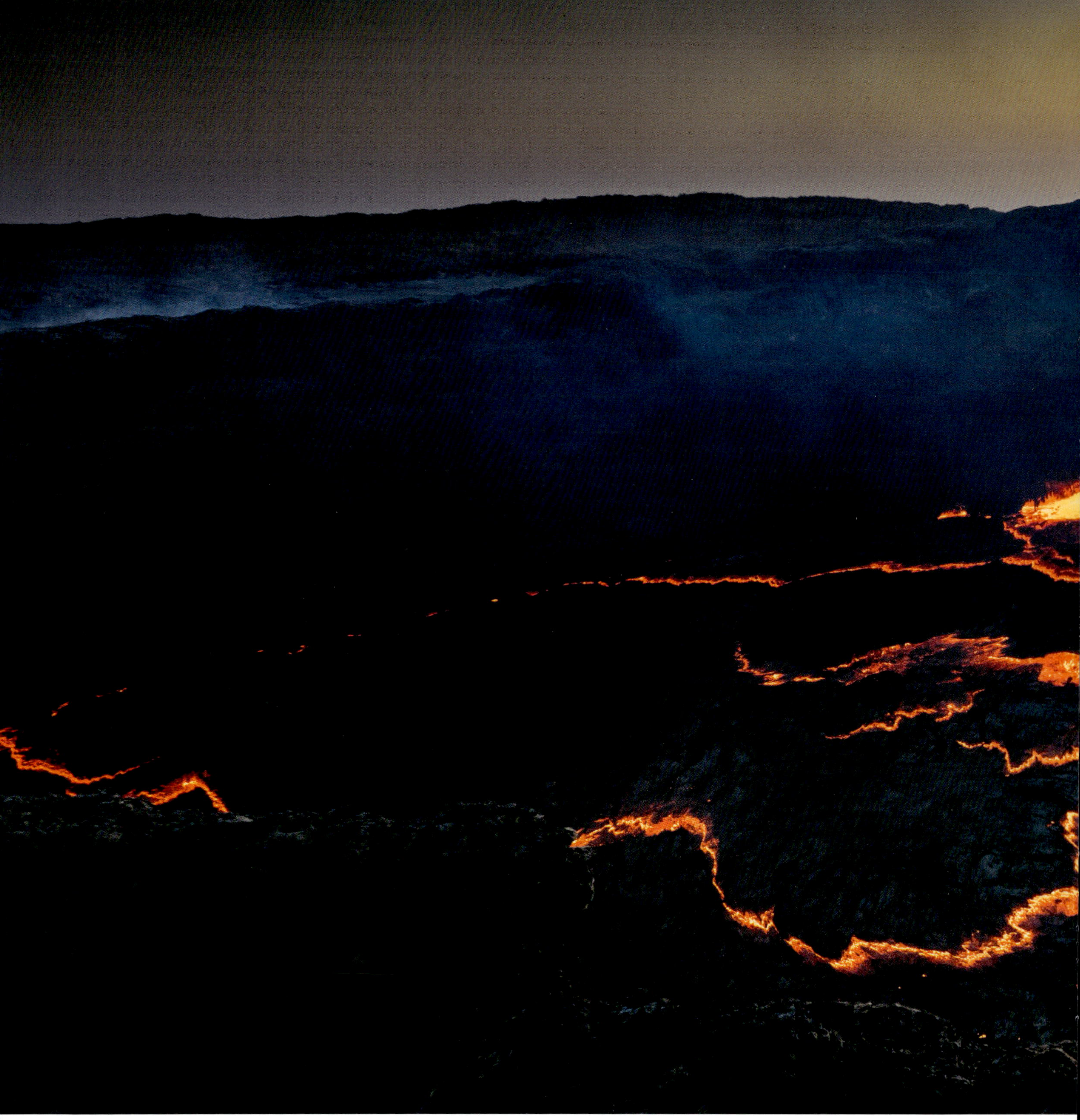

I encountered extreme conditions at Erta Ale in the Danakil Desert, eastern Ethiopia. The relentless heat crept into my equipment and within a short period of time, both my tripod and my camera were burning hot. I was enveloped in the pungent smell of volcanic gasses. Luckily, none of this was too much for my equipment to handle. Even after three days of shooting in these adverse conditions, the camera and lenses still worked perfectly.

On top of this, it proved impossible to get as close to the crater's rugged rim as I would have hoped. To get a better vantage point and still take the picture I had envisaged, I securely

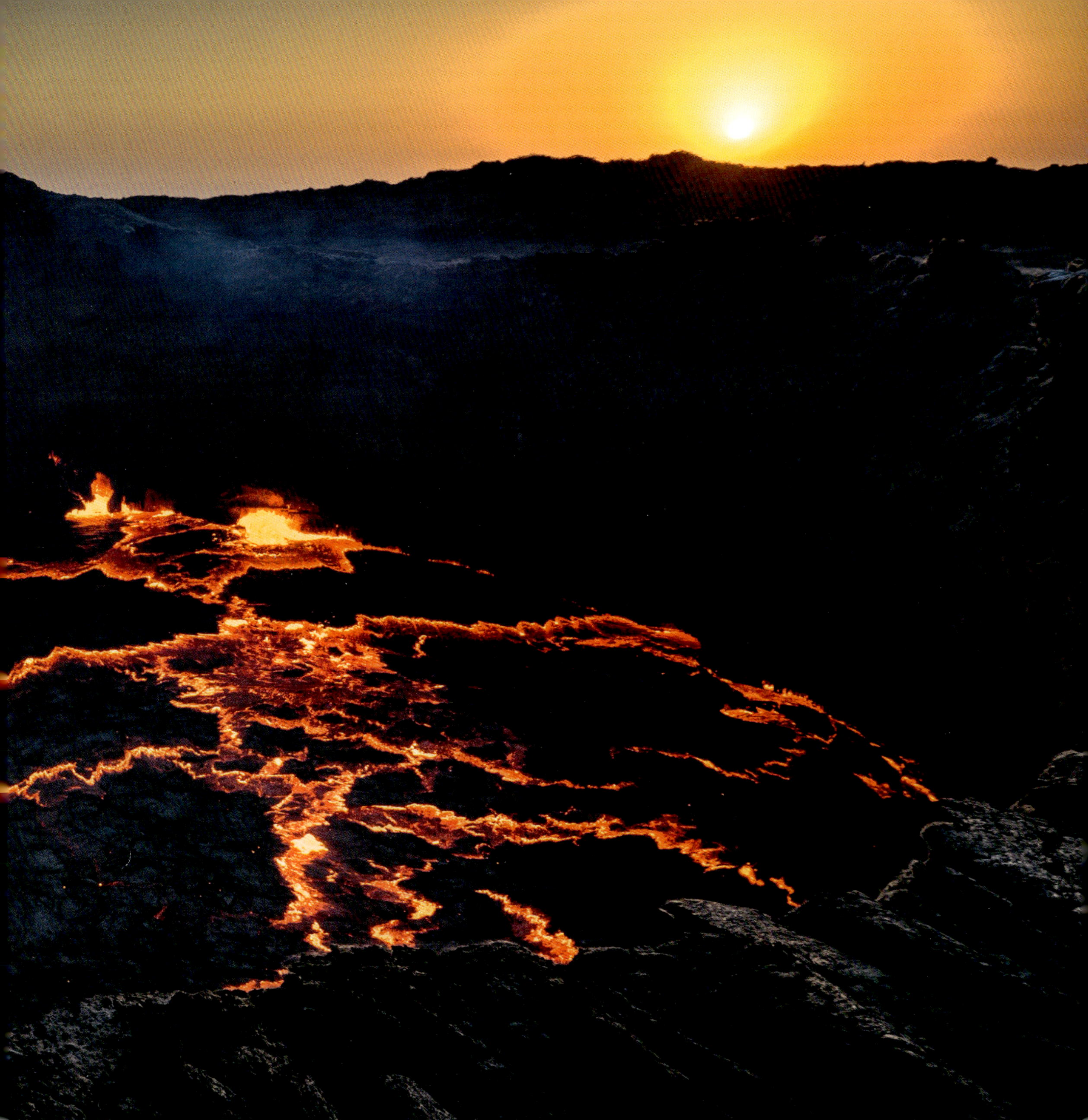

connected camera and tripod and held them
up in the air with just one arm outstretched.
This was only possible because the Olympus is
extremely lightweight and compact due to its
mirrorless system.

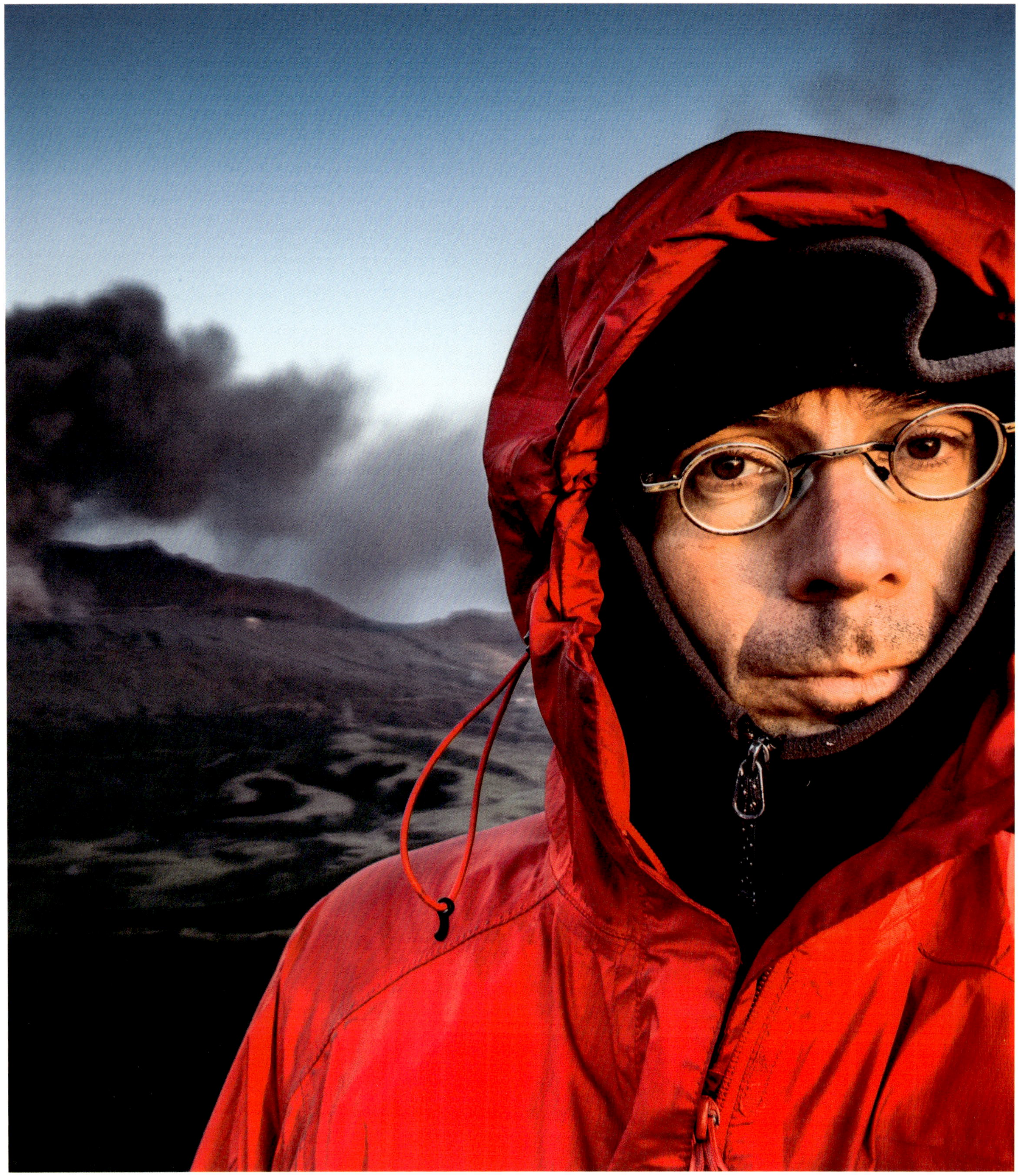

ADRIAN ROHNFELDER

Adrian Rohnfelder, born in 1968, is a landscape, travel, and extreme nature photographer with a passion for fire and ice. Since 2005, he has focused on reportage from the most remote places on the planet, with a particular passion for volcanoes. His biggest project to date is the ascent of the highest volcanoes across the seven continents.

Adrian Rohnfelder is a Visionary and Ambassador for Olympus. His stories and photographs have been published and awarded internationally. He also documents his travels in exhibitions and multimedia shows and is now a sought-after guest on talk shows. He lives in Bad Homburg, Germany.

Imprint

© 2019 Adrian Rohnfelder
© 2019 teNeues Media GmbH & Co. KG, Kempen
All rights reserved.

Editorial coordination by Roman Schmid
Translations by Judith Kahl
Creative Direction by Martin Graf
Design by Robin John Berwing
Production by Nele Jansen
Color separation by Robin Alexander Hopp

ISBN 978-3-96171-174-1
Library of Congress Number: 2019933041

Printed in Italy

Picture and text rights reserved for all countries.
No part of this publication may be reproduced in any manner whatsoever.
While we strive for utmost precision in every detail,
we cannot be held responsible for any inaccuracies, neither for any subsequent
loss or damage arising.Every effort has been made by the publisher to contact
holders of copyright to obtain permission to reproduce copyrighted material.
However, if any permissions have been inadvertently overlooked, teNeues
Publishing Group will be pleased to make the necessary and reasonable
arrangements at the first opportunity.
Bibliographic information published by the Deutsche Nationalbibliothek
The Deutsche Nationalbibliothek lists this publication in the Deutsche
Nationalbibliografie; detailed bibliographic data are available on the Internet
at http://dnb.dnb.de.

Kindly supported by

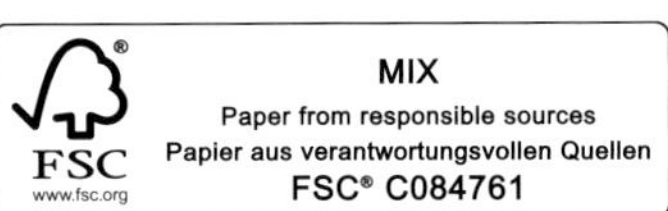

Published by teNeues Publishing Group

teNeues Media GmbH & Co. KG
Am Selder 37, 47906 Kempen, Germany
Phone: +49-(0)2152-916-0
Fax: +49-(0)2152-916-111
e-mail: books@teneues.com

Press department: Andrea Rehn
Phone: +49-(0)2152-916-202
e-mail: arehn@teneues.com

Munich Office
Pilotystraße 4, 80538 Munich, Germany
Phone: +49-(0)89-443-8889-62
e-mail: bkellner@teneues.com

Berlin Office
Kohlfurter Straße 41–43, 10999 Berlin, Germany
Phone: +49-(0)30-4195-3526-23
e-mail: ajasper@teneues.com

teNeues Publishing Company
350 7th Avenue, Suite 301, New York, NY 10001, USA
Phone: +1-212-627-9090
Fax: +1-212-627-9511

teNeues Publishing UK Ltd.
12 Ferndene Road, London SE24 0AQ, UK
Phone: +44-(0)20-3542-8997

teNeues France S.A.R.L.
39, rue des Billets, 18250 Henrichemont, France
Phone: +33-(0)2-4826-9348
Fax: +33-(0)1-7072-3482

www.teneues.com

teNeues Publishing Group
Kempen
Berlin
London
Munich
New York
Paris

teNeues